Brief Contents

Fourth Edition

International Relations
Perspectives, Controversies & Readings

Keith L. Shimko

PURDUE UNIVERSITY

WADSWORTH
CENGAGE Learning·

Australia • Brazil • Japan • Korea • Mexico • Singapore • Spain • United Kingdom • United States

International Relations: Perspectives, Controversies & Readings, Fourth Edition, International Edition
Keith L. Shimko

Senior Publisher: Suzanne Jeans

Executive Editor: Carolyn Merrill

Assistant Editor: Laura Ross

Editorial Assistant: Scott Greenan

Media Editor: Laura Hildebrand

Associate Media Editor: Kate MacLean

Marketing Program Manager: Caitlin Green

Design Direction, Production Management, and Composition: PreMediaGlobal

Print Buyer: Fola Orekoya

Rights Acquisitions Specialist: Jennifer Meyer Dare

Cover Designer: Craig Ramsdell

Cover Image: Barbed wire over a blue sky © Shutterstock

For product information and technology assistance, contact us at **Cengage Learning Customer & Sales Support, 1-800-354-9706**

For permission to use material from this text or product, submit all requests online at **www.cengage.com/permissions**. Further permissions questions can be e-mailed to **permissionrequest@cengage.com**.

Library of Congress Control Number: 2011938551

International Edition:

ISBN-13: 978-1-111-83314-5

ISBN-10: 1-111-83314-1

Cengage Learning International Offices

Asia
www.cengageasia.com
tel: (65) 6410 1200

Australia/New Zealand
www.cengage.com.au
tel: (61) 3 9685 4111

Brazil
www.cengage.com.br
tel: (55) 11 3665 9900

India
www.cengage.co.in
tel: (91) 11 4364 1111

Latin America
www.cengage.com.mx
tel: (52) 55 1500 6000

UK/Europe/Middle East/Africa
www.cengage.co.uk
tel: (44) 0 1264 332 424

Represented in Canada by Nelson Education, Ltd.
www.nelson.com
tel: (416) 752 9100 / (800) 668 0671

Cengage Learning is a leading provider of customized learning solutions with office locations around the globe, including Singapore, the United Kingdom, Australia, Mexico, Brazil, and Japan. Locate your local office at: **www.cengage.com/global**.

For product information and free companion resources:
www.cengage.com/international

Visit your local office: **www.cengage.com/global**

Printed in the United States of America
1 2 3 4 5 6 7 15 14 13 12 11

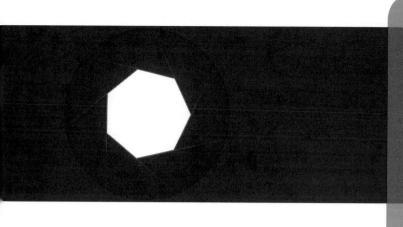

Contents

Chapter 8 Globalization and Sovereignty   189

Chapter 9 International Law   215

Chapter 13 The Global Commons   323

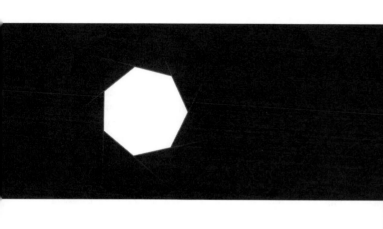

Preface: For
the Instructor

International Relations: Perspectives, Controversies & Readings, Fourth Edition, grows out of two decades of teaching the course for which it is intended—introductory international relations. I struggle to find the right balance of fact and theory, current events and historical background, as well as breadth and depth of coverage in an accessible manner without caricature or condescension. I constantly need to remind myself that even though the latest theoretical fad or methodological debate may interest me and my colleagues, it is usually of little interest or value to my students. Conversely, though many issues might be old and settled for those of us who have been immersed in the discipline for decades, they can still be new and exciting for students.

Goals

An introduction to international relations should accomplish several basic tasks: first, provide the essential information and historical background for an incredibly wide and diverse range of issues; second, instill the necessary conceptual and theoretical tools for students to analyze historical and contemporary issues from a broader perspective; and third, demonstrate the relevance of seemingly abstract academic theories and concepts for understanding the "real world."

In providing the necessary information and historical background, the major obstacle is the sheer volume of material. Because there is so much history that seems essential and so many issues to cover, it is always easy to find material to add but nearly impossible to identify anything to eliminate. Every textbook author knows this problem well: reviewers inevitably offer numerous suggestions for additions but few for deletions. Unfortunately, quantity is sometimes the enemy of quality. Presented with an endless catalog of facts, names, theories, and perspectives students risk drowning in a sea of detail. In trying to teach everything, we run the risk that students end up learning nothing. Choices need to be made.

These choices should be guided by the fundamental objective of getting students to *think* about international relations, instilling an appreciation for ideas and argument. If students understand the arguments for and against free trade, for example, it is not essential that they know the details of every WTO meeting or GATT round. Discussion of the WTO might be a useful entry point, but it is the ideas and arguments underlying the debate over free trade that are most critical.

© Geoffrey Holman / iStockphoto.com

Such ideas need to be presented in a manner that enables students to truly engage the arguments and grasp their implications. It is not enough that students are able to provide a paragraph summary of balance of power theory or the theory of comparative advantage: they need to understand the basic assumptions and follow arguments through their various stages, twists, and turns. This requires that ideas and theories must be developed at some length so students can see how their elements come together. As a result, it may be better to present two or three theories/positions in some depth rather than brief summaries of a dozen.

Since most undergraduates hope the class will help them understand the realities of international relations, the challenge of demonstrating relevance is critical. This is often achieved by supplementing a traditional text with a reader organized in a "taking sides" format. Though readers can be useful, they are seldom designed to accompany a particular text. As a consequence, the fit between readers and texts is usually imperfect. An additional problem with the text/reader combination is that it requires the purchase of two books. This text offers a unique solution to both problems: each of the substantive chapters incorporates readings that would normally appear in a supplementary reader, creating a single volume that is *both* a traditional textbook and a reader. The benefit for the instructor and students is that the readings are chosen specifically to reflect the discussion in each chapter. The additional benefit for students is that there is no additional reader to purchase.

Approach

The format of *International Relations: Perspectives, Controversies & Readings* reflects its approach to addressing these major challenges. Chapters 1 and 2 provide the basic historical and theoretical foundations for thinking about international relations. The remaining chapters are framed differently than in most other texts in that each chapter revolves around a central question/debate embodying an important and enduring controversy in international relations:

- Does international anarchy inevitably lead to conflict? (Chapter 3)
- Are democracies more peaceful? (Chapter 4)
- Is war part of human nature? (Chapter 5)
- Does free trade benefit all? (Chapter 6)
- What are the obstacles to economic development? (Chapter 7)
- Does globalization erode national sovereignty? (Chapter 8)
- Does international law matter? (Chapter 9)
- Is humanitarian intervention justified? (Chapter 10)
- How dangerous is nuclear proliferation? (Chapter 11)
- What is the appropriate response to terrorism? (Chapter 12)
- Is the global commons in danger? (Chapter 13)

Once the question is posed and the essential historical/factual background provided, alternative answers to the question are developed. The questions and "debate" format provide focus, prompting students to follow coherent and contrasting arguments. The goal is to present sustained arguments, not snippets. Finally, to help students move beyond abstract debates, each chapter concludes with the previously discussed readings that bring to life debates discussed in the chapter. For example, in the chapter dealing with democracy and war, the Points of View documents debate whether more democracy would bring peace to the Middle East. Given the successful protests against authoritarian rule in the Arab world in 2011 (e.g., Tunisia and Egypt) and the prospect of more democratic forms of government in the region, this should help students appreciate the real world implications of theoretical arguments.

Features

Beginning with Chapter 3, students will notice a standard set of pedagogical features that will guide their studies of the enduring controversies in international relations.

- An **opening abstract** introducing students to the chapter and its central question.
- An **introduction** providing historical background.
- **Key terms** are boldfaced where they are first introduced in the chapter, defined in the margin and listed at the end of the chapter.
- The **Points of View** section includes two readings related to the chapter's issues, often presenting both sides of the debate. An introduction to the readings provides questions for students to ponder as they read the selections.
- A **chapter summary** provides a brief review of the chapter.
- **Critical questions** ask students to apply the concepts they learned in the chapter.
- **Further readings** provide citations of additional sources related to the chapter material.
- Related **Web sites** give students the opportunity to explore the Internet for more information.

Highlights of This Fourth Edition

International Relations: Perspectives, Controversies & Readings, Fourth Edition, has been thoroughly updated. Key revisions include the following:

- New and updated Point of View sections. For Chapter 3 new readings focus on the implications of China's rising power and the likelihood of increased conflict with the United States. For Chapter 4 the readings reflect the debate over whether the fall of traditional authoritarian regimes and spread of democracy in the Arab world increases or decreases the prospects for peace. New readings for chapter 13 explore the continuing failure to reach an effective international accord on emissions and climate change at either Copenhagen (2009) or Cancun (2010).

■ Chapters are revised and updated to include, for example: debates about the implications of increasing Chinese economic and military power (Chapter 3), the process of democratization (as opposed to existence of established democracies) and peace in the context of recent developments in the Middle East (Chapter 4), the movement for "fair trade" rather than free trade (Chapter 6), the intensifying debate about Iran's nuclear weapons program (Chapter 11), and updated information on issues of climate change and global resources, particularly energy and food supplies/prices (Chapter 13).

■ Updated statistics throughout the book.

■ New and updated Web links throughout to provide useful resources in exploring chapter-related issues beyond the text.

■ New and updated end-of-chapter critical questions to prompt deeper student analysis and engagement with the concepts.

Instructor Resources

International Relations: Perspectives, Controversies & Readings, Fourth Edition, offers the following ancillary materials for instructors:

■ **Online Instructor's Resource Manual/Test Bank**
  ISBN-10: 1111769729 | ISBN-13: 9781111769727
  The comprehensive online instructor's resource manual features lecture outlines as well as an extensive array of well-crafted multiple-choice, true/false, fill-in-the-blank, and essay questions, along with answers and page references.

■ **Instructor Companion Web Site**
  ISBN-10: 1133001289 | ISBN-13: 9781133001287
  Students will find open access to learning objectives, tutorial quizzes, chapter glossaries, flashcards, and crossword puzzles, all correlated by chapter. Instructors also have access to the Instructor's Manual and PowerPoints.

■ **CourseReader: International Relations**
  1111480605 | 9781111480608 CourseReader 0-30: International Relations Printed Access Card
  1111480591 | 9781111480592 CourseReader 0-30: International Relations Instant Access Code
  1111480583 | 9781111480585 CourseReader 0-30: International Relations SSO
  111168068X | 9781111680688 CourseReader 0-60: International Relations Printed Access Card
  1111680671 | 9781111680671 CourseReader 0-60: International Relations Instant Access Code
  1111680663 | 9781111680664 CourseReader 0-60: International Relations SSO
  111168071X | 9781111680718 CourseReader Unlimited: International Relations Printed Access Card
  1111680701 | 9781111680701 CourseReader Unlimited: International Relations Instant Access Code

1111680698 | 9781111680695 CourseReader Unlimited: International Relations SSO

CourseReader for International Relations is a fully customizable online reader which provides access to hundreds of readings, audio, and video selections from multiple disciplines. This easy to use solution allows you to select exactly the content you need for your courses, and is loaded with convenient pedagogical features like highlighting, printing, note taking, and audio downloads. YOU have the freedom to assign individualized content at an affordable price. CourseReader: International Relations is the perfect complement to any class.

- **International Politics Atlas**

  ISBN-10: 0618837132 | ISBN-13: 9780618837137

  Free when bundled with a Wadsworth textbook, this atlas offers maps of the world showing political organization, population statistics, and economic development; maps highlighting energy production and consumption, major world conflicts, migration, and more; and extensive regional coverage. Students will find it useful for understanding world events and to supplement their studies with *International Relations: Perspectives, Controversies & Readings, 4th Edition.*

Student Resources

- **Student Companion Web Site**

  You will find open access to learning objectives, tutorial quizzes, chapter glossaries, flashcards, and crossword puzzles, all correlated by chapter.

- **CourseReader: International Relations**

  CourseReader enables instructors to create a customized reader so that you buy only the readings that are assigned in class. With this online reader you can take notes, highlight, and print content in a convenient, modern, and economical way.

- **International Politics Atlas**

  This atlas offers maps of the world showing political organization, population statistics, and economic development; maps highlighting energy production and consumption, major world conflicts, migration, and more; and extensive regional coverage. You will find it useful for understanding world events and to supplement your studies with *International Relations: Perspectives, Controversies & Readings, 4th Edition.*

Acknowledgments

The process of writing an introductory international relations text has been a rewarding, yet at times frustrating, experience. I suspect this is the case in any field. Although my name is on the cover, the end product involved the input of many people over the course of several editions. First and foremost are all those people who have read and commented on various drafts along the way. Many friends and colleagues at Purdue University, specifically Berenice Carroll, Harry Targ, Louis René Beres, and Aaron Hoffman, have made valuable suggestions for improving several chapters. Cynthia Weber of Leeds University provided useful input on my discussion of international relations theory, especially feminism. Although my debts to Stanley Michalak of Franklin and Marshall College go all the way back to my undergraduate days, for this text he read numerous chapters that are now much better as a result of his insightful, considerate advice and friendly criticism. Stanley was also one of my main sources of encouragement at times when I wondered whether the world really needed another introductory international relations text. Randy Roberts also gave valuable advice on navigating the maze of textbook publishing.

In addition to these friends, there is a list of reviewers for this edition arranged through my editors at Cengage:

Emmanuel Obuah, Alabama A&M University
Mariya Omelicheva, University of Kansas
Amanda Rosen, Webster University

Though it was obviously not possible to incorporate all of the ideas and suggestions provided by these reviewers, I can honestly say that this is a much better book as a result of their input.

Finally, this book is dedicated to my mother and father, Riitta Shimko and Leonard Shimko. My mother passed away halfway through the writing of the first edition. Although she was not here to see the final product, I know she would have been happy that after many years of talking about it, I finally got off my duff and wrote it. I only regret that she was not here to see it. My father saw the first edition but passed away just before I wrote the second edition. I miss them both terribly.

Keith L. Shimko

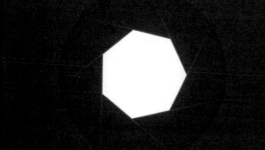

Introduction for the Student: Why Study International Relations?

You and the World

There are times when international events dominate the daily news, displacing the more immediate domestic issues and economic concerns that usually occupy peoples' attention. Despite the continuing recession and persistently high unemployment, domestic issues were bumped from the headlines in the Winter of 2011 as widespread protests throughout the Middle East focused news coverage once again on that volatile region. On television, YouTube, the blogosphere and a host of social media outlets, the world was flooded with images of unrest and occasional violence. American students could watch their Egyptian counterparts playing a critical role in protests that toppled of Hosni Mubarak after more than thirty years in power.

For U.S. policymakers, who have frequently espoused the benefits of democracy while enjoying the strategic stability offered by friendly but autocratic regimes, the prospect of greater democracy in parts of the Arab world put one of their cherished convictions to the test. The notion that democracies are inherently peaceful has been a deeply ingrained element of American thinking about international relations for decades. But in early 2011 not everyone was certain that a more democratic Egypt would advance the cause of Middle East. In such circumstances, not only are international issues thrust into the headlines, but seemingly dry and arcane academic research becomes relevant both for evaluating the consequences of democratization.

But even in more tranquil times, when international affairs recede into the background, our lives are touched by events beyond our shores. Whether the United States is at peace or at war, almost one in five of your tax dollars goes to defend the nation's security. If you are a farmer or work for a company that exports its products, your livelihood may depend on continued access to international markets. As a consumer, you pay prices for food and clothes from abroad that are influenced by how much access other nations have to our markets. A crisis on the other side of the globe may require you to shell out more money for the gas you pump into your car. And if you or a loved one is a member of the armed forces, international affairs can literally become a matter of life and death. Indeed, in the wake of September 11, 2001, Americans now know something people in less secure parts of the world have always known—one need not be wearing a uniform to become a casualty. There may have been a time before bombers, ballistic missiles, and the global economy when friendly neighbors and the isolation provided by two oceans allowed Americans to ignore much of what happened around the world. That world is long gone. Today we are reminded at almost every turn that our lives are affected, sometimes dramatically, by what goes on thousands of miles from home.

International Relations

What is *international relations*? At first glance this appears to be a relatively straightforward and easy question. In a narrow sense, *international* relations is the behavior and interaction of states. Those inclined to this somewhat restrictive definition often prefer the label international *politics* instead of international *relations*. Today the more commonly used *international relations* connotes a much broader focus. Although no one denies that state behavior is *a*, perhaps even *the*, central focus of international relations, few believe this adequately defines the boundaries of the discipline. There are simply too many important actors (e.g., multinational corporations, religious movements, international organizations and terrorist groups) and issues (e.g., climate change) that do not fall neatly into a state-centric vision of the world. But as we conceptualize international relations more broadly, it is hard to know where to stop. The line between domestic and international politics blurs as we realize that internal politics often influence a state's external conduct. The distinction between economics and politics fades once we recognize that economic power is an integral component of political power. In the end, it may be easier to specify what, if anything, does *not* fall within the realm of international relations. Indeed, according to one definition international relations is "the whole complex of cultural, economic, legal, military, political, and social relations of all *states*, as well as their component populations and entities."[1] This covers an awful lot of territory.

Fortunately, we need not settle on any final definition. Though it might be an interesting academic exercise, it serves no useful purpose at this point. It is enough that we have a good idea of the subjects included in any reasonable definition. It is hard to imagine a definition of international relations that would not, for example, encompass questions of war and peace, sovereignty and intervention, and economic inequality and development. As an introductory text, this book deals with perspectives and issues that almost all agree fall well within the core of international relations.

Learning and Thinking About International Relations

This text is designed to help you think systematically and critically about international affairs in a way that allows you to understand today's headlines as well as yesterday's and, more importantly, tomorrow's. Once you are able to see familiar patterns in unfamiliar situations, identify recurring puzzles in novel problems, and recognize old ideas expressed in new debates, international relations ceases to be a disjointed and ever-changing series of "events." The names and faces may change, but many of the fundamental problems, issues, and debates tend to reappear, albeit in slightly different form.

The first step in thinking systematically about international politics is realizing that our present is the product of our past. What happened today was influenced by what happened yesterday, and what happens today will shape what happens tomorrow. Even unanticipated and surprising events do not occur out of the blue: there are always antecedent developments and forces that produced them. The outbreak of World War I, the collapse of the Soviet Union and the end of the Cold War, or the terrorist attacks of September 11, 2001, cannot be understood apart from their historical roots. Understanding contemporary problems requires an appreciation of their historical origins. History is also essential for evaluating the significance of contemporary events/changes. Without history we would have no way of judging whether a proclaimed "new world order" is really new or merely a mildly updated version of the old world order.

The second step in thinking systematically about international relations is moving beyond *description* to the more difficult task of *explanation*. The move from description to explanation is rarely easy. Anyone who has ever taken a history class knows that agreement on the "facts" does not necessarily translate into consensus on explanation. Historians might be in total agreement about exactly what happened before and during World War I—who assassinated whom, which nation declared war first, and who won what battles—yet nonetheless disagree about what "caused" the war. These debates occur because historical facts do not speak for or explain themselves. Explanation requires that events be interpreted and linked together, and there is always more than one plausible explanation/interpretation.

Competing interpretations are the result preexisting beliefs/worldviews that act as lenses or filters enabling people to *look* at the same things yet *see* them differently. As a result, understanding debates about international relations requires knowledge of not only the "facts" but also these lenses through which people interpret and understand them. Only then is it possible to understand, for example, why some see the United Nations as an invaluable institution for creating a more civilized world while others dismiss it as a pompous and ineffective debating society. International relations is marked not only by conflicts among nations but also by conflicting worldviews.

An appreciation of these competing worldviews is also an essential aspect of critical thinking, which necessarily entails looking at issues and problems from many perspectives. This is why students in debating clubs and societies are required to defend positions regardless of their personal opinions. Presenting and defending positions other than your own is an intellectual exercise that aids critical analysis, encourages you to think about the structure of argument and the nature of evidence, and makes you aware of the strengths and weaknesses of your own position. Someone who cannot understand or faithfully present an opposing point of view can never really understand his or her own.

Thus, in order to cultivate this sort of critical analysis, a textbook needs to accomplish at least three tasks. First, it must provide a foundation of knowledge enabling you to think about current events in a broader *historical context*. Second, it has to make you aware of the differing worldviews that influence analyses of international affairs so they can analyze events in a broader *intellectual context*. And third, it should examine issues from multiple perspectives so that you can get into the habit of seeing international relations from many different angles.

Plan of the Book

This text has two sections. The first provides the historical and theoretical foundation. It begins (Chapter 1) with a broad survey of the development of international relations, focusing on the emergence and evolution of what we call the "modern state system." Although any attempt to summarize more than five centuries in a single chapter inevitably sacrifices much detail, it is still possible to convey the most significant elements of change and continuity. This historical survey is followed by an introduction to the major perspectives offering alternative ways of explaining and understanding international relations (Chapter 2).

The second section, which forms the bulk of the text, is devoted to enduring and contemporary controversies in international relations. Individual chapters focus on a central international issue, ranging from the very abstract and theoretical (e.g., war and human nature) to the extremely concrete and policy oriented (e.g., nuclear proliferation and terrorism) and everything in between. Whatever the specific issue, the format of each chapter is similar: A brief historical and factual introduction is followed by a discussion of competing perspectives or arguments.

It is, of course, impossible to do justice to every conceivable position on each issue. In the real world there are never just two sides to an argument or debate. There are always nuances of emphasis and gradations of belief in academic and policy debates. But before we can deal with nuances, we need to appreciate the more basic and fundamental differences. Thus, rather than covering the full range of positions on every topic, the focus will be on two or three major positions reflecting differences on fundamental questions. This allows us to concentrate on the most significant points of disagreement, develop arguments and discuss evidence in some depth.

The transition from the classroom to the "real world" is provided by each chapter's Points of View section, which includes an eclectic mix of official foreign policy statements, government documents, news stories, and editorials. What are you supposed to get out of these documents? Sometimes they are intended to demonstrate that ideas, which can often appear very theoretical, have real-world consequences. Other documents require you to think outside the box a little by presenting positions that depart somewhat from those presented in the chapter. Finally, some documents are straightforward news stories providing real world examples of various phenomena.

After the Final Exam

Few of you will make a career of studying international relations. This may be both the first and the last international relations course you will ever take, though hopefully not. But whether you like the subject or not, your life will be influenced by international affairs. Long after the exams and quizzes are an unpleasant memory, many of the issues and problems you studied will be encountered again. Even if you do not emerge with a burning interest in international relations and a passionate desire to learn more, I hope you will come away with an appreciation of the important issues at stake, that you will listen to candidates and their proposed policies, and that you can identify and understand the assumptions and beliefs that inform them. You should be able to analyze arguments and evidence rather than accept them at face value. You should aim to become an interested, informed, articulate, and thoughtful citizen of a nation and world in which all of our lives and fates are increasingly intertwined and dependent.

NOTE

[1.] Cathal J. Nolan, *The Longman Guide to World Affairs* (White Plains, NY: Longman, 1995), p. 178.

1

Change and Continuity in International History

Change and Continuity

The terrorist attacks of September 11, 2001, are the most recent in a series of events or crises considered critical turning points in international relations. Slightly more than a decade earlier, in 1989, the tearing down of the Berlin Wall signaled the beginning of the end of the Cold War, eliminating the conflict that had defined international relations for almost four decades. Some argued that the demise of communism removed the final obstacle to the eventual global triumph of liberal democracy. This optimism was reinforced in 1991 when a broad international coalition under the authority of the United Nations reversed the Iraqi invasion of Kuwait, prompting talk of a "new world order." The horrors of war in the former Yugoslavia and genocide in Rwanda during the 1990s dispelled much of this optimism. If there was a new world order, it seemed little better than the old one. Then came the assessment that the attacks of September 11 and the subsequent invasions of Afghanistan and Iraq had "changed everything."

These events and reactions highlight a recurring problem for students of international relations: How do we evaluate the significance of events and changes in the world? In the abstract, the question of whether a "new world order" is emerging depends not merely on those aspects of international relations that are changing, but also on those that are constant. What matters is the relative significance of changes compared to continuities. Unfortunately, continuities are often overlooked. Looking primarily at current and recent events, it is all too easy to focus on change because it is interesting and dramatic. The danger is that we will miss important elements of constancy. For this reason it is important to approach current issues from a larger historical perspective, with an appreciation of the events and forces that have shaped the world in which we live.

The Emergence of the Modern State System

We take certain features of our world so much for granted that they fade into an unremarkable background. Some things are almost too obvious to mention. If asked what a friend looks like, we are unlikely to describe them as having two arms and two legs. That may simply be too basic, but it is no less important for being so. To avoid overlooking the obvious, it is sometimes useful to play a mind game and imagine how someone with no previous knowledge of our world might see it. An alien visiting planet Earth would notice first some of the basic features of our world that most of us take for granted. In terms of our planet's political order, most striking would be the division of all of the planet's inhabitants (some 6.5 billion of them) and all the world's territory (about 58 million square miles) into a relatively small number of large political entities called *states* or *countries* (about 200), claiming to be independent. There is no central political authority that unites these different political entities. In pointing out these facts, the alien would be describing the fundamental features of the **modern state system**: a relatively small number of relatively large independent political units recognizing no higher political authority. But had the visitor arrived a thousand years ago, he would have seen a very different world, and if he returns a thousand years from now, it will certainly look different still. A good place to begin looking at the history of world politics is with how, why, and when the modern state system came into being.

The modern state system has been around (at least in the Western world) for about four hundred years. Some date the beginning of the modern state system to 1648, the year the **Thirty Years War** (1618–1648) ended with the **Peace of Westphalia**. Although 1648 is a convenient dividing point, the modern state system did not just appear overnight in that year: The world of 1647 did not look much different from the world of 1649. The emergence of the modern state system was in reality a slow, gradual process driven by important economic, religious, and military developments that eventually undermined the feudal order and replaced it with a new way of organizing European politics. As European influence spread throughout the world in subsequent centuries, this new way of organizing things would come, for better or worse, to characterize international politics on a global scale.

A tourist cruising down Germany's Rhine would see the remnants of the feudal order—picturesque castle ruins every few miles. Along the 120 miles from Cologne to Mainz alone, there are 39 castle ruins. Nothing more than quaint tourist attractions today, in its day each castle was the center of one of the many small kingdoms and fiefdoms that dotted the landscape of feudal Europe. That there are so many castles so close together indicates that these political units tended to be quite small (see Map 1.1). Each unit was ruled by some member of the nobility—princes, dukes, or other potentates—who ran them largely as personal property. They did not enjoy formal independence but rather were connected to one another in a complicated, chaotic, and often confusing pattern of obligations. Even though one might look at a map of the period and see a few larger countries (e.g., France or England), their appearance is misleading. Political power was not as centralized as the maps suggest. Central governments and rulers were usually very weak and

modern state system The international state system characterized by a relatively small number of relatively large independent or sovereign political units. Though the modern state system is the result of several complex economic, religious, and military changes, a convenient date for its foundation is 1648, when the Thirty Years War ended with the Peace of Westphalia.

Thirty Years War Name given to a series of bloody and devastating wars fought largely on German lands between 1618 and 1648. Though several complex causes and motivations fueled these wars, the conflict between Protestants and Catholics over the authority of the Catholic Church and the pope was a central issue.

Peace of Westphalia The agreement that officially closed the Thirty Years War (or wars). Significant in that it marked the origins of modern principles of sovereignty.

This map of Europe in 1300 illustrates the political fragmentation of the medieval period.

struggled constantly with lesser nobles over whom they supposedly held authority. In general, "the pattern of politics in medieval Europe was ... a crazy quilt of multiple and overlapping feudal authorities and reciprocal allegiances.... Central governments, when they existed at all, were consequently very weak."[1]

Holy Roman Empire The larger political entity that brought some political unity to medieval Europe under the authority of the pope and the Holy Roman Emperor.

As if this division of power were not messy enough, much of Europe was theoretically united under the **Holy Roman Empire**. The basis for unity was Europe's common Catholic identity. To make things even more complicated, the Holy Roman Empire had both religious and secular leaders (the pope and Holy Roman Emperor), and it was not always clear where their authority began and ended. Furthermore, the empire itself was a very weak entity in which local nobles and religious figures enjoyed substantial independence from the Emperor and Rome. Thus, feudal Europe was a fragmented place of numerous small political entities entwined in a confusing and complicated mishmash of political authority.

Three major developments began to transform Europe beginning in the 1200s or 1300s (it is impossible to pick any specific date). These three "revolutions" would ultimately create much larger political units, organized on the basis of sovereignty and independence. First, the **commercial revolution** (not to be confused with the industrial revolution) provided a powerful economic impetus for the creation of larger entities. Second, the **gunpowder revolution** dramatically altered the requirements for defense in ways that gave substantial advantages to larger entities. Finally, the **Protestant Reformation** and the resulting Thirty Years War (1618–1648) destroyed the Catholic unity of Europe and led to the modern notion of sovereignty. Let us deal with each of these revolutions in turn.

commercial revolution The revival of trade and commerce as Europe began to emerge from the stagnation that characterized much of the period after the fall of Rome in 476 CE. This was one of the forces for the creation of larger and more centralized political units, one of the essential features of the modern state system.

gunpowder revolution The dramatic military, social, and political changes accompanying the introduction and development of gunpowder weapons in Europe, beginning in the fourteenth century, made previous means of defense less reliable and placed a premium on land and larger political units.

Protestant Reformation Martin Luther's challenge to the Catholic Church in 1517 marked the emergence of a non-Catholic version of Christianity. The growing conflict between Protestants and Catholics was one of the major contributing forces to the Thirty Years War.

The Commercial Revolution

Beginning in the thirteenth and fourteenth centuries, Europe began its slow emergence from the stagnation that had prevailed after the fall of Rome 700 years earlier. Part of this resurgence was the revival of commerce and the growth of a new commercial class whose livelihood lay not in production but in trade. The commercial class faced obstacles because an extremely fragmented Europe was unable to provide many of the prerequisites for commerce. Law enforcement was weak, making the transport of valuable commodities very risky indeed. The infrastructure was in a terrible state of disrepair—roads, ports, and marketplaces had all deteriorated since the fall of Rome. Small fiefdoms did not possess the resources to build the infrastructure, and political fragmentation made coordination very difficult. Finally, systems of measurement and currency were unreliable.

All of these obstacles to commerce could be traced to the small size of political units. The emerging commercial class realized that larger political units with more effective central governments were essential. Ambitious rulers also desired larger kingdoms and increased power over local nobility. The result was a convergence of interests in favor of larger political units with more powerful central governments. A tacit alliance emerged between the commercial class and rulers who wanted to expand and centralize their authority. The commercial class provided the resources in the form of taxes, and in return the rulers provided the roads, ports, markets, law enforcement, and reliable currencies needed for trade. Thus, the economic imperatives of trade and commerce contributed to the emergence of larger political units with more effective central governments.

The Gunpowder Revolution

The weapons of the feudal age are familiar to us from movies about the period—knights in shining armor on horseback carrying swords, lances, and spears and archers on foot wielding crossbows. War between kingdoms often turned into long sieges, with the attackers surrounding a fortified castle within which people sought safety. Once surrounded, the goal was to harass and starve the inhabitants until they surrendered. The military problem was that the attackers could do little about the thick castle walls—spears and arrows did not make much of a dent, though catapults might propel fireballs over the walls to wreak havoc within. This type of warfare began to change with the introduction of gunpowder from China. Gunpowder weapons such as guns and cannons significantly altered the military equation. Most importantly, a kingdom could no longer resist attack by retreating behind castle walls because "from the 1430s onwards the cannons deployed by the major states of Western Europe could successfully reduce most traditional vertical defenses [i.e., walls] to rubble within a matter of days."[2] Consequently, an adequate defense required much more complicated (and expensive) fortifications and/or enough land to be able to absorb an attack and marshal one's own forces in time to meet the attack and defeat it. A kingdom only 40 or 100 miles across with a castle in the middle was now extremely vulnerable. Only larger states had the land and wealth necessary to conduct war and defend themselves in the gunpowder age.

The Protestant Reformation

Until 1517, Christianity was synonymous with Catholicism. Because the Catholic Church was such a central feature in the social and political life of feudal Europe, the rise of Protestantism had a profound effect on European societies and politics. Martin Luther's challenge to the authority of the Catholic Church marked the emergence of a Christian alternative to Catholicism that spread throughout Central and Northern Europe. The political problem was that many of the newly Protestant areas were located within the Catholic Holy Roman Empire. Protestants eventually sought freedom from the authority of the pope and Catholic rulers, resulting was a series of wars known collectively as the Thirty Years War (1618–1648). Though most of Europe was involved, the fighting occurred largely on German lands. By any measure, it was a war of unusual brutality and savagery. Estimates of the German population killed in the war range from 30 to 50 percent. Part of the barbarity and savagery of the war can be traced to its religious underpinnings: "Combatants on all sides thought that their opponents were, in a literal sense, instruments of the devil, who could be exterminated, whether they were soldiers or not. Indeed extermination of civilians was often preferred, precisely because it was easier to do away with civilians."[3] One need look no further than Martin Luther's German translation of the Bible to see the depth of this hostility. The only illustrated section was the book of Revelation, which foretells the coming of the Antichrist. Illustrations made the identity of the Antichrist perfectly clear— the pope. After thirty years of devastating and unspeakably brutal warfare, not much of Europe's sense of a common Christian identity survived.

The Thirty Years War ended in 1648 with the Peace of Westphalia, which solved the religious question by granting ruler the right to exercise authority over his or her territory. Each ruler would now determine questions of religion on their territory. They no longer had to answer to any higher, external authority such as the pope. This new freedom, however, did not imply religious tolerance or freedom—rulers often brutally suppressed religious dissidents in their countries. What the treaty established was the modern notion of **sovereignty**—that rulers were not obligated to obey any higher, external authority.

Thus, between the 1300s and the late 1600s the commercial revolution, the gunpowder revolution, and the Protestant Reformation combined to alter the nature of European societies, states, and international relations. The first two revolutions helped usher in larger political entities, and the Protestant Reformation and the Thirty Years War led to the notion of national sovereignty, creating the modern state system—a relatively small number of relatively large independent political units. These features continue to define our world. This basic continuity does not imply the absence of important changes. Even though certain essential features of international politics may have endured, the modern state system has certainly evolved in many important respects. And one needs to understand not merely the emergence of the modern state system, but also how it has evolved over the past four centuries.

The Age of Absolutism and Limited War (1648-1789)

The period between the Peace of Westphalia and the French Revolution (1789) was relatively uneventful compared to what came before 1648 and what was to come after 1789. There were no major continent-wide wars or political revolutions. Though frequent, wars tended to be modest affairs—small professional armies fighting limited wars for limited objectives, with limited casualties and destruction. This period is sometimes viewed as a golden age of diplomacy in which negotiation, compromise, and the balance of power prevented any repetition of the horrors of the Thirty Years War. This relative calm, however, depended on a certain political and social order that would not long survive the erosion of that order in the decades after the French Revolution.

When people tour Europe today, they inevitably visit one of the grand palaces that make for beautiful postcards, such as the Palace of Versailles on the outskirts of Paris. Situated on massive estates with finely manicured gardens and dramatic fountains, these mansions have hundreds of rooms covered in gold and valuable art. They are the physical manifestations of the social and political order of **absolutist monarchism**. Between 1648 and 1789, monarchs claiming absolute power and authority ruled virtually every nation in Europe. They claimed authority under the doctrine of the **divine right of kings**, which held that their legitimacy was derived from God, not the people over whom they ruled.

The prevalence of absolutist monarchism helps explain the relative calm of the period. Domestically, this was not a form of government that fostered loyalty between rulers and their subjects. Indeed, the very term *subjects* hints at the critical point. People who lived in France during this period were not in any meaningful

sovereignty In international relations, the right of individual states to determine for themselves the policies they will follow.

absolutist monarchism The political order prevailing in almost all of Europe before the French Revolution in which kings and queens claimed divine sources for their absolute rule and power unrestricted by laws or constitutions.

divine right of kings The political principle underlying absolutist monarchism in which God, not the people over whom leaders ruled, granted the legitimacy of rulers.

sense "citizens" of France; they were "subjects" of the monarch. But even though their power was absolute, in reality monarchs made limited demands on their people. They did not, for example, expect their subjects to serve in the military and fight wars. For this task the monarchs of Europe maintained professional armies. Unlike volunteer armies of today, soldiers did not have to be from the countries in whose armies they served; these were mercenary, not volunteer, armies. On the eve of the French Revolution in 1789, for example, nearly a quarter of the French army consisted of foreign soldiers.[4] Such armies were very expensive to maintain. Even the wealthiest rulers supported armies of only around 100,000 in peacetime, though this could swell to 400,000 in wartime. Given armies of this size, it was quite rare for battles to involve more than 80,000 soldiers.[5]

The professional and mercenary nature of European armies of the period reveals a reality in which the masses of people were excluded from politics, which was synonymous with royal court scheming and intrigue, not elections, political parties, interest groups, opinion polls, and so on. In the absence of any emotional sense of loyalty and connection between people and their rulers, nationalism as we know it did not exist. It was an era of dynastic nationalism, not popular or mass nationalism. Wars during this period were not conflicts involving entire nations; they were conflicts among royal families. France *as a nation* did not go to war with Spain or Austria; instead, the Bourbons, France's ruling dynasty, went to war with Austria's Hapsburgs.

The absence of mass nationalism helped keep wars and conflicts limited. The major issues leading to war were territorial disputes, economic and commercial interests, and questions of dynastic and royal succession.[6] Because European monarchs adhered to the same basic principles regarding how societies should be organized and ruled, wars were not waged over ideology. Consequently, "they were not concerned with religion as their seventeenth-century predecessors had been, nor political ideology as their post-1789 successors were to be."[7] The monarchs fought over *things*, not ideas, and wars over things are often less intense and bloody than wars over beliefs.

A final reason wars did not erupt into incredibly destructive affairs was the ability of European monarchs to maintain a balance of power through a constantly shifting pattern of allegiances and alliances. Throughout this period there were usually five or six major powers in Europe—some combination of England, France, Spain, Prussia, Russia, Austria, the Ottoman Empire (Turkey), Sweden, and the United Provinces (i.e., Holland)—that were successful in preventing any one power from becoming powerful enough to dominate all of Europe. Whenever one became too powerful or ambitious, the other major powers would align against it. Because the power of monarchs was absolute and they had no real ideological differences, allegiances could shift rapidly when the balance was threatened. Absolutism did have its advantages.

The Age of Revolutions (1789–1914)

As the 1700s drew to a close, few had any inkling of the dramatic changes about to transform European society, politics, and international affairs. Within a span of 120 years, Europe would cease to be a place where monarchs waged limited wars with professional armies, becoming one in which popular governments fought wars with millions of men, resulting in casualties and destruction on an almost unimaginable scale. The story of how the comparatively genteel world of the 1700s gave way to the horrors of World War I's trenches involves two interrelated developments. The first was the rise of modern nationalism, which altered the relationship between people and their governments, thus eroding the foundations of absolutist monarchism. And as absolutist monarchism faded, the international order it supported began to change. The second development was the industrial revolution, which would alter the social and political character of European societies and increase dramatically the destructive potential of warfare. Modern nationalism would eventually combine with industrialism on the bloody battlefields of World War I. This is a complicated story that begins with two political revolutions, one in the new world and the other in the heart of monarchical Europe.

The American and French Revolutions

French Revolution The popular revolt against the French monarchy in 1789 that resulted in the establishment of the French Republic. Along with the American Revolution (1776), it marked the emergence of modern nationalism.

popular sovereignty The principle that governments must derive their legitimacy from the people over whom they rule. Embodied in the French and American Revolutions, this doctrine challenged the principle of the divine right of kings.

The American Revolution of 1776 and the **French Revolution** of 1789 signaled the introduction of a new idea that would in time unravel the political order of European societies. Before these revolutions, the rulers of Europe claimed divine sources of legitimacy: Louis XVI ruled over the people of France not because they wanted him but because God willed it. At the core of the American and French revolutions was the dangerous, indeed revolutionary, idea of **popular sovereignty**— the notion that governments needed to derive their authority and legitimacy from the people over whom they ruled.

The French Revolution did not start as a revolution but merely as resistance to King Louis XVI's attempts to raise taxes (largely to pay off debts incurred when the French sided with American colonists in their war for independence). The resistance rapidly snowballed into a revolt against the monarchy itself, resulting in the overthrow of Louis XVI in 1792 and the establishment of the French Republic. A "Reign of Terror" eventually ensued in which thousands of nobles and supposed enemies of the revolution met with a gruesome end, usually via the infamous guillotine. Even Louis XVI and his queen, Marie Antoinette, were not spared the blade.

To grasp the significance of the French Revolution, we need to appreciate that the King of France was not just another king; he was *the* king, the most powerful and prestigious monarch in all of Europe. As a result, the Revolution and overthrow of the French monarchy came to be seen as a threat to the entire system of absolutist monarchism. As one might expect, this was viewed as an undesirable development in the royal courts of Europe, though it did take a while for the enormity of what had happened to sink in. The initial reaction was not one of great alarm, perhaps because the Revolution was seen as weakening France and unlikely to succeed in the long run. Thus, at first the response was largely to ignore and isolate revolutionary France.[8]

As it became apparent that the Revolution would succeed and maybe even spread, the monarchs concluded that they had a vested interest in crushing the revolt and restoring the French monarchy. The revolutionary government anticipated hostility and prepared to defend itself. France's first step was the creation of a massive citizen army. The call went out for volunteers, with the appeal being made not on the basis of financial reward but rather loyalty to the revolution and nation. When this failed to produce sufficient forces, the government instituted the **levée en masse** in 1793, conscripting all able-bodied men between the ages of 18 and 25 into military service. As a result of the *levée en masse*, "by the summer of 1794 the revolutionary army listed a million men on its rolls, of whom 750,000 were present under arms—a great force which, in terms of social class, occupation, and geographical origin, accurately reflected French society. It was the nation in arms composed of the best young men France could offer."[9] Unlike the pre-Revolutionary French army, French citizenship was a prerequisite for service. This was now the *nation's* army.

Though the citizen army of the French Republic successfully defended the revolution against its foreign enemies, the Republic had other problems. Constant fighting, some military setbacks, domestic political conflicts, and economic difficulties led to political instability. Exploiting domestic strife, Napoleon Bonaparte, an ambitious revolutionary general known for military brilliance and personal arrogance, staged a coup in 1799. Though he eventually crowned himself Emperor, there was a critical difference between Napoleon and his monarchical predecessors. Echoing the ideals of the Revolution, Napoleon maintained that his right to rule was derived from the French people. In claiming nearly absolute power while also insisting that his rule derived its legitimacy from the people, Napoleon became the first (but certainly not the last) populist dictator in modern Europe.

After consolidating power, Napoleon embarked on a program of conquest cloaked in the rhetoric and ideals of the French Revolution. The **Napoleonic Wars** (1802–1815) plunged Europe into another thirteen years of war. Given the unprecedented size of the French army, motivated by emotional appeals to spread the revolution, it was war on a grand scale. Napoleon's forces swept across Europe until France controlled most of the continent. It was not until his armies reached the outskirts of Moscow in 1812 that the tide finally turned. Napoleon's ambitions had gotten the better of him. His invasion of Russia proved to be a fatal mistake. A series of military defeats for France ended with the final failure at the Battle of Waterloo in 1815.

In many respects, the battles of the Napoleonic Wars looked very much like those of the 1700s—the soldiers and their weapons all looked the same. The major difference was scale. France's ability to mobilize and conscript men by the hundreds of thousands forced the other nations of Europe to respond in kind. Before the French Revolution, a battle involving 80,000 troops would have been extremely rare. Such battles were dwarfed by the major clashes of the Napoleonic Wars. The Battle of Leipzig (1813) involved more than 200,000 French and another 300,000 Austrian, Russian, Prussian, and Swedish forces.[10] With more than half a million troops on the field, the Battle of Leipzig involved at least five times as many men as a very large battle of the pre-Revolutionary era. The scale of war had changed to the point where it was no longer just a different level of warfare but a fundamentally new way of preparing for and waging war.

This expanding scale of war was possible because people were increasingly willing to fight and make sacrifices for their governments—and governments were

levée en masse The mobilization (conscription) of all able-bodied French males to defend the French Republic from attempts by European monarchs to restore the French monarchy.

Napoleonic Wars The French wars of European conquest following Napoleon's rise to power. Demonstrated the potential impact of modern national-ism through total national mobilization for war and widespread conscription.

more willing and able to ask people to make these sacrifices. The French Revolution was a turning point because it marked the beginnings of modern nationalism. The willingness of people from all levels of society to make sacrifices on behalf of their nation was a profoundly important development because "it was this psychological change—this popular sense of identification with the nation—that enabled the French to wage the new kind of war."[11]

After the Napoleonic Wars, the victorious monarchs of Europe formed the **Concert of Europe**, promising to resolve their disputes without resort to force and maintain a balance of power so that no one power would be tempted to dominate the whole continent, trying to recreate the order of pre-Revolutionary Europe. But no matter how much they yearned for the days of absolute monarchism, professional armies and limited wars, a permanent return would prove to be impossible. The nationalism of the French Revolution and the knowledge of how to organize and fight wars on a grand scale could not be forgotten. Furthermore, Europe was poised on the brink of another revolution that would transform the domestic societies and international order they sought to preserve.

Concert of Europe The informal system in which the monarchs of Europe tried to restore international order after the defeat of Napoleon in 1815. The victors agreed to settle their differences through diplomacy, not war, and maintain a balance of power.

The Meaning of Nationalism

Born with the French Revolution, **modern nationalism** has three major components. First, nationalism entails an emotional or psychological sense of affinity among people who share an ethnic, cultural, and linguistic heritage. A Frenchman who lives in Paris may never meet a countryman from Lyon, but they nonetheless feel connected as part of a distinct social grouping. Second, modern nationalism embraces the doctrine of popular sovereignty, according to which the only basis for legitimate government is the will of the people. This was the essence of the French and American revolutions. Finally, modern nationalism places a high value on **ethnic** or **national self-determination**. Each ethnic or national group has a right to determine its own destiny, have its own government or state, and rule itself. Thus, nationalism has both domestic and international implications. Domestically, it defines what is considered a legitimate political order. Internationally, it demands that political boundaries coincide with ethnic or national boundaries.

modern nationalism A political creed with three critical aspects: a sense of connection and loyalty between people and their rulers or governments; the belief that governments must derive their legitimacy from the people over whom they rule; and a commitment to national or ethnic self-determination.

national self-determination The principle that each national or ethnic group has the right to determine its own destiny and rule itself.

The idea of national or ethnic self-determination was a political time bomb in nineteenth-century Europe because its political map did not reflect its ethnic composition and distribution. There were a few places, such as France, where political and ethnic boundaries overlapped fairly well. Even in this case, however, the fit was not perfect: there were small populations of Germans as well as Basques and others in parts of France. The ideal of self-determination is hard to meet in reality. More problematic were Europe's major **multinational states** or empires, incorporating many ethnic and national groups within the boundaries of a single state. Austria-Hungary, the Ottoman (or Turkish) Empire, and the Russian Empire were the most prominent examples. Within Austria-Hungary, for example, there were at least ten different ethnic groups (Germans, Hungarians [also called Magyars], Romanians, Slovenes, Croats, Czechs, Poles, and so on) (see Map 1.2). In addition to the multiethnic empires, there were also several **multistate nations** in which one national or ethnic grouping was divided into several states. The Germans were the

multinational states A single state or government ruling over people of many distinct ethnic identities.

multistate nations A single ethnic group divided into several different, independent political units or states.

MAP 1.2 Distribution of ethnic groups, 1871-1908

This map showing the distribution of ethnic groups in the Austrian-Hungarian Empire illustrates the failure of political boundaries to coincide with ethnic boundaries.

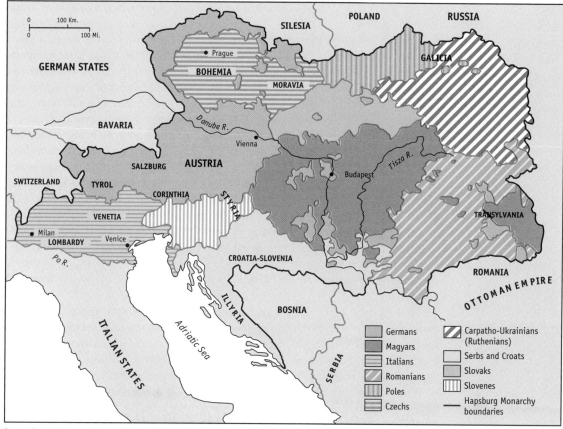

most significant example of a multistate nation through most of the nineteenth century. Before 1871, no such country as Germany existed; the area that we know as Germany was divided in several states (Prussia, Bavaria, Hanover, etc.). Nationalism would have a different impact depending on the particular ethnic or political configuration.

In the case of the Austrian-Hungarian and Ottoman empires, nationalism was a disintegrative force. As different ethnic groups demanded greater autonomy, power, and even independence, central governments found it necessary to expend resources and effort to suppress nationalist movements. The spread of nationalism would gradually weaken states composed of many different ethnic groups. But nationalism proved to have the opposite effect in places like Germany, where it led to the creation of new, larger, and more powerful political entities. The unification of Italy in 1861 and that of the German states in 1871 were logical consequences of the doctrine of ethnic self-determination. Thus, nationalism was both a destructive, disintegrating force and a creative, integrating force. The weakening of some states and the creation of others altered the map of Europe, upsetting the balance of power in ways that would create new problems and lead Europe down the path to World War I.

Between 1864 and 1871, the Prussian general Otto von Bismarck waged a series of quick and decisive wars to unify the German states. This was a monumental geopolitical development. The unification of Germany in only seven years marked the almost overnight creation of a new great power in the heart of Europe. With its substantial population, industrial output, efficient government administration, and military power based on the renowned Prussian army, Germany was a force to reckon with, and German power only increased in the decades following unification.

By the turn of the century, German industrial output had soared past Great Britain's. Within Germany, this led to demands for a more assertive foreign policy and the creation of sufficient military power to sustain it. Most troublesome, especially to Britain, was increasing German naval power, which was seen as a threat to British naval supremacy. Michael Mandelbaum explains the problem: "Germany's enormous growth was the disturbing element in European affairs. It was a development that could not be accommodated within the existing order.... Although surpassing the other powers in military and economic terms, they lagged behind in what were supposed to be the fruits, as well as the sources of power: territorial possessions."[12]

How did the other nations of Europe respond to German power? France in particular was not happy being replaced as the dominant continental power and sought allies to balance off Germany's growing power. Germany, on the other hand, feared "encirclement" by hostile powers (France to the west, Austria-Hungary to the south, and Russia to the east). Germany hoped to keep France isolated by forging alliances with Austria-Hungary and Russia. This proved to be very difficult because Russia and Austria-Hungary were often in conflict over issues in the Balkans (the southern part of Eastern Europe). Eventually, Germany formed an alliance with Austria-Hungary and Italy in 1882. After years of searching for a partner, France finally formed an alliance with Russia in 1892. This basic division of Europe remained intact until the outbreak of World War I (see Map 1.3).

The Industrial Revolution

The industrial revolution changed so much about the way people lived that it is almost impossible to know where to begin or end a discussion of its impact. In terms of understanding the evolution of international relations, three aspects of the industrial revolution are critical. First, the industrial revolution changed European societies in ways that reinforced many of the developments associated with nationalism, particularly the erosion of monarchical rule and the rise of mass politics. Second, the industrial revolution allowed for the production of commodities cheaply and in vast quantities. Not just clothes, canned goods, and railroad cars poured off the assembly lines but also guns, cannons, ammunition, and military uniforms. Third, the wealth, weapons, and technology created during the industrial revolution

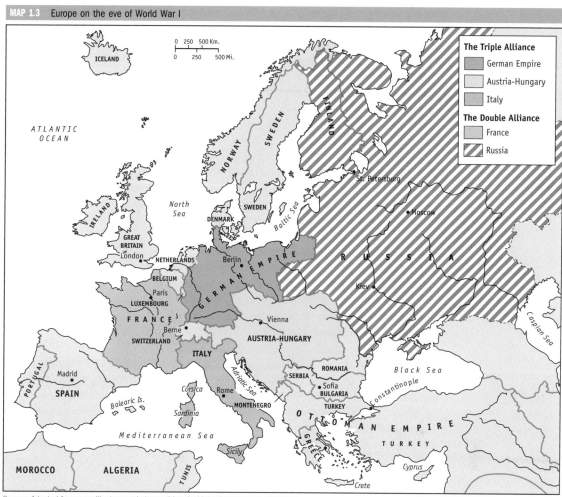

MAP 1.3　Europe on the eve of World War I

Source: Adapted from www.lib.utexas.edu/maps/historical/shepherd/europe_1911.jpg.

widened the power gap between Europe and the non-Western world, contributing to the expansion of European influence to all corners of the world.

Before the mid-1800s, European societies were primarily agricultural. But with the spread of industrialism, people began leaving farms and pouring into cities to work in factories. Just as important as urbanization, the industrial revolution also created new economic and social classes—a small elite of wealthy barons of industry; a substantial middle class of managers, entrepreneurs, and skilled workers; and an ever-increasing and organized urban working class. As these new groups increased in size and power, they demanded a greater voice in government and politics. The monarchs of Europe were increasingly confronted with a dilemma: how to preserve the existing political order in the face of such dramatic social and economic changes. In the long run, they failed to resolve the dilemma. As the nineteenth century progressed, the power of monarchs gradually eroded as the power of more representative political institutions increased. Although very few European countries could be considered genuinely democratic by the end of the century, there were also very few genuinely absolutist monarchs. The force of nationalism, the requirements and strains of industrial society, and demands for wider political inclusion slowly transformed European societies from elitist, absolutist monarchies to polities characterized by mass political inclusion and involvement.

One of the clearest manifestations of the dilemma the monarchs faced was the exclusion of people from political power while asking them to sacrifice on behalf of the state. The most onerous sacrifice governments demanded of their (male) citizens was military service. Conscription was practiced in virtually every nation, some demanding up to six or eight years of service. Only Britain among the major powers refrained from conscription. By the end of the nineteenth century, European powers maintained peacetime armies that dwarfed even the wartime armies of the century before. But despite the tremendous social and political changes of the nineteenth century, the period between 1815 and 1914 was deceptively calm. Other than the Crimean War (1854–1856), war among major powers was avoided. The most devastating war, the American Civil War, occurred on the other side of the world. By the end of the nineteenth century, every major power in Europe lived in a state of nearly permanent war readiness. No one knew when or why war might come or what it would be like when it did, but they knew it would come.

In terms of the wider world, increasing European wealth and military power combined with improvements in naval technology and communications to create a scramble for overseas colonies during the second half of the nineteenth century. By 1900, very few areas of Asia or Africa were free of European domination (see Map 1.4). England's Queen Victoria could accurately claim that the sun never set on her empire. This was the second major wave of European imperialism. The first, immediately following the discovery of the New World in the 1500s and 1600s, was concentrated on North and South America.

Historians differ on what forces drove the second wave of imperialism. Some argued that the major cause was industrial capitalism's need for overseas markets and access to cheap raw materials, resources, and labor. Others saw imperialism as a primarily cultural phenomenon, arguing that notions of ethnic, racial, and religious superiority led Europeans to conquer the "backward" parts of the world in a missionary attempt to spread the virtues of Christianity and Western culture. Whatever the motivation, "Europe's domination of the world…reflected the ability of sophisticated weapons and advanced techniques to overcome the inherent advantages of native populations…. The machine-gun was only the most concrete military expression of the tactical superiority enjoyed by European armies in Asia and Africa."[13] European wealth and weapons "vastly increased the gap between the West and the Rest, making it easy for a handful of Europeans to conquer much of Asia and Africa."[14]

At the dawn of the twentieth century the world had been transformed. The age of absolutist monarchism was on its last legs. The spread of nationalism was reconfiguring the map of Europe, creating new powers while weakening old ones.

MAP 1.4 European overseas empires in 1913

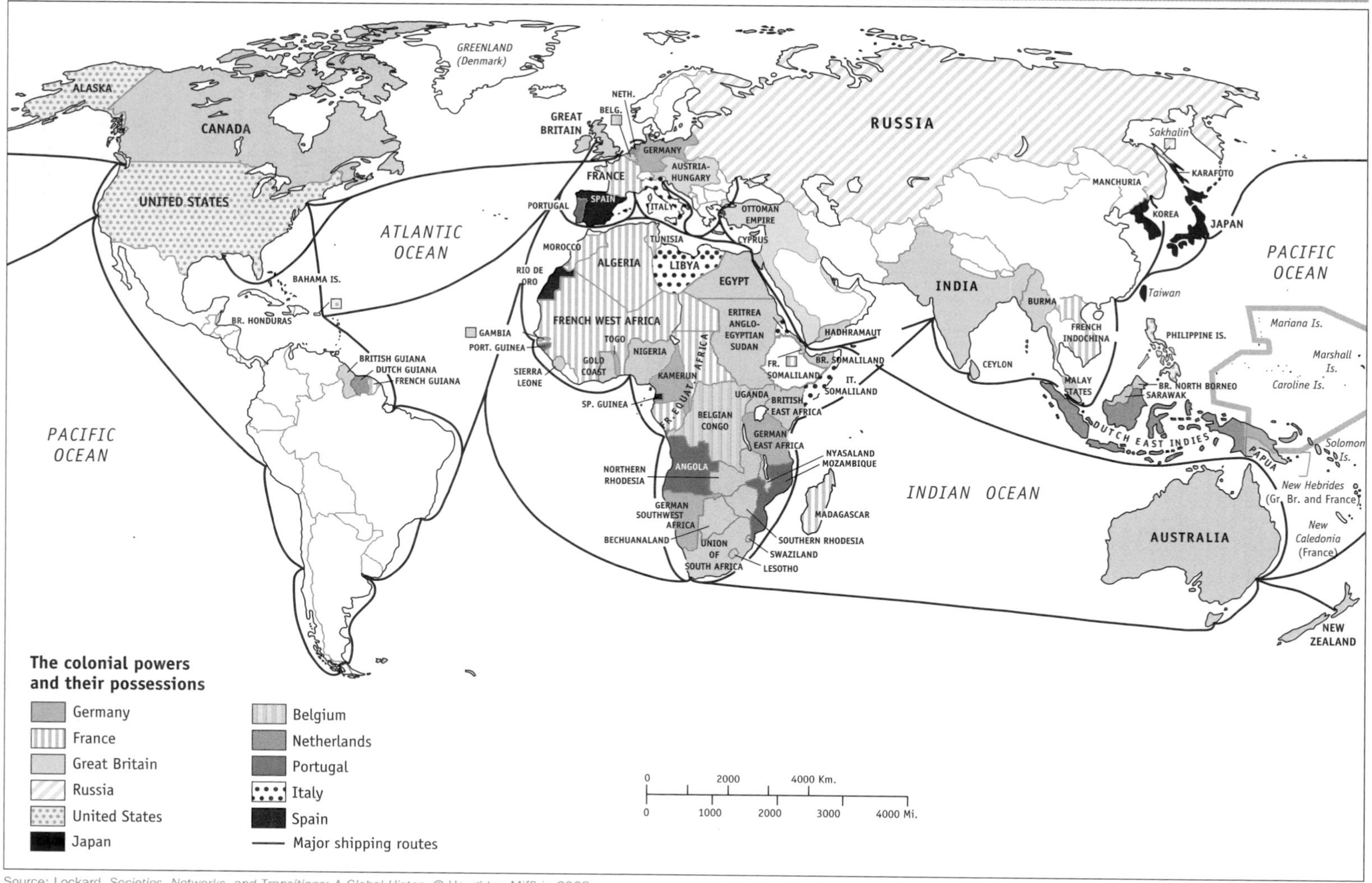

The colonial powers
and their possessions

Germany

France

Great Britain

Russia

United States

Japan

Belgium

Netherlands

Portugal

Italy

Spain

Major shipping routes

PACIFIC OCEAN

PACIFIC OCEAN

ATLANTIC OCEAN

INDIAN OCEAN

ALASKA

CANADA

UNITED STATES

GREENLAND (Denmark)

BR. HONDURAS

BAHAMA IS.

BRITISH GUIANA
DUTCH GUIANA
FRENCH GUIANA

GREAT BRITAIN

PORTUGAL

SPAIN

FRANCE

NETH.

BELG.

GERMANY

AUSTRIA-HUNGARY

OTTOMAN EMPIRE

CYPRUS

ITALY

TUNISIA

MOROCCO

RIO DE ORO

ALGERIA

LIBYA

EGYPT

GAMBIA
PORT. GUINEA

SIERRA LEONE

GOLD COAST

TOGO

FRENCH WEST AFRICA

NIGERIA

KAMERUN

SP. GUINEA

FR. EQUATORIAL AFRICA

ANGLO-EGYPTIAN SUDAN

ERITREA

FR. SOMALILAND

BR. SOMALILAND

IT. SOMALILAND

HADRAMAUT

UGANDA

BRITISH EAST AFRICA

GERMAN EAST AFRICA

BELGIAN CONGO

NORTHERN RHODESIA

ANGOLA

GERMAN SOUTHWEST AFRICA

BECHUANALAND

SOUTHERN RHODESIA

NYASALAND

MOZAMBIQUE

MADAGASCAR

SWAZILAND

LESOTHO

UNION OF SOUTH AFRICA

RUSSIA

Sakhalin

KARAFUTO

JAPAN

KOREA

MANCHURIA

Taiwan

INDIA

CEYLON

BURMA

FRENCH INDOCHINA

MALAY STATES

PHILIPPINE IS.

BR. NORTH BORNEO

SARAWAK

DUTCH EAST INDIES

PAPUA

Mariana Is.

Marshall Is.

Caroline Is.

Solomon Is.

New Hebrides (Gr. Br. and France)

New Caledonia (France)

AUSTRALIA

NEW ZEALAND

0	1000	2000	3000	4000 Km.
0		2000		4000 Mi.

Source: Lockard, Societies, Networks, and Transitions: A Global History © Houghton Miffl in 2008.

Nationalism and the industrial revolution allowed governments to create war machines capable of unparalleled destruction. European political and military power had spread to even the most remote reaches of the world. On the surface things remained calm, but the calm would not last long.

The Road to War

The division of Europe into rival alliances almost guaranteed that a war involving anyone would eventually involve everyone. The only question was which conflict would bring the precarious peace to an end. The chances were good that a general war would emerge from the conflicts in the Balkans in Southeastern Europe. It was here that the power of the Austrian-Hungarian, Ottoman, and Russian empires intersected in political waters muddied by the conflicts of nationalism. One of the most volatile conflicts was between Austria-Hungary and Serbia. Recall that there were substantial populations of Serbians living within the borders of Austria-Hungary (see Map 1.2). Consistent with the sentiments of nationalism, powerful forces within Serbia called for the creation of a Greater Serbia incorporating all the Serbian people, something that did not sit well with Austria-Hungary. When a Serbian nationalist extremist assassinated Archduke Franz Ferdinand of Austria-Hungary (next in line to the throne) in Sarajevo on June 28, 1914, the first step on the road to war was taken. What followed was a dizzying round of threats and ultimatums that failed to resolve the crisis. Austria-Hungary declared war on Serbia on July 28, 1914. Russia, which generally supported Serbia, mobilized its army on July 30, setting off a chain reaction in Germany and France. By August 4, all of Europe was at war, with Britain joining France and Russia. The peace that had lasted since the defeat of Napoleon was over.

The Age of Total War (1914–1945)

When the Great War (as World War I was known before there was any need to number such conflicts) finally came, most expected the troops home by Christmas. Men flooded into recruiting stations to get in on the big adventure. Enthusiastic crowds saw the trainloads of men off to war. This was still an age in which romantic images of chivalrous war clouded the popular imagination. The enthusiasm did not long survive the realities of industrial warfare. Instead of the glorious battles of war novels, the soldiers found a bleak, bloody, and impersonal battlefield. The war that was supposed to be over by the holidays dragged on for four indecisive years, turning into a horrific war of attrition that destroyed and scarred an entire generation. Machine guns, artillery, massive quantities of ammunition, poisonous gas, and muddy trenches robbed war of glamour and romance.

Whereas the Battle of Leipzig a century earlier represented war on an unprecedented scale because it involved 500,000 *soldiers*, during World War I it was not uncommon for single battles to result in more than 500,000 *casualties*. At the Battle of Verdun (1916), over 400,000 men were killed or wounded. The British lost almost 20,000 men on the very first day of the Battle of the Somme (1916).

Given the population of Britain at the time, this would be the equivalent of 80,000 Americans dying on the first day of the 2003 Gulf War. Proportionally, the British lost more men in one day at the Battle of the Somme than the United States did during all fifteen years of the Vietnam War. In the end, British casualties exceeded 400,000 at the Somme. At the Battle of Passchendaele (1917), the allies and the Germans suffered over 600,000 casualties. Such casualties are even more astounding given the modest gains achieved. At the Somme the British captured a mere 120 square miles of territory.[15] Industrial total war also transformed the manner of death. James Sheehan relates the grim fact that 100,000 of the 379,000 French casualties at Verdun were classified as "missing" because "the majority had been interred in the mud or simply blown to bits by artillery fire, their bodies unrecovered or unrecognizable."[16] This was not what the enthusiastic recruits of 1914 expected.

If it was the enthusiasm of nationalism that brought men to the battlefields, it was the factories of the industrial revolution that supplied them with a seemingly endless supply of guns, bullets, cannons, and artillery shells. People not fighting the war on the battlefields worked at home in factories supplying the soldiers. To wage war on this scale, governments mobilized entire populations and seized control of industry. War bonds were sold; prices and wages were controlled; consumer goods were rationed; new taxes were imposed; women came out of the home to work in the factories; and even children collected scrap metal to be turned into weapons and ammunition. World War I became the first **total war**, in which every element of society and every aspect of national life were consumed by the conduct of war.

total war A war in which participants mobilize all available resources, human and material, for the purpose of waging war.

Total war represented the coming together of the two developments transforming European societies and politics over the previous century—nationalism and industrialism. Nationalism allowed governments to make unprecedented demands of their citizens. Industrialization provided the material to equip, transport, and sustain armies on a vast new scale. Bruce Porter explains how, "The feverish nationalism that engulfed Europe in 1914 attested to the status that the nation-state had attained as the supreme claimant on human loyalty…. The nationalism of the war and its consequent unifying effect enabled states to mobilize their human resources on a scale previously unthinkable."[17] When combined with the ability of industry to produce limitless quantities of weapons and ammunition, the result was slaughter as "all the technological and organizational genius of the industrial age culminat[ed] in the mass production of mass destruction."[18]

The carnage continued for three years, and by 1917 the nations and armies of Europe were close to exhaustion. Three pivotal events finally brought the war to an end. First, the armored tank, a new weapon introduced by the British in 1917, offered a way out of the stalemate of trench warfare. Tanks provided protection, enabling soldiers to advance across battlefields and through barbed wire more safely and rapidly. Second, largely because of the devastation of the war, the demoralization of the army, and the weakness of the government, the Bolsheviks (the communists) seized power in the Russian Revolution of November 1917 and quickly made good on their promise to withdraw Russia from the war. Third, although peace with Russia seemed like good news for Germany, this was offset by American entry into the war on the side of France and Britain. German submarine warfare against ships crossing the Atlantic with supplies for Britain finally enraged the United States

Trench warfare during World War I. German troops try to advance (top) while a British soldier peers onto the battlefield. Glorious visions of war did not long survive the harsh realities of industrial warfare: barbed wire, machine guns, fire from distant artillery day and night, and life in a muddy ditch shared with corpses and vermin.

Source: Hulton Archive/Getty Images

sufficiently to bring it into the war in April 1917. The tide turned against Germany by August 1918, and Germany was defeated by November. The tragedy of the Great War was over. The troops, psychologically and physically scarred by the bleak horrors of industrialized warfare, limped home. It was now up to the statesmen to pick up the pieces and create a world in which the Great War might be the last one, the "war to end all wars," as it was referred to optimistically at the time. In the end it is hard to disagree with Simon Schama's assessment of World War I as the "original sin" of the twentieth century, a horror from which a host of other horrors, including Hitler and another World War, would soon follow.[19]

The Road to War (Again)

Two major power wars within a single generation is unusual in international history. That Europe would again be plunged into war merely two decades after World War I suggests a connection between the conflicts. World War II cannot be understood without an appreciation of the previous war's impact on both the victors and the vanquished. World War I cast a long, dark shadow. It is impossible to exaggerate the impact of the war on European societies. The legacy of the war was not uniform, however. For some, the horrors of World War I forged a determination to avoid a repeat at any cost. Modern war had become so terrible that nothing could justify another war. For others, the perception that the Great War's settlement was unfair and unjust fueled resentment. These contrasting views of the war proved a dangerous mix.

Major wars always pose the problem of creating a postwar order, a task that usually falls to the victors. The first step in this direction was the **Treaty of Versailles** (1919), which spelled out the final peace terms. The treaty was in many senses a quintessential "victor's peace"—harsh on the losers, easy on the winners. Germany was required to accept conditions that applied to no one else—relinquishment of territory, restrictions on the size of its armed forces, and payment of huge reparations. Most important, Germany was forced to accept sole and total blame for the war. This provision was particularly galling and humiliating for the Germans, who came to feel that they had been unfairly singled out for harsh treatment simply because they were the losers. As a result, "all German parties and statesmen … took it for granted that the Treaty of Versailles required drastic revision."[20] A decade later, Hitler and the Nazis were able to take advantage of and exploit these sentiments during their rise to power.

In Great Britain and France, the war's legacy was somewhat different. Having gone to war in 1914 expecting a short conflict, they instead found themselves trapped in a war of unprecedented horror. Though victorious, victory came at a staggering cost. From their perspective, the overriding priority was avoiding another war. During the 1970s in the United States, people often spoke of a Vietnam syndrome, referring to a supposed hesitance to use force abroad for fear of becoming bogged down in another Vietnam. But if we compare the human and economic costs of the Vietnam War to the United States to the costs of World War I, there really is no comparison. The casualties suffered by Britain in World War I (adjusted for the differences in population) were 80 times greater than those of the United States in Vietnam. Imagine the impact of Vietnam if the United States had suffered 4,000,000 casualties instead of 50,000.

Many yearned for the creation of a postwar order that might prevent another war, and U.S. President Woodrow Wilson attempted to provide one. The cornerstone of his postwar order was the **League of Nations** to provide a collective, international response to future threats to peace. The League eventually proved ineffective. Several obstacles doomed the League. First, despite the organization's connection to Woodrow Wilson, the United States failed to join when the U.S. Senate refused to ratify the treaty. Second, the Soviet Union retreated into isolation. Third, and most important, the League's members were unwilling to do what was necessary to

Treaty of Versailles Codified the terms on which World War I was concluded. These terms were particularly harsh on the loser, Germany. In addition to requiring the payment of reparations, restrictions on German armed forces, and territorial concessions, the treaty stated that Germany bore full responsibility for World War I. Germans viewed this stipulation across the political spectrum as one-sided and unjust.

League of Nations International organization created in the aftermath of World War I. Tried to ensure that there would be a collective, international response to any future threats to peace.

respond to threats to peace. The League was a voluntary organization of states, not a world government. It did not have its own military forces. If it were to mount a credible response, it would need to convince its member to do so. In the end, they were unwilling to respond when needed.

As the 1920s drew to a close, a dangerous brew was already simmering—Germany was dissatisfied with the terms of Versailles; Western European nations were weary of war and determined to avoid any repetition; and the principal post-war institution designed to preserve the peace was not living up to expectations. The Great Depression made things worse, creating economic hardship and political turmoil everywhere. Hitler and the Nazis exploited German resentment and the hardships of the depression to expand their political appeal. Many forget that although the Nazis quickly destroyed German democracy, they came to power initially through democratic means. Fascist, military-oriented dictatorships emerged in Italy, Japan, and Spain as well. These regimes provided the final tipping point that plunged the world into war for the second time in a generation.

Traditional accounts date the start of World War II to Germany's invasion of Poland on September 1, 1939, although Japan's takeover of Manchuria (part of China) in 1931 or its invasion of China in 1937 can also mark the starting point. As Japan was expanding its empire in Asia, Hitler came to power in Germany in 1933. Ravaged by the Great Depression and limited by the Treaty of Versailles, Germany remained too weak in the early years of Nazi rule to cause much trouble. By 1935, however, the German economy was recovering and Hitler began to implement his plan to restore and expand German power. Conscription was resumed and the new German air force (the Luftwaffe) was unveiled. Though both actions violated the Treaty of Versailles, Germany's neighbors did nothing. Hitler's first major international move occurred in 1936, when German forces reentered the Rhineland (German territory on the border with France), violating the Treaty of Versailles. Again, Germany's neighbors did nothing.

Hitler became increasingly bold. Between 1936 and 1938 German military spending increased dramatically and went largely unmatched and unchallenged. Instead of resisting these initial German moves, Western nations engaged in a policy of **appeasement**. Rather than risk war over demands that could be seen as legitimate, France and Britain acquiesced. Though a few lonely voices, such as Winston Churchill in Britain, expressed concern, the policy of appeasement remained popular, in part because the idea of another war was so unpopular. The most infamous act of appeasement occurred in the fall of 1938. The problem (or pretext) was the presence of ethnic Germans living in a part of Czechoslovakia known as the Sudetenland. With the encouragement of Hitler and the German government in Berlin, the Sudeten Germans demanded to be unified with Germany. As the situation approached war, a conference was held in Munich in which France and Britain (without the consent of the Czechs) gave Hitler what he wanted. Upon his return home, British Prime Minister Neville Chamberlain waved the agreement aloft, proclaiming proudly the achievement of "peace in our time." A few months later, in March 1939, Germany surprised the world again by invading and capturing the rest of Czechoslovakia. The **Munich Agreement** had not satisfied Hitler. Now it was clear to all that his goals went well beyond revising the Treaty of Versailles.

appeasement A policy in which nations deal with international conflicts by giving in to the demands of their opponents. The term acquired an extremely negative connotation as a result of attempts to appease Hitler and Nazi Germany in the years before World War II.

Munich Agreement Often cited as the most egregious example of appeasement, this was an agreement in which France and England allowed Germany to take over the Sudetenland (a portion of Czechoslovakia where many ethnic Germans lived).

Few could escape the conclusion that war would come again. But when? And when war came, would the nations of Europe be ready to fight Hitler's revived Germany?

The Next "Great War"

Europe did not have to wait long for answers. After signing a nonaggression pact with the Soviet Union, German troops invaded Poland on September 1, 1939. Britain and France declared war on Germany. After making quick work of Poland, Hitler turned westward, conquering Holland, Belgium, Luxembourg, and most of France, leaving Britain virtually alone to prevent total German domination of Western Europe. Though the United States provided critical supplies to Britain, isolationist sentiment kept the United States out of the war. The Germans bombed London and other parts of Britain, which many feared was a prelude to an invasion. Though the bombing caused substantial damage and hardship, the anticipated invasion never came.

In 1941, two developments altered the course of the war. In June, Hitler broke his nonaggression pact with Stalin and invaded the Soviet Union. Then, in December, the Japanese struck at Pearl Harbor, leading the United States to declare war on Japan. In response, Japan's ally Germany declared war on the United States, bringing the United States into the European conflict as well. The United States and the Soviet Union were now allies along with Britain in the struggle against Germany (Stalin promised to join the war against Japan shortly after Germany was defeated).

Though the United States declared war on Germany, the vast majority of the fighting in Europe between 1941 and 1944 took place on the Eastern Front between Germany and the Soviet Union. Stalin pressured Churchill and U.S. President Franklin Delano Roosevelt to relieve the burden of fighting on the Soviet Union by opening a "second front" in Western Europe, but this would not happen until June 1944. In the meantime the Soviet Union suffered massive casualties. Whereas previous estimates of Soviet casualties (military and civilian) were around 20 million, "new research growing out of the more open atmosphere in recent years has been pointing to figures closer to, and possibly in excess of, 25 million deaths."[21] It is impossible to overstate the level of devastation and its impact on the Soviet Union. Even though the United States shouldered the burden of fighting Japan in the Pacific, its casualties were modest in comparison, totaling approximately 330,000 in Europe and the Pacific combined, less than 2 percent of Soviet casualties. Because the attack on Pearl Harbor was the only military engagement on U.S. territory, civilian casualties and physical destruction were minimal. The experience of the countries that emerged from World War II as the two major world powers was strikingly different.

The invasion of France on the beaches of Normandy on June 7, 1944, opened the long-awaited second front, requiring Hitler to fight on two fronts. As allied troops advanced on Germany from the west and Soviet troops closed in from the east, the eventual outcome of the war in Europe became clear. In June 1945, American, British, and Soviet troops met in Berlin and Germany's defeat was final. The war against Japan continued for a few months after the German surrender, with the United States' use of atomic bombs on Hiroshima and Nagasaki in early August 1945 finally triggering Japan's surrender (just in time to prevent Soviet entry into the war against Japan, a fact some believe to be more than coincidence).[22] The second total war in the generation had come to its conclusion.

The Cold War (1945–1989)

After waging two wars in the span of thirty years with combined casualties approaching 100 million, the obvious concern was avoiding yet another war. As World War II ended, it was still unclear what sort of world would emerge from the wreckage. Would the victors be able to construct a postwar order that could avoid a descent into World War III? Would they be able to construct an international organization that might fulfill the failed promise of the League of Nations? Could the world finally learn to avoid the calamity of total war?

Though no one knew the answers, most realized everything depended on whether the United States and the Soviet Union would be able to build on the cooperative relationship established during the war. Everyone knew that these two countries would emerge from the war as the dominant powers, and the general character of any international order is usually defined by the nature of relations among its major powers. Before World War II, the relationship between the United States and the Soviet Union had been strained; the United States had refused even to recognize the Soviet government until 1933. Nonetheless, some hoped that their wartime alliance might form the basis for a better relationship. Others remained doubtful, seeing the wartime alliance as a product of unusual circumstances—namely, the presence of a common threat in Nazi Germany. Once that threat was eliminated, conflicts between the United States and the Soviet Union were expected to resurface.

During the war there were indications of future trouble. One can look to the U.S. atomic bomb program, the Manhattan Project, for one sign of the problems to come. Even though Great Britain was kept informed about the progress of the project, Britain and the United States decided not to share the information with the Soviet Union, though Stalin certainly knew about the project from spying. Despite the alliance President Roosevelt "saw no reason to take the Soviets into American confidence about a weapons system of potentially great significance in the post-war years."[23]

Keeping the atomic secret was only one sign that the Soviet Union was not viewed as an ally in the same sense as Britain. Another sign of trouble was disagreements about the postwar fate of Eastern Europe (e.g., Poland, Romania, Hungary, and others). The military reality was that at war's end Soviet forces would control these countries. The United States insisted that Stalin hold free elections in Eastern Europe after the war. In fact, Stalin signed the Declaration on Liberated Europe (1945), which called for free and open elections. Stalin, however, wanted governments friendly to the Soviet Union. Given Soviet losses in World War II, Stalin thought this was a reasonable demand to protect Soviet security in the future. Unfortunately, these two objectives could not be met simultaneously: freely elected governments in Eastern Europe would not have been friendly to the Soviet Union. As John Lewis Gaddis explains, "F.D.R.'s superficial knowledge of Eastern Europe kept him from fully recognizing the contradiction between freely elected and pro-Russian governments."[24]

The secrecy surrounding the Manhattan Project and disagreements about the future of Eastern Europe were not the only sources of tension between the two allies (the delayed opening of the second front in Europe was another), but they are enough to indicate that the United States–Soviet alliance during World War II was more a product of a common threat than of broader common interests and outlooks. To use a familiar adage of international politics: the enemy of my enemy is my friend. It is more accurate to view the United States and Soviet Union as co-belligerents in the war against Germany, not allies in any deeper sense of the term.

The Cold War Begins: Conflict and Containment

United States–Soviet relations deteriorated rapidly after the war. The impossibility of reconciling the Western desires for free elections in Eastern Europe with Soviet expectations of friendly regimes became obvious as Stalin moved to impose communist governments. It was increasingly clear that Stalin had no intention of abiding by the democratic provisions of the Declaration on Liberated Europe. Political dissent throughout Eastern Europe was ruthlessly crushed. Soviet actions prompted Winston Churchill's famous warning that "from Stettin in the Baltic to Trieste in the Adriatic, an iron curtain has descended across the continent."[25]

In response to these developments, an American diplomat in Moscow, George Kennan, composed an analysis of Soviet policy. Conveyed to Washington as a diplomatic telegram in early February 1946, it was later published in the influential journal *Foreign Affairs* under the title "The Sources of Soviet Conduct" (signed only as "X"). Kennan argued that the United States needed to understand the expansionist nature of Soviet policy and the threats it posed to U.S. interests. The sources of Soviet expansion, he argued, were deeply rooted in Russia's historical insecurity, Stalin's paranoid personality, the communist regime's need for external enemies, and the imperatives of Soviet ideology. Though in the long run these expansionist tendencies could be modified or tamed, the only immediate option available to the United States was a policy of **containment**. The United States needed to use its power—political, economic, and military—to prevent further expansion of Soviet influence. Kennan's analysis struck a chord in Washington.[26]

Because of political pressure to bring American troops home from Europe as soon as possible, many feared a military threat from the Soviet Union. But even those who were less concerned with a direct military attack worried that postwar economic hardship would provide fertile ground for communist parties loyal to the Soviet Union to come to power. Virtually everyone agreed that the economic reconstruction of Western Europe was vital to its security. The primary instrument for recovery was the **Marshall Plan**, announced in May 1947. The Marshall Plan offered massive economic aid to all the countries of Europe (including the Soviet Union) devastated by the war. The Soviet Union refused the aid because some of

containment The United States' policy of resisting the expansion of Soviet/communist influence during the Cold War.

Marshall Plan The program of economic assistance to rebuild the nations of Western Europe in the after-math of World War II.

the conditions were deemed incompatible with its socialist economy. The Soviet-imposed governments in Eastern Europe were pressured to do likewise. In the end, the Marshall Plan was a stunning success. By 1952, Western Europe's productive output was almost double its prewar levels.

At roughly the same time, the United States also became concerned about a civil war in Greece because the British informed the United States that they could no longer give assistance to the Greek government combating a communist insurgency. In a speech to Congress explaining his decision to aid the Greek government (as well as the Turkish government), President Harry Truman laid out his policy goals in broad and grandiose terms: "I believe it must be the policy of the United States to support free people who are resisting attempted subjugation by armed minorities or outside pressures."[27] This pronouncement, embodying an expansive vision of containment, came to be known as the **Truman Doctrine**. Thus, by the end of 1947 the hope for a cooperative superpower relationship was dead. The **Cold War** had begun in earnest.

The Cold War Expands

Despite the rhetoric of the Truman Doctrine, which suggested that the United States would assist *all* "free peoples," it was unclear whether containment would apply everywhere or only in strategically significant parts of the world. It was also unclear what types of aid would be provided and whether the United States was prepared to go to war to contain communist influence. The fall of China to the communists in 1949 and the North Korean attack on South Korea in 1950 would have the effect of expanding the scope of containment well beyond Europe. The United States decided to take military action under the aegis of the United Nations to prevent the expansion of communism into South Korea. The Korean War, which eventually involved China as well, lasted four years at the cost of more than 50,000 American casualties. The net effect of the Korean War was to globalize containment. Even if a given country was not strategically very significant, the fear was that if any country fell, others were sure to follow. This became known as the **domino theory**. The Korean War also shifted the emphasis of containment. Now the threat and response were seen increasingly in military terms, with one result being the creation of a military alliance, the **North Atlantic Treaty Organization (NATO)**, in Europe.

The logic of containment and the domino theory would be most severely tested in the Third World. World War II had seriously weakened the colonial powers of Britain and France, and the immediate postwar years witnessed the rise of independence and national liberation movements throughout Asia and Africa. The process of **decolonization**, however, was not free of conflict: sometimes the colonial power tried to hold on, usually in vain. But conflicts continued after independence as different groups, including communists, struggled for power.

The most important such conflict occurred in Vietnam. A former French colony, Vietnam was divided between the communist north, supported by China and the Soviet Union, and the noncommunist, though hardly democratic, south. In the late 1950s and early 1960s, a communist insurgency supported by North Vietnam

Truman Doctrine Announced by President Harry Truman in 1947, this policy committed the United States to assist foreign governments threatened by communist forces. It represented an expansive vision of the policy of containment.

Cold War The conflict between the United States and the Soviet Union from the late 1940s until the late 1980s (the fall of the Berlin Wall) or early 1990s (the collapse of the Soviet Union).

domino theory The belief (and fear) that the spread of communism to one country almost automatically threatened its expansion to neighboring countries.

North Atlantic Treaty Organization (NATO) The Cold War alliance, including the United States, Canada, and many Western European nations, against the Soviet Union and its allies. It has survived the end of the Cold War, even expanding to include many former Soviet allies in Eastern Europe.

decolonization The achievement of political independence by European colonies, especially in Asia and Africa, in the two decades following World War II.

threatened the regime in South Vietnam. United States policymakers were determined to support the South Vietnamese government, first in the form of aid and military advisers. It was not long before the United States was actively involved in fighting, and by 1968 there were over 500,000 American combat forces on the ground. Despite repeated promises that victory was at hand, the war dragged on year after year. Public support eroded and protests against the war spread and grew. Despite more than ten years of fighting, the world's most "powerful" nation was unable to prevail. In 1975, communist forces captured Saigon, the capital of South Vietnam, and television screens around the world were filled with scenes of desperate people climbing to the roof of the U.S. embassy to reach helicopters carrying the last people out before the communist victory was total.[28]

Easing the Cold War

Even as the Vietnam War was being waged, there were attempts to ease the superpower conflict. Elected president in 1968, Richard Nixon and his chief foreign policy adviser, Henry Kissinger, embarked upon a policy of **détente** toward the Soviet Union. They believed the United States possessed tools that could be used as leverage to moderate Soviet behavior. There were things the Soviet Union wanted from the United States. The Soviet Union sought recognition as a power on par with the United States and greater opportunities to trade. In return, the United States wanted greater respect for human rights and restraint in support for communist governments and insurgencies in the Third World. Détente was based on the assumption that these different interests and objectives of the two powers could be "linked" in order to create a relationship based not only on conflict, but also on cooperation.

détente A policy and period of relaxed tensions between the United States and Soviet Union during the 1970s.

Détente was controversial, even within Nixon's own party. A group of conservative Republicans and Democrats, including former governor of California Ronald Reagan, were convinced that détente was a one-way street. They pointed in particular to a dramatic increase in the Soviet nuclear arsenal during the 1970s. To make matters even worse, the promised benefits of détente failed to materialize as the Soviet Union continued to expand its influence in the Third World, including Latin America. Détente had merely lulled the United States into a false sense of security. Whatever the merits of this argument, the Soviet Union's invasion of Afghanistan in 1979 seemed to lend it credence. The invasion was the death knell for détente, an end further ensured by Ronald Reagan's election to the presidency in 1980.

The Resurgence and End of the Cold War

Reagan was convinced that détente allowed the Soviet Union to surge ahead of the United States in military power and expand its political influence in the Third World while the United States naïvely waited for Soviet moderation. His administration pursued policies that many viewed as a return to the coldest days of the Cold War, including an ambitious increase in military spending in both the conventional and nuclear areas. Nuclear arms control with the Soviet Union was placed on hold. The administration increased assistance to anticommunist governments and insurgency movements in Third World countries. Most controversial was aid to the "contras" fighting to overthrow the communist government in Nicaragua. Opponents in the United States feared that Reagan's policies risked an expensive and dangerous arms race with the Soviet Union as well as possible military intervention in a Third World conflict, another Vietnam. Administration supporters claimed these policies were a necessary demonstration of American power to deter an ambitious Soviet Union. Some may have even hoped that the Soviet Union, suffering from severe economic problems, could never afford to stay in a renewed arms race.

Soviet leadership was in a state of transition during Reagan's first term. Leonid Brezhnev, in power since the 1960s, died in 1982. He was followed by two geriatric remnants of the old guard before a much younger and vibrant figure, **Mikhail Gorbachev**, appeared on the scene. In 1984, Gorbachev impressed Prime Minister Margaret Thatcher of Great Britain as someone she could "do business with." People realized quickly this was a new type of Soviet leader. Not only were he and his wife relatively young and outgoing figures, but he also appeared determined to reform the stagnant Soviet system through his twin policies of **perestroika** and **glasnost**. *Perestroika* (restructuring) was intended to loosen government control over the economy and move it in a market-oriented direction. *Glasnost* (openness) was designed to open the Soviet political system to greater dissent and discussion of the problems that plagued Soviet society.

Much to the dismay of many conservatives in the United States, Reagan, like his friend Margaret Thatcher, became convinced that Gorbachev was for real. Chummy summits complete with smiling photo ops followed. Progress was made in nuclear arms control talks for the first time in over a decade. But despite the reduction in tensions, the question of how Gorbachev would respond to a real crisis or challenge remained. If "openness" got out of hand, would Gorbachev move to crush dissent, as past Soviet leaders had? Was he really different from his predecessors?

By the end of the 1980s, Gorbachev faced a dilemma at home and in Eastern Europe: *Glasnost* was a smashing success, whereas *perestroika* was a dismal failure. The result, as David Reynolds explains, was that "[a]s the economy collapsed, freedom to protest grew. Reconstruction became deconstruction."[29] As economies foundered and domestic criticism mounted, the communist regimes in Eastern Europe grew increasingly fragile. How would Gorbachev respond when pro-Soviet regimes found themselves on the wrong end of *glasnost*?

The answer came in East Germany, one of the most hard-line regimes in Eastern Europe until the very end. East Germany's leader, Erich Honecker, viewed Gorbachev and his reforms with alarm—and with good reason, because Honecker, his cronies, and the infamous secret police (the "Stasi") were despised by the East German people. When Gorbachev visited in October 1989, crowds chanted "Gorby" as Honecker, utterly clueless, stood at his side. Within weeks, opposition to Honecker's regime led to his ouster and desperate attempts to prevent an outright revolution. It was clear that Gorbachev was not going to save the East German regime from the wrath of its own people. By the middle of November, the Honecker regime was long gone and the Berlin Wall was being torn down.

Mikhail Gorbachev Leader of the Soviet Union from 1985 until its dissolution in 1991.

perestroika Mikhail Gorbachev's reforms during the second half of the 1980s, aimed at reforming the Soviet economic system.

glasnost Mikhail Gorbachev's political reforms in the Soviet Union during the second half of the 1980s, allowing for greater freedom of expression and dissent.

Although Gorbachev did not order the wall torn down, he did not prevent it. People around the world watched in amazement as Berliners streamed back and forth under the Brandenburg Gate between East and West Berlin, celebrating on the very spots where they would have been shot days before. The same forces that unraveled communism in Eastern Europe would eventually do the same in the Soviet Union. By 1991, the Soviet Union itself joined the list of former communist nations when Boris Yeltsin, Gorbachev's successor, declared communism dead and the Soviet Union disintegrated.

The Curious Peace of the Cold War

Students of international relations spend a lot of time trying to understand things that actually did happen, but sometimes it is just as interesting and important to learn about those things that did not happen. The peace of the Cold War provides a good example of just such a "nonevent." For more than forty years, two of the greatest military powers in history, divided by an intense ideological rivalry, struggled against each other across the globe. But despite the intensity of the conflict, they never went to war. In many ways this is a very curious outcome: It is unusual in international history for two great powers to compete against one another on such a scale and never fight. If any "non-event" cries out for an explanation, it is the curious peace that was the Cold War.

The citizens of East and West Berlin converge to tear down the Berlin Wall in November 1989.

Source: Jan-Peter Boening/Zenit/Laif/Redux Pictures

Why did the Cold War never turn hot? Explanations of why something fails to occur are by their very nature speculative. In thinking about what one scholar has called the **long peace**, a variety of possible explanations have been put forward.[30] John Mearsheimer highlights two factors, the presence of only two major powers (**bipolarity**) and nuclear weapons.[31] His argument is simple: The chances for war increase when there are more than two major powers because this increases the number of avenues through which war might break out. If there are five major powers, a war could break out between any two of them. When only two major powers are present, there is only one route to war. The more opportunities there are for something to happen, the more likely it will. Furthermore, the fact that the two countries had enough nuclear weapons to annihilate each other made them extremely cautious in their dealings with each other. Many scholars, however, remain skeptical that nuclear weapons were critical in preventing war from breaking out. John Mueller argues that conventional war had become so destructive that this alone was enough to make the two powers extremely hesitant to risk war.[32]

long peace The "peace" or absence of war between the United States and the Soviet Union during the Cold War.

bipolarity The existence of two major powers in international politics. Usually refers to the structure of the Cold War.

A balance of power between the two superpowers is also sometimes credited as the basis for peace. Because the countries were roughly equal in military strength, neither side could be confident of victory in war. As a result, neither side was tempted to start a war. Turning this argument somewhat on its head, Stephen Walt sees the peace as resting on a dramatic imbalance of power, claiming that the combined power of the United States and its allies (Japan, West Germany, France, Britain, etc.) was substantially greater than that of the Soviet Union and its allies (Poland, Hungary, Romania, etc.).[33] Given this imbalance, it was never necessary for the United States to resort to war. Soviet leaders realized their inferiority and never challenged genuinely vital American interests, thus avoiding any direct confrontation. Whatever the reason, the absence of war between the United States and the Soviet Union is certainly a remarkable (and a very fortunate) feature of the Cold War and its end.

The Post-Cold War World

In the first few years of the post–Cold War period, expectations about the future of international relations diverged. Some expected a more stable world marked by the triumph of liberal democracy, economic prosperity, peace dividends, and the reduction of war and conflict. Others lamented the Cold War's passing, fearing that its stability and predictability would be replaced by national and ethnic conflict, rouge regimes and nuclear weapons proliferation that would be more dangerous than the superpower rivalry. More than two decades into the post–Cold War era, these debates continue. Nonetheless, it is possible to make some general observations about the shape of international politics in the post–Cold War era to which most, if not all, would subscribe. An evaluation of the post–Cold War world is an exercise in examining and judging the relative significance of changes and continuities. Thus, we can approach the post–Cold War era by asking ourselves two questions: What changed since the end of the Cold War? What remained unchanged?

The demise and eventual dissolution of the Soviet Union was unquestionably a major event that transformed critical aspects of international relations, especially in Europe. Germany is unified again for the first time since 1945. Former allies of the Soviet Union are now members of NATO. The division of Europe has ended; the iron curtain, lifted. Outside the confines of Europe, the United States and Russia retain only a fraction of the nuclear weapons they possessed at the height of the Cold War, and this number is set to go lower still. One cannot underestimate the importance of these transformations.

But the end of the Cold War did not change everything, and the world of 2010 would not look totally unfamiliar to someone who had been asleep for twenty years. As John Ikenberry explains, "Only a part of the post–World War II order—the bipolar order—was destroyed by the dramatic events of 1989–1991."[34] There are still significant elements of continuity, especially in terms of the American influence in the world and the perpetuation of the institutions created under American tutelage during the Cold War.[35]

Indeed, the ending of the Cold War did not bring any fundamental alteration in the scope of American military power and commitments throughout the world. U.S. forces remain in Japan, Korea, and Europe, though in somewhat smaller numbers, just as they were at the height of the Cold War. The passing of the Soviet military alliance in Europe, the Warsaw Pact, has not brought an end to the American alliance, NATO. The 1991 Gulf War, considered at the time a possible harbinger of a "new world order," demonstrated the continuing centrality of the United States. Though the war involved an international coalition with the sanction of the United Nations, it was fundamentally an American enterprise. A handful of other nations contributed military forces, money, and military bases, but the outcome was determined by the military power of the United States. The 2003 Iraq War was, with the significant exception of Great Britain, almost entirely an American undertaking. No other nation possesses the necessary combination of capability and willingness to challenge the military power of

FIGURE 1.1

Global distribution of Military Expenditure in 2010

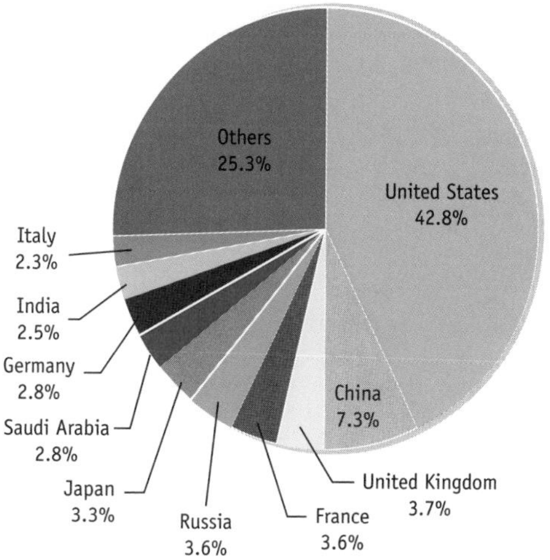

Source: Stockholm International Peace Research Institute

the United States. Indeed, in 2010 the United States accounted for more than forty percent of the world's military expenditures, more than the next dozen biggest spenders combined (see Figure 1.1). Whether one wishes to refer to this as American "hegemony," "dominance," or "unipolarity," the basic point remains the same. Ian Clark highlights this point in remarking on the "essential continuity in the role of American power…. There are institutions that were created during the Cold War, and which were almost defining attributes of it, [that] still endure into the post–Cold War era."[36]

When Clark refers to American power he does not mean just military power. The United States also remains the world's largest and most powerful economy (see Table 1.1). Some initially thought that economic integration in Europe may have created an single economic unit that would rival the United States. A series of economic crises in countries that use the common European currency (the Euro), especially Greece and Ireland, in 2010 have since dampened these expectations. The greatest economic challenge to the United States is now more likely to emerge from Asia. Though two decades ago some thought Japan might overtake the United States, today it is the rapid growth of India and China that poses the long-term challenge to American economic dominance. A potential milestone in the post-Cold War era may have occurred in 2010 when China finally surpassed Japan as the world's second largest economy. A controversial report from the International Monetary Fund (IMF) released in May 2011 even predicted that China might surpass the United States as the world's largest economy as early as 2016 if measured in terms of purchasing power. Consequently, even though the U.S. economy is still almost three times larger than China's and the average American almost ten times wealthier than

TABLE 1.1

2010 IMF Ranking of World's 15 Largest Economies (and the EU)

—World	62,909,274
—*European Union*	16,282,230
1 United States	14,657,800
2 China	5,878,257
3 Japan	5,458,872
4 Germany	3,315,643
5 France	2,582,527
6 United Kingdom	2,247,455
7 Brazil	2,090,314
8 Italy	2,055,114
9 Canada	1,574,051
10 India	1,537966
11 Russia	1,465,079
12 Spain	1,409,946
13 Australia	1,235,539
14 Mexico	1,039,121
15 South Korea	1,007,084

GDP (Gross Domestic Product) measured in millions of U.S. Dollars.

Source: International Monetary Fund, World Economic Outlook Database April 2011: Nominal GDP list of countries. Data for the year 2010.

the average Chinese, some see a possible transformation of the broader post-Cold War order resulting from China's rapid economic growth, particularly if greater economic power translated into military capabilities and political influence.

The world, however, is a big place, and we must remember that, for the vast majority of the world's people, life continues much as it did before the end of the Cold War or September 11. The passing of the Soviet Union has not narrowed the gap between the world's rich and its more numerous poor. Large portions of humanity go to bed hungry every night and have no access to the basic necessities of life. The global environmental problems that were emerging before the Cold War's end remain as pressing as ever. Deadly national and ethnic conflicts throughout the world continue to rage. In the second part of this text we will focus a range of issues, many of which highlight possibly important changes in our world such as globalization, terrorism, and the spread of democracy. But as we appreciate and try to understand the significance of these changes, we should not lose sight of the perhaps equally important things that remain the same.

CHAPTER SUMMARY

■ The modern state system, characterized by a small number of relatively large sovereign political units, gradually took shape as Europe began to emerge from the medieval period around 1300. The economic pressures of the commercial revolution and the military dynamics of the gunpowder revolution contributed to the creation of larger and larger political units. The Protestant Reformation and the Thirty Years War (1618–1648) brought the origins of the modern conception of sovereignty as embodied in the Peace of Westphalia (1648).

■ The period between the Peace of Westphalia and the French Revolution (1789) was a period of relative calm in which wars and conflicts tended to be limited, modest affairs. This calm was rooted in the nature of European societies and politics, particularly absolutist monarchism, the lack of any strong sense of loyalty or connection between people and their rulers, and the absence of ideological conflict.

■ The American and French revolutions marked the beginning of modern nationalism and its doctrine of popular sovereignty. Over time, this idea contributed to the erosion of absolutist monarchism and the international order it sustained.

■ At the same time, the industrial revolution of the 1800s transformed European societies in ways that had a profound effect on international politics. Increasing wealth and advances in technology solidified European dominance of the globe. Nationalism and the industrial revolution combined to create the "total war" of World Wars I and II.

■ In the aftermath of two devastating wars in the span of a single generation, the conflict between the United States and the Soviet Union dashed hopes for a more peaceful world order based on cooperation among the great powers. Although the Cold War never resulted in direct military conflict between the superpowers, it did bring several smaller wars as the United States and Soviet Union engaged in sometimes-fierce competition for influence throughout the world, including the recently decolonized nations of Africa and Asia.

■ The superpower conflict, political conflict in postcolonial societies, and the policy of containment would eventually lead the United States to war in Vietnam.

■ Attempts to moderate the Cold War and control the growth of nuclear arsenals lead to détente and several arms limitation agreements during the 1970s. This thaw in the Cold War was short-lived. The Soviet invasion of Afghanistan in 1979 and the election of Ronald Reagan in 1980 ushered in a period of renewed hostility and conflict between the superpowers.

■ By the mid-1980s, the stagnation of communism in the Soviet Union and Eastern Europe prompted a new generation of leaders, particularly Mikhail Gorbachev, to conclude that radical reforms were essential. His policies of *perestroika* and *glasnost*, however, ultimately doomed the very communist system they were designed to save. The unraveling of communism was most vividly displayed in Berlin, where the city's citizens demolished the wall between East and West in the fall of 1989. This event marked the end of the Cold War.

■ Though we have experienced several crises since the end of the Cold War (e.g., the 1991 Gulf War, the terrorist attacks of September 11, 2001, and the Iraq War that began in 2003), the fundamental nature of the post–Cold War world remains in doubt.

CRITICAL QUESTIONS

1. What aspects of international relations have changed the most and least over the last 350 years?

2. What are the most significant changes in the contemporary world?

3. One of the most important developments of the past 200 years has been the rise and spread of nationalism. In what ways has nationalism changed international relations? Do you think nationalism remains as important and powerful as 50 or 100 years ago?

4. One of the enduring questions in international relations concerns the linkage between domestic and international politics. Historically, how have changes in the domestic character of states altered international relations?

5. Is it possible to judge the significance of an event such as September 11 or the end of the Cold War at the time it occurs or does this sort of assessment require the benefit of hindsight?

KEY TERMS

absolutist monarchism, 6

appeasement, 20

bipolarity, 27

Cold War, 24

commercial revolution, 4

Concert of Europe, 10

containment, 23

decolonization, 24

détente, 25

divine right of kings, 6

domino theory, 24

French Revolution, 8

glasnost, 26

gunpowder revolution, 4

Holy Roman Empire, 4

League of Nations, 19

levée en masse, 9

long peace, 27

Marshall Plan, 23

Mikhail Gorbachev, 26

modern nationalism, 10

modern state system, 2

multinational states, 10

multistate nations, 10

Munich Agreement, 20

Napoleonic Wars, 9

national self-determina-
tion, 10

North Atlantic Treaty
Organization (NATO), 24

Peace of Westphalia, 2

perestroika, 26

popular sovereignty, 8

Protestant Reformation, 4

sovereignty, 6

Thirty Years War, 2

total war, 17

Treaty of Versailles, 19

Truman Doctrine, 24

FURTHER READINGS

A classic work on the rise of the modern state system that emphasizes the military aspects is John Herz, "The Rise and Demise of the Territorial State," *World Politics* 9 (July 1957): 473–493. Two more recent treatments are Bruce D. Porter, *War and the Rise of the State* (New York: Free Press, 1994), especially chapters 2 and 3, and Hendrik Spruyt, *The Sovereign State and Its Competitors* (Princeton, NJ: Princeton University Press, 1996).

For the period between the Peace of Westphalia and the French Revolution, few works surpass the classic account by Edward V. Gulick, *Europe's Classical Balance of Power* (New York: W. W. Norton, 1967).

The rise and impact of nationalism have been the focus of a very large body of literature. Good starting points include Ernest Geller, *Nations and Nationalism* (Oxford: Blackwell, 1983); Eric Hobsbawn, *Nations and Nationalism Since 1780* (Cambridge: Cambridge University Press, 1990); and Benedict Anderson, *Imagined Communities: Reflections on the Origin and Spread of Nationalism* (New York and London: Verso, 1991).

The events leading to the outbreak of World War I are given a very straightforward treatment in Laurence LaFore *The Long Fuse: An Interpretation of the Origins of World War I* (New York: J. P. Lippincott, 1971). A more recent account is Niall Ferguson, *The Pity of War: Explaining World War I* (New York: Basic Books, 1999). An interesting discussion of the legacies of World War I is provided in Porter, *War and the Rise of the State*, chapters 5 and 6.

Not surprisingly, there are many works on the origins and course of World War II. Perhaps the best and most accessible overview is Gerhard Weinberg, *A World at Arms: A Global History of World War II* (Cambridge: Cambridge University Press, 1994). On U.S. policy during this period, see Robert Dallek, *Franklin D. Roosevelt and American Foreign Policy, 1932–1945* (Oxford: Oxford University Press, 1979). An excellent book on the war against Japan is Saburo Ienaga, *The Pacific War, 1931–1945* (New York: Pantheon, 1978).

A widely respected examination of the early years of the Cold War is John Lewis Gaddis, *The United States and the Origins of the Cold War, 1941–1947* (New York: Columbia University Press, 1971). A more imposing treatment is Melvyn Leffler, *A Preponderance of Power: National Security, the Truman Administration and the Cold War* (Stanford, CA: Stanford University Press, 1992). For a more general overview of the Cold War, see Ronald E. Powaski, *The Cold War, the United States and the Soviet Union, 1917–1991* (Oxford: Oxford University Press, 1998). The Vietnam War is covered in Robert D. Schulzinger, *A Time for War: The United States and Vietnam, 1941–1975* (Oxford: Oxford University Press, 1997). The end of the Cold War is covered in Raymond Garthoff, *The Great Transition: American–Soviet Relations and the End of the Cold War* (Washington, DC: The Brookings Institution, 1994). An excellent place to begin making sense of the Cold War's aftermath is Ian Clark's interesting yet theoretically rigorous *The Post–Cold War Order* (Oxford: Oxford University Press, 2001).

NOTES

[1]John Weltman, *World Politics and the Evolution of War* (Baltimore: The John Hopkins University Press, 1995), p. 21.

[2]Geoffrey Parker, "The Gunpowder Revolution, 1300–1500," *Cambridge Illustrated History of Warfare*, ed. Geoffrey Parker (Cambridge: Cambridge University Press, 1995), p. 107.

[3]Weltman, *World Politics and the Evolution of War*, p. 24.

[4]Bruce Porter, *War and the Rise of the State: The Military Foundations of Modern Politics* (New York: The Free Press, 1994), p. 124.

[5]See John A. Lynn, "States in Conflict, 1661–1763," *Cambridge Illustrated History of Modern Warfare* (Cambridge: Cambridge University Press, 2000), p. 164–185.

[6]Kalevi J. Holsti, *Peace and War: Armed Conflicts and International Order, 1648–1989* (Cambridge: Cambridge University Press, 1991), pp. 83–102.

[7]John Owen, "The Canon and the Cannon: A Review Essay," *International Security* 25 (Winter 1998/99): 161.

[8]Paul W. Schroeder, *The Transformation of European Politics, 1763–1848* (Oxford: Oxford University Press, 1994), pp. 68–69.

[9]John A. Lynn, "Nations in Arms, 1763–1814," *Cambridge Illustrated History of Warfare* (Cambridge: Cambridge University Press, 2000), p. 193.

[10]Ibid., p. 207.

[11]Weltman, *World Politics and the Evolution of War*, p. 42.

[12]Michael Mandelbaum, *The Fate of Nations: The Search for National Security in the Nineteenth and Twentieth Centuries* (Cambridge: Cambridge University Press, 1988), p. 40.

[13]Hew Strachan, "Military Modernization, 1789–1918," *The Oxford Illustrated History of Modern Europe*, ed. T. C. W. Blanning (New York: Oxford University Press, 1996), p. 75.

[14]Max Boot, *War Made New: Technology, Warfare and the Course of History, 1500 to Today* (New York: Gotham Books, 2006), p. 13.

[15]Casualty figures drawn from Williamson Murray, "The West at War, 1914–1918," *Cambridge Illustrated History of Warfare*, pp. 284–288; and Weltman, *World Politics and the Evolution of War*, p. 93.

[16]James J. Sheehan, *Where Have all the Soldiers Gone? The Transformation of Modern Europe* (Boston: Houghton Mifflin, 2008), p. 75.

[17]Porter, *War and the Rise of the State*, p. 170.

[18]Ibid., p. 150.

[19]Adam Hochschild, "I Tried to Stop the Thing," *The American Scholar* (May 6, 2010). Accessed at: www.theamericanscholar.org/i-tried-to-stop-the-bloody-thing/.

[20]Randall Schweller, *Deadly Imbalances: Tripolarity and Hitler's Strategy of World Conquest* (New York: Columbia University Press, 1998), p. 5.

[21]Gerhard Weinberg, *A World at Arms: A Global History of World War II* (Cambridge: Cambridge University Press, 1994), p. 894. About one-third of the casualties were military and two-thirds civilian.

[22]For the argument that the decision to use the atomic bomb was based on a desire to scare or impress the Soviet Union, see Gar Alperovitz, *The Decision to Use the Atomic Bomb and the Architecture of an American Myth* (New York: Alfred A. Knopf, 1995).

[23]Ibid., p. 573.

[24]John Lewis Gaddis, *The United States and the Origins of the Cold War* (New York: Columbia University Press, 1972), p. 173.

[25]Ibid., p. 308.

[26]"X" [George F. Kennan], "The Sources of Soviet Conduct," *Foreign Affairs* 25 (July 1947): 566–582. The best discussion of Kennan's view of containment can be found in John Lewis Gaddis, *Strategies of Containment* (Oxford: Oxford University Press, 1982), chapter 2.

[27]Gaddis, *United States and the Origins of the Cold War*, p. 351.

[28]On the Vietnam War, see Robert D. Schulzinger, *A Time for War: The United States and Vietnam, 1941—1975* (Oxford: Oxford University Press, 1997). An insightful explanation of the reasons for the United States' defeat is presented in Andrew Mack, "Why Big Nations Lose Small Wars: The Politics of Asymmetric Conflict," *World Politics* 27 (1975): 175–200.

[29]David Reynolds, "Europe Divided and Reunited, 1945–1995," *The Oxford Illustrated History of Modern Europe*, ed. T. W. C. Blanning (New York: Oxford University Press, 1996), p. 299.

[30]John Lewis Gaddis, *The Long Peace: Inquiries into the History of the Cold War* (Oxford: Oxford University Press, 1987).

[31]John Mearsheimer, "Why We Will Soon Miss the Cold War," *The Atlantic* (August 1990): 35–50.

[32]John Mueller, "The Essential Irrelevance of Nuclear Weapons: Stability in the Postwar World," *International Security* 13 (Fall 1988): 55–79.

[33]Stephen M. Walt, *The Origins of Alliances* (Ithaca, NY: Cornell University Press, 1987), pp. 274–278.

[34]John Ikenberry, *After Victory: Institutions, Strategic Restraints, and the Rebuilding of Order After Major Wars* (Princeton, NJ: Princeton University Press, 2000), p. 215.

[35]This point is emphasized effectively in Ian Clark, *The Post Cold War Order: The Spoils of Peace* (Oxford: Oxford University Press, 2001).

[36]Ibid., p. 23.

2

Contending Perspectives on International Politics

Many Questions, Even More Answers

Students of international relations are often frustrated by the absence of precise answers to questions and problems. On one level, this frustration is justified: we usually lack answers in the same sense that problems in a calculus text have solutions at the end of the text. On another level, the problem is misidentified: frustration emerges not from the absence of answers but from their proliferation—too many answers, not too few. The problem is not that we lack an answer to the question of why nations go to war, but rather that we have five, six, seven, or more answers. To further complicate the issue, some explanations that appear different but are actually complementary, meaning they can be reconciled if one thinks carefully enough about how they might fit together, while others cannot because they reflect more fundamental and incompatible assumptions about how the world works.

This existence of alternative and competing paradigms, theories, philosophies, and worldviews characterizes all social sciences: international relations is no different. As a general rule, different perspectives have two interrelated components: an analytical component explaining why things work the way they do, and a prescriptive element dictating what should be done. The prescriptive element should flow from the explanation: what someone thinks needs to be done to reduce armed conflict (the prescription) depends on why he or she thinks we have war in the first place (the explanation).

Students of international relations disagree intensely about explanations for, and possible solutions to, critical international problems. They may even disagree on what the most critical problems are. Disagreements about specific issues usually reflect deeper differences about the nature of international relations, which are often unarticulated debates on concrete issues. As Stephen Walt explains, "Everyone uses theories—whether he or she knows it or not—and disagreements about policy usually rest on more fundamental disagreement about the basic forces that shape international outcomes."[1]

This chapter introduces the major perspectives on international relations that will be reflected in specific debates throughout the remainder of this book. These differing views of the nature and dynamics of international relations are themselves rooted in more fundamental social and political philosophies. That is, they represent the application of more general ideas and assumptions about the nature of people and society to the specific realm of international politics. In order to fully appreciate debates about international relations, we will examine the underlying social or political theory or philosophy upon which each perspective is based as well as the application of those ideas to international relations.

Over the past two centuries, three dominant philosophies have framed debates about social, economic, and political issues: conservatism, liberalism, and Marxism. Each rests on a set of assumptions or ideas that provides a general intellectual framework for understanding how the social world works, and each has also been applied to understanding the dynamics of international relations. But these three perspectives do not exhaust the range of potential worldviews, and in recent years alternative approaches, particularly feminism and constructivism, have begun to challenge these traditional perspectives.

Realism

realism A conservative perspective on international politics emphasizing the inevitability of conflict among nations, the centrality of power, and the ever-present threat of war.

The most influential perspective on international relations, especially in the United States since the end of World War II, is **realism**, an approach with intellectual roots in conservative social and political philosophy. If we want a deeper understanding of realism as an outlook on the world, we need to appreciate its conservative foundations. Though conservatism, like all the philosophies we will examine, is a rich and complex system of thought developed over centuries, and there are dangers in summarizing an entire philosophy in a few pages, we can highlight several of conservatism's central beliefs/assumptions.

The first critical element of a conservative social and political philosophy is a *pessimistic view of human nature*. The conservative worldview sees people as flawed, imperfect, and imperfectible creatures. Human nature is a mix of good and bad features, and the latter can never be completely eliminated. Conservatives of a more religious orientation emphasize the notion of original sin traced to the biblical story of Genesis and humankind's fall from grace with God in the Garden of Eden. This is why Christians who attend church every Sunday pray for forgiveness of their sins. The minister or priest does not ask just those who have sinned in the past week to pray; the assumption is that no one in attendance could possibly have made it through an entire week free of sin. The Christian view of people as tainted by original sin is one of humans as flawed creatures. More secular versions of conservatism emphasize that even though people are capable of rational, thoughtful, and ethical behavior, they are also motivated by the less noble impulses of lust, passion, and greed. As Edmund Burke (1729–1797), the founder of modern conservatism, noted, "politics ought to be adjusted, not to human reason, but to human nature, of which reason is but a part, and by no means the greatest part."[2]

The second critical element of a conservative philosophy is a view of people as social creatures, meaning that people are driven, and have a deep-seated need, to identify with and belong to social groups. People do not want to be isolated, unattached beings. People are not individualists; they derive a necessary sense of belonging and comfort from group and social identities. Family groups, social groups, political groups, and so on define who we are and allow us to feel like part of something larger than ourselves. In and of itself, this impulse is not a bad thing. The problem is that group identity entails both inclusion and exclusion. Groups are defined not merely by whom they include but also by whom they exclude. A group to which everyone belongs is not really a group at all, at least not one that provides any special sense of belonging. This is why social groups almost always exist with opposing groups. How many colleges or universities have only one sorority? Why do so many religions spend as much time talking about the nonbelievers outside the group as they do the believers in the group? The tendency for people to form group identities has the inevitable consequence of dividing human societies. But even this might not be necessarily bad. The existence of groups and the recognition of differences are essential for diversity, which can often be a very good thing.

The more problematic aspect of people's social nature is the almost irresistible tendency for people to view themselves and their groups as not merely different but also as superior. We refer to this as **collective** or **group egoism**. How many people view themselves as belonging to one religious group while thinking another religion is actually the true one? How many people believe that their fraternity or sorority is the worst on campus? It is very difficult for people to see themselves consistently as merely different but in no sense superior to others. This sets the stage for all sorts of problems and conflicts.

The third critical element of conservative social and political philosophy is a belief in the *inevitability of social conflict*. Why is conflict inevitable? Social conflict has both *rational* and *irrational* bases. Group or collective egoism is one of the irrational sources of conflict. When people and groups believe that they are not merely different but also better than others, this is a recipe for conflict. But conflict does not result solely from irrational impulses. Conflict also results from the impossibility of creating a social, economic, and political order that benefits all equally. In every society there are people and groups that benefit from the status quo and other people and groups that would benefit from a change in the status quo. Those who would benefit from changing the status quo will always come into conflict with those who benefit from the existing order. This is the essence of social, economic, and political conflict. Politics is about managing social conflict, not a utopian quest to eliminate conflict. There may be more or less effective ways of managing social conflict, but social conflict has always existed and always will. American theologian and social commentator Reinhold Niebuhr (1892–1971) provided the most succinct statement on the inevitability of social conflict: "the easy subservience of reason to prejudice and passion, and the consequent persistence of irrational egoism, particularly in group behavior, make social conflict an inevitability in human behavior, probably to its very end."[3] Here we see the three critical elements of conservatism: flawed human nature, group identity and egoism, and the inevitability of conflict.

collective or **group egoism**
The tendency of social groups to view themselves as not only different from other groups but also better in some respect. An element of conservative or realist thought particularly important for understanding the dynamics of social conflict.

Realism originated as an application of these conservative insights to the study and understanding of international relations. Though realism can be traced as far back as the ancient Greek historian **Thucydides** (c. 460–c. 400 BCE), a number of twentieth-century thinkers have exerted a more profound and direct impact on the development of realism, including British historian Edward Hallet Carr (1892–1982), political scientist **Hans Morgenthau** (1891–1976), and the American diplomat **George Kennan** (1904–2005). Carr, Morgenthau, and Kennan are often considered *classical* realists whose ideas are more explicitly conservative in orientation than many contemporary realists. This distinction can be seen most dramatically in the classical realists' view of human nature. Hans Morgenthau thought, "It is the ubiquity of the desire for power which … constitutes the ubiquity of evil in all human action. Here is the element of corruption and sin which injects itself into the best of intentions at least a drop of evil and thus spoils it." It is this inevitable element of power lust and sin that accounts for "the transformation of churches into political organizations, of revolutions into dictatorships, [and] love of country into imperialism."[4] George Kennan wished he "could believe that the human impulses which give rise to the nightmares of totalitarianism were ones which providence had allocated to other people and to which the American people had graciously been left immune." Unfortunately, "the fact of the matter is that there is a little bit of totalitarian buried somewhere, way deep down, in each and every one of us."[5] Although some classical realists placed greater emphasis on flawed human nature than others, the conservative view of humans as imperfect and imperfectible creatures was clearly central to their view of international relations. In Morgenthau's words, "the world, imperfect as it is from a rational point of view, is the result of forces inherent in human nature."[6]

Similarly, realists see group identity and conflict as essential to understanding international relations. According to Robert Gilpin, "Realism … holds that the foundation of political life is what Ralf Dahrendorf has called 'conflict groups.' … This is another way of saying that in a world of scarce resources and conflict over those resources, human beings confront one another ultimately as members of groups, not as isolated individuals."[7] At the international level the primary group identity is the nation-state. For realists, contemporary international relations is fundamentally about the interactions and conflicts between and among states. Certainly realists recognize the existence of other identities and nonstate actors. Such groups and actors can sometimes be important and influential. But for realists they have yet to replace the nation-state as the key actor. The nation-state has been and remains the major actor, or *conflict group*, at the global level.

Finally, realists argue that just as conflict is an inevitable feature of social life, so is it among nations. The reasons why are straightforward extensions of the irrational and rational sources of social conflict more generally. First, feelings of national, ethnic, and cultural superiority are sources of irrational international conflict. Second, there is no such thing as international order that benefits all nations equally. E. H. Carr warned scholars and statesmen that it was a dangerous wishful thinking to ignore "the unpalatable fact of a fundamental divergence of interest between nations desirous of maintaining the status quo and nations desirous of changing it."[8] The central conflicts of international politics are those between *status quo* states—that is, those that derive benefits from the existing international order—and *revisionist* states—that is, those states that would benefit by revising the existing order. Put even more simply, "Like all politics, international politics involves conflicts between those who want to keep things the way things are and those who want to change them."[9]

The fact that conservatives and realists view social or group conflict as inevitable does not mean that we must simply throw up our hands in despair. Though conflicts are inevitable, there are ways to manage social conflicts to minimize the chances of them becoming violent. At the national level, governments manage conflict through laws, police, and courts. This leads us to what realists see as perhaps the most critical feature of international relations—international **anarchy**. Though many realists, especially *neorealists*, have abandoned the classical realist emphasis on human nature, all realists place international anarchy at the center of their understanding of international politics. *Anarchy* means the absence of a central authority or government. Anarchy is not to be confused with chaos and a lack of order—there is a lot of order in international relations. It is the absence of government on a global level that distinguished international politics from domestic politics. E. H. Carr was succinct on this point: "In domestic affairs it is clearly the business of the state to create harmony if no natural harmony exists. In international politics, there is no organized power charged with the task of creating harmony."[10] This, according to Stanley Michalak, is "the first fact of life about international politics: The international system is a system without government."[11]

> **anarchy** The absence of a central governmental/political authority.

To understand why anarchy is so important for our understanding of international relations we need only consider all the things our government does for us. The most important function of government is to provide protection. If you see an armed band of thugs coming down the street toward your home, you call the police; people do not rely on neighbors with whom they negotiated previous alliances for mutual aid. Upon receiving your call, the police do not sit around at the station for hours debating whether it is in their interest to come help. It is their job and obligation to help protect you.

Though the absence of a world government means that states are not obligated to obey any higher authority, it also means that no state can rely on others to come to their aid. As Kenneth Waltz, perhaps the most influential neorealist, observes: "Citizens need not prepare to defend themselves. Public agencies do that. A national system is not one of self-help. The international system is."[12]

International anarchy in turn creates a **security dilemma** in which states "must be, and usually are, concerned about their security from being attacked, subjected, dominated or annihilated" by other states. As states acquire the power and means to defend themselves, "this, in turn, renders the others more insecure and compels them to prepare for the worst. Since no one can ever feel entirely secure in a world of competing units, power competition ensues, and the vicious cycle of power accumulation is on."[13] The dilemma nations face is how to increase their security without making other nations less secure. On the domestic level, the police provide security to all simultaneously; as a result, one person's security does not come at the expense another's. This is not the case for nations. For realists, the anarchic nature of international relations and resulting security dilemma are the cornerstones for understanding how and why states behave as they do.

> **security dilemma** The problem nations face when the actions taken to make one nation feel more secure inevitably make other nations feel less secure.

How, then, do realists propose we manage international conflict? Create a world government? At a theoretical level, realists concede this would be a solution to the security dilemma, though they are skeptical that this theoretical solution can be translated into reality. Historically, realists have focused on more modest solutions such as the balance of power. When nations find themselves in a conflict, realists have traditionally argued that the chances for war are lessened if the parties are relatively equal in power. The reasoning is quite simple. We assume that nations start wars because they expect to win, not lose. Nations are more likely to anticipate victory when they are more powerful than their opponent. Thus, when two sides are relatively equal, neither side will be confident of victory, so neither is likely to initiate war. There is some debate about this point among realists—some argue instead that peace is actually more likely when there is a great imbalance of power. The logic here is also simple: A very powerful nation need not resort to war to get what it wants and the much weaker states avoid war because they recognize how futile war would be. Despite these differences among realists (which will be explored in more detail in the next chapter), there is general agreement that the management and distribution of power is critical for realists when they think about international conflict and the chances for war.

Realism presents us with one way of understanding the world that grows out of conservative assumptions about the nature of people and human societies. It is a vision of world politics in which states interact and manage conflicts without the benefit of a central authority to do for them what governments do for their citizens. It is a world in which some states benefit from the existing world order and find themselves in conflict with others who would benefit from changing the existing order. Though conflicts of interest are common, violent conflict among nations remains relatively rare. Nevertheless, the anarchic nature of international politics drives nations to prepare for and occasionally fight wars. Robert Gilpin provides a very succinct expression of the realist point of view: "the fundamental nature of international relations has not changed over the millennia. International relations continues to be a recurring struggle for wealth and power among independent actors in a state of anarchy."[14]

liberalism Social, political, and economic philosophy based on a positive view of human nature, the inevitability of social progress, and the harmony of interests.

idealism An approach to international politics based on liberal assumptions and principles. Its more optimistic (or utopian) versions envision a world in which law, institutions, and diplomacy replace power competition and the use of force.

liberal internationalism Another term, along with **idealism**, for the application of liberal assumptions and principles to international relations.

Liberalism, Idealism, and Liberal Internationalism

The dominant alternatives to conservatism and realism are **liberalism** and **idealism**. In some sense the latter term is unfair because it suggests that people who hold "idealist" views are woolly-headed dreamers devising fanciful plans for world peace while ignoring the hard realities of world politics. Though this may have been the case for some of the more utopian idealists of the interwar period who hoped that international treaties could outlaw war, it is generally an unfair characterization. Idealism is merely a different way understanding the world that grows out of different beliefs and assumptions than those underpinning realism. It is better to label this alternative to realism as **liberal internationalism** or, more simply, *liberalism*, which refers to the political and philosophical tradition from which it emerged.

Liberalism is a social and political philosophy that began to flourish as Europe emerged from the medieval world that existed from the fall of the Roman Empire in 476 CE until the beginnings of the Renaissance in the 1300s and 1400s.

The Renaissance was a period of scientific, artistic, intellectual, and cultural revival that ended the stagnation of medieval times. It was a period of renewal, and liberalism provided a more optimistic outlook that challenged conservativism. Among the thinkers influential in the development of liberal thought were John Locke (1632–1704), Jean Jacques Rousseau (1712–1778), and Immanuel Kant (1724–1804), although the historical roots of liberal thought can be traced to the ancient Greeks.

Like conservatism, liberalism is a rich and varied intellectual tradition not easily reduced to a few paragraphs. That having been said, there does appear to be a core set of beliefs that define a liberal worldview and set it apart from a conservative outlook. "In simplest terms," David Sidorsky explains, liberalism is "first, a conception of man as desiring freedom and capable of exercising rational free choice. Second, it is a perspective on social institutions as open to rational reconstruction in the light of individual needs. It is, third, a view of history as progressively perfectible through the continuous application of human reason to social institutions."[15] Liberalism, thus, parts company with conservatism on almost every critical point. In contrast to conservative philosophy, liberalism views people as essentially rational, ethical, and moral creatures capable of controlling their baser impulses. No doubt people have often behaved in irrational and immoral ways, but this is not seen as the inevitable result and manifestation of a flawed human nature. Liberals usually see such behavior as being the result of ignorance and misunderstanding, which can be overcome through education and reforming social and political institutions.

In addition to possessing a more optimistic view of human nature, liberals are much less inclined to view social and individual conflict as inevitable. Liberals believe that it is possible to create a social, political, and economic order that benefits everybody—an order that maximizes individual freedom and material/economic prosperity. This element of liberal thought is sometimes referred to as the **harmony of interests**. The harmony of interests, for example, is the cornerstone of the liberal belief in the free market: When people left alone to pursue their individual economic interests, the long-term result is growth and prosperity benefiting everyone. Yes, Bill Gates has become a multibillionaire, but his wealth did not come at the expense of anyone else's well-being. In fact, his creations and inventions have improved the lives of others. There is no conflict between his interests and mine. Much of what we see as social conflict results not from an inevitable clash of interests, but from the failure to recognize deeper mutual interests.

harmony of interests A central element of liberal thought emphasizing the existence of common interests among people and nations. This contrasts with the conservative assumption of the inevitability of social conflict.

Thus, when realists look at the world, they tend to focus on conflicts of interests and the clashes that result; liberals are more drawn to the common interests that people and nations share and the prospects for cooperative activities that will satisfy these interests. Liberals see the realist emphasis on international conflict and war as a distortion of reality. The overwhelming majority of interactions among nations are cooperative or at least nonconflictual. Certainly wars occur, but the vast majority of nations spend the vast majority of their time at peace for reasons that have little to do with balances of power. Is it a balance of power, liberals would ask, that preserves peace between Finland and Sweden, the United States and Mexico, or Argentina and Chile? Emphasizing conflict and war in trying to understand international relations while paying less attention to cooperation and peace would be like trying to understand New York City by focusing on the several hundred people murdered every year while ignoring the other 8-plus million who get along without killing one another. Not that wars and murders should be ignored; it is a matter of looking at such things in the context of the totality of relations. International relations is not all about conflict and war; in fact, it is not even mostly about conflict and war.

Finally, and perhaps most important, liberals believe in the possibility, perhaps inevitability, of human progress. The human condition is better today than it was two hundred years ago, and it is likely to be better still two hundred years from now. Why? In part, because people are essentially rational creatures who learn more about their physical or natural world (e.g., the causes of disease) as well as their social world (e.g., the causes of poverty, prejudice, and violent conflict). As people learn more, they use this knowledge to solve problems. Human history is a story of the application of reason and knowledge to the solution of problems. There are, of course, temporary setbacks (e.g. no one argues that Nazi Germany constituted "progress" over what came before), but the general trend of human history is one of scientific, social, and moral progress.

Those who follow American politics can be forgiven if they are slightly perplexed by this discussion of liberalism and conservatism. The confusion stems from the fact that the labels *conservative* and *liberal* are used somewhat differently in everyday political debate than in discussions of political philosophy. For example, in American political discourse we categorize free market capitalism and limited government as conservative principles, with liberals favoring greater regulation and big government. Philosophically, however, free markets and limited government are central tenets of liberalism. What we have in the United States is really gradations and variations of liberalism. Ronald Reagan may have been a conservative president and Edward ("Ted") Kennedy may be a liberal senator, but both embrace the more fundamental and basic assumptions of liberalism.

In the realm of international relations, this belief in progress is central to the liberal view of the world. Although realists argue that the main features and dynamics of international politics are relatively enduring, liberals believe that we are in the midst of profound changes reducing the importance of force and war in relations among states while increasing the significance of such things as human rights as major concerns. One such change is the spread of democratic institutions around the world. Not only is this a good thing for the people within newly democratic states, it is also good news for international relations. **Democratic liberalism** argues that democracies are more peaceful than are nondemocracies, particularly in their dealings with one another. As a result, a more democratic world will also be more peaceful.

The spread of democracy has also been accompanied by another trend—the growth of economic interdependence. This interdependence takes many forms—from the more obvious and recognizable growth in trade among states to the somewhat less obvious increase in investments that people and corporations make in other countries. According to **commercial liberalism**, trade and interdependence are forces for peace. The logic is simple—greater economic interdependence

Democratic liberalism A strain of international liberal thought that claims democracies are more peaceful than are nondemocracies, especially in their relations with each other.

commercial liberalism A version of liberal international thought that stresses the importance of interdependence in trade and investment as a force for peace.

means one nation's well-being depends on another nation's well-being, creating common interests. As Richard Rosecrance argues in one of the most forceful and persuasive statements of commercial liberalism: "interpenetration of investment in industrial economies provides a mutual stake in each other's success that did not exist in the nineteenth century or before World War I."[16] As a result, "the incentive to wage war is absent in such a system for war disrupts trade and the interdependence on which trade is based."[17]

The growth of international institutions has also helped ameliorate many of the conflicts and insecurities that traditionally characterized international politics. One of the dilemmas that states have historically faced is the difficulty of cooperating even in the face of common interests because of the lack of trust in an anarchical environment. According to **liberal institutionalism**, international organizations can help states reduce these uncertainties by building trust. Perhaps nowhere is this more evident than in Europe, which is a much different than it was fifty or sixty years ago. Whereas suspicion, rivalry, conflict, and war were once normal among Europe's major powers, war among Germany, France, and Britain today would be ludicrously unimaginable in large part because post–World War II institutions such as the European Union have helped nurture and sustain peace, cooperation, and commerce. The citizens of modern Europe no longer live in a state of perpetual readiness for war as their grandparents and great-grandparents did.

A final positive development is the growth of international ethical and moral norms. In particular, the way people view war has changed dramatically over the previous two centuries. John Mueller argues that this transformation has been so profound that war is rapidly becoming obsolete in large parts of the world. He begins by noting that only two hundred years ago people tended to view war as noble, invigorating, exciting, and romantic. This view did not long survive the horrors of World Wars I and II. War then came to be viewed as a regrettable necessity in certain circumstances, not something to be valued and welcomed. Increasingly, the prevailing view of war is shifting to something more resembling our current view of dueling or slavery—a barbaric and outdated institution. Mueller explains "dueling finally died out not so much because it became illegal, but because it became ridiculous—an activity greeted not by admiration or even grudging acceptance, but by derision and contempt." Similarly, "when the notion of war chiefly inspires ridicule rather than fear, it will have become obsolete. Within the developed world at least, that condition seems to be gradually emerging."[18]

We can see in these liberal perspectives on international relations the more basic elements of liberal philosophy—assumptions of basic human rationality and morality, the belief in reforming institutions as solutions to problems, and, most important, a belief in human progress. Liberals reject the realist assumption that the dynamics and fundamental realities of international relations remain unchanged. People are rational enough to know that certain things (e.g., war) are irrational and undesirable, and they are capable of learning how to eliminate these practices. Robert Gilpin noted that realism "is founded on a pessimism regarding moral progress and human possibilities."[19] In contrast, liberalism is founded on a belief that "the changing interests of inhabitants of states.... [and] the underlying forces for change are creating opportunities for increased cooperation and a greater realization

liberal institutionalism A version of liberalism that stresses the positive role of international organizations and institutions in promoting cooperation and peace.

of peace, welfare and justice."[20] Perhaps this is the best way to distinguish realism from liberalism. Liberals are generally optimistic about the prospects for positive change and progress, whereas realists are fundamentally pessimistic about the chances for any lasting improvement in the nature of international relations.

Marxism

Marxist Social theory emphasizing the importance of class conflict for understanding social relations, including international politics.

It can be difficult to talk about a **Marxist** approach to international relations, largely because Marx himself had relatively little to say about it. Marx was mainly concerned with describing and analyzing the internal dynamics of capitalist societies. Indeed, some of what Marx did say about international relations, such as treating British imperialism as a progressive force, would not sit too well with most contemporary Marxists. Rather than being the product of Marx himself, the Marxist view of international relations is largely the result of attempts by subsequent thinkers—some Marxists, some merely influenced by Marx—to apply his basic ideas and concepts to the realm of international relations. Some prefer other labels, such as *radicalism* or *globalism*. But whichever label we choose, the foundations can be found in Marx's basic assumptions about the nature and dynamics of capitalism. It is ideas, not labels, that really matter.

Karl Marx German philosopher whose writings form the basis for the social, political, and economic theory that bears his name, Marxism.

Understanding Marxism requires an appreciation of the times and conditions in which Marx lived. **Karl Marx** (1818–1883) lived and wrote in the middle of the nineteenth century—that is to say, the early years of industrial capitalism. Indeed, it was Marx who coined the term *capitalism*. He spent most of his life in the cradle of the industrial revolution, England. Here he saw a world that bears little resemblance to the capitalist societies we live in today. It was a world of 60-and 70-hour workweeks, where children toiled alongside adults for low wages. Workers lived in slums and tenements, not comfortable suburbs. There were no child labor laws, no overtime, and no paid vacations. It was a world without laws and regulations to ensure that factories had fire exits and clean drinking water. It was a world without health insurance, from either government or employers. There was no unemployment insurance, no worker's compensation, no retirement accounts and 401Ks. It was a world in which the vast majority of people worked long hours for little reward, living lives of nearly unending misery and drudgery. But amidst the hardship and squalor of the masses, others enjoyed great affluence and comfort: mansions with fifty or hundred rooms for families of five or six people littered with expensive artwork and gold-plated bric-a-brac, summer villas, and private schools for children dressed in fancy clothes playing with ponies and swimming in private lakes. What made this disparity of living conditions even worse in Marx's eyes was that the very people leading miserable lives worked on the land and in the factories of those leading such opulent lives. The lifestyles and wealth of the elite relied upon the labor and effort of the impoverished.

bourgeoisie Karl Marx's label for the economic class that controls the "means of production." More colloquially known today as the *capitalist class*.

proletariat Karl Marx's label for those people who sell their labor to those who own the means of production (i.e., the bourgeoisie or capitalists). More colloquially known today as the *working class*.

Given the world in which he lived, it is not surprising that Marx saw class conflict as the defining feature of capitalist society, though this was not unique to capitalism. All previously existing societies were class societies, but the nature and basis of these class divisions changes over time. The classes that defined capitalism were the **bourgeoisie** (i.e., the capitalist class) and the **proletariat** (i.e., the working class) distinguished by their different *relationship to the means of production*. This simply means that the bourgeoisie control the means of production (i.e., the land, mines, factories, banks, etc.) whereas the proletariats earn their income by selling labor for wages to the bourgeoisie. The bourgeoisie owns the means of production; the proletariat works in or on the means of production. Marx argued that the relationship between the classes was not merely unequal but also exploitative because the workers produce all the goods and services but only a portion of the value in wages. The capitalists take the remainder as profit. This inequality and exploitation forms the basis of a fundamental conflict of interests. As long as some people exploit other people, conflict will result.

Marx viewed all aspects of capitalist society—art, culture, literature, religion, and politics—in the context of class conflict. A society's economic structure, or *base*, forms the foundation for everything else, the *superstructure*. Religious doctrines telling people that wealth and material well-being in this world are unimportant because it is spiritual health and the afterlife that really matter are actually part

In 2001 Germany was among the first nations to adopt the Euro, which replaced the German Mark. German citizens had to be educated about the transition, and convinced that it would be beneficial.

Source: Sean Gallup/Getty Images News/Getty Images

of the system of class domination. Ideas and doctrines that encourage people to accept the inequalities of capitalist society have the effect of supporting and perpetuating capitalism. This is why Marx characterized religion as the "opiate" of the masses, a drug that prevents them from seeing the world around them for what it really is.

Just as religion cannot be understood apart from class conflict, neither can politics because control of economic resources brings political power and control of political institutions. The state or government in capitalist society is controlled by and serves, protects, and advances the interests of the capitalist class. This concept is referred to as the **nonneutrality of the state**. The government is not a neutral actor—it is systematically biased in favor of the dominant economic class. As Gabriel Kolko explains, "the *essential, primary* fact about the American social system is that it is a capitalist society based on a grossly unequal distribution of wealth and income … *political power in America is an aspect of economic power* [emphasis added]."[21] Consequently, the actions and policies of capitalist governments, domestically and internationally, can be understood only in the context of class interests. Take, for example, social welfare programs that appear to benefit the working classes. Marxists view such reforms as minor crumbs placating the working class to prevent revolution. Although social welfare programs seem to undermine the logic of capitalism, their actual effect is to uphold and sustain an unequal and exploitative system. Eventually, Marx believed that the misery of the working class and the inequality inherent in the capitalist system would increase to such extent that the proletariat would revolt.

When these basic insights are applied to international relations, the result is a very different view of the world than that offered by realists or liberals. At the level of individual states, Marxism emphasizes the significance of their internal class structure. One cannot understand the policies of the United States without recognizing that it is a capitalist society whose government pursues policies to protect and advance the interests of its economic elite. Whether one is trying to understand why the United States was at war in Vietnam or the Persian Gulf or why it enacted the North American Free Trade Agreement (NAFTA), we must trace policies to the class interests they advance. This is very different from either a realist or a liberal perspective. A realist account of the U.S. involvement in Vietnam might not even mention the fact that it is a capitalist system, whereas for Marxists this is the essential starting point for analysis.

But Marxist analysis goes beyond this. Not only are the policies of individual states to be understood in terms of economic and class interest, but the international system as a whole is also conceptualized in class terms. The international system is first and foremost a capitalist system. Like domestic capitalist systems it is based on inequality, exploitation, and class conflict. Whereas realists and liberals look at the world and see roughly two hundred sovereign states interacting with one another, Marxists see its defining feature as the division of the world into the powerful **core** of states that control economic resources and use their power to exploit the states and people of the weak and powerless **periphery**. Whether one labels the division as core versus periphery, North versus South, haves versus have-nots, or First World versus Third World, the underlying reality of inequality remains the same.

nonneutrality of the state The Marxist assumption that the state or government inevitably serves, protects, and advances the interests of those with economic power.

core and periphery Terms that refer to the division of the world into classes somewhat analogous to Marx's bourgeoisie and proletariat. The **core** is the small group of wealthy and powerful states exploiting the larger group of weak and impoverished states (i.e., the **periphery**).

This vision of the world leads Marxists to a different set of concerns from those that normally animate realists and liberals. Despite profound philosophical and theoretical differences, realists and liberals usually focus on questions of war and peace. They may disagree about whether or not democracies are more peaceful, but the problem of war and conflict is at the core of both liberal and realist thought. Marxists focus on understanding the institutions and processes that sustain what they see as an unequal, exploitative, and unjust international order. Whether it is states (through military intervention or imperialism), quasi-state actors (such as the World Bank or International Monetary Fund), or nonstate actors (such as multinational corporations), Marxist analysis always returns to the central reality and problems—understanding the role these actors play in maintaining and perpetuating an unequal and exploitative global capitalist order.

Feminism

Feminist approaches to international relations share some things in common with Marxist approaches, even though the vast majority of feminists are not Marxists. One similarity is that both Marxism and **feminism** are dissident approaches in the sense that they are often ignored in debates where realist and liberal perspectives are assumed to exhaust the alternatives. Feminist and Marxist approaches also share a belief that the dominant approaches of realism and liberalism ignore the most significant variable for understanding social reality: for Marxists, that variable is economic class, whereas for feminists it is gender. When Marxists look at the world around them, they think it is obvious that class inequality and conflict are critical for understanding how that world works. When feminists look at the world, they think it is obvious that gender inequality and male dominance are, if anything, even more pervasive. Indeed, there are few areas where male dominance is more pronounced than international relations: One can count on a few fingers the women who have led their nations in the past fifty years (e.g., Britain's Margaret Thatcher, Israel's Golda Meir, India's Indira Gandhi, and Germany's Angela Merkel). How one can possibly understand international relations while ignoring this fact is incomprehensible to feminists. A final similarity is that Marxism and most varieties of feminism are self-consciously emancipatory perspectives in that both seek to create a social order free of the inequalities, domination, and injustices that characterize the contemporary world.

Although there is no single feminist theory of international relations, there is a core of concerns and beliefs that unites a variety of feminist perspectives. Feminists of all stripes agree that traditional approaches and research have systematically excluded women and issues of concern to them. For example, the literature on war in international relations could fill a large library. There are endless studies on whether war is more likely when there are one, two, three, or more major powers. However, the studies on how war affects the lives of women could fit on a very small shelf. Discussions of human rights in international relations focus on political rights such as free speech and extrajudicial executions, but much less attention is paid to the widespread and systemic violations of the human rights of

feminism A perspective on social phenomena focusing on issues of concern to women while theoretically emphasizing the importance of gender.

women, whether it be sexual slavery, genital mutilation, the denial of access to education, or the acceptance of violence against women. The imprisonment of political opponents prompts governments to protest and people to write letters, but the failure of governments to prosecute men who kill their wives because of insufficient dowries is written off as a cultural peccadillo. Whatever their other theoretical differences, feminists of all persuasions decry the exclusion of women and issues that affect women from the agenda of international relations scholars. But feminist perspectives go much further than simply demanding a greater focus on women.

In her article "Well, What Is the Feminist Perspective on Bosnia?" Marysia Zalewski explains that "there is an easy and a difficult answer to such a question. The easy, but no less important, answer is to look at what is happening to women in Bosnia. No one can deny that women suffer in gender specific ways in wartime."[22] Here Zalewski is talking about an empirical focus on women's experiences, such as the systematic use of rape as a weapon of terror in ethnic cleansing. But she goes on to note that "this, at first sight easy, answer feeds immediately into the difficult one…. Changing the empirical focus … make[s] us start questioning how beliefs

Angela Merkel, Germany's first woman Chancellor, is one of the few women to lead a major power.

Source: AP Photo/Bundeswehr, Michael Schulze

and myths about gender play an important role in creating, maintaining and ending war, including the one in Bosnia."[23] That is, one should not stop with detailing how certain practices and institutions affect women. The more fundamental question is how and why such practices and institutions came into being and are perpetuated. This requires that we look not only at women, but also at gender and the gendered nature of all social relations, including international relations.

If feminist approaches to international relations are marked by their empirical focus on women, feminist theories are distinguished by their focus on **gender**. This may seem a little confusing since in everyday language people often use *sex* and *gender* interchangeably. Feminists draw a distinction between the two. A person's *sex* is biological: The nurse could tell, with a few rare exceptions, whether you were a boy or a girl the moment you were born. *Gender*, on the other hand, has to do with those behavioral traits we associate with "masculinity" and "femininity." When we say that someone's "manhood" is being questioned, we are not referring to whether someone is a man in a strictly biological sense. His masculinity, not his sex, is being questioned. Gender refers to those socially constructed notions of what a "man" or a "woman" should be and how they should behave. As Steve Niva explains, "gender does not refer to biological differences between men and women but to a set of socially constructed and defined characteristics, meanings, and practices associated with being a man (masculinity) and being a woman (femininity)."[24]

gender Socially constructed categories and traits of "masculinity" and "femininity."

Although some feminists see behavioral differences between men and women as biologically based, most assume there are virtually no inherent or essential differences between men and women beyond the biological variations associated with procreation. The dramatic differences in social roles and power between men and women cannot be the result of these relatively minor differences. They result instead from socially formed conceptions of what it means to be a man or woman. Most of the traits or behaviors we commonly associate with men or women (e.g. men are aggressive, women are nurturing) are not biologically determined, but rather socially constructed.[25] This can be demonstrated anecdotally by the fact that we can all think of men who seem to embody many feminine traits and women who exhibit masculine traits.

Feminists go on to observe that masculine and feminine traits are typically defined in opposition to one another—that is, if men are competitive, women are cooperative; if men are aggressive, women are peaceful; if men are rational, women are irrational or hysterical; and if women are nurturing, men are emotionally distant. To be a man is not to be a woman, and vice versa. Furthermore, societies have systematically placed greater value on traits associated with masculinity than those associated with femininity. A woman who displays masculine behavior will be more accepted than a man who is considered feminine because masculine traits are preferable to feminine traits. Social reactions to boys who engage in typically feminine behaviors are more judgmental than reactions to girls engaging in typically masculine behaviors. When a woman politician, such as Margaret Thatcher, is combative, competitive, and confrontational, this is seen as a good thing, almost as if she had overcome her femininity. A male politician displaying feminine traits, on the other hand, is considered a wimp.

These socially constructed definitions infuse all aspects of social, political, and economic life and result in a myriad of gendered practices and institutions that effectively perpetuate male dominance. Take, for example, one of the gendered dualisms that has been part of our culture for centuries, if not millennia: that of the *private* versus the *public*. The idea that home and family life, the private sphere, is the natural domain of women whereas politics and commercial life, the public sphere, is the natural domain of men has had a profound impact on the status of women. The most glaring example was the exclusion of women from the right to vote in every democracy until the first quarter of the twentieth century, though even in the first part of the twenty-first century women are still wildly underrepresented in these areas. When one combines socially constructed notions of masculinity and femininity with the exclusion of women from the institutions of public power, this inevitably means that the institutions and practices of the public sphere will reflect masculine traits. If men are supposed to be competitive, aggressive, and rational, then the institutions dominated by men will reflect these traits. In this way, institutions and practices become gendered.

How do these insights relate to international relations? To begin with, there is no reason to think that the processes and dynamics of international relations are immune to the impact of gender. The nature and conduct of international relations is profoundly shaped by the effective exclusion of women and prevailing social constructions of masculinity. Feminists would ask us to explore both the reasons for, and consequences of, the exclusion of women. When masculinity is socially defined as competitiveness, lack of empathy, self-reliance, aggressiveness, and power seeking, it should come as no surprise that a realm of activity dominated by men will reflect these values and characteristics. Socially constructed notions of masculinity are projected onto world politics. But feminists maintain that there is nothing inevitable about this state of affairs, because neither male dominance nor social constructions of masculinity are unchangeable.

But it is not merely the "real world" that reflects this male dominance. Our philosophical and theoretical thinking about international relations has also been shaped almost completely by men. This fact affects both what we think constitutes international relations and how we think international relations works. This way of thinking helps account for why many of the issues of concern to women have typically been ignored as "not really international relations." Male dominance also influences prevailing theories and perspectives on international relations. When male theorists portray international relations as a naturally competitive realm marked by conflict and strategic rationality and calculation, they are treating as inevitable and universal something that is actually the consequence of socially constructed conceptions of gender and the exclusion of women. Feminists have been particularly critical of realism in this area because they see it as a theory of international relations of, by, and for men. Realism sees the world through a masculine lens but pretends to provide an "objective" portrait of how the world works. Realism treats a world shaped by men and permeated to its core by masculine gender assumptions as a genderless and universal reality.

A common misperception of feminist theories is that they are only about women. Given the label "feminist" theories, this is understandable. In reality, the focus on gender norms and their impact is just as much about men as it is about women. Though the empirical focus on women naturally leads to an emphasis on how women are adversely affected by these gendered norms, men are also frequently harmed as well. After all, if war is a consequence of the gendered nature of international politics, the millions of men who died on the battlefields of World War I were hardly beneficiaries of gendered practices.

Many find feminist approaches to international relations difficult to grasp. The main problem is that feminism presents a way of looking at international relations that is so different from the perspectives we have become accustomed to. It requires us to look at something—the consequences of male dominance—that is so obvious and pervasive that it often escapes our notice. What is staring us in the face is often the very thing we overlook. Though feminist approaches may appear difficult to grasp at first, the basic elements that shape a feminist approach are quite simple. First, the empirical fact is that men have dominated the institutions of public power. Perhaps, nowhere is this dominance greater than in those areas that have traditionally been the focus of international relations—foreign policy, diplomacy, and the military. And male dominance has consequences in terms of the conduct of international relations. Second, male dominance is no less absent among scholars who have shaped our theoretical thinking about international relations, whether it be realism (Morgenthau), liberalism (Kant), or Marxism (Lenin). This dominance has consequences for how we have traditionally thought about international relations. Third, there is no doubt that socially constructed gender roles and norms remain a central feature of our social and political life. Thus, to assume that the reality of male dominance and social conceptions of gender can be ignored in our attempts to understand international relations is simply not tenable.

Constructivism

Feminism, which stresses the socially constructed nature of gender norms, segues well into a discussion of the most recent approach to thinking about international relations, **constructivism**. Feminists argue that almost all behavioral differences between men and women are rooted in socially derived norms about the content and boundaries of acceptable or desirable male and female behavior. That is, men and women learn what it means to behave like a man or woman and act accordingly. Over time, however, changing norms alter behavior even though sexual biology remains the same, which in itself demonstrates the socially constructed nature of behavior.

constructivism A perspective that stresses the importance of identities and shared understandings in shaping the behavior of social actors.

One can restate feminist insights about the socially constructed nature of gender in a more general form: Any actor's behavior is shaped by socially transmitted and reinforced beliefs, norms, and identities that define that actor within the context of its society. Being a "man" is only one social identity. "College professor" is another. A professor's behavior is also shaped by prevailing beliefs, norms, and conceptions about what it means to be a professor and how professors should behave. And how professors relate to students and vice versa is shaped by their mutual identities and conceptions of how they should behave toward each other.

Thus, when we look at why people behave as they do, there is no escaping the overwhelming importance of beliefs, social norms, and identities.

Constructivists attempt to apply this basic insight to understanding international relations. Daniel Thomas explains: "According to … constructivist theories of international relations, actors [states] seek to behave in accordance with the norms relevant to their identities … [which are] definitions of the self in relation to others that provide guidance for how one should behave in a given context."[26] The focus is on how actors, in this case largely policymakers and elites, view themselves, others, and the norms of appropriate behavior. Richard Rosecrance explains that "one reason why no single theory of international politics has ever been adequate is that nations modify their behavior in face of experience and theory. If statesmen believe that the balance of power must determine their policies, then they will act in such a way as to validate the theory." And "because leaders and statesmen have been acting on different and contrasting theories of international politics," no single theory will be able to capture all of international politics.[27]

Rosecrance states the point so casually that its significance might be lost. Most theories of international relations, and especially realism, assume the existence of an objective reality that they seek to reveal. The preeminent realist Hans Morgenthau claimed that "political realism believes that politics, like society in general, is governed by objective laws … the operation of these laws being impervious to our preferences, men will challenge them only at the risk of failure."[28] Realists assume that states would act as they do independent of any theory telling them that is how they should behave. The realities of world politics exist; they are not "created." Constructivists disagree. They see no inherent and inevitable reason why states must behave in any particular way. States behave as they do because people adhere to certain notions of how they should and do behave. Their behavior is determined by their identities, which are neither given nor constant. "Constructivism," notes Cynthia Weber, "argues that identities and interests in international politics are not stable—they have no pre-given nature."[29] States behave as realists (or liberals) predict they will only so long as they accept and internalize the norms of state behavior embodied in these theories. This is not to suggest that there is no "real" world or that the world is and can become whatever we imagine it to be. There are realities: no world government exists; some nations do have nuclear weapons; and some nations are stronger than others. Constructivism holds, however, that the implications of these facts for the conduct of international relations depend on how people understand their significance.

An example may help illustrate the point. Constructivists accept the fact that there is no world government—that is, international politics is anarchic. Realists argue that anarchy creates insecurities and leads states into conflict with one another (the security dilemma). Constructivists are quick to note that this is not always the case. Sometimes the insecurity of anarchy leads states into conflict, but other times it does not. France and Great Britain, enemies or rivals for much of their history, no longer fear each other. Why? Has a world government been created to eliminate uncertainty and insecurity? No. What has changed is how British and French statesmen view themselves and each other. They have come to see themselves as democracies that do not threaten each other. In the words of a prominent constructivist, "anarchy is what states make of it."[30] That is, anarchy exists, but what this means in terms of how states relate to one another depends on what statesmen think, how they identify themselves and others, and how they believe they should act toward each other.

In this sense, constructivists highlight the distinction between theory in the natural sciences such as biology, chemistry, and physics as opposed to theory in the social sciences. The laws of physics, for example, operated long before we knew what they were. Gravity will force a dropped book to the ground regardless of whether we think this will or should happen. Theories about how cells behave or chemicals interact do not influence their behavior. But this sharp line between theory and behavior does not hold in the social realm. In the social sciences there is an intimate relationship between theory and practice, between what leaders think about how the world works and how they choose to behave in the world.

Perspectives and Levels of Analysis

There are several ways we can organize and make sense of the complexities of international relations. One is to identify distinct schools of thought or worldviews and see how they apply to particular issues and problems. This is the approach emphasized in this text. Others have found it useful to focus on different **levels of analysis** in which international phenomena such as war or foreign policy are examined from several different "levels." At the *individual level*, for example, we might focus on general aspects of human nature or traits of individual decision makers (e.g. perceptions, beliefs, and personalities). At the *state level*, we can try to understand how societal characteristics influence state behavior (e.g. are democratic states more peaceful or capitalist states more expansionist?). Finally, at the *international level*, we can attempt to understand the impact of international anarchy or given distributions of power (e.g. does a balance or imbalance of power lead to peace?).

Although various analysts tend to emphasize different levels, any reasonably complete understanding of international relations will incorporate all the levels of analysis. Indeed, the various perspectives discussed in this chapter usually cut across these different levels. Liberals, for example, make some assumptions about human nature (individual level) and the peacefulness of democracies (state level). Similarly, realists make assumptions about human nature (individual level) as well as the consequences of international anarchy (system level). Whether we organize our thinking about international relations primarily in terms of competing theories and philosophies or different levels of analysis is largely a matter of what seems most useful. Neither approach is necessarily better than the other; they are simply different organizational schemes for thinking about, and making sense of, international relations.

levels of analysis An organizational scheme for thinking about international politics. The most general focuses on causes and dynamics of the individual, state, and systemic levels.

Conclusion

Though this diversity of perspectives might seem confusing enough, matters actually get a little worse because even within each perspective there are differences of opinion on theoretical and practical policy issues. As a result, it is very rare that we can identify *the* realist, liberal, Marxist, feminist, or constructivist position. An answer to the question, "What is the realist position on such and such?" is not always straightforward. On a theoretical level, for example, realists disagree among themselves about whether the chances for war are lowest in a world with one, two, or multiple major powers. Using a policy issue as an example, there was no single realist position on the 2003 invasion of Iraq: some realists favored war, while others were staunch opponents. Muddying the waters further, representatives of differing perspectives may find themselves in agreement on an issue.

Thus, it is not always useful to think in terms of *a* realist, liberal, Marxist, feminist, or constructivist *position*. Instead, it is better to approach debates in terms of *arguments* or *rationales*. Let us again use the example of the 2003 invasion of Iraq to illustrate. Realists disagreed among themselves about the wisdom of the U.S. invasion. But if we look at the type of arguments and rationales offered in defense of their differing positions, certain similarities are evident. Realist opponents of the Iraq War claimed that the threat Iraq posed was insufficient to warrant the costs associated with war. Other realists found the threat posed by Iraq to be compelling and supported the war. In this case there was agreement that national and strategic interests needed to guide decisions to go to war—realists were united on this point—but they disagreed about whether war in Iraq was in the national interest. The underlying issues and concerns were the same, but their application to the specific case was different. On the question of Iraq, one could make an argument for or against the war on realist terms. It is the type of argument made, not necessarily the conclusion reached, that usually allows one to distinguish a realist from a Marxist or liberal. Thus, people who share the same basic assumptions may arrive at different positions. Conversely, people who start with different assumptions may arrive at the same position. Some liberals, for example, supported the war in Iraq largely on human rights grounds, arriving at the same position as pro-war realists but for very different reasons. Thus, we cannot always assume that realists will always agree with other realists (or liberals with liberals and so on) or that people from different perspectives will always be at odds. In textbooks such as this one, ideas are often neatly divided into sections and subsections. The real world, however, is not always so tidy.

CHAPTER SUMMARY

■ Theoretical and policy debates in international relations are usually rooted in competing perspectives or worldviews that provide differing ways to look at and understand the world around us. The chapter focused on five competing visions of international relations: realism, liberalism, Marxism, feminism, and constructivism.

■ Realism provides a somewhat pessimistic outlook that stresses the centrality and inevitability of conflict among nations. Many classical realists trace these conflicts to a flawed human nature, whereas neorealists are more inclined to see it as a consequence of an inherently insecure anarchical international system.

■ Liberalism is a more optimistic outlook that sees a greater scope for international cooperation and peace. Whether the stress is on expanding commerce, spreading democracy, changing ethical norms, or strengthening international institutions, liberals believe that common interests and shared values offer hope for a fundamentally better and more peaceful world.

■ Marxists analyze society, domestic and international, in terms of class interests and conflicts. The behavior and policies of states are seen as reflections of class

(not national) interests, and the dynamics of world politics as a whole are understood in terms of the unequal and exploitative relations between the wealthy, powerful nations of the global north and the impoverished, weak nations of the global South. Social conflict generally, and international conflict in particular, is an inevitable consequence of inequality and exploitation.

■ Feminists argue that social dynamics and institutions cannot be understood without the recognition of the reality of male dominance and the importance of gender. International relations is no exception, especially because there are few other areas where male dominance is so pronounced. Male dominance and socially constructed notions of masculinity and femininity have helped shape the reality of international politics as well as our theories of international politics.

■ Constructivists argue that the behavior of social actors (e.g., individuals, groups, nations) is shaped by ideas, norms, and identities. As a result, they are skeptical of theories that portray certain types of behaviors as inevitable.

CRITICAL QUESTIONS

1. Realism and liberalism are sometimes distinguished by the pessimism of the former and optimism of the later. Can the other perspectives discussed in this chapter be differentiated along the same lines?

2. To some extent do the perspectives on international relations differ in the questions they ask rather than the answers they provide?

3. It is important to recognize that sometimes different perspectives share things in common. Select various combinations (e.g., realists and Marxists or feminists

and constructivists) and identify points of agreement as well as disagreement.

4. How might representatives from the different perspectives explain the U.S. decision to go to war against Iraq in 2003?

5. Do you think it is possible to combine different perspectives in a way that makes sense? For example, can someone be both a realist and a Marxist or a feminist and a liberal? Do some combinations make sense but not others?

KEY TERMS

anarchy, 39
bourgeoisie, 44
collective egoism, 37

commercial liberalism, 42
constructivism, 51
core, 46

Democratic liberalism, 42
feminism, 47
gender, 49

George Kennan, 38
group egoism, 37
Hans Morgenthau, 38

FURTHER READINGS

A good place to begin is with two of the most influential statements of classical realism: Edward Hallett Carr, *The Twenty Years' Crisis, 1919–1939* (New York: Harper Collins, 1964 [1945]), and Hans Morgenthau, *Politics Among Nations: The Struggle for Power and Peace* (New York: Alfred A. Knopf, 1967). The essential presentation of neorealism is Kenneth Waltz, *Theory of International Politics* (Reading, MA: Addison-Wesley, 1979). A forceful recent restatement of realism is John Mearsheimer, *The Tragedy of Great Power Politics* (New York: W. W. Norton, 2000).

The literature on liberalism is more diverse. Some essential works reflecting various strains of liberal thinking include Bruce Russett, *Grasping the Democratic Peace* (Princeton, NJ: Princeton University Press, 1993); Richard Rosecrance, *The Rise of the Trading State: Commerce and Conquest in the Modern World* (New York: Basic Books, 1986); John Mueller, *Retreat from Doomsday: The Obsolescence of Major War* (New York: Basic Books, 1989).

Those interested in Marxist approaches should begin with Lenin's classic *Imperialism: The Highest Stage of Capitalism* (New York: International Publishers, 1939) and John Hobson's *Imperialism: A Study* (Ann Arbor: University of Michigan Press, 1965). A more recent survey is Anthony Brewer, *Marxist Theories of Imperialism: A Critical Survey* (London: Routledge, 1990).

Some important recent feminist works include J. Ann Tickner, *Gender and International Relations* (New York: Columbia University Press, 1993), and Christine Sylvester, *Feminist Theory and International Relations in a Post-Modern Era* (Cambridge: Cambridge University Press, 1994). One of the classic and most interesting feminist works is Cynthia Enloe, *Bananas, Beaches and Bases: Making Feminist Sense of International Relations* (Berkeley: University of California Press, 2001, updated edition). The essential work in the constructivist tradition is Alexander Wendt, *A Social Theory of International Politics* (Cambridge: Cambridge University Press, 1999).

NOTES

[1]Stephen Walt, "International Relations One World, Many Theories," *Foreign Policy* 110 (Spring 1998): 29.

[2]Quoted in Hans Morgenthau, *Scientific Man versus Power Politics* (Chicago: University of Chicago Press, 1946), p. ii.

[3]Reinhold Niebuhr, *Moral Man and Immoral Society: A Study in Ethics and Politics* (New York: Charles Scribner's Sons, 1934), p. xx.

[4]Morgenthau, *Scientific Man*, pp. 194–195.

[5]George Kennan, *Memoirs 1925–1950* (Boston: Little, Brown, 1967), p. 319.

[6]Hans Morgenthau, *Politics Among Nations: The Struggle for Power and Peace* (New York: Alfred A. Knopf, 1967), p. 3.

[7]Robert Gilpin, "The Richness of the Tradition of Political Realism," in *Neorealism and Its Critics*, ed. Robert Keohane (New York: Columbia University Press, 1986), p. 305.

[8]Edward Hallett Carr, *The Twenty Years' Crisis, 1919–1939* (New York: Harper & Row, 1964), p. 53.

[9]Stanley Michalak, *A Primer in Power Politics* (Wilmington, DE: Scholarly Resources, 2001), p. 45.

[10]Carr, *Twenty Years' Crisis*, p. 51.

[11]Michalak, *Primer in Power Politics*, p. 2.

[12]Kenneth Waltz, *Theory of International Politics* (Reading, MA: Addison-Wesley, 1979), p. 104.

[13]John Herz, *The Nation-State and the Crisis of World Politics* (New York: David McKay, 1976), pp. 72–73.

[14]Robert Gilpin, *War and Change in World Politics* (Cambridge: Cambridge University Press, 1981), p. 7.

[15]David Sidorsky, ed., *The Liberal Tradition in European Thought* (New York: Capricorn Books, 1970), p. 2.

[16]Richard Rosecrance, *The Rise of the Trading State: Commerce and Conquest in the Modern World* (New York: Basic Books, 1986), p. 148.

[17]Ibid., p. 24.

[18]John Mueller, *Retreat from Doomsday: The Obsolescence of Major War* (New York: Basic Books, 1989), pp. 217, 244.

[19]Gilpin, *War and Change in World Politics*, p. 305.

[20]Mark Zacher and Richard Matthew, "Liberal International Theory: Common Threads, Divergent Strands," in *Controversies in International Relations Theory*, ed. Charles W. Kegley (New York: St. Martin's Press, 1995), p. 140.

[21]Gabriel Kolko, *The Roots of American Foreign Policy* (Boston: Beacon Press, 1969), pp. 6, 9.

[22]Marysia Zalewski, "Well, What Is the Feminist Perspective on Bosnia?" *International Affairs* 71, no. 2(1995): 355. The interesting title of this article reflects the widespread frustration feminists feel when their work is attacked on the grounds that it lacks "real-world" relevance.

[23]Ibid., pp. 355–356.

[24]Steve Niva, "Tough and Tender: New World Order Masculinity and the Cold War," in *The "Man" Question in International Relations*, ed. Marysia Zalewski and Jane Parpart (Boulder, CO: Westview Press, 1998), pp. 111–112.

[25]There are those (mostly nonfeminists) who see many behavioral differences as biologically determined. See, for example, Francis Fukuyama, "Women and the Evolution of World Politics," *Foreign Affairs* 77, no. 5 (September/October 1998), and Richard Wrangham and Dale Peterson, *Demonic Males* (Boston: Houghton Mifflin, 1996).

[26]Daniel C. Thomas, *The Helsinki Effect: International Norms, Human Rights and the Demise of Communism* (Princeton, NJ: Princeton University Press, 2001), p. 13.

[27]Rosecrance, *Rise of the Trading State*, p. 41.

[28]Morgenthau, *Politics Among Nations*, p. 4.

[29]Cynthia Weber, *International Relations Theory: A Critical Introduction* (New York: Routledge, 2001), p. 60.

[30]Alexander Wendt, "Anarchy Is What States Make of It," *International Organization* 46, no. 2 (Summer 1992): 392–425.

3 Power Politics

Key Controversy: Does International Anarchy Lead to War?

International politics is often considered the realm of power politics. Without a world government, nations do not have the luxury of security and must strive for power or live at the mercy of their powerful neighbors. According to realists, international politics is fundamentally a struggle for power in which nations must always be wary of the power of other nations. Nations that naïvely ignore these realities and try to avoid power politics will suffer the consequences of their folly. Historically, liberals have rejected this pessimistic assessment and sought alternatives to power politics. Though some utopian liberals have embraced world government, most have proposed more modest alternatives. Assuming a widely-shared interest in peace, many liberals believe that the international community as a whole can effectively organize to deter aggression and war. Constructivists also reject the realist view that states must pursue power to ensure their security, pointing out that many states have created stable and secure relations that do not rest on calculations of power. ■

What are the causes of war? What, if anything, can be done to preserve and promote international peace? Although there is little agreement on the answers, at least there is consensus that these are the most important questions for students of international relations. Most would concede that some measure of international conflict is unavoidable. Nations are unlikely to agree about everything all the time. Accepting the inevitability of international conflict, however, does not necessarily entail the inevitability of *violent* international conflict. And even if it is unrealistic to eliminate all violent international conflict, it might still be possible to significantly reduce its likelihood. As we will see in the next chapter, some hold out hope that the spread of democracy in the world can reduce, or perhaps even eliminate, the chances for war. Others argue that the prospects for war and peace have more to do with the nature of the international system—including anarchy, the distribution of power, and/or the existence of international institutions—and suggest we need to look here for ways to preserve peace. But which international arrangements or institutions are conducive to peace? Does a balance of power lead to peace? Does peace require the presence of a hegemonic power capable of enforcing it (i.e., a great imbalance of power)? Can the global community as a whole come together to preserve peace? In short, what are alternative mechanisms for preserving peace, and how feasible are they?

Peace Through Strength?

It is almost impossible to get through a national political campaign in the United States without hearing the phrase "peace through strength." Unfortunately, this geopolitical catchphrase is more often employed than explained. The political attraction of the slogan is clear: Both peace and strength are desirable, especially in contrast to war and weakness. Peace and strength are like motherhood and apple pie, something very hard to oppose. For our purposes the interesting word in the phrase is *through*, because it suggests a causal connection between peace and strength. Perhaps this is meant to inoculate candidates who favor increasing military power from charges of warmongering: More military power will lead to peace, not war. Political motivations aside, is there any reason to believe that peace and strength go hand-in-hand, that the latter leads to the former? Is there any evidence, for example, that strong nations are involved in fewer wars than are weaker nations? Probably not: Research demonstrates that great powers are involved in more, not fewer, wars.

    Those who invoke peace through strength, however, probably do not intend it to be taken as a social scientific hypothesis. More likely, it is rhetorical shorthand for a foreign policy orientation emphasizing national power as the essential currency of international affairs. It conveys the message that nations must be concerned about their power if they value their independence and security. The expression "peace through strength" reflects a commitment to **power politics**, a perspective in which international politics inevitably entails "perceptions of insecurity (the security dilemma); struggles for power; the use of Machiavellian stratagems; the presence of coercion; attempts to balance power; and the use of war to settle disputes."[1] The guiding assumption is that nations have no choice, or at least no otherwise choice, but to engage in power politics. If nations neglect considerations of power and place their fate in the hands of international institutions or the good will of others, they imperil their survival. In the international realm, nations have two options: "the alternatives … [are] probable suicide on the one hand and the active playing of the power-politics on the other."[2] The imperatives and logic of international anarchy compel states to pursue power. As Stanley Michalak argues, "We like to think that solutions exist 'out there,' new ideas that … could usher in a new era of peace and amity among nations," but regrettably, "the truth is: none exists. The few alternatives to military force have been well known for centuries … and

power politics A perspective portraying international relations as inevitably a realm of conflict and competition for power among states.

whenever they have [been] tried, they have failed."[3] Thus, the operation or "play-ing" of power politics is not an alternative to international peace; it is the only feasible, though admittedly imperfect, means for achieving international peace.

Not surprisingly, Michalak's pessimistic conclusion is not universally shared. Though the wisdom of "peace through strength" may not be questioned on the campaign trail, there is an enduring debate about the wisdom and inevitability of power politics. Critics find the association of power and peace to be disingenuous at best and morally irresponsible at worst. If the history of international politics reveals anything, it is that the pursuit of power has not produced anything that deserves to be called peace, and the security it supposedly ensures is fleeting and illusory. Strong powers may be *less insecure* than others, but in a world of relentless power competition no nation enjoys security, simply varying degrees of insecurity. Critics also challenge the assertion that there are no alternatives to power politics as a dangerously self-fulfilling part of the realist catechism, a statement of faith and ideology rather than a reflection of reality.

There Is No Alternative to Power Politics

In vivid terms Kenneth Waltz tells us "the state among states … conducts its affairs in the brooding shadow of violence." Because "some states may at any time use force, all states must be prepared to do so—or live at the mercy of their militarily more vigorous neighbors." In international relations, as in any other sphere of social interaction, "contact without at least occasional conflict is inconceivable; and the hope that in the absence of an agent to manage or manipulate conflicting parties the use of force will always be avoided cannot be realistically entertained."[4] It is hard to imagine a more concise statement for the inevitability of power poli-tics: International politics is anarchic; nations must provide for their own security; nations can never be certain what others are up to; war is always a possibility; and alternatives to national power as the final guarantor of safety and independence are unrealistic. Let us examine the argument in more detail.

Anarchy Leads to Power Politics

Why do nations in international society worry about strength and power in ways that people and groups within nations usually do not? Is it because nations come into conflict, whereas as people and groups within nations manage to live in har-mony? Certainly not. Domestic societies are rife with all kinds of conflicts—personal, social, and political. Is it that people within domestic societies are never threatened with violence, whereas nations are? Again, this is obviously not the case. Even though nations differ greatly in their level of domestic violence, none is able to eliminate it entirely. The difference is that in domestic society conflicts and vio-lence occur in a context with a central political authority to deal with and manage these conflicts. Waltz explains "the difference between national and international politics lies not in the use of force but in the different modes of organization for doing something about it." In the domestic realm we have governments with

anarchic The absence of a central governmental or political authority.

"a monopoly on the *legitimate* use of force, and legitimate here means that public agents are organized to prevent and counter the private use of force." Because there is a government, "citizens need not prepare to defend themselves. Public agencies do that. *A national system is not one of self-help. The international system is.*"[5]

International society is **anarchic**, meaning there is no world government with the right, obligation and/or capacity to protect nations. The United Nations is an international governmental organization (IGO)—that is, a voluntary organization of states. The United Nations is not, nor was it ever intended to be, a world government. Without a central authority to protect them from threats, nations have no alternative but to protect themselves as best as they can. This contrasts with domestic society in which people are not responsible for providing their own security. This is why we have police. Even though police do not offer foolproof protection, "states … do not enjoy even an imperfect guarantee of their security unless they set out to provide it for themselves."[6] States can protect their security by relying on their own resources, or they can combine power with others. But either way, nations are responsible for their own security. There is no escaping the reality that

self-help The necessity for actors to make provisions for their own security in the absence of any central authority to protect them from potential threats.

"**self-help** is *necessarily* the principle of action in an anarchic order."[7] And, according to Frederick Dunn, "so long as the notion of self-help persists, the aim of maintaining the power position of the nation is paramount to all other considerations."[8]

security dilemma The problem nations face when the actions taken to make one nation feel more secure inevitably make other nations feel less secure.

If self-help is the necessary corollary of anarchy, the **security dilemma** is the logical consequence of self-help. The dilemma nations face, even those not intending to threaten others, is that many of the actions that make them more secure increase the insecurity of others. Even actions that appear purely defensive can seem menacing to others. It is difficult to imagine a defensive military force that does not have at least some offensive potential. As a result, one nation's security is often another's insecurity. Although every increase in one nation's security does not necessarily lead to an equivalent reduction in another nation's security, there is usually some tradeoff. The contrast with domestic society is critical. Governments solve the security dilemma by providing security to all simultaneously. As the police provide for your security, this does not increase your neighbor's insecurity. Because international politics is anarchic, there is no lasting solution to the security dilemma of nations.

The security dilemma has two facets. First, states must be aware of how their security measures will be viewed by others; there is no reason to provoke unnecessary anxiety since this might prompt other nations to take actions that will in turn reduce your security. Second, nations have to worry about the capabilities and intentions of other states. The relatively easy part of this assessment is determining capabilities. Trying to decipher intentions is another matter. There was not much uncertainty, for example, about the size of the Soviet nuclear arsenal during the Cold War: Spy planes and satellites gave the United States a fairly reliable picture of Soviet capabilities. Debates revolved around what the Soviet Union planned on doing with these capabilities. This is the unavoidable element of uncertainty in international politics, and uncertainty translates into insecurity, which easily escalates into fear. And because "fear is endemic to states in the international system … it drives them to compete for power so that they can increase their prospects for survival in a dangerous world."[9]

So the argument for the inevitability of power politics follows a clear line of development: "Because the international system has no central authority, every nation must fend for itself, and states can do that only by utilizing their power; therefore, they will always be trying to increase their power."[10] In other words, "the mere existence of states claiming sovereignty in a world without a central authority creates a dynamic that encourages competition and violence."[11]

Power Politics I: The Balance of Power

In the field of international relations, terms and concepts are often ambiguous and contested. *Power* and *balance of power* are two examples of commonly-used concepts whose meanings are not always crystal clear. Even though "power lies at the heart of international politics ... there is considerable disagreement about what power is and how to measure it."[12] At a conceptual level, we can think of **power** as the ability to prevail in conflict, to influence the behavior of other actors. Actually measuring power is more problematic. Most operating within the tradition of realism and power politics would be inclined to agree with Mearsheimer that "states have two kinds of power: latent power and military power. These two forms of power are closely related but not synonymous." Whereas military power is fairly self-explanatory, "latent power refers to the socio-economic ingredients that go into building military power; it is largely based on a state's wealth and overall size of its population. Great powers need money, technology and personnel to build military forces and to fight wars, and a state's latent power refers to the raw potential it can draw on when competing with rival states."[13] While some will undoubtedly find this definition a little narrow, it is a good starting point for a discussion on power politics.

> **power** Influence over the behavior of others and the ability to prevail in conflict.

The expression *balance of power* can also be confusing. As Inis Claude notes, "balance of power is assigned a number of different, and not always compatible, meanings in discourse on international relations."[14] This can be illustrated by looking at two common uses of the term. In some cases, it is clear that the balance of power refers to a situation in which two nations or alliances are roughly equal—that is, when the power of one nation or alliance is literally balanced by the equal power of another. Here balance of power indicates an *equilibrium* of power. But there are also instances in which people refer to a "favorable balance of power." This usage seems like a contradiction in terms, since the very idea of "favorable" balance suggests that power is not balanced at all. In this case, the balance of power actually refers to a *distribution* of power that is not in balance. So when we see references to the balance of power between X and Y, it is necessary to look closely to determine if balance in fact means a balance or an imbalance.

Definitions of these terms are critical because they are central to many theories of international relations, especially **balance of power theory**, sometimes referred to as "the grand old theory of international relations."[15] Indeed, "not only is the balance if power one of the most enduring concepts in the field, its also persists, by some considerable distance, as the most widely cited theory."[16] Balance of power theory begins with the basic premises of power politics: International relations is a struggle for power and security in an anarchic world. Kenneth Waltz, probably the

> **balance of power theory** Predicts that the pursuit of security by nations tends to result in the creation of balances of power on a systemic level. This is often accompanied by the prediction that war is less likely when power is balanced because no nation can be confident of winning a war (and, thus, no nation is tempted to initiate one).

theory's leading proponent, claims that "balance of power politics prevail wherever two, and only two, requirements are met: that the order be anarchic and that it be populated by units [states] wishing to survive."[17] Some states undoubtedly wish to do more, but survival is assumed to be the minimal objective of all states. Since no central authority provides protection and because intentions are always uncertain, states inevitably focus on the capabilities of other states. Balance of power theory predicts that states will do exactly what the theory's name suggests—balance against the power of other states. In order to prevent any one state or alliance from achieving dominance, states can do one of two things; increase their own power or band together with other states. These options are sometimes referred to as *internal* and *external* balancing. States do not always intend for a balance to emerge, but "according to the theory, balances of power tend to form whether some or all states consciously aim to establish or maintain a balance."[18] States merely set out to safeguard their security and in the process "the various nations group themselves together in such a way that no single nation or group of nations is strong enough to overwhelm the others."[19]

Chinese military power on display in a parade in Tiananmen Square in Beijing. May see China as the most significant military challenger to the United States in coming decades.

Source: ROBYN BECK/AFP/Getty Images

Balancing, however, is not the only option states have. There is also the possibility of joining forces with the stronger power—that is, states could *bandwagon* with, rather than balance against, the most powerful state or alliance. Balance of power theorists see **bandwagoning** as unlikely because "to ally with the dominant power means placing one's trust in its continued benevolence. The safer strategy is to join with those who cannot readily dominate their allies, in order to avoid being dominated by those who can." Furthermore, "joining the weaker side increases the new members' influence within the alliance, because the weaker power has greater need for the assistance."[20] To use an illustrative metaphor, the balance of power operates like a seesaw: Whenever one side gets powerful enough to tip the contraption in its favor, nations scoot over to the other side to keep it on an even keel.

> **bandwagoning** When less powerful actors align with (rather than against) the most powerful ones. Inconsistent with balance of power theory, which predicts that nations will align against (and hence "balance") the most powerful nation.

In addition to preventing a nation or alliance from becoming powerful enough to dominate the international system, the tendency for states to balance has the added benefit of contributing to peace and stability. The argument is straightforward. It begins by assuming that nations start wars because they expect to win them—that is, they expect gains to exceed losses. When potential antagonists are roughly equal in power, neither side can be confident of prevailing in a war. The cost of war with equals is likely to be high and the prospects for victory uncertain. In such a situation, the incentive to initiate war is low.

Balance of power theory is not universally accepted. Even many realists who think in terms of power politics question whether it presents an accurate picture of how the world works. Part of the problem is that the theory is very difficult to test. Waltz himself admits, "because only a loosely defined and inconstant condition of balance is predicted, it is difficult to say that any given distribution of power falsifies the theory."[21] Since the theory predicts only a *tendency toward* balancing, the absence of a balance of power at any point in time does not automatically undermine the theory. More significantly, critics of the theory point to many historical examples that appear to run counter to its predictions. In the early years of the Cold War, for example, the United States was undeniably the world's most formidable military and economic power. If ever there were an undisputed strongest power in the world, the United States was it. According to balance of power theory, other nations should have been flocking to align against the United States. This did not happen. Why not?

Power Politics II: Balance of Threat Theory

An alternative that still accepts the basic precepts of power politics is **balance of threat theory**. Balance of power theory assumes that states focus on power because intentions can never be known for certain. In balance of power theory, states assume that those with the greatest capabilities pose the greatest threat and balance against them. On an abstract level, this is probably true. All else being equal, the most powerful states do pose the greatest danger. In the real world, however, all else is never equal. States do not ignore intentions merely because they cannot be established beyond a reasonable doubt. States make assessments, however imperfect, of both power and intentions. Balance of threat theory agrees that states do

> **balance of threat theory** Predicts that nations align against whichever nation is seen as posing the greatest threat, not necessarily against the powerful nation.

in fact balance; the question is what they balance against (see Figure 3.1 for a summary and contrast of the two theories).

Stephen Walt, who provides the most persuasive statement of balance of threat theory, explains: "Perceptions of intent are likely to play an especially crucial role in alliance choices.... Even states with rather modest capabilities may prompt others to balance if they are perceived as especially aggressive."[22] Many historical examples that contradict balance of power theory appear more consistent with balance of threat theory. Again, Walt notes "balance of threat theory helps explain why the coalitions that defeated Germany and its allies in World War I and World War II grew to be far more powerful than their opponents.... The answer is simple: Germany and its allies ... were more threatening (though weaker) and caused others to form a more powerful coalition in response."[23] This approach also helps explain the alignment pattern of the early Cold War. Even in the face of its obvious advantage in virtually every component of power, most nations aligned with the United States rather than the Soviet Union because the latter was seen as posing the greater threat despite its more limited power.

An important caveat needs to be noted here: Nations balance against others that are *perceived* as posing a threat, and assessments of threat may be wrong, just as measurements of power can be mistaken. The failure of an adequate deterrent coalition to emerge against Nazi Germany in the mid-1930s is an example of just such a failure. Balance of threat theory does not claim that perceptions of threat are correct, merely that they play a critical role in alliance choices.

FIGURE 3.1

Balance of power versus balance of threat theory

BALANCE OF POWER THEORY

Imbalances of power   ——————— cause ———————→   Alliances against the strongest state

An imbalance of power occurs when the strongest state or coalition in the system possesses significantly greater power than the second strongest. Power is the product of several different components, including population, economic and military capability, technological skill, and political cohesion.

BALANCE OF THREAT THEORY

Imbalances of threat   ——————— cause ———————→   Alliances against the most threatening state

An imbalance of threat occurs when the most threatening state or coalition is significantly more dangerous than the second most threatening state or coalition. The degree to which a state threatens others is the product of its aggregate power, its geographic proximity, its offensive capability, and the aggressiveness of its intentions.

Source: Reprinted from Stephen Walt, *The Origins of Alliances*. Copyright © 1987 by Cornell University. Used by permission of the publisher, Cornell University Press.

Power Politics III: Preponderance Theory

A final version of power politics is **preponderance** or **hegemonic stability theory**, in which states are distinguished by their **degree of power** and **degree of satisfaction**. *Degree of satisfaction* refers to whether a state is essentially satisfied or dissatisfied with the current international order and its place in it. Satisfied states are interested in preserving the international status quo, whereas dissatisfied states are revisionist and want to change (i.e., revise) the existing order. On the basis of power and satisfaction, the theory identifies four types of nations: (1) the powerful and satisfied, (2) the powerful and dissatisfied, (3) the weak and satisfied, and (4) the weak and dissatisfied. At the top of the power hierarchy is the dominant power or hegemon, which typically emerged from the last major war as the victor. By definition, the hegemon is a status quo power interested in preserving the existing order (the United States can be viewed as the hegemon from the end of World War II until the present). Below the hegemon are great powers, middle powers, small powers, and dependencies. In each category there are typically both status quo ("satisfied") and revisionist ("dissatisfied") states.[24]

This theory holds that states tend to align on the basis of interests—that is, status quo nations against revisionist nations. Though the alliances may not always be formal, status quo states will come together if the existing order is threatened by revisionist states. In the mid-1930s, for example, the United States, France, and Great Britain (status quo powers) did not form an alliance against Nazi Germany (a revisionist power), but they did eventually align in the face of German aggression.[25]

Preponderance theory also parts company with balance of power theory on the issue of which power distribution is most conducive to peace. According to Organski, it is not a balance of power that leads to peace but rather an imbalance of power: "World peace is guaranteed when the nations satisfied with the existing international order enjoy an unchallenged supremacy of power … major wars are most likely when a dissatisfied challenger achieves an approximate balance of power with the dominant nation."[26] Though it is true that a balance of power "means that either side might lose, it also means that either side may win."[27] When there is a great imbalance of power, the challenger knows there is no chance of winning a war and the dominant status quo power has no need to resort to war. The peace that results when the dominance of the status quo powers is unquestioned "is not necessarily a peace with justice," but it is peace if we define this to mean the absence of war.[28]

To illustrate the differences among the theories, consider their predictions for the post–Cold War world. The collapse of the Soviet Union clearly left the United States as the dominant nation in the world. No other nation possessed the combination of economic and military power equivalent to that of the United States. The United States was the only nation with the ability to project military force on a global scale. Balance of power theory predicts that other nations, fearful of U.S. power and uncertain of its intentions, will eventually balance and align against the United States in order to prevent American domination. Balance of threat theory does not automatically predict the emergence of a counter-American coalition.

preponderance or **hegemonic stability theory** Argues that nations tend to align on the basis of interests—those that are satisfied with the status quo as opposed to those that are dissatisfied. Peace and stability are more likely when there is a great imbalance of power in favor of the status quo states—that is, when there is a preponderance of power in support of the existing order.

degree of power In power preponderance theory, refers to a state's position in the international power hierarchy—that is, whether it is a great power, a middle-range power, or a weak state.

degree of satisfaction In power preponderance theory, the extent to which a state is essentially satisfied or dissatisfied with the existing international order.

The important variable is not the power of the United States per se but whether it comes to be viewed as a threat. Hegemonic stability theory predicts that a counter-American coalition will not emerge because the other major powers (Japan, Germany, Britain, France), whatever their disagreements with the United States, are all essentially satisfied powers interested in preserving, not overturning, the existing international order.

The Common Vision of Power Politics

The differences among balance of power, balance of threat, and hegemonic stability theories are clearly significant. Whether states balance against power or threats or align on the basis of interests is a critical question both for historical understanding and current policy debates. But the issues on which these theories disagree should obscure their common underlying vision of international politics. For our purposes, the most important point is that all of these theories agree on the fundamental features and dynamics of international relations: Anarchy is the central fact shaping relations among states; nations have to be concerned about their power vis-à-vis other states; and the pursuit of power and security by independent states is the driving force of international politics. There is no suggestion of any feasible alternative to the reality of international power politics in a world of sovereign states.

Alternatives to Power Politics

Even those who believe there is no realistic alternative to power politics concede it is not ideal. Though a balance or imbalance of power may be more conducive to peace, there is no guarantee that peace can be preserved indefinitely. Eventually, the balance breaks down or revisionist states gain power and war results. Within a system of power politics, war is always possible and periodically inevitable. Even when peace prevails, states must conduct their "affairs in the brooding shadow of violence."[29] At least this is what realists tell us. But is it so? Is the world really doomed to power politics, with periods of peace and stability punctuated by spasms of war and violence? Or are there alternatives to the relentless and ruthless logic of power politics?

World Government?

To the extent that anarchy is the fundamental cause of power politics, the creation of a world government would constitute a frontal assault on the problem. On the level of theory and logic, the case for world government is impeccable and simple. Just as national governments eliminate the security dilemma for individuals by providing protection and mechanisms for dealing with conflicts, a world government is essential if the same result is to be attained on a global scale. A truly effective world government would entail "the establishment of an authority which takes away from nations, summarily and completely, not only the machinery of battle that can wage war, but also the machinery of decision that can start a war."[30]

Even if we assume that world government is desirable, however, the problem is getting there. As Inis Claude notes in his discussion of the prospects for world government, "I do not propose to deal extensively with the question of the *feasibility* of world government in the present era, or in the foreseeable future. This abstention is in part a reflection of my conviction that the answer is almost self-evidently negative." He sees "no realistic prospect of the establishment of a system of world government as a means for attempting to cope with the critical dangers of world politics."[31] Realists, such as Kenneth Waltz, concede that *in theory* world government presents a solution to the problems of anarchy. But world government is "unattainable in practice" because the world lacks the sense of shared values and community that are essential preconditions for effective government. "In a society of states with little coherence," Waltz predicts, "the prospect of a world government would be an invitation to prepare for world civil war."[32] Fortunately for those who seek an alternative to power politics, world government is not the only option.

Collective Security

Though there has never been a serious attempt to establish a world government, efforts have been made to transcend power politics through **collective security**, which refers to "a system of states that join together ... and make an explicit commitment to do two things: (1) they renounce the use of force to settle disputes with each other, and (2) they promise to use force against any of their number who reject rule 1."[33] "The animating idea of collective security," Earl Ravenal explains, "is that each outbreak of aggression will be suppressed, not by a partial alliance directed specifically against certain parties, but by a universal compact, binding *all* to defend *any*."[34] Under collective security, peace is preserved not by individual states shifting alignments to offset the power of potential aggressors, but rather by the prospect of the entire community of nations coming to the aid of victims of aggression. Collective security arrangements can be global in scope but need not be; they can also be confined to more limited regions such as Europe or Southeast Asia.

It is important to note what collective security does and does not do. Though there would certainly be institutions for making decisions about how and when to respond to aggression, collective security does not create a world government. Individual states are not disarmed and replaced by some global police force. International politics remains anarchic and states sovereign. Nor does collective security reject power and deterrence as vital components of preserving peace. Proposals for collective security "recognize that military power is a central fact of life in international politics, and is likely to remain so for the foreseeable future."[35] In fact, collective security seeks to keep the peace by threatening any aggressor with the overwhelming power of the international community as a whole.

Rather than transcending international anarchy, collective security tries to ameliorate its consequences. Because the protection of each state's security becomes the responsibility of the wider international community, states would no longer be in a pure self-help situation. In committing themselves to aid any state threatened with aggression, all nations become part of an international police force, albeit one more like a volunteer fire department than a full-time police department. The element of

collective security A system in which states renounce the use of force to settle disputes and also agree to band together against states that resort to the use of force. In such a system, the threat of collective response by all states deters the use of force by individual states. Collective security was the initial goal of the League of Nations.

self-help is removed because states are obligated to help whenever peace is threatened, not merely when it is in their interests to do so. And the fact that aid would be available to all members of the community allows states to escape the security dilemma. The security afforded to all does not come at anyone else's expense.

The most significant experiment with collective security was the League of Nations during the 1920s and 1930s. In urging the creation of the League, U.S. President Woodrow Wilson laid out the basic logic of collective security: "If the peace presently to be made is to endure, it must be a peace made secure by the organized major force of mankind.... Right must be based upon the common strength, not the individual strength, of nations upon whose concert peace will depend."[36] Though the League of Nations provided for means short of force to punish and deter aggressors, such as economic sanctions, the military option remained the ultimate deterrent. According to Article 16 (1) of the League Charter, "Should any Member of the League resort to war ... it shall *ipso facto* be deemed to have committed an act of war against all other members of the League," and after other measures had failed to restore the peace, "the Members of the League should severally contribute to the armed forces to be used to protect the covenants of the League."[37]

Though the League failed to achieve its objectives, there is debate about why it failed so miserably. Some trace its failure to specific historical circumstances, particularly the unwillingness of the United States to join. It is also clear that even though members paid lip service to the principles of collective security, they proved time after time unwilling to actually do what needed be done to make it work. There was a huge gulf between the rhetoric and treaty on one hand and the real world of policy on the other. Others go further and attribute the League's failure to the inherent weaknesses of collective security that render it unworkable in almost any context.

A few of the problems likely to be encountered in any collective security system are obvious from the outset. One is the identification of the "aggressor." Sometimes this is relatively clear, such as when Iraq invaded Kuwait in 1990. But there are also many instances in which there is disagreement. A vote in the United Nations on whether Israel is an "aggressor" vis-à-vis the Palestinians would certainly not be unanimous. A vote on whether the United States was the aggressor in Vietnam would have also yielded a similarly divided verdict. The point is not that these judgments are right or wrong, but merely that such things are not always unambiguous in international politics. And if nations cannot agree on who the aggressor is, how can they be expected to fall into line in punishing and/or deterring the aggressor?

Critics see even deeper flaws in collective security. In rejecting as illegitimate any forceful change of the existing order, collective security is inevitably biased in favor of the status quo and those that benefit from it. Hochman observes that the League's goal of collective security "was, of course, identical with the defense of the post–World War I status quo."[38] Unfortunately, Germany and other nations viewed the World War I settlement as illegitimate, and they eventually possessed the power to challenge and change it. From the perspective of nations disadvantaged by the existing international order, collective security arrangements look very different. Rather than seeing collective security as a noble and high-minded attempt to preserve peace, they view it as a scheme for protecting the status quo. As E. H. Carr argues, "just as the ruling class in a community prays for domestic

The League of Nations meets in 1923. It was one of the most ambitious attempts to implement the principles of collective security. Unfortunately, the world's great powers failed to live up to expectations. World War II followed sixteen years later.

Source: Hulton-Deutsch Collection/Historical/Corbis

peace, which guarantees its own security and predominance … so international peace becomes a special vested interest of predominant powers."[39] Interestingly, both realists and Marxists tend to dismiss the lofty pronouncements about preserving peace as mere smokescreens for the underlying interests of dominant states.[40]

Even those who support collective security admit that it only works if the major powers share an interest in upholding the status quo. In considering whether collective security could work in post–Cold War Europe, for example, Charles and Clifford Kuchan hold out the possibility that "Russia will emerge as a benign democratic great power and that all of Europe's major states will share similar values and interests." If this happens, "the underpinnings for the successful functioning of a collective security system" will be in place.[41] Note the critical concession: In order for collective security to work, all major powers must "share similar values and interests." Skeptics are quick to note that if all major powers share the same basic values and interests, the chances for war are exceedingly low to begin with. Thus, collective security arrangements are most likely to work under conditions where there is no major threat to peace and most likely to fail when they are needed most.

Finally, in order for collective security systems to work, nations must be willing to deter and counter acts of aggression whether or not their interests are threatened. Woodrow Wilson recognized that "the central idea of the League of Nations was that States must support each other *even when their national interests are not involved.*"[42] Wilson could have gone one step further: In some circumstances collective security could require states to act in *opposition to* their national interests. This is what differentiates collective security from power politics: the idea that nations can and will refrain from the use of force to advance their national interests and will use force when their interests are not at stake. Putting aside for the moment the issue of whether nations *should* do this, realists in particular doubt that they *will* because there is no evidence that states ever have. Thus, realists argue that collective security arrangements are bound to fail for two basic reasons: The necessary common interests and values among great powers will rarely be achieved, and states will place their national interest above the security of others.

If realists have been the traditional critics of collective security, its supporters have been found among liberal ranks. The basis for liberal support should be fairly obvious. Though few liberals have been so naïve as to believe that conflicts among nations do not exist, they have always been more inclined to see common interests as a basis for international cooperation. Collective security assumes that the common interest in preserving peace outweighs particular interests that might be advanced through war. Advocates of collective security concede that the League of Nations was a failure, but they warn against assuming that every effort at collective security is doomed. Though not part of a formal collective security arrangement, the international coalition that reversed the Iraqi conquest of Kuwait in 1991 is often cited as an example of the world community coming together to resist aggression. In 1991 there were plenty of nations that committed to use force even though it would be difficult to indentify any national interests in the outcome of the crisis. Can collective security prevent all wars? Certainly not. Collective security offers no guarantees of a peaceful world. But what does? Certainly not the balance of power.

Security Amidst Anarchy

Even if we conclude that world government and collective security are not terribly practical alternatives to power politics, we are still not without hope. Despite international anarchy, Inis Claude notes "in sober fact, most states co-exist in reasonable harmony with most other states, most of the time; the exceptions to this passable state of affairs are vitally important, but they are exceptions nonetheless."[43] Consider for a moment relations among the Nordic states of Norway, Sweden, and Finland. No one seriously believes there is any chance these nations will go to war with each other, and even though they each have armed forces, there is no evidence they worry about the potential threat these forces pose. Why not? Is it a Nordic balance of power that preserves the peace? Is it because one nation enjoys a preponderance of power? Is there a central Nordic government? Have they created a collective security system? No, no, no, and no.

Scandinavia provides an example of what Karl Deutsch referred to as a **security community**, a group of nations sharing a reasonable and prevailing expectation of

security community A group of nations among whom exists the prevailing and widely accepted expectation of nonviolence.

nonviolence.[44] There is nothing that makes violence impossible—they are still sovereign states possessing offensive military capabilities. It is simply that the use of force has become sufficiently improbable that it no longer guides or shapes their relations. Deutsch identified several critical factors for the development of security communities; the most important being shared political and social values among political elites and a history of reliable and predictable behavior. Someone who tried to convince a Finnish president of the need to prepare for war with Sweden by giving a lecture about anarchy, self-help, and uncertainty would be confronted with a question: Sure, Sweden could invade tomorrow, but since it has not invaded on any other day over the past two centuries, why worry about it doing so now? Assuming that a Swedish invasion is not in the cards is a gamble in some sense, but a pretty safe one. Though the emergence of security communities may be uncommon, they nonetheless make a significant point: international anarchy does not *inevitably* lead to power politics. There have been and still are parts of the world that are anarchic yet "seem not to be subject to the kind of interstate relations that realists talk about."[45]

One could also look to the larger pattern of European politics in the postwar era. Though individual nations continue to maintain armed forces, there is no sense of security competition and the risk of war is almost nonexistent. Despite a long history of war and conflict, nations such France, Spain, and Britain no longer live in the "brooding shadow of violence." There is a security community in the sense of an expectation of nonviolence. This may stem from the creation of institutions that brought about greater integration, the most significant being the **European Union (EU)** or European Community. The EU had its origins in the European Coal and Steel Community (1952) in which France, West Germany, Italy, Belgium, the Netherlands, and Luxembourg agreed to reduce barriers to trade in coal and steel. The hope was that this would start a gradual process of economic integration as a foundation for greater political cooperation. Over time the economic integration has become wider and deeper. Membership in the EU now stands at twenty-seven and several other nations are in the process of becoming full members. Economic cooperation has reached the point at which seventeen states (Austria, Belgium, Cyprus, Estonia, Finland, France, Germany, Greece, Ireland, Italy, Luxembourg, Malta, the Netherlands, Portugal, Slovakia, Slovenia, and Spain) share a common currency, the euro. How far the members of the EU will be able and willing to move toward political unification, something akin to a United States of Europe, remains an open question.

Even though the EU is not a European government in a strict sense, it also seems a bit misleading to think of Europe as anarchic. Several observers have offered terms such as "pooled" or "shared" sovereignty to describe the somewhat uncertain political status of European states. Because the real world does not always conform to established definitions and dichotomies, common notions of anarchy and sovereignty might not capture the complexities and subtleties therein. It is also difficult to evaluate the role of the EU in helping European states overcome the intense security competition that marked their relations between the rise of the modern state system and World Wars I and II. But there it seems plausible that such institutions can help states escape power politics even if they are not true governments in the strictest sense.

European Union A regional intergovernmental organization of European states designed to promote greater trade and economic integration. Those who founded its precursors hoped that economic cooperation and prosperity would lead to greater political cooperation and a reduction in the conflict and competition that had marked European politics before World War II.

In recent years, constructivists have offered a more direct challenge to the realist proposition that international anarchy necessarily leads to power politics. Alexander Wendt states the question succinctly: "Does the absence of centralized political authority force states to play competitive power politics?" Realists answer this question in the affirmative. Wendt's answer is equally straightforward: "Self-help and power politics do not follow logically or causally from anarchy."[46] Understanding exactly why not is somewhat complicated.

Constructivism assumes that the behavior of social actors, be they individuals or nations, is shaped by their identities and prevailing beliefs and norms about how they should behave. Constructivists argue that nations (or the people who make decisions in their name) are influenced by prevailing beliefs and norms about how states should behave. On the question of power politics, John Vasquez offers a good summary of the constructivist perspective. He begins with a simple restatement of constructivism's basic premise: "I assume that any theory of world politics that has an impact on practice is not only a tool for understanding, but also helps construct a world." If nations engage in power politics it is "not because that behavior is natural or inherent in the structure of reality, but because realism has been accepted as a guide that tells leaders (and followers) the most appropriate way to behave." Thus, if we tell ourselves that nations should and will act in certain ways, we create "a kind of self-fulfilling prophecy."[47] It is not anarchy but rather "realist folklore [that] has provided a guide and cultural inheritance for Western states that has shaped and patterned the behavior of major states."[48] It is no accident that realism seems most accurate when we look at the behavior of European states over the past few centuries, since this is where realist theory has been most influential. But "once you move to the periphery where nations were not socialized to realist theory, states do not behave this way."[49] So even within the context of anarchy, there appear to be alternatives to power politics. There is nothing about anarchy that dictates that states continue to engage in power politics. If Finland and Sweden view each other as peaceful social democratic states that pose no threat to each other, there is nothing about anarchy that forces them into a competitive relationship. Anarchy does not have to lead to power politics. "Anarchy," according to Wendt, "is what states make of it."[50]

Conclusion

Even those who see no alternative to power politics do not exactly sing its praises; it is treated as a regrettable inevitability, like death and taxes. It is hard to make a case in favor of insecurity, power struggles, and war. A recent statement of the inevitability of power politics begins with the caveat: "Nothing in this primer should be taken as an endorsement or glorification of power politics."[51] If we asked whether there were any *desirable* alternatives to power politics, almost everyone would answer "yes." It is easy to imagine systems of international relations preferable to the one that has produced violence, death, and destruction on such a massive scale. The shortcomings of power politics are plain for all to see. The critical question, however, is whether there are any *feasible* alternatives.

It is often in the aftermath of great wars that people begin to reevaluate the nature of international politics and create institutions that might help prevent the recurrence of war: the creation of the Concert of Europe in the wake of the Napoleonic Wars, the League of Nations after World War I, and the United Nations after World War II are cases in point. Though the Cold War never resulted in a literal war, its ending has also prompted a reexamination of international politics. President George H. W. Bush's vision of a "new world order" after the 1991 Gulf War was typical of the hopes for a better world that frequently emerge after major wars. But have we seen the emergence of a new world order, or just a slightly reshuffled version of the old world order? And if a new world order proves unattainable, is this because efforts to transform the international system are inevitably doomed to failure? Is there a better and feasible way to preserve international peace? These are the fundamental and enduring questions addressed by the debate over power politics.

CHAPTER SUMMARY

- Fear and insecurity, the pursuit of power, the use of force, and the ever-present possibility of war—that is, power politics—are often presented as inevitable, if regrettable, realities of international politics. For realists in particular, there is no avoiding power politics in an anarchic international system that lacks any mechanism but self-help to provide security for states.

- Despite this agreement on the inevitability of power politics, realists differ on the dynamics of power politics. Balance of power theorists assume that states tend to align with the most powerful nations. Balance of threat theorists predict that states will align against whatever powers appear to pose the greatest threat, regardless of whether they are the most powerful. Similarly, preponderance theorists argue that nations align on the basis of interests, with the generic distinction being status quo versus revisionist states.

- Balance of power theory predicts the emergence of balances of power in international politics, whereas balance of threat and preponderance theories anticipate imbalances of power.

- Despite their differences, all three theories assume the inevitability of power politics.

- Liberals have historically rejected the realist claim that there is no alternative to power politics. Though some more idealistic liberals have advocated the creation of world government, most have sought more modest collective security arrangements.

- Collective security, which was the principle behind the League of Nations, posits an organized community of states whose combined power will preserve peace by deterring possible aggressors. Collective security transcends power politics, not by eliminating the need for power, but by replacing self-help with community assistance.

- Critics claim that collective security arrangements have rarely worked and have several fundamental flaws. The requirement that states be willing to use force even when their national interests are not threatened is considered unrealistic. Most important, collective security is unlikely to work when it is needed most—that is, when major powers reject the status quo and are willing to change it by force.

- More recently, constructivists have argued that world government and/or complex collective security arrangements are not essential to overcome power politics. Power politics can be (and has been) transcended by shared expectations, beliefs, and images that allow states to see each other as nonthreatening.

CRITICAL QUESTIONS

1. What do we mean by "power politics" and do realists consider it an inevitable consequence of international anarchy?

2. What are the similarities and differences between power politics and collective security?

3. Is world government necessary to overcome the negative consequences of anarchy?

4. Why does the immediate post-World War II period pose a problem for balance of power theory? How would other power politics theories explain alignment patterns during this period?

5. Does the post–Cold War world appear to conform to balance of power, balance of threat, or preponderance theory?

KEY TERMS

anarchic, 62	collective security, 69	power politics, 60	security dilemma, 62
balance of power theory, 63	degree of power, 67	preponderance, or hegemonic stability theory, 67	self-help, 62
balance of threat theory, 65	degree of satisfaction, 67		
bandwagoning, 65	European Union (EU), 73	security community, 72	
	power, 63		

FURTHER READINGS

A classic analysis of power politics and balance of power theory that remains essential reading despite the passage of time is Inis Claude, *Power and International Relations* (New York: Random House, 1962). A recent argument for the inevitability of power politics is presented in Stanley Michalak, *A Primer in Power Politics* (Wilmington, DE: Scholarly Resources, 2001). An influential restatement of balance of power theory is Kenneth Waltz, *Theory of International Politics* (Reading, MA: Addison-Wesley, 1979). Balance of threat theory is most clearly presented in Stephen Walt, *The Origins of Alliances* (Ithaca, NY: Cornell University Press, 1989). Randall Schweller's *Deadly Imbalances: Tripolarity and Hitler's Strategy for World Conquest* (New York: Columbia University Press, 1998) is a fascinating application of balance of power and threat theories for understanding the origins of World War II. The best statement of preponderance theory is still A. F. K. Organski and Jacek Kugler, *The War Ledger*

(Chicago: University of Chicago Press, 1980). In addition to Inis Claude's *Power and International Relations*, a good (though critical) overview of collective security is presented in Earl Ravenal, "An Autopsy of Collective Security," *Political Science Quarterly* 90 (Winter 1975–1976): 697–714. A more favorable assessment is provided by Charles Kupchan and Clifford Kupchan, "The Promise of Collective Security," *International Security* 60 (Summer 1995): 52–61. The constructivist critique of power politics can be found in Alexander Wendt, *Social Theory of International Politics* (Cambridge: Cambridge University Press, 1999), especially chapter 6, and John Vasquez, *The War Puzzle* (Cambridge: Cambridge University Press, 1993), especially chapter 3. A recent examination of the consequences of China's rise by a prominent realist and former Secretary of State is Henry Kissinger, *On China* (New York: Penguin Press, 2011).

POWER POLITICS ON THE WEB

www.globalsolutions.org/wfi/index.html
Web site of the World Federalist Institute, which seeks the "establishment of a democratic federal world government."

http://avalon.law.yale.edu/20th_century/leagcov.asp
The full text of the Covenant of the League of Nations, a classic statement of the ideals of collective security, especially Article 16.

www.globalpolicy.org/reform/index.htm
Web site with extensive coverage of both the history of, and debates about, United Nations reform.

www.sipri.org/databases
Though military power is not all there is to national power, most power politics theories emphasize this aspect of power. The databases of the Swedish International Peace Research Institute (SIPRI) provide a wealth of information on world military expenditures and power.

NOTES

[1]John Vasquez, *The Power of Power Politics: From Classical Realism to Neotraditionalism* (Cambridge: Cambridge University Press, 1998), p. 168.
[2]Kenneth Waltz, *Man, the State and War* (New York: Columbia University Press, 1959), p. 205.
[3]Stanley Michalak, *A Primer in Power Politics* (Wilmington, DE: Scholarly Resources Books, 2001), p. 173.
[4]Kenneth Waltz, *Theory of International Politics* (Reading, MA: Addison-Wesley, 1979), p. 102.
[5]Ibid., pp. 103–104, emphasis added.
[6]Waltz, *Man, the State and War*, p. 201.
[7]Waltz, *Theory of International Politics*, p. 111, emphasis added.
[8]Quoted in Waltz, *Man, the State and War*, p. 160.

[9]John Mearsheimer, *The Tragedy of Great Power Politics* (New York: W. W. Norton, 2001), p. 345.
[10]Michael P. Sullivan, *Power in Contemporary International Politics* (Columbia: University of South Carolina Press, 1990), p. 76.
[11]Mark V. Kauppi and Paul R. Viotti, *The Global Philosophers' World Politics in Western Thought* (New York: Lexington Books, 1992), p. 11.
[12]Mearsheimer, *The Tragedy of Great Power Politics*, p. 55.
[13]Ibid., p. 55.
[14]Inis Claude, *Power and International Relations* (New York: Random House, 1962), p. 12.
[15]Geoffrey Blainey, *The Causes of War* (New York: The Free Press, 1973), p. 110.

[16]Richard Little, *The Balance of Power in International Relations: Metaphors, Myths and Models* (Cambridge: Cambridge University Press, 2007), p.3.

[17]Waltz, *Theory of International Politics*, p. 121.

[18]Ibid., p. 119.

[19]A. F. K. Organski, *World Politics* (New York: Alfred A. Knopf, 1968), p. 274.

[20]Stephen Walt, *The Origins of Alliances* (Ithaca, NY: Cornell University Press, 1989), pp. 18–19.

[21]Waltz, *Theory of International Politics*, p. 124.

[22]Walt, *Origins of Alliances*, p. 25.

[23]Ibid., pp. 264–265.

[24]The best overall statement of preponderance theory, which this discussion draws heavily on, is provided by A. F. K. Organski, *World Politics* (New York: Alfred A. Knopf, 1968), pp. 338–376; and A. F. K. Organski and Jacek Kugler, *The War Ledger* (Chicago: University of Chicago Press, 1980).

[25]See Randall Schweller, *Deadly Imbalances: Tripolarity and Hitler's Strategy of World Conquest* (New York: Columbia University Press, 1998).

[26]Organski, *World Politics*, pp. 371–372.

[27]Inis Claude, cited in Sullivan, *Power in Contemporary World Politics*, p. 79.

[28]Ibid., p. 370.

[29]Waltz, *Theory of International Politics*, p. 102.

[30]Norman Cousins, cited in Inis Claude, *Power in International Relations*.

[31]Ibid., p. 208.

[32]Cited in Thomas L. Prangle and Peter J. Ahrensdorf, *Justice Among Nations: On the Moral Basis of Power and Peace* (Lawrence: University Press of Kansas, 1999), p. 246.

[33]David W. Ziegler, *War, Peace and International Politics* (New York: HarperCollins, 1993), p. 302C.

[34]Earl C. Ravenal, "An Autopsy of Collective Security," *Political Science Quarterly* 90, no. 4 (Winter 1975–1976): 702.

[35]John Mearsheimer, "The False Promise of International Institutions," in *Theories of War and Peace*, ed. Michael Brown, Owen Cole, Sean Lynn-Jones, and Steven Miller (Cambridge, MA: MIT Press, 1998), p. 355.

[36]Cited in Claude, *Power in International Relations*, pp. 96–97.

[37]Charter provisions cited in Michalak, *Primer in Power Politics*, p. 195.

[38]Jiri Hochman, *The Soviet Union and the Failure of Collective Security* (Ithaca, NY: Cornell University Press, 1984), p. 174.

[39]Edward Hallett Carr, *The Twenty Years' Crisis, 1919–1939* (New York: Harper & Row, 1964), p. 82.

[40]For the Marxist view, see C. Dale Fuller, "Lenin's Attitude Toward an International Organization for the Maintenance of Peace, 1914–1917," *Political Science Quarterly* 64, no. 2 (June 1949): 245–261.

[41]Charles Kupchan and Clifford Kupchan, "The Promise of Collective Security," *International Security* 60, no. 1 (Summer 1995): 60.

[42]Quoted in Ravenal, "Autopsy of Collective Security," p. 712.

[43]Claude, *Power in International Relations*, p. 213.

[44]Karl Deutsch et al., *Political Community and the North Atlantic Area* (Princeton, NJ: Princeton University Press, 1957).

[45]Vasquez, *The Power of Power Politics*, p. 211.

[46]Alexander Wendt, "Anarchy Is What States Make of It: The Social Construction of Power Politics," *International Organization* 46, no. 2 (Spring 1992): 391, 394.

[47]John Vasquez, *The War Puzzle* (Cambridge: Cambridge University Press, 1993), p. 87.

[48]Ibid., p. 196.

[49]Ibid., p. 116.

[50]Wendt, "Anarchy Is What States Make of It," p. 391.

[51]Michalak, *Primer in Power Politics*, p. xii.

The Consequences of China's Rise

From a power politics perspective, the distribution of power among the great powers determines character of international relations. Since the end of the Cold War most have characterized the international system as unipolar, with the United States clearly the world's dominant military and economic power. Some saw this as a "unipolar moment" unlikely to last very long. Others were not so sure. Even though nothing lasts forever, the magnitude of American dominance, particularly in military terms, was such that the unipolar "moment" might last for some time, perhaps even decades. But whenever that moment ends, it will be because another great power has emerged to challenge American dominance. Given its population and potential economic power, the most likely candidate to knock the United States off its hegemonic perch is China. As we enter the second decade of the twenty-first century, there is no longer any doubting China's economic potential. The critical question is whether China's rapid growth continues and, if it does, what China intends to do with this power. Will economic power be translated into military power? Will China's rise pose a threat to its neighbors? And would this set China on a collision course with the United States? In the essays below John Lee and Yuriko Koike provide somewhat different takes on implications of China's rise, both for its regional neighbors and the United States. Though neither makes any confident predictions, Lee is much more pessimistic about the future than Koike. What does each author see as the most likely future for China? What is the basis for Koike's relative optimism? Why does Lee not share this optimism? And how do these differing perspectives relate to assumptions about the inevitably of power politics discussed in this chapter?

China's Rise and the Road to War (2010)

PERSPECTIVE 1

John Lee

Four years before World War I, British author and politician Norman Angell published "The Great Illusion," arguing that military conquests had become obsolete between modern economies. Many policy makers use the same logic today to predict that China and the United States can avoid war. Like their forebears, they may be wrong.

Source: John Lee, "China's Rise and the Road to War," Reprinted from The Wall Street Journal Asia, © 2011, Dow Jones & Company, Inc., All rights reserved.

That's the implicit argument of University of Chicago political scientist John Mearsheimer, who delivered the annual Michael Hintze Lecture at Sydney University this week. Politics, rather than economics, will decisively shape the future of Asia just as it did Europe in the previous century, he believes. China's ascent is likely to spark an intense security competition with the U.S., leading to the strong possibility of war between the world's two biggest economies.

This argument runs counter to today's conventional wisdom, which sees a benign future for U.S.-China relations. This view, still popular in Washington, is based on the idea that the U.S. can manage China by offering Beijing incentives to rise as a "responsible stakeholder" within the current U.S.-led global order. Like the educated and well-heeled elites in Europe whom Angell chronicled and who a century ago exhibited extreme reluctance to imagine the outbreak of major war, today's policy makers can't fathom war in the Pacific.

Yet history suggests that Mr. Mearsheimer's warnings should be heeded. Prior to World War I, Angell's logic—that the disruption to the international credit and trading system would mean that everyone loses in the event of war—was irrefutable. Prior to 1914, annual trade volumes of Britain, Germany and France was 52%, 38% and 54% of GDP respectively, with much of the trade being between these great powers. By 1913, Britain had become the leading market for German exports, with both countries largely benefitting from the economic relationship. In the decade leading to the Great War, trade and capital flows between these great powers increased by an estimated 65% and 84%, respectively. Yet, economic interdependence was not enough to prevent the tragic escalation of events that followed the assassination of Austria's Archduke Franz Ferdinand.

Today, China's self-proclaimed and widely accepted "peaceful development" similarly appears to be based on solid economic ground. China has re-emerged as a great trading nation but remains a poor country in terms of GDP per capita. China's export sector is responsible for the creation of hundreds of millions of jobs, and the country still remains deeply dependent on outside technology and know-how. To continue the country's rapid economic development, the Chinese Communist Party needs a peaceful and stable environment in Asia. On the U.S. side, no one in Washington wants to see a conflict with China erupt, especially at a time when America is fighting two wars and worries about Iran's intentions.

Yet Angell's optimism was ultimately wrong because it was based on an incomplete account of driving forces behind relations between the great powers. While the economic relationship created powerful incentives for peace, Angell did not take seriously the intense strategic competition—particularly the growing naval rivalry—between status quo powers like Britain and a rapidly rising and revisionist power like Germany. Nor did Angell's account allow for the human factor of strategic missteps and miscalculations—particularly by Germany's Kaiser Wilhelm II—that eventually plunged Europe into war.

What are the lessons for Asia? While economic interdependence and American attempts to "manage" China's rise has so far succeeded in preventing war, the recent diplomatic conflagration over the Chinese reiteration that its claims in the South China Sea are part of Beijing's "core interests" validates what scholars such as Aaron Friedberg have been saying for a decade: East Asia today has the potential to recreate the European situation at the turn of the previous century. When it comes to strategic goals, China is re-entering into a regional order not of its making after decades of self-imposed isolation. By virtue of Beijing's fundamental dissatisfaction with several of its land and maritime borders, it is a revisionist power. As it rises, the desperation to secure its "core interests" will deepen.

Chinese grand strategy since the days of former leader Deng Xiaoping has been to avoid conflict with a much more formidable competitor (i.e., America) while China builds its "comprehensive national power." In favor of "winning Asia without fighting," as Chinese General Ma Xiaotian once put it, are many of the older generation of leaders who see caution as prudence, even if they relentlessly seek "windows of opportunity" to extend Beijing's power at the expense of America's. They still remember the suffering and humiliation of the Mao Zedong years, when an isolated China tried to achieve too much too quickly.

Yet, as history reaffirms, a peace built on continued political skill, dexterity and restraint rather than a harmony of strategic interest is inherently precarious. Without personal experience of China's recent traumatic history, future generations of leaders will be more confident and assertive. Even now, emerging Communist Party and People's Liberation Army leaders argue that China is moving too slowly on securing its foreign-policy goals. The danger is that, just as Germany did in Europe a century ago, China's overestimation of its own capabilities, and underestimation of American strengths and resolve—combined with strategic dissatisfaction and impatience—is the fast way toward disastrous miscalculation and error.

Several years before the outbreak of the Great War, Kaiser Wilhelm II publicly declared that he considered the prospect of war with Britain "a most unimaginable thing." Despite deep economic interdependence, Europe could not avert a disaster. Leaders in Washington and throughout Asia should not commit the same failure of imagination.

John Lee is a Visiting fellow with Hudson Institute and a foreign-policy fellow at the Centre for Independent Studies in Sydney. He is the author of Will China Fail? (CIS, 2008).

Cold War With China is Not Inevitable (2011)   PERSPECTIVE 2

Yuriko Koike

MESMERISED by China's vast military build-up, a new constellation of strategic partnerships among its neighbours, and America's revitalised commitment to Asian security, many shrewd observers suggest last year saw the first sparks of a new cold war in Asia.

But is Cold War II really inevitable?

Although appeasing China's drive for hegemony in Asia is unthinkable, every realistic effort must be made to avoid militarisation of the region's diplomacy.

After all, there was nothing cold about the Cold War in Asia. First in the Chinese civil war and then in Korea, Indonesia, Malaysia, and Indochina — particularly Vietnam — the Cold War raged not as an ideological-propaganda battle between rival superpowers, but in dogged, often fratricidal combat that cost millions of lives and retarded economic development as well as political democratisation.

It is this grim history that makes China's present disregard for Deng Xiaoping's maxim that China "disguise its ambition and hide its claws" so worrying for Asian leaders from New Delhi to Seoul and from Tokyo to Jakarta. From its refusal to condemn North Korea's unprovoked sinking of the South Korean warship, Cheonan, and shelling of South Korean islands, to its claims of sovereignty over various Japanese, Vietnamese, Malaysian and Philippine archipelagos and newly conjured claims on India's province of Arunachal Pradesh, China has revealed a neo-imperial swagger.

So it should surprise no one that the concept of containment is coming to dominate Asian diplomatic discourse.

But it is wrong — at least for now — to think that a formal structure of alliances to contain China is needed in the way that one was required to contain the Soviet Union. Containment, it should be recalled, was organised against a Soviet totalitarian regime that was not only ideologically aggressive and in the process of consolidating its colonisation of eastern Europe (as well as Japan's Northern Territories), but also deliberately sealed off from the wider world economy.

Today's China is vastly different. Overt military imperialism of the Soviet sort has, at least historically, rarely been the Chinese way. Sun Tzu, the great Chinese theorist of warfare, focused on the weakening of an adversary psychologically, not in battle. Until recently, much of China's bid for regional hegemony reflected Sun's concepts.

More significantly, China abandoned economic autarky three decades ago.

Today its economic links in Asia are deep and — it is to be hoped — permanent. China's export machine sucks in vast quantities of parts and components for final assembly from across Asia: from Thailand, Malaysia, The Philippines and Indonesia, as well as richer Singapore, Taiwan, South Korea and Japan.

Membership of the World Trade Organisation has helped bind China to highly sophisticated pan-Asian production networks. Everybody has benefited from these ties.

Throughout China's three-decade rise from poverty to economic juggernaut, trade within East Asia has grown even faster than the region's trade with the rest of the world, suggesting deeper specialisation and integration.

Indeed, China's rise has profoundly altered the course of Asia's trade flows. Japan no longer focuses on exporting finished goods to Europe and North America, but on exporting parts and components for assembly in China. In turn, Japan now imports from China finished goods (such as office machines and computers) that once came from America and Europe.

Given that as many as half of China's 1.3 billion people remain mired in abject poverty, it is in China's interest to ensure that these economic relationships continue to flourish.

In the past, China has recognised the vital need for good neighbourly relations.

During the Asian financial crisis of 1997-98, Chinese officials did not engage in competitive devaluation of the yuan. Unfortunately, such clear-sighted and responsible policy-making is a far cry from what we are seeing today.

China's dizzying increase in its military capacity is another obvious source of concern in Asia.

But even according to the highest estimates, China's military budget is now about equal to that of Japan and, of course, much less than the combined military budgets of Japan, India and Russia, all of which border China; not to mention Indonesia, South Korea and a militarily modernising Taiwan. Moreover, Russia and India possess nuclear weapons and Japan has the technological wherewithal to reconfigure its defence posture to meet any regional nuclear threat.

So the challenge China poses today remains predominantly political and economic, not military. The test of China's intentions is whether its growing economic and, yes, military capacities will be used to seek to establish Asian hegemony by working to exclude America from the region and preventing regional partnerships from flourishing.

The alternative is a China that becomes part of a co-operative effort to bind Asia in a rules-based system similar to that which has underpinned long-term peace in Europe. In this sense, Asia's rise is also a test of US competitiveness and commitment in Asia.

America's historical opposition to hegemony in Asia — included as a joint aim with China in the Shanghai Communique of 1972 — remains valid. It will have to be pursued, however, primarily by political and economic means, albeit backed by US power.

Before 2010, most Asian countries would have preferred not to choose between China and the US. But China's assertiveness has provided enormous incentives to embrace an Asian multilateral system backed by America, rather than accept the exclusionary system that China seeks to lead.

This year we may begin to see whether those incentives lead China's rulers to reappraise their diplomatic conduct, which has left them with only the corrupt, basket-case economies of Burma and North Korea as reliable friends in Asia.

Yuriko Koike, Japan's former minister of defence and national security adviser, is chairwoman of the executive council of the Liberal Democratic Party.

4 War and Democracy

Key Controversy: Are Democracies More Peaceful?

The idea that democracies are more peaceful than nondemocracies has been part of liberal international thought for more than two hundred years, and it is one of those ideas that has seeped from the realm of theory to real-world policy. Though proponents of *democratic peace theory* offer a variety of reasons why democracies might be less willing and able to wage war, all versions of the theory share the basic prediction that democracies will not wage war against one another. If the theory is correct, a more democratic world will also be a more peaceful world. The commonly cited evidence in support of the theory is the absence of any wars between clearly democratic states. Skeptics question this evidence, pointing to what they see as convenient and shifting definitions that omit troublesome cases. Some even claim that there have been wars between democratic states. Realists in particular are generally unconvinced by the theory and its supporting evidence. Even if we have not yet seen a war between democratic states, realists think our luck is likely to run out. In time, democracies will be subject to the same insecurities and conflicts that have driven nondemocratic states to war. The coming decades are likely to put the theory to a real-world test as the number of democracies in the world continues to grow. ■

The spread of democratic political institutions has been one of the most remarkable trends in world politics over the past few decades (see Figure 4.1 and Map 4.1). In fact, the period around 1989 marked something of a watershed in global political history when, for the first time, a majority of the world's population lived under some form of democratic government. One might question the democratic credentials of a few countries, but the overall trend of global democratization seems clear. Most people, particularly in democracies such as the United States, view this as a good thing. But why? Why should anyone in the United States care whether people in other countries live under democratic forms of government? To the extent that democracy is associated with a greater respect for human rights, political

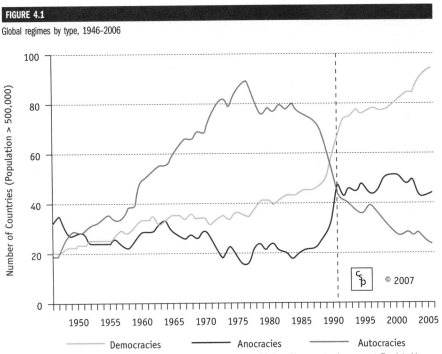

FIGURE 4.1

Global regimes by type, 1946–2006

Source: Center for Systemic Peace, Polity IV Project. For more information visit http://www.systemicpeace.org. Reprinted by permission.

and otherwise, the positive assessment of global democratization is welcomed as a triumph for those values that people in democracies hold dear and wish to be shared. The spread of democracy elsewhere is a good thing in and of itself, not necessarily because there is anything to be gained from it. Not everything boils down to self-interest.

Nonetheless, the spread of democracy around the world is often presented as a matter of national interest. But how are Americans in South Dakota better off if people in the Middle East, Latin America, Asia, or Africa live under democratic governments? Several possible connections might be drawn. To the extent that democracy is related to capitalism, free markets, and trade, one could argue that the spread of democracy contributes to global prosperity, something that might eventually improve the lives of Americans. This chapter, however, focuses on another claim, namely, that democracies are more peaceful than nondemocracies. It is the assumed peacefulness of democracies that generally provides the connection to American national interests: The United States has an interest in peace; democracies are more peaceful; and thus the spread of democracy is a vital interest. The notion that democracies are more peaceful than nondemocracies is so widely accepted—among the general public, policymakers, and academics alike—that it is often taken as an article of faith. Some have gone so far as to refer to this as perhaps the only "iron law" of international relations. But why would we expect democracies to be more peaceful? What do we mean when we say they are more peaceful? And does the historical evidence support democratic peace theory?

The Sources of Democratic Peacefulness

The proposition that democracies are more peaceful than nondemocracies is a central tenet of liberal international theory that can be traced to the writings of **Immanuel Kant** (1724–1804). Living in an era of absolutist monarchism, Kant argued in his classic work, *Perpetual Peace*, that the emergence and spread of "republican" (or liberal democratic) political institutions would be accompanied by the emergence of a zone of peace. Kant referred to this as a republican or **democratic pacific union**. Kant did not argue that democracies would totally refrain from waging wars; he simply argued that democracies would not wage war against other democracies. Peaceful must not be confused with pacifist. More democracies would mean a larger zone of peace, and universal democracy would usher in universal peace.

But why did he expect democracies to be more peaceful? Kant begins with the basic observation that in a republic or democracy people are citizens of the state as opposed to subjects of a monarch. As such, there are mechanisms that allow the desires and interests of citizens to influence government policy, including decisions about war and peace. Kant assumed that citizens have much more to lose than to gain from war because they shoulder the burdens of war. As essentially rational creatures (another fundamental assumption of liberalism), people are generally unwilling to support policies that do them harm. In *Perpetual Peace* Kant expressed his belief that democratic citizens "will have a great hesitation in embarking on so dangerous an enterprise [as war]" because "this would mean calling down on themselves all the miseries of war." These miseries include not only the obvious, such as "doing the fighting themselves, supplying the costs of war from their own resources," but also "making good the ensuing devastation, and, as the crowning evil, having to take upon themselves a burden of debts which will embitter peace itself and which can never be paid off on account of the constant threat of new wars."[1]

Kant's explanation is usually referred to as the **rational** or **pacific public thesis** because it sees democratic peacefulness as rooted in the rational self-interest of democratic publics. This view is no longer very popular as an explanation of democratic peace because the past two centuries provide too many examples of public support, even enthusiasm, for war. People in democratic states greeted World War I with tremendous enthusiasm. In some cases, such as the Spanish–American War of 1898, it was the public, spurred by a pro-war press, that pushed a reluctant political leadership into war.[2] As Robin Fox, a critic of democratic peace theory, observes, "there is rarely very effective opposition to a successful war."[3] For Fox, the absence of effective antiwar movements against successful wars suggests that there is no general preference for peace, merely a reluctance to fight losing wars. The hesitance for war, which seemed "natural" to Kant, appears not to exist in reality.

Even Kant was not content to rely on the assumption that popular opposition to war would be sufficient to create democratic peace. Kant and others also point to characteristics of democratic systems, namely their institutional structure and political-cultural underpinnings. In terms of institutions, the most important

Immanuel Kant German political philosopher who first proposed that democratic (or "republican" states) would be unlikely to wage war against each other.

democratic pacific union The separate peace that Immanuel Kant predicted would exist among democratic states. Many believe that this democratic peace has in fact emerged.

rational or **pacific public thesis** The view that democracies are more peaceful because their foreign policies reflect the desires of an inherently rational and peaceful public.

MAP 4.1   Map of Freedom, 2008

Source: http://www.freedomhouse.org/template.cfm?page=363&year=2010. Used with permission by Freedom House.

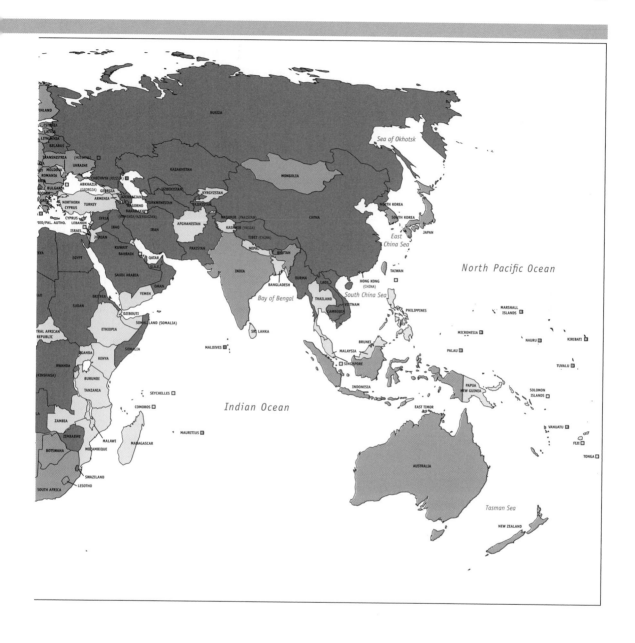

feature of democracies is that political power and decision making are distributed in a manner that presents obstacles to war making. In terms of political culture, democratic peace theorists note that successful democratic institutions depend on the widespread adherence to certain values that shape international behavior of democracies. These institutional and cultural constraints are generally seen as particularly significant in terms of relations among democratic states.

institutional thesis A variant of democratic peace theory that sees the dispersion of power in democracies (see checks and balances) as the most important reason they are less likely to wage war, especially against each other.

The **institutional thesis** emphasizes that democratic political systems are usually characterized by a dispersion of political power, whereas undemocratic systems usually concentrate power in the hands of a single person or small elite. Leaders such as Louis XIV, Joseph Stalin, or Saddam Hussein do not generally operate with many domestic constraints on their authority. When Saddam Hussein invaded Kuwait in 1991, he did not have to secure the approval of an elected legislature, hostile newspaper editorials, or the next election. This is not to say that he had no worries, because even undemocratic leaders can be overthrown. The point is simply that, as a general rule, leaders in nondemocratic societies face fewer political constraints than do those in democracies.

checks and balances The division of power in democracies among different branches of government (e.g., the president and Congress in the United States). The institutional version of democratic peace sees this dispersion of powers as the critical reason why democracies are less likely to engage in war, especially with each other.

Democratic societies, on the other hand, usually disperse political power. There are competing political parties, elections that can be lost, and public opinion that cannot be consistently ignored. There are also separate government institutions that limit the executive's freedom of action. Legislatures commonly possess budgetary authority, providing leverage over anything (like wars) that requires expenditures. In the United States we refer to this as the system of **checks and balances** between the executive (i.e., the president), the legislature (i.e., Congress), and the judiciary. Other democracies have slightly different institutional structures, but the general point remains valid. This dispersion of power makes it very difficult for democracies to do anything, whether it be reforming social security, changing the tax code, or going to war. As America's founders made it clear in *The Federalist Papers*, making government action difficult was precisely the point of dispersing political power. A certain degree of consensus is required for democratic governments to act, particularly when actions represent radical change or are very controversial. Thus, the essential element of the institutional thesis is that democracies will find it more difficult to go to war, and certainly more difficult to initiate a war, than will nondemocratic governments.

political-cultural thesis A variant of democratic peace theory that sees political and cultural norms or peaceful conflict resolution as the most important reason that democracies are less likely to wage war, especially against each other.

While the institutional constraint thesis stresses a democracy's diminished *ability* to wage war, the **political-cultural thesis** emphasizes the *unwillingness* of democracies to go to war. The argument is that democratic institutions are rooted in widely shared norms about how political conflicts are managed. Democracy requires a consensus that conflicts be resolved without resort to force: Democracies substitute the counting of heads for the breaking of heads. However deep the disagreements over certain issues, very few resort to violence once they lose in the political arena. Al Gore loyalists did not circle the White House with guns to prevent George Bush from moving in, despite their reservations about the election's outcome. Without a norm of peaceful conflict resolution, democracy is unlikely to prove very durable. In terms of international relations, the political-cultural thesis anticipates that democracies will externalize this norm from the domestic to the international realm. Thus, this norm of peaceful conflict resolution predisposes democracies to favor nonviolent approaches to international conflicts.[4]

Constructivists present a slightly different explanation for the democratic peace. It is not something inherent in democracies preventing them from waging war against each other. What keeps democracies at peace is the internalized norm that democracies do not fight each other. The prohibition on fighting other democracies has become part of what it means to be a democracy—that is, an integral component of the democratic self-image, how democracies identify themselves. When democracies share this self-image, an "intersubjective understanding" emerges and peace among democracies holds. In a sense, democratic peace theory is an almost self-fulfilling prophecy—the more people, especially elites, in democratic societies tell themselves that democracies do not fight with each other, the more their behavior reflects this belief.[5]

Most formulations of the democratic peace thesis, including Kant's, do not predict a generalized predisposition for peace. The democratic preference for peace is assumed to operate primarily (or maybe even only) when democracies deal with one another. Kant's pacific union was a zone of peace among democratic states: He fully anticipated that this would not extend to relations with nondemocratic states. But why would democracies prefer peace with each other but not with nondemocracies? Part of the reason is that the institutional and cultural factors that supposedly inhibit democracies from going to war will be more successful in preventing war when they are present in both nations as opposed to just one. But there is more to it than that.

Peace among democracies is also rooted in mutual expectations. When a democracy comes into conflict with another democracy, it is does so with the expectation of peaceful conflict resolution because it assumes the opposing democracy is doing likewise. As Spencer Weart explains, "Peace follows if leaders come to recognize that their preference for negotiation is shared."[6] This expectation of reciprocity allows the democratic peace to flourish. When the potential opponent is not a fellow democracy, the assumption of peaceful resolution cannot be made. In fact, democracies may assume the exact opposite—that nondemocracies will be unwilling to resolve disputes peacefully. The insight that what matters most is a democracy's expectations about the conduct it can expect from another nation has led one scholar to revise the democratic peace proposition slightly, pointing out that the critical factor is whether two states *perceive* each other as democratic, not whether they are democratic according to some previously set criteria. There are a few cases where this distinction may be critical. For example, it may be possible to argue that Germany was a democracy on the eve of World War I (we will have more to say about this shortly). Since Germany ended up fighting Great Britain and the United States, this could invalidate the democratic peace proposition. John Owen and Ido Oren, however, try to demonstrate that British and American leaders did not perceive Germany as democratic. Because they did not think they were dealing with a democracy, the obstacles to war were not operative.[7]

What Is "Democracy"?

The assertion that democracies are more peaceful seems straightforward, but several issues need to be resolved to put the proposition to the test. One of the trickiest is the meaning of *democracy*. Though casual observers are sometimes exasperated by the academic tendency to argue over the definition of terms whose meanings appear obvious, sometimes definitions really matter. While virtually any definition of democracy would encompass nations such as the United States, Japan, and India today, many other cases are less clear-cut.

If asked what makes a country democratic, most people would probably list universal adult suffrage (i.e., the right to vote) as an essential component. Though this seems uncontroversial, it is not always easily applied. A strict application of this standard would exclude the United States before 1920 when women were not allowed to vote at the federal level (they could vote only in some states). This standard might even exclude the United States in 1960, because in large parts of the country citizens of African descent were effectively denied their right to vote. Can a country be considered a democracy when a sizable portion of its adult population is excluded from the franchise by law or practice? The extent of suffrage, however, is not the only question. Another concerns the durability of democratic practices. Should a country be considered a democracy after a single round of elections, or do we need to see a pattern sustained over time? This is not the place to work through all the fine details and complications. It is enough to realize that matters of definition and classification are not always easy.

Despite some minor differences, most examinations of democratic peace theory have agreed on the essential features of democracy: regular elections for major government offices, competitive political parties, near universal adult suffrage, and certain basic political and individual rights.[8] The inclusion of basic rights that are protected even from democratic majorities leads many to prefer the description *liberal democratic states*. The criteria are usually relaxed somewhat when we move back to the nineteenth century, particularly on the issue of voting rights. A country that denied women and others the right to vote in 1900 can still be classified as a democracy, but similar practices today would be disqualifiers.

After we define democracy, we need some measure of "peacefulness." Again, this is not as easy as one might assume. Should we look simply at a crude measure, such as the number of wars that nations are involved in? This is certainly easy, but is it a valid measure of peacefulness? Perhaps a more meaningful indicator is not war involvement, but rather war initiation. But what about covert operations, threats of force, and military interventions that fall short of a formal state of war? And what about the provision of military aid and assistance that fuels wars? The range of behaviors we might look at to get a handle on the peacefulness is quite broad, and our conclusions might differ depending on the measure chosen.

The Evidence

At first glance, the claim that democracies are more peaceful seems odd. A long list of democracies waging war is easy to compile: the United States in the Vietnam War, British imperialism and all the wars that accompanied it, and the French war in Algeria, to name just a few. One of the initial studies of democracy and war demonstrated that over the last two centuries there was no difference between democracies and nondemocracies in the frequency or duration of their war involvement.[9]

Russians watch election returns for their 2008 elections. Though displaying all the trappings of democracy, many question Russia's democratic credentials.

Source: AP Photo/Mikhail Metzel

This was not the result of democracies always being attacked either, because there was no difference in war initiation. Rather than disputing these findings, democratic peace theorists have argued that they are not good tests. Kant and others did not predict that democracies would refrain from war. The expectation was that democracies would not fight one another. Thus, the test of democratic peace theory is whether democracies deal with their conflicts among themselves differently than they do with conflicts with non-democracies. So the question is not how many wars democracies have been involved in, but whether they have waged war against each other

The most commonly cited evidence in support of democratic peace theory is the absence of wars between democratic states. There have been many wars between democracies and nondemocracies as well as among nondemocracies. But, as Bruce Russett asserts, "there are no clear-cut cases of sovereign stable democracies waging war with each other in the modern international system."[10] Several important qualifications in this observation need to be highlighted. Russett's observation does not include civil wars, only wars involving *sovereign* states. War is defined as an armed conflict between sovereign states resulting in at least 1,000 battle casualties. Note also the qualifier of *stable* democracies, which might exclude wars involving new, fledgling democracies. Russett also shows that conflicts between democracies are less likely to involve threats of force, displays of force, and uses of force below the threshold of war, though there are some cases.[11] Interestingly, Russett makes an attempt to examine democratic peace theory in the premodern era by looking at ancient Greece, finding that democratic city-states were "reluctant to fight each other," though it did happen.

Russett and others recognize close cases that might be classified as wars between democracies: the War of 1812 between the United States and Great Britain, the American Civil War, the Spanish-American War (1896), and the allies against Finland in World War II. Upon closer inspection these end up not being wars between democracies. Britain was not yet a democracy in 1812, nor was Spain in 1896. The Confederacy was not a sovereign state during the American Civil War. And even though Finland was aligned with Germany in World War II because of its conflict with the Soviet Union, it never fought against the Western democracies. A more recent close case might be the 2008 conflict between Russia and Georgia, though this is likely to be rejected on the grounds that Russia is not really democratic, even though it holds regular elections. Freedom House, an organization whose classifications are often relied upon, categorizes Russia as "not free," which is usually taken to mean nondemocratic. Recent restrictions on the press and harassment of political opposition led Freedom House to talk about a "return to authoritarianism" in Russia. Georgia is considered "partially free."[12] Other supposed examples of democratic wars are usually rejected on similar grounds. Some boldly assert that democracies never have and never will wage war against each other, whereas others are content with the more limited claim that democracies are much less likely to fight one another. But whichever version one is examining, the empirical fact that no democracy has ever gone to war against another democracy appears to many as strong evidence supporting Kant's prediction vision of democratic pacific union.

Are Democracies Really Any Different?

Despite the apparently compelling fact that democracies have never fought each other, those who approach international relations from perspectives other than liberalism remain skeptical. This is to be expected because someone who sees war as the result of flawed human nature, international anarchy, the dynamics of capitalism, or the gendered nature of international politics would fail to see how these underlying causes are eliminated by altering the domestic political arrangements of states. In terms of the larger debate among the competing visions of international relations, the question of democratic peace is extremely significant. If, in fact, something about the nature of democratic regimes prevents them from going to war with each other, this would strongly support the liberal worldview and undermine other perspectives, particularly realism.

But how does one get around the "fact," as Russett describes it, of democratic peace? In reality, the "fact" of democratic peace is not universally accepted. First, it is possible to accept the empirical observation while questioning its significance. Second, some see the absence of democratic wars as an artifact of definitions of democracy and war that almost appear designed to exclude disconfirming cases. Finally, merely because two democracies have not fought each other does not automatically prove that their democratic nature explains the absence of war. Other factors may account for their failure to fight one another.

No Democratic Wars—So What?

The absence of war between stable democratic states is the most striking piece of evidence in support of democratic peace theory. It is, after all, rare in a discipline filled with qualifications that we are able to say something has *never* happened. This nonevent seems to cry out for an explanation. Then again, maybe it does not. Perhaps the nonoccurrence of democratic war is not as surprising as it first appears.

To understand why some remain unimpressed by this apparently striking bit of evidence, let us draw an analogy. If you have never won the big jackpot in the state lottery, would anyone find this at all surprising? Would this nonevent be viewed as unusual, as something requiring explanation or investigation? Probably not. The mere fact that something has never happened does not automatically create a puzzle. Because the odds of winning the lottery are so small to begin with, the fact that you have never won is to be expected and is explained by the statistical improbability of winning. In fact, winning the lottery is the real anomaly, and winning twice would require some investigation. Thus, the nonoccurrence of an event is surprising only if there was a good reason to expect it to happen in the first place.

David Spiro has made this argument about the absence of democratic war. The logic is quite simple and rests on two basic observations. First, over the last two hundred years there have been very few democratic states. No more than a handful could be considered democratic prior to 1945, and it is only in the last two decades or so that democracies have constituted a majority of the world's states. Until recently, democratic institutions have been rare. Second, war is also a rare event. Even though a war is usually going on somewhere in the world at any given moment, virtually all countries spend most of their time at peace, not war. Peace is the norm in international relations; war is the exception. Spiro demonstrates that when we take into account the statistical rarity of both democracy and war, the absence of a war pitting one democracy against another is not in the least surprising. In fact, this is precisely what we should have expected. Thus, this absence of war is not an anomaly that cries out for an explanation.[13] The "puzzle" of democratic peace is explained by the statistical improbability of war between two democracies.

Empirical Fact or Definitional Artifact?

Proponents of democratic peace theory usually recognize the existence of some potential examples of war between democracies. They also go to great lengths to explain why these cases are not what they seem. The typical response is that either one of the states in question was not really democratic or sovereign. Critics, however, see a pattern of shifting and loose definitions that always manage to save the theory. Sometimes the requirements for being classified as a democracy appear quite lenient (e.g., the United States in 1840), whereas at other times they become curiously stringent (e.g., Germany in 1914).

The commonly employed definition of war is a very restrictive one. Proponents of democratic peace theory, for example, usually reject the American Civil War as an instance of democracies fighting because the Confederacy was not a sovereign state recognized as such by other states. This is true. But given the underlying logic of democratic peace theory, it is not clear why this matters. Why should the theory not hold merely because the states in question are not recognized as independent by other states? This objection seems to be relying on a theoretically irrelevant technicality. Russett appears to admit as much when he notes that the American Civil War is "readily eliminated" as an exception "by the straightforward use of the definitions."[14] But for critics of democratic peace theory, the American Civil War raises serious questions that cannot be dismissed by its definitional elimination. Ted Galen Carpenter points to "the inconvenient matter that Southerners considered their new confederacy democratic (which it was by the standards of the day) and that most Northerners did not dispute that view (they merely regarded it as beside the point) is simply ignored. The willingness of democratic Americans to wage enthusiastic internecine slaughter fairly cries out for more serious discussion." The experience of the Civil War leads him to ask "if democratic people could do that to their own, how confident can we be that two democracies divided by culture or race (e.g., the United States and Japan) would recoil from doing so?"[15]

The example of Germany and World War I is undoubtedly the most controversial case, largely because of the magnitude of the conflict. As Christopher Layne explains, "Even if World War I were the only example of democracies fighting each other, it would be so glaring an exception to democratic peace theory as to render it invalid."[16] To some, Germany in 1914 seems reasonably democratic— there were regular and competitive elections, political parties represented a full range of political views from far left to far right, there was a free and vigorous press, and adult males were allowed to vote. In a largely undemocratic world, this was not too bad.

So why is Germany, labeled "Imperial" Germany in these discussions, not generally considered a democracy? The problem is that German foreign and defense policy was determined by unelected government officials not responsible to the legislature. Germany as a whole may have been somewhat democratic, but its foreign policy apparatus was not. Though this may be true, Layne believes Germany is being held to a higher standard and subjected to a degree of scrutiny that France, Britain, and the United States manage to escape. Looking more closely at these democracies, Layne concludes that most foreign policy decisions in London and Paris were also made with little or no legislative involvement, oversight, or control. Maria Meginnes reaches the same conclusion: "Through universal male suffrage, Germans elected a legislature, the Reichstag, in contested elections between multiple parties. German civil rights, protected under the constitution, were consistently observed." Though conceding that "the issue of foreign policy control is slightly problematic," she notes that "minimal popular influence was common practice among other 'liberal' states of the era. In short, Imperial Germany was indeed 'democratic.'"[17] Democratic peace theorists, however, will have none of this. Spencer Weart reacts almost angrily, insisting that anyone classifying Germany in 1914 as a democracy "display[s] either their ignorance of modern history, or a willful indifference to the explicit meaning of this proposition."[18]

Critics of democratic peace theory counter Weart's charges of ignorance or willful indifference by noting that all democracies in 1914 were imperfect. One would not have to look very long to find legitimate grounds to deny the democratic credentials of any country in 1914, starting with the denial of the right to vote to women. Many democracies look a lot less democratic under the magnifying glass that always seems to be pulled out in the close cases. Thus, there are suspicions that new criteria emerge because the classification of Germany as a democracy in 1914 would, as Layne observes, be a fairly devastating blow to the theory. But just as the American Civil War was "readily eliminated" by using a certain definition of war, World War I is eliminated by using a certain definition of democracy. A charitable interpretation of the whole debate would highlight the inherent problems of making clear distinctions between democratic and undemocratic states in a messy world. A less charitable interpretation is that democratic peace theorists are more interested in finding ways to eliminate troublesome cases than subjecting their theory to rigorous examination.

The charge that democratic peace theorists play fast and loose with definitions in order to protect their theory from problematic cases is frequently made by realists, who are anxious to demonstrate that democracy has no significant impact. But there are also criticisms from the political and theoretical left. From this perspective it is the manner in which terms such as *peaceful* are used that comes under fire. On one level, democratic peace theory makes a very specific claim: democracies are unlikely to fight other democracies. Unfortunately, this very narrow theoretical prediction and (maybe) empirical fact almost imperceptibly is inflated into self-congratulatory assertions about being more "peaceful" in general. Robert Latham, for example, argues that there is a tendency to see refraining from war as synonymous with being peaceful, which allows people to ignore the myriad ways in which democratic states contribute to war and conflict all over the world. In his view, "Islands of liberal democratic peace have not only waged war on nondemocracies, they have also been responsible for—and are uniquely successful at generating—high levels of global militarization in, and conflict among, nondemocratic states." He focuses in particular on the role of democratic states in the development and spread of arms in the world: "In the post second–World War period liberal democratic states—above all, the U.S.—have been in the lead in arms sales and the development and transfer of technology." As a result, Latham concludes that "liberalism is the most effective interstate social organization for the production of military force in modern history."[19] Latham does not disagree with the fact that no two democracies have fought each other. He is simply unable to get terribly excited about it. For Latham, the absence of a democratic war is a relatively insignificant point that indicates little about the peacefulness of democracies in any broader and more meaningful sense of the term.

One could add to this evidence of democracies using covert action to undermine or overthrow other democratically elected regimes. As Ted Galen Carpenter notes, "during the Cold War the United States government overthrew democratic regimes in other countries." Even though democratic peace theorists would be quick to point out that these efforts did not count as "wars," he sarcastically quips that "this will come as a tremendous comfort to the people of Iran, Guatemala and other countries that were saddled with thuggish dictatorships." Technically, of course, such policies do not undermine the narrow claim that democracies will refrain from war with each other, but it does seem relevant to democratic peace theory's underlying assumptions of how democracies would view and treat each other. In these cases, "U.S. policy exhibited extreme hostility to democratic regimes that were not deemed 'friendly' to the United States."[20] That is, strategic considerations dictated U.S. policy, and the fact that these regimes were democratic did not save them. This being the case, critics wonder, can we really be so sanguine about the future of the democratic peace?

Cause or Coincidence?

Let us accept that no two democracies have ever fought each other. Would we be able to infer from this claim that they have avoided war *because* they were democracies? Not necessarily. *New York Times* columnist Thomas Friedman also points out that "no two countries that both had a McDonald's has fought a war against each other because each got its McDonald's."[21] Would anyone seriously infer from this that eating fast-food burgers and fries leads nations to be more peaceful? Probably not. Though the "McDonald's peace thesis" is obviously somewhat frivolous, the underlying point is critical: empirical correlation is not sufficient grounds for inferring a causal relationship. There is always the possibility that the relationship is **spurious**—that is, explained by other variables.

spurious In statistics, a relationship that might appear to indicate a causal relationship but that actually reflects the impact of a third variable. For example, democracies may not fight each other for reasons other than the fact that they are democracies (e.g., wealth).

in-group/out-group hypothesis The proposition that the internal unity of a social group increases when it is faced with an alternative social group, particularly if that other group is seen as posing a threat.

In many respects peace among democracies has been "overdetermined"—that is, there are many contributing factors. Until the post–World War II era the rarity of democracies and their distance from each other severely restricted even the possibility of going to war. Peace between Finland and New Zealand in 1920 can be explained by geography, not shared democracy. There is also the existence of common, unifying threats. One could point to what sociologists refer to as the **in-group/out-group hypothesis**, which predicts internal cohesion in the face of an external enemy. It is plausible that peace among democracies in the twentieth century can be explained by the presence of such external threats—fascism in the 1930s and early 1940s and communism throughout most of the post–World War II period. That is, the democratic peace has been the product of strategic circumstances that provided a powerful incentive for cooperation. Still others have argued that peace is a consequence of economic wealth, growth, and prosperity, and because most democracies have been relatively wealthy and prosperous, this seems plausible as well.

Perhaps one way to look at the influence of alternative factors is to examine closely the cases in which democracies came close to war but refrained. This might reveal what considerations prevented the outbreak of war. Christopher

Crowds in the West Bank celebrate Hamas' election victory in 2006. The electoral victory of Hamas, classifi ed by the United States government as a terrorist organization, leads some to wonder whether democracy always increases the prospects for peace.

Source: Paul Vinten/Shutterstock.Com

Layne examined several such crises between 1861 and 1923. The United States and Great Britain came close to war twice: in 1861, after the North's naval blockade prevented British commerce with the Confederacy, and again in 1895–1896, in a border dispute between Great Britain and Venezuela. Great Britain was also a party to the third close call, though this time with France in a contest for advantage in Egypt and the critical Suez Canal in 1898. The final crisis pitted France against Germany in 1923, when France militarily occupied German territory known as the Ruhr. Though none of these crises escalated to war, Layne thinks they are relevant for two reasons. First, the democracies involved seriously contemplated going to war with one another, which in and of itself seems inconsistent with democratic peace theory. Second, the reasons they managed to avoid war had little, if anything, to do with the fact that they were democracies. In each case, the decision against war was based on assessments of what the interests at stake were and the relative power of the states in conflict. Even Russett concedes that "in each of Layne's cases, power and strategic considerations *were* predominant."[22] That is, the democracies remained at peace, but not necessarily for the reasons suggested by democratic peace theory.

Democratization versus Democracy

A final wrinkle in the democratic peace debate focuses on the distinction between *democratic* and *democratizing* states and their respective propensities to war. Even those who agree that mature, stable democratic states are more peaceful in their relations with each other note that democracies do not just appear overnight fully formed. There is almost always a period of transition in which democracies emerge from some form nondemocratic polity. This can be a very long and tumultuous process that increases the likelihood of both domestic and international conflict as old and new political groups adjust to the change in their status that democracy often entails. Examining these periods of democratic transition in the nineteenth and twentieth centuries, Jack Snyder and Edward Mansfield conclude that "in this transitional phase of democratization, countries become more aggressive and war-prone, not less, and they do fight wars with democratic states."[23] Regarding the case of Germany in World War I discussed previously, for example, Snyder and Mansfield explain this as an example of an aggressive democratizing state not yet restrained by the forces the keep mature democracies from waging war against each other.

Applying these conclusions to contemporary debates, Snyder and Mansfield warn against excessive optimism regarding the spread of democracy in the Arab/Islamic world. Even before the 2011 uprisings in Tunisia, Egypt and elsewhere, they cautioned that "although democratization in the Islamic world might contribute to peace in the very long run…pressing for a quick democratic opening is unlikely to lead to peaceful democratic consolidations." Instead, "unleashing Islamic mass opinion through sudden democratization might raise the likelihood of war."[24] At the time Snyder and Mansfield were trying to dampen expectations about the consequences of democratization in Iraq, because this was often presented by supporters of the 2003 Iraq war as one of the potential benefits of regime change. There is no reason to think, however, that their warnings are any less applicable to possible democratization elsewhere in the region in the wake of the ouster several undemocratic regimes. While in the long run a more democratic Middle East may be a much more peaceful place, there are reasons to worry. In the first place, it is too early to know the political trajectory of the current uprisings. There may be hopes for greater democracy, but there are no assurances. But even if the result is democracy and peace in the long run, we have no idea how long that run might be or what the interim period will look like.[25]

Conclusion

We began this chapter by noting the recent trend of global democratization and ended with some speculation about recent uprisings and hopes for greater democracy in the Arab world. Although the historical evidence concerning the democratic peace remains controversial, the next few decades might go a long way to resolving the debate. For the first time, there are a lot of democracies in the world representing many different cultures and levels of economic development.

Many of these democracies are next to each other with histories of conflicts and war. Democratic peace theory might face its greatest test in places such as the Middle East. Referring back to the argument about the statistical insignificance of the democratic peace thus far, every year that passes without a democratic war makes for greater significance. If a hundred or more democracies around the world can go the next four or five decades without a war among them, it would be hard to deny the reality of democratic peace. In this sense, we are about to live through a massive real-world test of democratic peace theory.

As the world becomes a giant laboratory, the debate over the democratic peace is sure to rage in the interim, with implications for both international relations theory as well as the real world of policymaking. On the level of theory, Russett goes so far as to claim that "the theoretical edifice of realism will collapse" if democratic peace theory is proven correct.[26] Though not everyone would see the stakes in such extreme terms, there is a general recognition that the issues raised strike near the heart of different theories. If internal democracy has a profound effect on the behavior of states, this would clearly undermine realist notions that international anarchy or human nature are the fundamental causes of war. But it is not only realism on the theoretical chopping block: Marxism is also challenged because liberal democratic states are for the most part capitalist states. Because Marxism sees the underlying dynamics and requirements of capitalism as a basic cause of expansionism, militarism, and war, we can extend Russett's warnings about the collapse of realism to Marxism as well. Perhaps it is the realization that the stakes are so important that explains why the debate over the democratic peace has become so central to contemporary research in international relations. The high stakes involved may also explain why the debate is sometimes so testy.

In terms of policy, critics of democratic peace theory see its acceptance by policymakers as dangerous. Some worry that it will lead to misguided attempts to spread democracy throughout the world, and others fear that it will blind the United States to emerging strategic threats because of the optimistic assumption that other democracies cannot possibly be threatening. Even the realist, Christopher Layne warns that "if American policymakers allow themselves to be mesmerized by democratic peace theory's seductive—but false—vision of the future, the United States will be ill-prepared to formulate a grand strategy that will advance its interests in the emerging world of multipolar great power competition."[27] For Russett, however, the failure to "grasp the democratic peace" would represent a tragedy of historic proportions, a lost opportunity to create and nurture a more civilized and peaceful world.

CHAPTER SUMMARY

■ The idea that democracies are more peaceful than non-democracies, which has long been central to liberal thinking about international politics, can be traced to Immanuel Kant's vision of a "democratic pacific union" in which democratic (or "republican") states would refrain from war in their relations with each other.

■ With the end of the Cold War and the dramatic spread of democracy in the 1980s and 1990s, there has been renewed interest in democratic peace theory among academics and policymakers alike.

■ Democratic peace theory has two major variants. The institutional variant claims that the division or dispersion of power in democratic states makes it very difficult for them to initiate and wage war. The cultural version argues that the norms and values that permeate democratic societies, especially the commitment to resolving political disputes without resort to force, also shape the foreign policies of democratic states. These institutional and cultural constraints are particularly powerful when democracies deal with one another.

■ The empirical record appears to support democratic peace theory because there is no example of an unambiguously democratic state engaging in war with another unambiguously democratic state.

■ Critics and skeptics remain unconvinced by the evidence. The rarity of war and (until recently) the rarity of democracy mean that we should not have expected to see wars among democracies. As a result, the lack of war between democracies is neither surprising nor compelling.

■ Skeptics also see a very convenient pattern of constantly shifting definitions, particularly when it comes to the requirements for classifying a country as a democracy. Whether or not Germany on the eve of World War I deserves the label of democracy is the most controversial example of these definitional problems.

■ The spread of democracy over the past two decades will provide for a real-world test of democratic peace theory in coming years because many new democracies are geographically close to each other and have long histories of conflict.

CRITICAL QUESTIONS

1. Does historical experience support the proposition that democracies do not go to war against other democracies?

2. What other factors might explain the absence of war among democratic states?

3. Why is democratic peace theory inconsistent with realism?

4. Why might the next few decades be critical for establishing the validity of democratic peace theory?

5. Why is World War I such a controversial case in the debate over democratic peace theory?

KEY TERMS

checks and balances, 90
democratic pacific union, 87
Immanuel Kant, 87

in-group/out-group
 hypothesis, 98
institutional thesis, 90

political-cultural thesis, 90
rational/pacific public
 thesis, 87

spurious, 98

FURTHER READINGS

Contemporary interest in democratic peace theory was sparked by Michael Doyle's seminal "Liberalism and World Politics," *American Political Science Review* 80

(December 1986): 1151–1169. Several subsequent works have since become standards in support of the democratic peace theory, including Bruce Russett, *Grasping the*

Democratic Peace (Princeton, NJ: Princeton University Press, 1993), and Spencer Weart, *Never at War: Why Democracies Will Not Fight One Another* (New Haven, CT: Yale University Press, 1998). Stressing the importance of mutual perceptions of democracy is John Owen, *Liberal Peace, Liberal War: American Politics and International Security* (Ithaca, NY: Cornell University Press, 1997). Critiques from several different perspectives can be found in Christopher Layne, "Kant or Cant: The Myth of the Democratic Peace," *International Security* 19 (Fall 1994): 5–49; Joanne Gowa, *Bullets and Ballots: The Elusive Democratic Peace* (Princeton, NJ: Princeton University Press, 1999); and Robert Latham, "Democracy and War-Making," *Millenium: A Journal of International Affairs* 22 (1993): 139–164. On the propensity of democratizing states for war see Edward D. Mansfield and Jack Snyder, *Electing to Fight: Why Emerging Democracies Go to War* (Cambridge, MA: MIT Press, 2007).

WAR AND DEMOCRACY ON THE WEB

www.hawaii.edu/powerkills
Explores the relationship among freedom, democracy, and war.

www.worldaudit.org
Evaluates and ranks the nations of the world on various scales, including democracy, press freedom, civil liberties, and others.

www.freedomhouse.org
Classifies nations of the world on a scale of "free," "partially free," and "not free." Categorizing nations as "free" is often taken by researchers as tantamount to classification of democratic.

www.systemicpeace.org/polity/polity4.htm
Classifies nations of the world according to their type of government.

NOTES

[1] Quoted in Michael Doyle, *The Ways of War and Peace* (New York: W. W. Norton, 1997), p. 280.

[2] This not a universally shared interpretation. See Louis A. Perez, *The War of 1898* (Chapel Hill: University of North Carolina Press, 1998), pp. 70–77. Still, even those who reject the notion that popular opinion pushed President McKinley into war over Cuba cannot plausibly argue that public opinion was a force for peace in the crisis.

[3] Robin Fox, "Fatal Attraction: War and Human Nature," *The National Interest* 30 (Winter 1992/1993): 17.

[4] The best summary of the institutional and cultural theses can be found in Bruce Russett, *Grasping the Democratic Peace* (Princeton, NJ: Princeton University Press, 1993), pp. 29–42.

[5] Thomas Risse-Kappen, "Democratic Peace—Warlike Democracies: A Social Constructivist Interpretation of the Liberal Argument," *European Journal of International Relations* 34, no. 1(1995): 489–515.

[6] Spencer Weart, *Never at War: Why Democracies Will Not Fight One Another* (New Haven, CT: Yale University Press, 1998), p. 90.

[7] John Owen, *Liberal Peace, Liberal War: American Politics and International Security* (Ithaca, NY: Cornell University Press, 1997), and John Owen, "How Liberalism Produces the Democratic Peace," *International Security* 19, no. 2 (Fall 1994): 87–126. Also Ido Oren, "The Subjectivity of the Democratic Peace: Changing U.S. Perceptions of Imperial Germany," *International Security* 20, no. 2 (Fall 1995): 147–184.

[8] More radical or Marxist theorists might take issue with this statement. They would be inclined to argue that the formal processes mask the fundamentally undemocratic nature of most contemporary democracies because the skewed nature of economic power prevents the emergence of anything that could be considered democratic in the deeper sense of the term.

[9] J. D. Singer and Melvin Small, "The War Proneness of Democratic States," *Jerusalem Journal of International Relations* 1 (1976): 49–69.

[10] Bruce Russett, *Grasping the Democratic Peace* (Princeton, NJ: Princeton University Press, 1993), p. 11.

[11] Ibid., p. 21.

[12] See http://www.freedomhouse.org/template.cfm?page=22&country=7475&year=2008

[13] David Spiro, "The Insignificance of the Liberal Peace, *International Security* 19, no. 2 (Fall 1994): 50–86.

[14] Russett, *Grasping the Democratic Peace*, p. 16.

[15] Ted Galen Carpenter, "Review Essay: Democracy and War," *Independent Review* 2 (Winter 1998): 435–441.

[16] Christopher Layne, "Kant or Cant: The Myth of Democratic Peace," *International Security* 19, no. 2 (Fall 1994): 41.

[17] Maria A. Meginnes, "Defining the Democratic: Imperial Germany and Democratic Peace Theory," *The Undergraduate Journal of Politics and Government* 1, no. 2 (Spring 2001): 32.

[18] Weart, *Never at War*, pp. 311–312. In general, Weart provides a comprehensive overview of the "close" cases and the reasons why he thinks none of them invalidates the democratic peace proposition (pp. 297–318).

[19] Robert Latham, "Democracy and War-Making: Locating the Liberal International Context," *Millenium: A Journal of International Affairs* 22, no. 2 (1993): 139, 153, 154.

[20] Ted Galen Carpenter, "Democracy and War: Reply," *Independent Review* 3 (Summer 1998): 107.

[21] Thomas Friedman, *The Lexus and the Olive Tree* (New York: Farrar, Straus and Giroux, 1999), p. 195.

[22] Bruce Russett, "And Yet It Moves," *International Security* 19, no. 4 (Spring 1995): 166.

[23]Edward D. Mansfield and Jack Snyder, "Democratization and the Danger of War," *International Security* vol. 20, no. 1 (Summer 1995), p. 5.

[24]Edward D. Mansfield and Jack Snyder, "Prone to Violence: The Paradox of Democratic Peace," *The National Interest* no. 82 (Winter 2005/06), p. 40.

[25]Another skeptical view is Piki-Ish Shalom, "'The Civilization of Clashes': Misapplying the Democratic Peace in the Middle East," *Political Science Quarterly* 122, no. 4 (Winter 2007-08), pp. 533–54.

[26]Russett, "And Yet it Moves," p. 164.

[27]Layne, "Kant or Cant," p. 49.

Would Democracy Bring Peace to the Middle East?

Though it is one thing to understand the logic of democratic peace theory in the familiar context of Europe or North America, there is no reason this logic should be so restricted. The interesting question is whether the introduction of democracy into places of intense war and conflict would have a similarly pacifying effect. When we think of conflict in the contemporary world, perhaps the first place that comes to mind is the Middle East. This raises the inevitable question: Would the spread of democracy bring peace to the Middle East? The conviction that it would was part of the rationale for regime change in Iraq in 2003. This general question is addressed in the following two essays. In a 2005 editorial, former U.S. Secretary of State Condoleezza Rice makes the case that war and terrorism in the Middle East would be substantially reduced by the introduction and spread of democratic institutions. She does so, of course, largely in the context of justifying the decision to use force in pursuit of regime change in Iraq. More recently, uprisings in the Arab world have raised hopes such optimistic expectations might finally become reality. Perhaps nowhere are potential consequences of democratization greater than in the case of Egypt and its relations with Israel. Because the two countries enjoyed more than two decades of peace with undemocratic regimes in Egypt, there are understandable concerns about the future. Benny Morris voices the fears shared by many in Israel that democratization in Egypt might actually endanger the peace between the two countries. The region may very soon become a real world laboratory for various versions of democratic peace theory. In what ways do Rice and Morris reflect the various arguments presented in this chapter? Which view of democracy and peace in the Middle East do you find more persuasive and why?

The Promise of Democratic Peace

Secretary Condoleezza Rice
Op-Ed
Washington Post
December 11, 2005[1]

Soon after arriving at the State Department earlier this year, I hung a portrait of Dean Acheson in my office. Over half a century ago, as America sought to create the world anew in the aftermath of World War II, Acheson sat in the office that I now occupy. And I hung his picture where I did for a reason.

[1] Source: Condoleezza Rice, "The Promise of Democratic Peace," *Washington Post* (December 11, 2005). Accessed at http://www.state.gov/secretary/rm/2005/57888.htm

Like Acheson and his contemporaries, we live in an extraordinary time—one in which the terrain of international politics is shifting beneath our feet and the pace of historical change outstrips even the most vivid imagination. My predecessor's portrait is a reminder that in times of unprecedented change, the traditional diplomacy of crisis management is insufficient. Instead, we must transcend the doctrines and debates of the past and transform volatile status quos that no longer serve our interests. What is needed is a realistic statecraft for a transformed world.

President Bush outlined the vision for it in his second inaugural address: "It is the policy of the United States to seek and support the growth of democratic movements and institutions in every nation and culture, with the ultimate goal of ending tyranny in our world." This is admittedly a bold course of action, but it is consistent with the proud tradition of American foreign policy, especially such recent presidents as Harry Truman and Ronald Reagan. Most important: Like the ambitious policies of Truman and Reagan, our statecraft will succeed not simply because it is optimistic and idealistic but also because it is premised on sound strategic logic and a proper understanding of the new realities we face.

Our statecraft today recognizes that centuries of international practice and precedent have been overturned in the past 15 years. Consider one example: For the first time since the Peace of Westphalia in 1648, the prospect of violent conflict between great powers is becoming ever more unthinkable. Major states are increasingly competing in peace, not preparing for war. To advance this remarkable trend, the United States is transforming our partnerships with nations such as Japan and Russia, with the European Union, and especially with China and India. Together we are building a more lasting and durable form of global stability: a balance of power that favors freedom.

This unprecedented change has supported others. Since its creation more than 350 years ago, the modern state system has always rested on the concept of sovereignty. It was assumed that states were the primary international actors and that every state was able and willing to address the threats emerging from its territory. Today, however, we have seen that these assumptions no longer hold, and as a result the greatest threats to our security are defined more by the dynamics within weak and failing states than by the borders between strong and aggressive ones.

The phenomenon of weak and failing states is not new, but the danger they now pose is unparalleled. When people, goods and information traverse the globe as fast as they do today, transnational threats such as disease or terrorism can inflict damage comparable to the standing armies of nation-states. Absent responsible state authority, threats that would and should be contained within a country's borders can now melt into the world and wreak untold havoc. Weak and failing states serve as global pathways that facilitate the spread of pandemics, the movement of criminals and terrorists, and the proliferation of the world's most dangerous weapons.

Our experience of this new world leads us to conclude that the fundamental character of regimes matters more today than the international distribution of power. Insisting otherwise is imprudent and impractical. The goal of our statecraft is to help create a world of democratic, well-governed states that can meet the needs of their citizens and conduct themselves responsibly in the international system. Attempting to draw neat, clean lines between our security interests and our democratic ideals does not reflect the reality of today's world. Supporting the growth of democratic institutions in all nations is not some moralistic flight of fancy; it is the only realistic response to our present challenges.

In one region of the world, however, the problems emerging from the character of regimes are more urgent than in any other. The "freedom deficit" in the broader Middle East provides fertile ground for the growth of an ideology of hatred so vicious and virulent that it leads people to strap suicide bombs to their bodies and fly airplanes into buildings. When the citizens of this region cannot advance their interests and redress their grievances through an open political process, they retreat hopelessly into the shadows to be preyed upon by evil men with violent designs. In these societies, it is illusory to encourage economic reform by itself and hope that the freedom deficit will work itself out over time.

Though the broader Middle East has no history of democracy, this is not an excuse for doing nothing. If every action required a precedent, there would be no firsts. We are confident that democracy will succeed in this region not simply because we have faith in our principles but because the basic human longing for liberty and democratic rights has transformed our world. Dogmatic cynics and cultural determinists were once certain that "Asian values," or Latin culture, or Slavic despotism, or African tribalism would each render democracy impossible. But they were wrong, and our statecraft must now be guided by the undeniable truth that democracy is the only assurance of lasting peace and security between states, because it is the only guarantee of freedom and justice within states.

Implicit within the goals of our statecraft are the limits of our power and the reasons for our humility. Unlike tyranny, democracy by its very nature is never imposed. Citizens of conviction must choose it—and not just in one election. The work of democracy is a daily process to build the institutions of democracy: the rule of law, an independent judiciary, free media and property rights, among others. The United States cannot manufacture these outcomes, but we can and must create opportunities for individuals to assume ownership of their own lives and nations. Our power gains its greatest legitimacy when we support the natural right of all people, even those who disagree with us, to govern themselves in liberty.

The statecraft that America is called to practice in today's world is ambitious, even revolutionary, but it is not imprudent. A conservative temperament will rightly be skeptical of any policy that embraces change and rejects the status quo, but that is not an argument against the merits of such a policy. As Truman once said, "The world is not static, and the status quo is not sacred." In times of extraordinary change such as ours, when the costs of inaction outweigh the risks of action, doing nothing is not an option. If the school of thought called "realism" is to be truly realistic, it must recognize that stability without democracy will prove to be false stability, and that fear of change is not a positive prescription for policy.

After all, who truly believes, after the attacks of September 11, 2001, that the status quo in the Middle East was stable, beneficial and worth defending? How could it have been prudent to preserve the state of affairs in a region that was incubating and exporting terrorism; where the proliferation of deadly weapons was getting worse, not better; where authoritarian regimes were projecting their failures onto innocent nations and peoples; where Lebanon suffered under the boot heel of Syrian occupation; where a corrupt Palestinian Authority cared more for its own preservation than for its people's aspirations; and where a tyrant such as Saddam Hussein was free to slaughter his citizens, destabilize his neighbors and undermine the hope of peace between Israelis and Palestinians? It is sheer fantasy to assume that the Middle East was just peachy before America disrupted its alleged stability.

Had we believed this, and had we done nothing, consider all that we would have missed in just the past year: A Lebanon that is free of foreign occupation and advancing democratic reform. A Palestinian Authority run by an elected leader who openly calls for peace with Israel. An Egypt that has amended its constitution to hold multiparty elections. A Kuwait where women are now full citizens. And, of course, an Iraq that in the face of a horrific insurgency has held historic elections, drafted and ratified a new national charter, and will go to the polls again in coming days to elect a new constitutional government.

At this time last year, such unprecedented progress seemed impossible. One day it will all seem to have been inevitable. This is the nature of extraordinary times, which Acheson understood well and described perfectly in his memoirs. "The significance of events," he wrote, "was shrouded in ambiguity. We groped after interpretations of them, sometimes reversed lines of action based on earlier views, and hesitated long before grasping what now seems obvious." When Acheson left office in 1953, he could not know the fate of the policies he helped to create. He certainly could never have predicted that nearly four decades later, war between Europe's major powers would be unthinkable, or that America and the world would be harvesting the fruits of his good decisions and managing the collapse of communism. But because leaders such as Acheson steered American statecraft with our principles when precedents for action were lacking, because they dealt with their world as it was but never believed they were powerless to change it for the better, the promise of democratic peace is now a reality in all of Europe and in much of Asia.

When I walk past Acheson's portrait upon departing my office for the last time, no one will be able to know the full scope of what our statecraft has achieved. But I have an abiding confidence that we will have laid a firm foundation of principle—a foundation on which future generations will realize our nation's vision of a fully free, democratic and peaceful world.

PERSPECTIVE 2 | Arab Spring, Israeli Winter (2011)

Benny Morris[2]

The National Interest
http://nationalinterest.org/commentary/arab-spring-israeli-winter-5229

April 28, 2011
Egypt is steadily backing away from its peace treaty with Israel, with possible dire consequences for the region's stability and Israeli-Arab relations in general.

Yesterday's demolition of the Egyptian-Israeli gas pipeline near El Arish, in Sinai, was only the latest in a series of ominous signs.

Many in the West waxed enthusiastic as thousands of Cairenes took to the streets two months ago to topple their aged dictator, President Hosni Mubarak: The revolution was hailed—along with the other outbursts of popular anger across the Arab world—as the birth of freedom in a long-dormant, long-unfree world.

And while none could remain unmoved at the sight of multitudes claiming their political voice for the first time, the ultimate outcome of this human turbulence is as yet unclear.

But, for Israelis, the Arab spring, as some call it—though it might yet turn out to have been an Arab autumn—had a clear, dark subtext, which many in the West preferred to ignore or deny. "What is happening is about the Arab world, internally; it has nothing to do with Israel," they claimed.

But I'm afraid it has, and in spades, and the chickens are beginning to come home to roost. From the start, at least as regards Egypt, Israel was there as an issue, if not absolutely in the foreground then certainly not in a faraway background. Pictures occasionally appeared of Mubarak surrounded by a Star of David; occasionally, the crowds chanted that he was a lackey of America and Israel.

Now the issue is definitely moving to the foreground. The Pew Research Center for the People and the Press this week published a poll about what Egyptians think and want. *The New York Times* preferred to head its report in the matter by pointing to the overwhelming optimism of post-revolutionary Egyptians about their collective future. But the poll's more striking feature was the finding that 54% of Egyptians want to annul the country's 1979 peace treaty with Israel, a key symbol of the gradual dissipation (at the time) of the pan-Arab-Israel conflict and the precedential cornerstone of any possible Israeli-Palestinian accommodation in the future. The percentage of nay-sayers rose among less educated Egyptians, though a full 45% of educated Egyptians also sought the annulment of the treaty.

(The poll also showed that 36% of Egyptians favored Islamic fundamentalism—a smaller number opposed such fundamentalism—and more than half believed that the Koran or Islamic sharia law should be the basis or guideline for the country's constitution.)

On the energy front, two of Mubarak's former energy ministers, Mahmoud Latif and Sameh Fahmy, are to stand trial for selling the gas to Israel at a discount (and, presumably, personally profiting in the process). Mubarak himself is today regularly portrayed as a dupe—or Zionist agent—and may be held to account in this connection. The bilateral $2.5 billion agreement, signed in 2005 though never popular with the Egyptian public, was for fifteen years, with an option for five additional years. The Egyptians began supplying the gas through the overland pipeline in 2008.

Yesterday's explosion severing the pipeline—it provided about half of the fuel for Israel's electricity-generating plants—was but the latest instalment in the saga. About two months ago, the gasline was reportedly damaged by saboteurs and Egypt ceased supplying gas to Israel (and Jordan) for about a month. It was unclear then whether the line was really damaged or by whom. Now the supply has completely stopped. For yesterday's sabotage the Egyptian military, which runs the country, have blamed "unknown, armed" assailants—though conspiracy theorists, who abound in the region, might suggest that one of their own squads perpetrated the explosion, to put an end to the unpopular energy link while being able to deny responsibility. Simply stopping the gas supply would be a breach of contract and might well go down poorly in Washington.

All of this may augur a definitive Egyptian-Israeli rift following the establishment of a new government in Egypt after the scheduled September general elections. Whether that government would go so far as formally to cancel the peace treaty and renew the state of belligerence between the two countries is unclear. But without doubt Israel will no longer enjoy the certainty and strategic benefit of a quiescent and dependable neighbor on its southern front as it faces its enemies to the east and north (Hezbollah and Iran/Syria). How such a new Egyptian regime will handle Hamas (and the Israeli-Hamas conflict) along the Gaza Strip border is anyone's guess—though much will depend on the size of the Muslim Brotherhood contingent in the future Egyptian government. (Hamas is the Palestinian offshoot of the brotherhood, Egypt's largest Islamist party.)

And one last word about the Pew poll, which many of the participants appear to have missed. There may well be a clear contradiction, for Egyptians, between viewing their future optimistically and scrapping the peace with Israel. Put another way, the annulment of the treaty might lead to Egypt rejoining the Arab confrontation front against Israel and even to participation in new wars. And I doubt if this would result in a roseate future for Egyptians.

5

War and "Human Nature"

Key Controversy: Is War Part of Human Nature?

Is there something about human nature that leads to war? Given its obvious irrationality, many believe there must be an uncontrollable force that drives people to engage in warfare. For centuries, contrasting philosophical and religious views of human nature have framed this debate. More "scientific" versions of this argument focus on psychological and biological impulses or instincts that supposedly lead to aggression and war. Though most realists do not explicitly endorse instinctual theories of war, there are some obvious parallels with their negative view of human nature, especially for classical realists. The opposing view sees war as a culturally learned practice, a form of collective violence rather than a manifestation of an individual-level aggressive instinct. This perspective is more consistent with liberalism's positive assessment of human nature as well as feminist and constructivist perspectives stressing the socially constructed nature of many human behaviors. Though much of this debate has been defined in terms of the familiar nature-*or*-nurture divide, in the final analysis it might be more useful to think in terms of a combination of nature *and* nurture. ∎

Whatever students of international relations might have to say about anarchy or the lack of democracy being fundamental causes of war, many if not most people suspect a deeper cause. It is almost impossible to get very far in discussing the causes of war before someone ventures their opinion that war is just part of "human nature." Psychologist Anthony Storr appears to agree: "That man is an aggressive creature will hardly be denied. With the exception of certain rodents, no other vertebrate habitually destroys members of his own species. No other animal takes positive pleasure in the exercise of cruelty upon another of his own kind."[1] Observing that humans behave like animals in war is something of an insult to animals, since there are virtually no other creatures who do to their own kind what we do to ours. The question of why human beings systematically prepare for and carry out the large-scale slaughter of members of their own species is perhaps the central question for anyone interested in our fate on this planet.

Though Anthony Storr's indictment is certainly harsh, it seems to be supported by the depressing statistics of war. By one estimate, there have been only 292 years of peace in the world over the last 5,600 years, and during that time more than 3,500,000,000 people have died in, or as a result of, more than 14,000 wars.[2] This includes not only the obvious military and civilian casualties, but also deaths from the common consequences of war—disease, famine, and civil violence. Other studies arrive at somewhat different figures but do not change the overall picture: War is almost certainly the second leading cause of death in human history, behind only the diseases and conditions associated with old age. Even though explanations supporting the view of war being part of human nature have fallen out of favor with scholars and academics, they remain part of the common wisdom. Exactly what it is about human nature that supposedly leads to war varies, and the concept of human nature is itself quite fuzzy and elastic. Some treat human nature in a philosophical or theological sense involving foundational assumptions about human motivation, whereas others approach it from a biological perspective, emphasizing instincts and evolutionary imperatives. For some, the element of human nature that leads to war is an innate aggressive drive or instinct. Others see war as resulting not from aggression per se, but rather from human greed, irrationality, or group-forming tendencies. Whatever the specifics, human nature explanations of war imply, either explicitly or implicitly, the inevitability of war. On the other side of the debate are those who see war as learned behavior, the culmination of a socialization process that encourages us to think about aggression, violence, and other social groups in ways that make systematic killing acceptable, even desirable in some situations. War does not come "naturally," like sex; it is something people learn, and must sometimes be coerced to do. It is more like slavery and wearing black to funerals, learned social practices that can change, than it is sex, which is a biological drive. In very simplistic terms, disagreements about the relationship between war and human nature are specific examples of the age-old **nature-versus-nurture** debate over which human behaviors are inevitable reflections of some unchangeable part of the human makeup and which are social practices amenable to alteration. Although any explanation for something as complex as war inevitably combines elements of both nature and nurture, there is usually a sufficient difference in emphasis so that it is possible to place different theories on either side of this divide.

nature-versus-nurture The debate over which human behaviors are biologically or instinctually determined as opposed to being socially or culturally conditioned.

Aggression, Instincts, and War

Philosophical and theological assumptions about human nature are not susceptible to scientific test; they are simply foundational beliefs that one either accepts or rejects. There have, however, been attempts to trace the origins of human aggression and war to biological and physiological instincts, creating modern or scientific versions of philosophical and theological doctrines. Sigmund Freud, for example, argued that people have both a life instinct (Eros) and a death instinct (Thanatos), with aggression, whether it is directed toward oneself in the form of suicide or toward others as violence, resulting from the deep-seated death instinct. Though he would later express doubts about this position, in his *Civilization and*

Its Discontents Freud was clear about his view of human nature: "Men are not gentle creatures who want to be loved, and who at most can defend themselves if they are attacked; they are, on the contrary, creatures among whose instinctual endowment is to be reckoned with a powerful share of aggressiveness.... [this instinct] manifests itself spontaneously and reveals man as a savage beast."[3]

The most coherent and influential attempts to theorize about war in terms of human instincts have been advanced by **ethologists** (those engaged in the study of animal behavior). Books such as Desmond Morris's *The Naked Ape*, Lionel Tiger and Robin Fox's *The Imperial Animal*, and Robert Ardrey's *The Territorial Imperative* portray war as a manifestation of an aggressive instinct that humans share with other animals.[4]

The most prominent and influential exponent of this viewpoint was **Konrad Lorenz**, a German ethologist, whose book *On Aggression* provided the intellectual and theoretical foundation for the more popularized works of Morris, Tiger, Fox, and Ardrey.[5] Lorenz's approach to understanding war begins with the implicit puzzle in Anthony Storr's observation about the near uniqueness of human slaughter: How do we explain the fact that human beings kill each other with such frequency and enthusiasm? "Undeniably, there must be," Lorenz concludes, "superlatively strong factors which are able to overcome the commands of individual reason so completely and which are so obviously impervious to experience and learning."[6] What might these factors be? To answer this question, it is useful to break the big puzzle into two smaller ones. First, why do humans fight with one another? Second, why do they frequently kill one another? The distinction between aggression and *lethal* aggression is critical. If people just fought without killing, the problem of war would not be nearly that important.

ethologists The study of animal behavior. Many ethologists have been influential proponents of the view that war has an instinctual basis in human behavior.

Konrad Lorenz Influential and controversial German ethologist famous for drawing the distinction between lethal and nonlethal animals and placing humans in the latter category. Claimed that the ability of humans to craft lethal weapons upset the balance between our ability to kill and inhibitions against killing.

The "Functions" of Aggression

Lorenz and his fellow ethologists begin with the assumption that humans are animals in the sense that we are living, breathing creatures. Though different from other animals in important respects, we are animals nonetheless. Like other animals we are a product of evolutionary processes that have endowed us with certain instincts. We may have fewer instincts than other animals, but we still have them. These assumptions raise a number of misleadingly simple questions. First, what is an instinct? And second, how does one distinguish instinctual actions from learned behaviors? These questions are not easy to answer.

An **instinct** is typically defined as a psychologically and biologically predetermined behavioral response to external stimuli. Hibernation, for example, is an instinct in some animals because it is a predetermined response to changes in the weather announcing the coming of winter. Lorenz and Morris distinguish instinctual from learned behaviors by the presence or absence of biological or physical "symptoms." Sexual arousal provides one example: External stimuli, such as the appearance of an attractive mate, elicit specific physical changes and activate desires to engage in certain behaviors. For Lorenz and Morris, it is significant that aggression and fighting are also accompanied by physiological changes, such as rapid breathing, increased blood pressure, accelerated heart rate, higher levels of

instinct A biologically or psychologically predetermined behavioral response to external stimuli.

adrenaline, a cessation of food digestion, muscle tension, and various neurological changes.[7] These are all indicators of an instinctual response. In comparison, culturally learned behaviors, such as wearing black to funerals, are not associated with similar physiological indicators.

Ethologists view instincts in the context of evolutionary theory in that they emerge and survive because they serve useful purposes. To use more technical terminology, instincts exist and persist because they are "adaptive"; they help assure the survival of a species. Among the instincts that virtually all animals possess are fear, sex, hunger, and aggression. The usefulness of sex and hunger for species survival is obvious. Fear helps protect animals from unknown dangers. The evolutionary purpose of aggression is not as immediately clear and requires some explanation.

Ethologists see aggression as fulfilling several useful functions. The first is **spacing**. Any environment has sufficient resources to support a limited population. As the animal population expands, fights over resources (e.g., land, food, and mates) increase. These fights tend to repel the animals, driving them away from each other, distributing or spacing them out to prevent overpopulation. The second function is the establishment of a **hierarchy** in animal groups. Fights among animals within their groups determine who rules, who is at the top and bottom of the social heap. This hierarchy is an integral element of social structure. It is also usually linked to reproduction in that animals at the top have the most access to mates, ensuring that the strongest and fittest mate the most. Finally, aggression is necessary for the defense of the young. According to Lorenz and his followers, there is every reason to believe that aggression performed these same basic functions in human evolution. Humans have developed an aggressive instinct over the course of evolution for very much the same reasons as other animals.

The critical puzzle, however, is not why human beings fight each other but rather why we kill each other. It is not aggression that makes us stand out but rather our lethal aggression. All animals fight with their own kind; the difference is that they rarely kill members of their own species. This is the genuinely puzzling thing about war. It is in his explanation of the uniqueness of human lethal aggression that Lorenz made his most original and controversial contribution.

The Curse of Intelligence: Weapons

In looking at the animal kingdom as a whole, Lorenz makes a fundamental distinction between two types of animals. On one hand, there are animals that lack the physical endowments necessary to kill with ease. Doves, gerbils, and rabbits, for example, do not possess the powerful limbs and jaws or sharp claws and teeth required for lethal aggression. On the other hand, animals such as lions, tigers, wolves, and bears do possess the physical tools necessary to kill. Explaining why doves, gerbils, and rabbits do not run around slaughtering each other is easy: They cannot. They fight, but they are unable to kill. No puzzle there.

The real puzzle is why animals with ability to kill members of their own species rarely do. As Desmond Morris observes, "Species that have evolved special killing techniques for dealing with their prey seldom employ these when fighting their own kind."[8] Why not? Why aren't the plains of Africa littered with the corpses of

---

spacing The tendency of animals to disperse themselves over a given territory so as to prevent overpopulation and depletion of resources. Cited by ethologists as one of the useful functions of aggression in animals.

hierarchy The unequal distribution of power and authority in an animal grouping. In-group fighting often establishes the social hierarchy. Cited by ethologists as one of the useful functions of aggression in animals.

great game killed by their own kind? The answer, according to Lorenz, is that lethal animals have developed in the course of evolution a set of signals, repertoires, and behaviors that inhibit the killing of members of their own species. In a fight between potentially lethal members of the same species, there is almost always a point where the fight ends well short of death. This happens in one of two ways. The most obvious means of avoiding death is flight; the loser simply runs away and the victor seldom chases to inflict further harm. In instances where flight is not feasible, the loser "must somehow signal to the stronger animal that he is no longer a threat and that he does not intend to continue the fight…. But if he can signal his acceptance of defeat … he will be able to avoid further serious punishment." According to Morris, "this is achieved by the performance of certain characteristic submissive displays. These appease the attacker and rapidly reduce his aggression, speeding up settlement of the dispute."[9]

This submissive posture is sometimes referred to as an **appeasement gesture**. It might involve lying down passively and/or exposing a vulnerable part of the body. Such gestures signify, and are recognized as symbols of, defeat. Death rarely follows. Thus, potentially lethal animals rarely kill members of their own species because "all heavily armed carnivores possess sufficiently reliable inhibitions which prevent the self-destruction of the species."[10] The ability to kill one's own kind without inhibition is a recipe for evolutionary failure.

appeasement gesture A concept popularized by Konrad Lorenz involving displays or signals made by lethal animals while fighting with members of their own species in order to indicate defeat and avoid death.

How do human beings fit into this analysis? In terms of the division between lethal and nonlethal animals, humans fall into the latter category. Our natural physical endowments are not terribly menacing. We do not have sharp teeth, powerful jaws, strong limbs, or dangerous claws. Two naked people would find it very difficult to kill each other using only their physical capabilities. In this sense we are more like rabbits than wolves. As essentially nonlethal creatures, we should have no need for mechanisms that prevent us from killing each other. The problem is that our intellect, creativity, and ingenuity have allowed us to develop tools that make us exceptionally lethal. In the 150,000 or so years humans have been around, we have gone from using sticks and rocks to cannons and missiles. Although 150,000 years seems like a long time to you and me, from an evolutionary perspective this is an eye blink. And it has been less than ten thousand years from the development of many close-range weapons to the development of bombers and missiles. So in an evolutionary sense, we have gone from being relatively harmless to being incredibly lethal almost overnight. Lorenz lays out the basic problem: "All of his [mankind's] trouble arises from his being a basically harmless omnivorous creature, lacking in natural weapons with which to kill prey, and, therefore, devoid of the built-in safety devices which prevent 'professional' carnivores from abusing their killing power." Unfortunately, "in human evolution, no inhibitory mechanisms preventing sudden manslaughter were necessary because quick killing was impossible … the invention of artificial weapons upset the equilibrium of killing potential and social inhibitions."[11]

On some level there undoubtedly do exist certain inhibitions. Many people would find it very difficult to kill someone in hand-to-hand combat when they were crouching and crying helplessly in a corner begging for mercy. Many would take this behavior as a sufficient appeasement gesture. The problem, however, is that humans have fashioned weapons that allow them to be lethal from great distances: a few dozen feet with spears and arrows, a few hundred feet with guns, a mile or two with artillery, several miles from above with a bomber, and thousands of miles away with missiles. A few individuals pressing buttons in an underground bunker can vaporize millions of their fellow human beings without even seeing a drop of blood or a single anguished expression. Again, Lorenz makes the implications of this clear: "The distance at which all shooting weapons take effect screens the killer against the stimulus situation which would otherwise activate his killing inhibitions…. The man who presses the releasing button is so completely screened against seeing, hearing or otherwise emotionally realizing the consequences of his action, that he can commit it with impunity."[12] Physical distance encourages emotional distance.

evolutionary lag or **disequilibrium** Konrad Lorenz's idea that humans' intellectual evolution and ability to kill has not been matched by the development of inhibitions against using these abilities to kill members of our own species.

Thus, according to Lorenz and Morris, what we have is a form of **evolutionary lag** or **disequilibrium**. Human intellectual evolution, reflected in our ability to build increasingly destructive weapons that allow us to kill from greater and greater distances, has outstripped our moral evolution. We are the evolutionary equivalent of bunny rabbits running around with machine guns, amazed at their newfound lethality while lacking the internal devices that stop them from killing their own kind. This is not a very pretty picture.

In some respects, theories of instinctual human aggression seem to mirror conservative/realist views. If people have an aggressive instinct that leads to war, this would seem to be consistent with the conservative/realist view of humans as an imperfect and imperfectible species. Very few realists, however, have explicitly adopted any particular biologically based theory of human aggression. Realists who emphasize the imperfections of human nature are generally content to rely on generic assertions of human lust, greed, passion, and will to power. Nonetheless, it is difficult to avoid the similarities. And when those who believe in the innateness of human aggression turn their attention to international relations, they tend to adopt a decidedly realist approach. The arguments of Lorenz, Ardrey, and Fox appear to echo George Kennan's lament that humankind cannot do anything about the beast within.

The Curse of Intelligence: Abstract Thought

Even if Lorenz is correct about the presence of an aggressive instinct and the consequences of our ability to produce lethal weapons, this in and of itself could not completely account for war. The argument presented thus far could just as easily lead to the expectation that individuals would be running around killing each other *as individuals* on a grand scale, but this is not what happens. War is not merely lethal aggression; it is a particular form of lethal aggression. It is lethal aggression among, and in the name of, organized political or social entities. The aggressive instinct alone cannot account for the prevalence of war. It may be a necessary part of explaining war, but it is not sufficient. As Robin Fox explains, "There is no question that aggression is related to war, just as sex is related to prostitution…. but neither *institutional* form follows directly from the basic instinctive drive."[13] If we want to understand why people use particular types of lethal aggression, we need to add something to the equation. In a sense, there are three questions we need to answer in order to understand war: Why do people engage in aggression? Why do they engage in lethal aggression? Why do they engage in that type of lethal aggression we call war? Thus far, we have only answered the first two questions. Lorenz and Morris give the final explanatory answer by incorporating our capacity for abstract, symbolic thought and our innate sociability. These things combine with our innate aggressiveness to explain war.

Though Lorenz and those who agree with him see people as animals with instincts, they would also concede that we are probably less instinctual than other creatures because of our intelligence and capacity for abstract, conceptual thought. It is this intelligence that distinguishes us from other creatures and has allowed us to thrive in an evolutionary sense. Paradoxically, it is also our intelligence, our greatest asset, that is the root cause of our war problem. It is our intelligence, after all, that provides us with the ability to invent the weapons that place our species in danger. It is also this intelligence that "aids and abets" our innate aggressiveness to produce war as we know it. Not only does our intelligence allow us to think of new ways to kill each other, it allows us to conceive the world in ways that are part of the equation of war. As Lionel Tiger and Robin Fox explain, "Only an animal with brain enough to think of empires and try to manage them could conceive of war. Only an animal so wedded to the truths inside his skull could travel many miles and expend endless, precious calories and hours and artifacts to destroy others."[14] Animals fight over things—mates, food, territory—but people fight over ideas: "Since we are an animal that lives primarily by ideas and only secondarily by instincts … we react fanatically when our basic ideas—those that decide our identities individual and collective—are threatened."[15] And as Lorenz states with characteristic boldness, "All the great dangers threatening humanity with extinction are direct consequences of conceptual thought."[16]

The notion of a collective identity hints at another fundamental human motivation—our "natural tendency to form in-groups."[17] Though not necessarily an instinct, this is a basic human motivation deeply ingrained in our psyche over the course of human evolution. Again echoing ideas we saw in conservative and realist thought, people are seen as inherently social creatures who inevitably identify themselves with social groups. These social groups provide people with a sense of belonging. Earlier in human history, they were also essential to survival in very harsh environments in which individuals on their own stood little chance. Group identity, however, requires differentiating one's in-group from out-groups. Anthony Storr elaborates: "We define ourselves, psychologically as well as physically, by comparison and differentiation. Colour does not exist except in relation to another colour; personality has no meaning except in relation to other personalities…. The maintenance of human identity requires oppositions."[18] People are generally able to maintain peaceful relations within their in-group when an out-group exists upon whom aggression can be directed. But it is this division of human society into distinct social groupings combined with our attachment to ideas that accounts for the particular form of lethal aggression we call war. Fox combines these elements in observing that "the occasions for each particular will vary … but ultimately 'we' fight 'them' because they are different, and their difference is threatening in its challenge to the validity of these ideas we live by. Thus, all wars are ideological wars."[19]

For Lorenz, Morris, Fox, and Storr, war results from this combination of an innate aggressive instinct, the ingenuity that produces artificial weapons, our capacity for conceptual thought, and the divisive consequences of social group formation. Our creativity and intelligence are at the same time humankind's greatest blessing and curse. The result is gloomy assessments about the fate of humankind. Though Lorenz tries to maintain a cautious optimism that human reason and culture may eventually prevail over instincts, he is usually drawn to more pessimistic conclusions: "An unprejudiced observer from another planet, looking upon man as he is today, in his hand the atom bomb, the product of his intelligence, in his heart the aggressive drive inherited from his anthropoid ancestors, which this same intelligence cannot control, would not prophesy long life for the species."[20]

Culture, Social Learning, and War

Those who believe that war is the inevitable result of human nature are fond of pointing to the frequency of war in human history. Using the figures cited at the beginning of this chapter, we can point to less than three hundred years of peace in the last fifty-six centuries. Robin Fox confidently asserts that "war has been a constant of human history."[21]

But what do we mean that war has been a constant? That every person, every society, and every nation is "constantly" engaged in warfare? This is patently not the case. Even though war is constant in that at any given moment a war is probably going on somewhere in the world, this is not the same as saying that people and nations are constantly at war. Others look at the evidence and are struck by war's rarity, not its constancy. In any given year, the vast majority of people and nations are at peace, not war. The majority of the world's people has never fought in a war, has never killed anyone, and probably never will. Furthermore, few people will go to their graves considering their life diminished and incomplete if they have never engaged in warfare. Does this sound like aggression, lethal aggression, and war are an integral part of human nature? Could we say the same thing about other supposedly instinctual behaviors such as sex? Thus, many reject the empirical characterization of war as a constant feature of human existence. And if war is actually a rare event, then its inevitability and connection to what we call human nature can be called into question.

Beyond the fact that war does not seem to be a constant, those who fall on the nurture side of the debate see several other major flaws in human nature explanations. First, the presence of peaceful societies contradicts the expectations of human nature theories. Second, when we look at the actual behavior of those who fight wars, there are reasons to believe that people may in fact possess a fundamental aversion to lethal aggression. Third, even if there is an individual instinct of aggression, this may have nothing to do with war. Finally, it is more compelling to view aggression, lethal aggression, and war as the result of social learning, cultural norms, conditioning, peer influence, and other environmental forces that shape our behavior.

Peaceful Societies

If a behavior is an inherent part of human nature, it seems reasonable that it would be universal. That is, the behavior, or the desire to engage in that behavior, should be evident across time and space in human existence. Again, sex provides a less controversial example. Almost every human being has sexual desires and every human society we know of has engaged in sexual behavior. Those groups that refrain, such as religious leaders or sects that take vows of celibacy, do not claim to be free of sexual impulses but merely pledge to resist the desire. There are no examples of sexless human societies.

One piece of evidence that seems to contradict the notion that war is inherent in human nature is the presence of so-called **peaceful societies**. Anthropologists have identified contemporary and historical human societies that appear to have no experience with anything we would recognize as war, lacking even a word or concept for it. Commonly cited examples include the Copper Eskimo in Canada, the Polar Eskimo of Greenland, the King Bushman of the Kalahari Desert in Africa, and the Hutterites and Zuni Indians in North America.[22] These are obviously societies of human beings, but they seem to have no war. In the modern world, there are also countries that have gone generations without any involvement in war, such as Sweden and Switzerland. If there is such a thing as human nature and human instincts, we can assume people in these societies share them. Nonetheless, war does not seem to be part of their world. For many, this refutes the idea that war is the consequence of some essential, inherent human characteristic.

Studies of peaceful societies remain controversial. A few supposed examples, such as the Tasaday in the Philippines, a primitive society supposedly discovered in the 1970s, have been exposed as frauds. Most, though genuine, raise questions of interpretation. For example, does any act of violence by someone from one group against someone from another group constitute an act of war? When a group attacks another group and takes food or captures mates, are these raids or wars? These debates aside, there are certainly a few examples of human societies that appear to have been free of war. But many remain skeptical of their larger significance, pointing to both their rarity and very unusual characteristics. After emphasizing that only a handful of peaceful societies exist "in all the world and all history," Joshua Goldstein observes that "these societies all exist at the fringes of ecological viability, in circumstances where small communities are scattered in a harsh environment with little contact with each other. These cases demonstrate the extremes to which one must go to find a society where war is absent."[23] Still, their existence cannot be denied. Examining the evidence on peaceful societies, Lawrence Keeley concludes that "while it is not inevitable, war is universally common and usual."[24] The fact that war does not seem to be inevitable is a theoretically significant finding, even if it does not offer much of a basis for practical hope.

The Reluctance to Kill

An intriguing body of evidence that might help us assess the relative merits of the nature–nurture positions is studies of how people behave in battle, a subject often ignored by those interested in the causes of war. Do people in battle behave as

peaceful societies Historical and contemporary human communities that do not engage in war or even have a concept for it. These rare examples are often used to counter the argument that human nature or instincts make war an inevitability.

innate aggression theories would lead us to expect? There are reasons for doubt. In fact, some argue that the evidence seems to point exactly in the opposite direction: people possess an instinctual aversion to lethal aggression.

There are surprisingly few systematic studies of how soldiers behave in battle, though anecdotal accounts are common. Before World War II there were no such studies. To fill this gap, the U.S. Army decided that it needed to understand what soldiers did in combat in order to train them better. Under the direction of General S. L. A. Marshall, soldiers were asked what they did in combat. Their answers came as something of a shock. Marshall found that only 15 to 20 percent of soldiers actually took part by firing their weapons at the enemy. The majority, in even situations where their lives might be endangered, refrained. Though they did not run from battle, they would simply not fire their weapons or would do so in ways that posed little danger of actually killing anyone. In recent years Marshall's work has come under intense criticism, with some even questioning whether he really conducted the research on which his conclusions rest.[25] Despite these critiques, many continue to accept Marshall's findings, particularly because they seem consistent with other historical evidence of large amounts of ammunition fired resulting in comparatively few casualties.

The idea that soldiers might purposely try to miss the enemy did not occur to most people. But unless they were simply very bad shots, this should have been the unavoidable conclusion. There is also evidence that soldiers are particularly unlikely to fire their weapons when they are isolated—that is, when others are unable to witness their refusal to shoot.[26] This has become known as the phenomenon of **nonfirers**, or the reluctance of soldiers to fire their weapons to kill the enemy.

nonfirers Soldiers who refuse to fire their weapons in battle (or deliberately try to avoid killing enemy soldiers). Those who reject instinctual theories of aggression and war often cite the frequency of this phenomenon.

How are we to interpret this evidence? For critics of the innate aggression thesis, this avoidance of lethal aggression hardly seems consistent with the notion that the violence of war is the consequence of some uncontrollable instinct. The fact that soldiers are even more reluctant to engage in lethal aggression when they are isolated from commanding officers and comrades suggests that social pressures are essential to get soldiers to do things they would prefer not to do. What sort of instinct can this possibly be when social pressure is so important and when so many soldiers refuse to kill, even when their own lives are in danger?

Some have gone so far as to suggest that studies on nonfirers point in precisely the opposite direction. General Marshall himself concluded that "the average and healthy individual … has such an inner and usually unrealized resistance towards killing a fellow man that he will not of his own volition take life if it is possible to turn away from the responsibility."[27] From these studies, the military learned that its training had been based on the faulty assumption that a soldier's fear of death was the major obstacle that the military needed to overcome. Marshall's study demonstrated that the real problem was countering the average soldier's reluctance to kill. And even after all the drills, training, indoctrination, social pressure, and threat of discipline, the military is not always successful in doing so. What kind of instinct is this when so much effort meets with so little success in eliciting the desired behavior?

War Is Violence, Not "Aggression"

One of the more powerful criticisms of the Lorenzian thesis begins with the seemingly odd assertion that war has nothing (or very little) to do with aggression in the first place. Ashley Montagu, perhaps the harshest critic of theories of instinctual innate aggression, makes the startling argument that "the truth is—and this is perhaps the greatest paradox of all—motivationally, war represents one of the least aggressive forms of man's behavior."[28] This is an observation that takes some time to digest. How can the slaughter of millions on the battlefields of World War I represent one of the *least* aggressive forms of human behavior? There are two keys to understanding Montagu's argument—his careful use of the word *motivationally* and the distinction between violence and aggression.

An analogy might help illuminate Montagu's point. If asked why people eat, we might say that they do so to satisfy their hunger: Hunger provides the motivation for the behavior of eating. But does this mean that every time someone eats they were hungry? No. Certainly hunger leads people to eat, but people often eat for reasons that have nothing to do with hunger, such as habit, social custom, or some psychological compulsion. Sometimes we eat lunch just because it is lunchtime. Other times we might sooth our depression with a pint of ice cream. Everyone eats at social functions such as wedding receptions, though it is unlikely they all happen to be hungry at the same time. Thus, even though hunger drives people to eat, we cannot assume that every act of eating is motivated by hunger.

Similarly, although aggression may lead to violence, we cannot assume that every act of violence is motivated by aggression. To use another analogy, a robber who shoots a bank teller refusing to hand over the cash is using violence to get something, not because of any internal desire or drive to violence. Had the teller handed over the cash, the shooting would not have taken place. The robber was motivated by greed, not aggression. This is sometimes referred to as **instrumental violence** to accomplish a particular objective. It is very different, for example, from someone who kills in an aroused state of anger in the midst of a heated argument. Though there is certainly some relationship between violence and aggression, they are not one and the same.

instrumental violence
Violence used in pursuit of some identifiable objective.

Montagu sees the violence of war much as we would the bank robber shooting the teller. War is the organized, planned use of violence by political units in pursuit of political, economic, or social objectives. People who make the decision to go to war are rarely participants themselves, and the soldiers who engage in the violence are picked out of their normal settings (often by force) and transported to distant battlefields. Montagu quotes French biologist Jean Rotund: "In war ... man is much more like a sheep than a wolf. War is servility ... but not aggressiveness."[29] The soldier's behavior "is not instinctively but state-directed toward the enemy."

Montagu's argument is clever and formidable. Even if one concedes almost all of Lorenz's major points, Montagu's basic position still stands. Even if people do have instincts, and even if aggression is one of them, this does not necessarily bring us any closer to understanding war. Theories of human aggression only help us understand war if war is aggression. It is the linkage between war and aggression

Basic training at Paris Island, North Carolina, designed to turn civilians into soldiers. The transformation is as much psychological as physical.

Source: ©Andrew Lichtenstein/The Image Works

that Montagu rejects, which makes theories of aggression interesting but largely irrelevant. To understand war one needs a theory of violence, not a theory of aggression. For Montagu, war has as much, or as little, to do with aggressive instincts as gluttonous Roman feasts where people stuffed their faces for hours and days on end had to do with their hunger.

Social Learning and Conditioning

Human nature, by definition, is constant. War, on the other hand, is variable. Some periods in history reveal more frequent and intense wars than others: The first half of the twentieth century was much bloodier than the last half of the nineteenth century. Certain countries and societies have been extremely warlike in the past but are relatively pacific today: The Swedes, for example, used to be fierce warriors. Within societies some groups are more warlike than others: The Amish refused to fight in World War II, even though almost all other citizens participated enthusiastically. Whenever we see behavior that varies over time, across societies, and even within societies, we are dealing with something that has a significant social or cultural component. The variability of war across and within societies and cultures leads anthropologist Margaret Mead to conclude that warfare "is an invention like any of the inventions in terms of which we order our lives, such as writing, marriage, cooking our food instead of eating it raw, trial by jury, or burial of the dead, and so on."[30] If war is an invention, it can be "uninvented"; if it is learned, it can be unlearned.

When we say that war is a learned behavior, we do not mean in the narrow sense of classroom instruction. Learning refers to the complex process by which people are socialized—that is, how they learn what behaviors are acceptable in what settings. People learn in a variety of ways. One mechanism is observation and imitation. As children grow in any culture, they see how others behave in certain situations and they are likely to behave likewise in similar settings. People also learn through a process of **stimulus and response** based on the consequences of a particular behavior. If people are rewarded for a behavior, they are more likely to engage in it. Conversely, if people are punished for a behavior, they are inclined not to repeat it. "Rewards" and "punishments" need not be financial but can also be praise, prestige, adulation, criticism, denigration, and social ostracism. To use a common example, no instinct leads most kids to dress alike, but they inevitably follow the same trends and fads. Why? Because they fear the social "punishments" and value the social "rewards" that result from various forms of dress.

These processes of socialization that shape our behavior are so pervasive and subtle that people are usually not even conscious of what is going on.

There are potentially many forms and manifestations of aggression. All cultures have norms and rules regarding what types of aggression are acceptable. Almost nobody believes that it is permissible to beat up a cashier who gives you the wrong change or kill someone who cuts you off on the highway. These are forms of aggression our society rejects and punishes. As a result, they are also extremely rare. But if the government sends you a draft notice, cuts your hair, puts you in uniform, and sends you thousands of miles away to kill people you have never met, you are praised. If you are very good at it, you may even get medals. Richard Barnet put his finger on the irony that "Individuals get medals, promotions and honors for committing the same acts for the state for which they would be imprisoned in any other circumstance."[31] Even if there is some instinctual basis for aggression, the forms this aggression will take and the contexts in which it is deemed acceptable are shaped by our culture. These sorts of distinctions are culturally, not biologically, determined.

Many also see a connection between a culture's treatment of aggression and violence in general and war. In this context, it is interesting to look at the subtle and not-so-subtle messages our culture conveys about violence. War films provide an obvious example. At any time of day we can turn on the television and see films that portray the mass slaughter of people in war in positive and heroic terms. Such films are not relegated to late-night viewing accompanied with warnings about mature content. The same holds for video stores, where there are usually never any restrictions on who may rent films containing incredible levels of violence in the name of "entertainment." David Grossman emphasizes in graphic terms society's disparate treatment of violence and sex by pointing out that "in video stores the horror section repeatedly displays bare breasts (often with blood running down them), gaping eye sockets, and mutilated bodies. Movies rated X with tamer covers are generally not available in many video stores and, if they are, are in separate adults-only rooms. But horror videos are displayed for every child to see."

stimulus and response Used in social learning theory to indicate that human behavior is shaped by social stimuli—that is, people engage in those behaviors for which they receive social rewards and refrain from behaviors that bring social punishment.

The implicit lesson is that "breasts are taboo if they are on a live woman, but permissible on a mutilated corpse."[32]

What message does this send about acceptable and unacceptable behavior? Why is boxing, in which two men (and, now, women) beat each other up, considered a "sport" that can be seen on television at any time of day but certain types of nudity need to be reserved for after 9 p.m.? Why do people automatically become tempting presidential candidates because they successfully fought a war and not because they avoided one? These examples can be multiplied many times over. What is the cumulative effect of these images, messages, and practices over the course of a lifetime?

Though images and messages conducive to war are prevalent even in times of peace, in times of war they become dominant in the form of propaganda. How war propaganda portrays the enemy is particularly significant. In his study *Faces of the Enemy*, Sam Keen demonstrates that societies at war tend to use very similar visual and rhetorical imagery to portray the enemy as less than human.[33] Whether the picture is a savage brute or, at the most extreme, the depiction of the enemy as an animal or vermin, the prevalence of such imagery, and perhaps the need for it, might tell us something. The process of constructing enemy images has been characterized as **dehumanization** or **pseudo-specification**, which is the tendency to view members of our own species as if they are not members of our species—that is, to falsely (hence *pseudo*) divide the human race into different species.[34] Keen and others argue that the process of dehumanization is an almost necessary component of war because "as a rule, human beings do not kill other human beings. Before we enter into warfare or genocide, we must first 'dehumanize' those we mean to eliminate.... The hostile imagination systematically destroys our natural tendency to identify with others of our species.... The purpose of propaganda is to paralyze thought ... and to condition individuals to act as a mass."[35] This dehumanization is particularly important for soldiers who have to do the actual fighting and killing. As Richard Holmes explains, "The legitimate need to defuse deep-seated cultural and psychological taboos against killing is an inseparable part of military training." Part of this "defusing" of taboos is the "almost obligatory dehumanisation of the enemy."[36] William Broyles, an author and veteran of the Vietnam War, pointed out that the soldier's greatest weapon was not his rifle but rather his idea of the enemy.[37]

The ubiquity of dehumanization in war is both depressing and grounds for hope. It is depressing in the sense that we are able with such ease to create and accept images of other people as less human than ourselves. On another level, however, the fact that we do this suggests that people may indeed have a resistance to killing other people whom they recognize as like themselves. If we were able to kill other human beings on a grand scale while viewing them as being on a par with ourselves, this would be even more troubling. This process of dehumanization also suggests the importance of culture and socialization for understanding war. It is obvious that inhibitions against killing, the social "taboos" Holmes refers to, can be created. The fact that efforts need to be taken to overcome these taboos suggests there is nothing natural or inevitable about it. The images and ways of thinking that allow or encourage people to do the killing that is part of war are

dehumanization The portrayal and/or perception of other people as less than human.

pseudo-specification Viewing other humans as if they were not members of one's own species. Wartime propaganda depicting the enemy as animals or insects facilitates this process. Those who see war as a culturally and socially learned phenomenon often cite this tendency.

social and cultural artifacts. There is nothing inevitable or biologically instinctual about them. Part of the answer to problems of war, then, is how we make the "taboos" against killing stronger while refraining from actions to "defuse" these taboos. If we can consciously "defuse" these taboos, we can also reinforce them.

Are People Peaceful?

If people are not by nature aggressive and warlike, does this mean that we are by nature peaceful? Most alternatives to instinctual theories of aggression do not make this leap. It does not automatically follow that a negative view of human nature needs to be replaced with a positive one. Logically, one can also claim that people have no "nature" at all—that is, we are not naturally good or bad, moral or immoral, rational or irrational, peaceful or warlike. Exactly where social learning theorists come down on this question is often unclear. When David Grossman refers to the difficulties of overcoming people's fundamental resistance to killing, he does appear to suggest the existence of an innate peaceful disposition. Similarly, in pointing to the essential role played by dehumanizing rhetoric and propaganda, Sam Keen also seems to lean in this direction because he suggests that people would be much less inclined to kill other people if they recognized them for what they are—other people. If ethological theories of instinctual aggression lent support to conservatism and realism, these approaches would appear more in line with liberalism's optimistic view of human nature.

Most social learning theories, however, reject the very notion that we can identify a "human nature" independent of social circumstances. There are no (or almost no) human behaviors that are not socially derived. It is not a matter of social forces or pressures reinforcing or defusing preexisting drives, but rather of creating them in the first place. Skepticism about the utility of the concept of human nature is a characteristic of Marxist, feminist, and (obviously) constructivist approaches. These approaches may differ in terms of which social forces are viewed as most important in shaping human behavior. For Marxists it is the underlying economic forces that drive behavior, whereas for feminists it is beliefs about gender roles and gendered social and political institutions. From these perspectives, debates about the relationship between war and human nature are pointless and distracting.

"Death to the Fascist Beast" proclaims a Soviet poster from World War II. The enemy, of course, is not another human being but a snake. Who mourns the death of snake? Such dehumanization of the enemy is a common feature of war propaganda.

Source: Laski Diffusion/Getty Images News/Getty Images

Conclusion

Within this debate about whether war is a biological, instinctual phenomenon or a cultural and social invention there is actually more common ground than might be assumed. We can see the point of convergence in Robin Fox's admission that war as an institutional form of aggression does *not* follow directly from what he sees as the basic instinctual drive. In order to make the link between the supposed instinct of aggression and war, Lorenz, Fox, and Morris are compelled to add cultural and social factors. The causal arrow is not a direct one. That is, even though they see aggression, like sex, as an instinct, they admit that culture conveys norms about the contexts in which aggression is acceptable. War is seen as the result of both nature and nurture—a basic drive and a culture that channels it. The question then becomes whether those cultural and social factors that complete the link between the aggressive instinct and war can be altered. If so, the instinctual drive, even if it exists, becomes irrelevant. One need not always eliminate the "root" cause in order to deal with a problem. We do not need to get rid of the sun to eliminate skin cancer; sunscreen can do the job. Thus, the real debate is not about whether there is an aggressive instinct that leads to war, but rather whether those social and cultural forces that everyone seems to agree are a significant part of the equation of war can be altered.

To say that war is a learned behavior is not necessarily a basis for much optimism if the practical obstacles to unlearning war are insurmountable. Tiger and Fox are led in this direction when they ask: "If we are not by nature violent creatures, why do we seem to inevitably create situations that lead to violence?" After conceding that a substantial element of learning and social conditioning goes into war, they conclude that "we are creatures who are by nature *easily* aroused to violence, we *easily* learn it, and we are wired to create situations in which the arousal and learning readily take place and in which violence becomes a necessity [emphasis added]."[38] When Tiger and Fox look at the world, they are amazed by how little it takes to get people to fight and kill. The ease with which they think this is done indicates to them that it strikes a cord with a deep and fundamental part of our being.

Others are struck by how difficult it is to get people to kill: a lifetime of socialization into a culture of violence, social pressure, and government compulsion to get soldiers to serve, and a continual dehumanization of the enemy. According to Sam Keen, "*Homo hostilis* must be created by the media and the institutions that subject him to a constant indoctrination by way of hero stories, ideology, rationalizations, tribal myths, rites of passage, and icons of the enemy ... The entire institutional and symbolic apparatus of society is necessary" to get people to engage in war. And even after all this, "the effort is successful for only a small minority." Rather than being easy, Keen thinks "it is so *difficult* to mold us into killers [emphasis added]."[39]

CHAPTER SUMMARY

■ The nature–nurture debate is one that appears in some guise in virtually all social sciences. At issue is which behaviors are best understood as reflections of basic and unalterable aspects of human nature or instincts as opposed to cultural conditioning and socialization. Whether or not the persistence of war can be explained by some element of human nature is only one specific manifestation of this more general debate.

■ A "nature" or instinctual explanation for war often begins with the assumption that the persistence of such an irrational and destructive behavior must be rooted in some uncontrollable drive.

■ The ethologist Konrad Lorenz claimed that human beings possess an aggressive instinct, just like virtually every animal. For animals this instinct is "adaptive" because it helps preserve, protect, and perpetuate species.

■ Lorenz divided the animal kingdom into two categories—lethal and nonlethal creatures. In the case of nonlethal animals, there is no danger that aggression will become lethal aggression. Hamsters do not kill each other because they cannot. Though lethal animals can kill members of their species, over the course of evolution they tend to develop inhibiting mechanisms that prevent them from killing.

■ The problem is that humans are essentially nonlethal animals who have become lethal because of the technology afforded by our intellectual evolution. Humans can now kill their own kind with great efficiency and often at great distances. This adaptation has happened so quickly, however, that inhibiting mechanisms have not emerged to prevent humans from killing members of their own species.

■ When we add the basic human need for social belonging and identity to this aggressive instinct and weapons, the result is war.

■ The proposition that war is an inevitable reflection of human nature or instincts can be criticized in several ways. The existence of peaceful societies and others that can go for very long periods without war suggest that war is not an integral feature of human existence. The lengths to which societies and governments must go to get soldiers to engage in war seems to undermine the instinctual argument. Finally, some question whether it even makes sense to view war as aggression. Perhaps war is better viewed as instrumental, socially organized violence that has little or nothing to do with individual aggression.

■ Instead of viewing war as rooted in human nature or instincts, it can also be viewed as a cultural or social practice shaped and reinforced in countless and often subtle ways as people are bombarded with messages, lessons, images, and ideas about violence and war.

■ Perhaps a better approach is to understand war as a result of instincts *and* learning. In this view, aspects of human nature certainly can lead to war, but they do not do so on their own. It is a matter of whether those elements of human nature that contribute to war are reinforced or discouraged by learning and socialization.

CRITICAL QUESTIONS

1. Why does it matter if war is instinctual or learned?

2. Assuming that war is a learned behavior, how is it "learned"?

3. Why might it be best to view war as the result of both instinctual and learned behaviors??

4. What does the phenomenon of "pseudo specification" tell about the instinctual basis of war?

5. Why is the distinction between aggression and violence potentially critical for understanding the causes of war?

KEY TERMS

appeasement gesture, 115   evolutionary lag, 116   Konrad Lorenz, 113   pseudo-specification, 124

dehumanization, 124   hierarchy, 114   nature-versus-nurture, 112 spacing, 114

disequilibrium, 116   instinct, 113   nonfirers, 120   stimulus and response, 123

ethologists, 113   instrumental violence, 121 peaceful societies, 119

FURTHER READINGS

The classic statement of the instinctual aggression thesis is Konrad Lorenz, *On Aggression* (New York: Harcourt, Brace and World, 1963). The major critique of this position is Ashley Montagu, *The Nature of Human Aggression* (Oxford: Oxford University Press, 1976). The classic statement of the social/cultural perspective is Margaret Mead, "Warfare Is Only an Invention—Not a Biological Necessity," *Asia* 40 (1940): 402–405. A more recent example of this position is David Grossman, *On Killing* (Boston: Little, Brown, 1995). Another interesting perspective on this debate is found in Joanna Burke, *An Intimate History of Killing* (New York: Basic Books, 1999). And Barbara Ehrenreich's *Blood Rites: Origins and History of the Passions of War* (New York: Henry A. Holt, 1998) tries to integrate and transcend the nature–nurture divide.

WAR AND HUMAN NATURE ON THE WEB

www.conflicthistory.com
Though not focused on human nature, a very interesting site detailing the history of war beginning in 680 A.D.

www.culture-of-peace.info
Organization dedicated to creating a "culture of peace" to replace the "culture of war." The group's perspective in terms of the issues discussed in this chapter is obvious.

www.seedsofpeace.org
Organization dedicated to promoting peace by teaching children to "develop trust and empathy for another."

The underlying assumption guiding the organization's mission obviously places it on the "nurture" side of the debate over war and human nature.

www.globalissues.org/HumanRights/Media/Military.asp
Discusses and illustrates media coverage of war issues as well as propaganda.

www.classroomtools.com/faces2.htm
Contains some good examples of the dehumanizing propaganda that is often part and parcel of modern war.

NOTES

[1]Anthony Storr, *Human Aggression* (New York: Atheneum, 1968), introduction, n.p.

[2]These are the conclusions of Norman Cousins cited in Francis Beer, *Peace Against War* (San Francisco: Freeman, 1981), p. 20.

[3]Sigmund Freud, *Civilization and Its Discontents* (New York: W. W. Norton, 1961), p. 58.

[4]Desmond Morris, *The Naked Ape: A Zoologist's Study of the Human Animal* (New York: McGraw-Hill, 1967); Lionel Tiger and Robin Fox, *The Imperial Animal* (New York: Holt, Rinehart and Winston, 1971); and Robert Ardrey, *The Territorial Imperative* (New York: Atheneum, 1966).

[5]Konrad Lorenz, *On Aggression* (New York: Harcourt, Brace and World, 1963).

[6]Ibid., p. 237.

[7]James A. Schellenberg, *The Science of Conflict* (New York: Oxford University Press, 1982), p. 32; Morris, *Naked Ape*, pp. 149, 159.

[8]Morris, *Naked Ape*, p. 156.

[9]Ibid., p. 156.

[10]Lorenz, *On Aggression*, p. 241.

[11]Ibid., p. 241.

[12]Ibid., p. 242.

[13]Robin Fox, "Fatal Attraction: War and Human Nature," *The National Interest* (Winter 1992/1993), p. 15.

[14]Tiger and Fox, *Imperial Animal*, p. 212.

[15]Fox, "Fatal Attraction," p. 17.

[16]Lorenz, *On Aggression*, p. 238.

[17]Morris, *Naked Ape*, p. 176.

[18]Storr, *Human Aggression*, p. 57.

[19]Fox, "Fatal Attraction," p. 16.

[20]Lorenz, *On Aggression*, p. 49.

[21]Fox, "Human Attraction," p. 13.

[22]David Fabro, "Peaceful Societies," in *The War System: An Interdisciplinary Approach*, ed. Richard Falk and Samuel Kim (Boulder, CO: Westview, 1980), pp. 180–203; Lawrence Keeley, *War Before Civilization: The Myth of the Peaceful Savage* (New York: Oxford University Press, 1996), pp. 27–32.

[23]Joshua Goldstein, *War and Gender* (New York: Cambridge University Press, 2001), pp. 32–33.

[24]Keeley, *War Before Civilization*, p. 32.

[25]See Roger J. Spiller, "S. L. A. Marshall and the Ratio of Fire," *RUSI Journal* (Winter 1988), pp. 63–71.

[26]See S. L. A. Marshall, *Men Against Fire* (New York: Morrow, 1967). The implications of this study are addressed by David Grossman, *On Killing* (Boston: Little, Brown, 1995), pp. 15–16, 29–30; Sam Keen, *Faces of the Enemy: Reflections of the Hostile Imagination* (San Francisco: HarperCollins, 1986), p. 178; and Richard Holmes, *Acts of War: The Behavior of Men in Battle* (New York: The Free Press, 1985), pp. 325–327.

[27]Quoted in Grossman, *On Killing*, p. 29.

[28]Ashley Montagu, *The Nature of Human Aggression* (New York: Oxford University Press, 1976), p. 273.

[29]Ibid., p. 272.

[30]Margaret Mead, "Warfare Is Only an Invention—Not a Biological Necessity," in *War*, ed. Leon Bramson and George Goethals (New York: Basic Books, 1964), p. 270.

[31]Richard Barnet, *Roots of War* (New York: Atheneum, 1972), p. 13.

[32]Grossman, *On Killing*, p. 310.

[33]Keen, *Faces of the Enemy*, p. 25.

[34]See David Barash and Judith Eve Lipton, *The Caveman and the Bomb* (New York: McGraw-Hill, 1985), pp. 139–140.

[35]This dehumanization is particularly.

[36]Holmes, *Acts of War*, p. 366.

[37]From the documentary video by Sam Keen, *Faces of the Enemy*, produced in 1987 and based on the previously cited book.

[38]Tiger and Fox, *Imperial Animal*, p. 208.

[39]Keen, *Faces of the Enemy*, p. 178.

Are People (or Men) "Hard Wired" for War?

The relationship between war and human nature is one of those abstract and theoretical topics that people rarely talk about explicitly. Assumptions about human nature are more likely to remain implicit in most discussions of war and peace. Occasionally, however, those who reject or endorse the notion of a tie between innate human aggressiveness and war feel compelled to restate their position. One of the more powerful and succinct attempts to refute the instinctual theory of violence and war in recent decades is the Seville Statement on Violence. Drafted in 1986 by a group of natural and social scientists, the statement was subsequently adopted by the United Nations Educational, Scientific and Cultural Organization (UNESCO) as an official expression of its position on war and violence. This statement, included here, clearly reflects the view that war is a culturally learned and conditioned practice. Yet there are those who remain convinced that some connection must exist between aggressive instincts and war, though the exact nature of the connection is sometimes unclear. This viewpoint is evident in the ABC News report that follows, on recent research relating to the question of whether people (or men in particular) are "hard wired" for war.

In many respects, these two documents reflect the basic positions presented in this chapter, though often with different emphases and evidence. To what extent do they reflect the familiar arguments in the nature–nurture debate, and in what ways do they move beyond the traditional positions? In particular, how might the evidence about war and violence for societies with a high proportion of young males fit into the larger nature–nurture debate? Though this evidence is presented as if it supports an instinctual theory of violence and war, can one also argue that it is more in line with cultural theories (and even feminist theories)?

PERSPECTIVE 1 Seville Statement on Violence, Spain, 1986

Subsequently Adopted by UNESCO at the Twenty-fifth Session of the General Conference on November 16, 1989[1]

Believing that it is our responsibility to address from our particular disciplines the most dangerous and destructive activities of our species, violence and war; recognizing that science is a human cultural product which cannot be definitive or all-encompassing; and gratefully acknowledging the support of the authorities of Seville and representatives of the Spanish UNESCO; we, the undersigned scholars

[1] Source: Seville Statement on Violence, Spain, 1986, subsequently adopted by UNESCO at the Twenty-fifth Session of the General Conference on November 16, 1989 © 1986. Used by permission of UNESCO.

from around the world and from relevant sciences, have met and arrived at the following Statement on Violence. In it, we challenge a number of alleged biological findings that have been used, even by some in our disciplines, to justify violence and war. Because the alleged findings have contributed to an atmosphere of pessimism in our time, we submit that the open, considered rejection of these misstatements can contribute significantly to the International Year of Peace.

Misuse of scientific theories and data to justify violence and war is not new but has been made since the advent of modern science. For example, the theory of evolution has been used to justify not only war, but also genocide, colonialism, and suppression of the weak.

We state our position in the form of five propositions. We are aware that there are many other issues about violence and war that could be fruitfully addressed from the standpoint of our disciplines, but we restrict ourselves here to what we consider a most important first step.

IT IS SCIENTIFICALLY INCORRECT to say that we have inherited a tendency to make war from our animal ancestors. Although fighting occurs widely throughout animal species, only a few cases of destructive intra-species fighting between organized groups have ever been reported among naturally living species, and none of these involve the use of tools designed to be weapons. Normal predatory feeding upon other species cannot be equated with intra-species violence. Warfare is a peculiarly human phenomenon and does not occur in other animals.

IT IS SCIENTIFICALLY INCORRECT to say that in the course of human evolution there has been a selection for aggressive behavior more than for other kinds of behavior. In all well-studied species, status within the group is achieved by the ability to co-operate and to fulfill social functions relevant to the structure of that group. 'Dominance' involves social bindings and affiliations; it is not simply a matter of the possession and use of superior physical power, although it does involve aggressive behaviors. Where genetic selection for aggressive behavior has been artificially instituted in animals, it has rapidly succeeded in producing hyper-aggressive individuals; this indicates that aggression was not maximally selected under natural conditions. When such experimentally-created hyper-aggressive animals are present in a social group, they either disrupt its social structure or are driven out. Violence is neither in our evolutionary legacy nor in our genes.

IT IS SCIENTIFICALLY INCORRECT to say that humans have a "violent brain." While we do have the neural apparatus to act violently, it is not automatically activated by internal or external stimuli. Like higher primates and unlike other animals, our higher neural processes filter such stimuli before they can be acted upon. How we act is shaped by how we have been conditioned and socialized. There is nothing in our neurophysiology that compels us to react violently.

IT IS SCIENTIFICALLY INCORRECT to say that war is caused by "instinct" or any single motivation. The emergence of modern warfare has been a journey from the primacy of cognitive factors. Modern war involves institutional use of personal characteristics such as obedience, suggestibility, and idealism, social skills such as language, and rational considerations such as cost-calculation, planning, and information processing. The technology of modern war has exaggerated traits associated with violence both in the training of actual combatants and in the preparation of support for war in the general population. As a result of this exaggeration, such traits are often mistaken to be the causes rather than the consequences of the process.

We conclude that biology does not condemn humanity to war, and that humanity can be freed from the bondage of biological pessimism and empowered with confidence to undertake the transformative tasks needed in this International Year of Peace and in the years to come. Although these tasks are mainly institutional and collective, they also rest upon the consciousness of individual participants for whom pessimism and optimism are crucial factors. Just as a "wars begin in the minds of men," peace also begins in our minds. The same species who invented war is capable of inventing peace. The responsibility lies with each of us.

Seville, 16 May 1986

David Adams, Psychology, Wesleyan University, Middletown, CT, U.S.A.
S.A. Barnett, Ethology, The Australian National University, Canberra, Australia
N.P. Bechtereva, Neurophysiology, Institute for Experimental Medicine of Academy of Medical Sciences of the U.S.S.R., Leningrad, U.S.S.R.
Bonnie Frank Carter, Psychology, Albert Einstein Medical Center, Philadelphia (PA), U.S.A.
José M. Rodriguez Delgado, Neurophysiology, Centro de Estudios Neurobiologicos, Madrid, Spain
José Luis Diaz, Ethology, Instituto Mexicano de Psiquiatria, Mexico D.F., Mexico
Andrzej Eliasz, Individual Differences Psychology, Polish Academy of Sciences, Warsaw, Poland,
Santiago Genovés, Biological Anthropology, Instituto de Estudios Antropologicos, Mexico D.F., Mexico
Benson E. Ginsburg, Behavior Genetics, University of Connecticut, Storrs, CT, U.S.A.
Jo Groebel, Social Psychology, Erziehungswissenschaftliche Hochschule, Landau, Federal Republic of Germany
Samir-Kumar Ghosh, Sociology, Indian Institute of Human Sciences, Calcutta, India
Robert Hinde, Animal Behavior, Cambridge University, Cambridge, U.K.
Richard E. Leakey, Physical Anthropology, National Museums of Kenya, Nairobi, Kenya
Taha H. Malasi, Psychiatry, Kuwait University, Kuwait
J. Martin Ramirez, Psychobiology, Universidad de Sevilla, Spain
Federico Mayor Zaragoza, Biochemistry, Universidad Autonoma, Madrid, Spain
Diana L. Mendoza, Ethology, Universidad de Sevilla, Spain
Ashis Nandy, Political Psychology, Centre for the Study of Developing Societies, Delhi, India
John Paul Scott, Animal Behavior, Bowling Green State University, Bowling Green, OH, U.S.A.
Riitta Wahlstrom, Psychology, University of Jyvlskyla, Finland

PERSPECTIVE 2   Hard-Wired for War? Violence Part of Being Human (1999)

June 2, 1999[2]

Humankind has lived through a hideously violent century.

World War I, World War II, wars in Vietnam, Cambodia, China, Bangladesh, Korea, Nigeria and elsewhere have extinguished millions upon millions of lives. The killings continue today in Sierra Leone, East Timor and Sudan, to name a few.

[2] Source: Hard-Wired for War? Violence Part of Being Human from ABCNEWS.com (June 2, 1999). Courtesy of ABC NEWS.

Waging war is nothing new for us humans. Bloody conflicts from the Crusades to Kosovo have been a hallmark of our history. Which raises the questions: Is such behavior simply part of human nature? Are we hard-wired for war?

There's certainly no definitive answer. But enough scientists have looked into our past—and present—to shed a bit of light on why we do what we do.

New Environment, Old Brain

When interpreting human behavior, it's best to remember that the strongest human instincts are to survive and reproduce. What we need to satisfy those instincts hasn't changed much since our primitive ancestors roamed the globe; it's about getting enough food, water and mates.

Like it or not, write Leda Cosmides and John Tooby, co-directors of the Center for Evolutionary Psychology at University of California, Santa Barbara, "our modern skulls house a Stone Age mind."

Though modern-day aggressors may not be aware of it, those primitive instincts drive their behaviors too. A strong group benefits from attacking a weaker group if in the process the aggressors gain fertile lands, reliable water, and greater market share—any resources that improve their collective livelihood.

There's no denying that aggression has been a good survival strategy. Which is why we humans are genetically hard-wired to fight.

But what triggers that aggression and what can magnify it to the point of a Rwanda or a Kosovo?

Richard Wrangham of Harvard University sees two conditions necessary for what he calls "coalitional aggression," or violence perpetrated by groups rather than individuals. One condition is hostility between neighbors.

Human aggression got more organized with the introduction of agriculture about 10,000 years ago, says J. William Gibson, author of *Warrior Dreams: Violence and Manhood in Post-Vietnam America*. With farming came the concept of land ownership—and defense—and the development of more complex and organized societies. Suddenly, there was more to covet, more to protect and more people around to help do both.

The other condition for group violence is an imbalance of power great enough that aggressors believe they can attack with virtually no risk to themselves. Majorities have persecuted minority groups, whether religious, ethnic or tribal, again and again, believing they're immune from punishment. The tangled turmoil in the former Yugoslavia is only the most immediate example.

Animals Do It, Too

Humans aren't the only ones who gang up. Chimpanzees, with whom we share 98.4 percent of our DNA, are another. Wrangham, who wrote *Demonic Males: Apes and the Origins of Human Violence*, describes five chimps attacking one. Four will hold the victim while the fifth breaks bones and rips out the victim's throat or testicles.

Examples of taking such advantage of imbalances of power are rare in the animal kingdom because that kind of behavior requires a sophisticated level of coordination and cooperation. However, both chimps and humans are certainly capable of it.

"There's always conflict in societies," says Neil Wiener, an associate professor of psychology at York University, "The issue is, when do these conflicts erupt into violence?"

Young Men More Likely to Wage War

According to Wiener, a critical factor in the escalation from conflict to violence, is the percentage of young, unmarried males in a population. He and co-author Christian Mesquida studied the demographics of 153 nations since the 1960s, comparing those that have remained peaceful and those that have been at war. Turns out, there is a difference.

"Whenever young people represent a relatively small portion of the population … times are relatively tranquil," they wrote in their study. "But when a large portion of a country's population is young there is likely to be turmoil and political violence."

Examples include the Congo, Rwanda, Sudan, even the former Yugoslavia.

Aggressive wars seem to happen when the percentage of young men—ages 15 to 29—reaches 35 to 55 percent of the adult male population. "I think that young males are hard-wired to form groups … and under the right circumstances, to act aggressively in groups," Wiener says.

If Wiener is right, some areas ripe for conflict are China and India—the world's two most populous nations—as well as Pakistan, parts of the Middle East and Africa.

So, with evolution and demographics against us, what can be done to lessen the chances of war?

Natural selection over millions of years has brought us to this violent point and it won't be swinging the other way any time soon.

Besides, says Wiener, "what drives this stuff ultimately is demographics."

That may be, but there are certain actions that can be taken to derail our baser human tendencies.

Peace has a better chance in a more interconnected world, where all nations keep tabs on one another. International watchdogs big and small—the United Nations, NATO, Amnesty International and others—are already helping to keep imbalances of power in check.

Population control can reduce conflicts by making sure that every nation has adequate resources.

Such efforts may not bear fruit for generations, but they do provide seeds of hope for a more peaceful twenty-first century.

6

Free Trade

Key Controversy: Does Free Trade Benefit All?

A basic principle of the post–World War II global economic order, free trade has been part of a liberal prescription for international relations for almost two hundred years. Free trade is seen as desirable because it allows consumers to buy what they need and want for the lowest price regardless of where in the world it is produced. Free trade serves the interests of consumers (and everyone is a consumer) while promoting economic efficiency. Just as nations practice free trade within their borders, they should practice free trade across their borders. Critics reply that there are times when, and very good reasons why, nations might not want to pursue free trade. Marxists and feminists (and even many liberals) fear the impact of free trade on economically vulnerable segments of society. Even if free trade does promote economic efficiency, there may occasionally be other social considerations and values that take precedence. Realists, who tend to think about international economics in terms of national security, worry about becoming dependent on other nations for essential commodities. These intellectual conflicts are likely to fuel political conflicts over trade for some time to come. ■

During the 2008 primary contests for the Democratic presidential nomination, there was a lot of talk about negative impact of trade on American industries and workers. As Senators Obama and Clinton stumped for votes in the industrial Midwest "rust belt," "the campaign has looked like a contest over who hates free trade more: Obama has argued that free trade agreements like NAFTA are bought and paid for by special interests, while Clinton has emphasized the need to 'stand up' to countries like China." Opposition to free trade, or at least concern about its consequences, is neither new nor limited to Ohio and Michigan. Public opinion polling reveals why the Democratic candidates were so anxious to voice skepticism about free trade. In a 2008 poll, for example, more than two-thirds of respondents said they supported trade restrictions to protect American industries threatened by foreign competition, the highest level of support for such measures since pollsters started asking the question in the 1980s.[1]

Though supporters of free trade usually rely on the same arguments, opposition is more varied. Some fear that global trade is increasingly benefiting wealthy nations and multinational corporations at the expense of already the poor and marginalized in the world economy, locking developing nations in a cycle of poverty and misery. Others worry that workers in the advanced industrialized nations are seeing their wages and social welfare benefits reduced as they are forced to compete with cheaper labor in places like China and Vietnam. Many argue that the world's environment and resources are being sacrificed to satisfy the demands of growth and corporate profits. And still others charge that international economic institutions and multinational corporations are taking power and authority away from democratically elected governments, eroding national sovereignty in the process.[2] Whatever the specifics might be, anxiety about trade is likely to remain at the forefront of political debate in the United States and elsewhere for some time to come. Thus, it is important that we understand the historical origins of free trade, as well as the arguments for and against it.

The Liberal International Economic Order

How, when, and why did free trade become so central to the global economy? In general terms, the current global economy was created after World War II under the leadership of the United States, which emerged from the war as the world's dominant military power and most powerful economy. The global economy it created was shaped by the recent historical experience of war and depression, U.S. economic interests, and a commitment to liberal economic theory. The system became known as the **Liberal International Economic Order (LIEO)**, the cornerstone of which is the principle of free and open trade. As Stephen Krasner explains, "The fundamental objective of American foreign economic policy after the Second World War was to establish a regime in which the impediments to the movement of capital and goods were minimized."[3]

In formal terms, several institutions were designed to help create and sustain a liberal international order. The **World Bank**, officially known as the International Bank for Reconstruction and Development, and the **International Monetary Fund (IMF)** were established in 1944. The World Bank is a global lending agency whose initial purpose was, as its official name suggests, to assist postwar reconstruction. The IMF's major function was to provide short-term assistance to nations with balance of payments difficulties. The final element of the postwar liberal order was the **General Agreement on Tariffs and Trade (GATT)**. Created in 1947, GATT was the most important institution for international trade because its fundamental goal was the reduction of international tariffs (taxes on goods imported from other countries) to the lowest possible level. After 1947, there was a series of negotiations (known as GATT *rounds*) to reduce tariffs. Today, largely as a result of these efforts, "the average tariff on U.S. imports is a meager 3 percent—down from 20 percent in

Liberal International Economic Order (LIEO) The post-World War II international economic order embodying the traditional liberal preference for free and open trade as a means of promoting economic efficiency and prosperity.

World Bank Originally the International Bank for Reconstruction and Development, now one of the major institutions of the post-World War II international economic order. Its initial function of providing aid in the rebuilding of societies destroyed by the war has been replaced with a more controversial focus on aiding and assisting the world's developing nations.

International Monetary Fund (IMF) One of the critical institutions of the post-World War II Liberal International Economic Order. Initially intended to help nations deal with balance of payments deficits, since the 1960s it has played an increasing and controversial role in assisting developing nations.

General Agreement on Tariffs and Trade (GATT) World organization of nations created in 1947 for the purpose of reducing tariffs and other obstacles to international trade. Resulted in a series of meetings and agreements in subsequent decades (so-called GATT Rounds) that reduced tariffs. Replaced in 1995 with the World Trade Organization (WTO).

1940."[4] In January 1995, GATT became the **World Trade Organization (WTO)**. Even though the world has never achieved a completely free and open trading system with no barriers to the sale of goods and services among nations, this is the ideal, the principle, upon which these institutions are based.

The critical question, however, is *why* the United States and others believe that a liberal order based on free and open trade is a desirable objective. What was the motivation behind the creation of the LIEO? Part of the explanation lies in the perceived lessons of the Great Depression and World War II. After World War II, American decision makers traced the causes of the Great Depression of the 1930s to the **economic nationalism** of the 1920s. That is, throughout the 1920s the world's major economies, the United States included, used ever-increasing tariffs and quotas to protect domestic industries from foreign competition. These tariffs and quotas in the United States and elsewhere undermined world trade, contributing to the Great Depression. The Great Depression, in turn, was seen as critical to the failure of democracy and the rise of fascism, which then led to world war. Free trade, it was believed, was necessary to prevent a repetition of this course of events. In this way free trade was seen as providing political as well as economic benefits: If economic nationalism brought depression, fascism, and war, free trade would bring prosperity, democracy, and peace.

There was also a good measure of self-interest driving the creation of the LIEO. Since the United States emerged from World War II as the only intact industrial economy, free trade was clearly in its interests—after all, where else would other nations buy things? But the commitment to free trade was also based on a broader conviction that it would benefit all in the long run. By promoting economic growth and prosperity, a system of free and open trade would be, to use a common metaphor, a rising tide that lifts all boats. It is this assumption of mutual gains from free trade that derives from the intellectual rationale for the postwar liberal order.

The Case for Free Trade

"About two hundred years ago," Douglas Irwin observes, "free trade achieved an intellectual status unrivaled by any other doctrine in the field of economics." And even though it has "been subjected to intense scrutiny over the two centuries since that time, free trade has, by and large, succeeded in maintaining this special position."[5] Why have economists generally embraced free trade? To answer this question, we must return to the economists who first made the case for free trade, particularly **Adam Smith** (1723–1790) and **David Ricardo** (1772–1823). Even though Smith and Ricardo lived two centuries ago, the arguments in favor of free trade have changed little over the intervening centuries.

In their time Smith and Ricardo advocated free trade in place of prevailing policies and doctrines of **mercantilism**, a policy designed to increase the wealth of each state by rigging trade rules to promote exports and reduce imports. The rationale was that if more goods were sold than bought, more gold would flow in than out, increasing the state's wealth. Mercantilist doctrine viewed trade as a means to

World Trade Organization (WTO) Created in 1995 as a successor to GATT, the World Trade Organization is supposed to enforce international trade rules promoting free and open trade.

economic nationalism Policies designed to protect domestic industries from foreign competition, usually by using tariffs and quotas as barriers to imports.

Adam Smith (1723-1790) A liberal economist and philosopher who argued for free trade. Coined the famous expression "the invisible hand" to describe the operation of a free market economy.

David Ricardo (1772-1823) English economist known for his defense of international free trade and theory of comparative advantage.

mercantilism Trade policies designed to increase the wealth and power of a state vis-à-vis other states.

increase a state's relative wealth and power. It was economics in the service of politics. Smith and Ricardo opposed mercantilism, because such trade restrictions reduced economic competition, promoted economic inefficiency, and harmed consumers by making them pay more for goods.

The Origins of Free Trade

Corn Laws In the first half of the 1800s, these laws gave English farmers protection from foreign competition. Supporters of free trade claimed they protected inefficient farmers and forced consumers to pay too much for basic food items. Attempts to repeal these laws succeeded in 1846.

Richard Cobden (1804–1865) Prominent figure in the British Liberal Party and a leading crusader for free trade and the repeal of the Corn Laws.

division of labor Individuals and/or nations specializing in the production of certain commodities.

theory of comparative advantage The idea that all nations benefit when they produce those commodities each produces most efficiently. David Ricardo argued that free trade allows nations and consumers to benefit from their different comparative advantages.

Conflicts over mercantilism came to a head in the middle of the 1800s, when England faced intense domestic debate over the repeal of what were known as the **Corn Laws**. These laws gave British growers of wheat, corn, and other grains a monopoly on the domestic market through government subsidies as well as restrictions on the export and import of grains. Mercantilist policies resulted in British consumers paying higher prices for grain and bread because access to cheaper products from abroad was restricted. These laws benefited wealthy landowners at the expense of the poor, who were still excluded from politics. Influenced by the writings of Smith and Ricardo, **Richard Cobden** (1804–1865), a prominent figure in the British Liberal Party, pushed for the repeal of the Corn Laws on the grounds that they benefited a few at the expense of many. Though the Anti-Corn Law League had been around since 1838, it wasn't until 1846 that the laws were repealed, marking the emergence of free trade as a theory converted into policy.[6] The historical popularity of free trade has fluctuated ever since. For the next few decades of the mid-to late 1800s, trade barriers declined, especially within Europe. The last decades of the nineteenth century saw waning enthusiasm for free trade. The years between World War I and World War II also witnessed increasing barriers to international trade.

Smith and Ricardo's defense of free trade was based on two relatively simple economic concepts, the division of labor and comparative advantage. The **division of labor** refers to the simple fact that people do not (and should not) produce everything they need and want. Few of us build our own houses, make our own clothes, educate our children, or even change the oil in our cars. In all but the most primitive economies, there is a division of labor: People specialize in the production of certain commodities and trade what they produce with the producers of other commodities. In modern economies this exchange occurs through the medium of currency, not barter. When we buy things with money, we are really exchanging what we produce (and got paid for) for things others have produced. This is the most efficient way to organize an economy. If we all had to make and provide for ourselves the things we need and want, we would end up with fewer of the things we want and need. Thus, an efficient economic system at any level (local, national, or international) is based on a division of labor. And if there is a division of labor, trade is necessary to meet people's wants and needs.

But why does this trade have to be free, unencumbered by taxes, tariffs, and other barriers? To answer this we look to Ricardo's **theory of comparative advantage**, which has been described as "the greatest gift that economic wisdom ever bestowed upon humankind."[7] Simply stated, the theory holds that people and nations should produce whatever they produce most efficiently and cheaply (i.e., those commodities for which they have an advantage compared to others) and trade with others specializing in what they do best. Nations possess different resources and assets that lead to different comparative advantages—some nations produce oil or other scarce commodities, some have plentiful and cheap labor, some have agriculturally productive land, and others have favorable geographical locations for trade. Japan will probably never produce its own oil. Saudi Arabia will never grow rice. Landlocked Chad will never be a center of shipping. And Canada is unlikely to produce much coffee. If these nations want to meet their peoples' needs and desires, they need to specialize in the trade of particular commodities. **Autarky**, or complete self-sufficiency, is not a practical or economical option.

Autarky A policy of self sufficiency in which a state attempts to cut itself off from the outside world. A policy of economic autarky would attempt to meet all of society's needs from its own resources.

In his *Principles of Political Economy and Taxation*, Ricardo illustrated his theory using the example of Portugal and England producing wine and cloth, arguing that Portugal produced good, cheap wine (while England did not) and England produced good, cheap cloth (while Portugal did not). It is a division of labor and free trade that allows English and Portuguese consumers to have both good and cheap wine and cloth.[8] In the words of Adam Smith, "If a foreign country can supply us with a commodity cheaper than we ourselves can make it, better buy it of them."[9]

Let us use a more familiar example to illustrate the economic logic of comparative advantage. The citizens of Vermont and Florida occasionally like to have maple syrup and orange juice as part of their breakfast. How should these desires be satisfied? One option is that each state could produce both juice and syrup. Producing maple syrup would be no problem for Vermont because the climate conditions are ideal. Orange juice would be another matter, requiring the construction of huge greenhouses to grow orange trees. This can be done. Vermonters *could* make their own orange juice. But the cost of production would be high. The reverse can be said of orange juice (easy) and maple syrup (difficult and expensive) production in Florida. What to do? Ricardo's answer was simple—each state should specialize in producing that commodity for which it has a comparative advantage and trade the commodity with others producing commodities for which they have an advantage. Vermonters make maple syrup, Floridians make orange juice, and they trade. Everyone gets what he wants for the lowest price.

Not everyone will be happy, however. Free trade will chase Vermont's orange juice producers out of business. Who, after all, would pay several more dollars a gallon for orange juice from Vermont than juice from Florida? For the orange juice producers of Vermont to survive, an import tax would have to be applied to artificially raise the price of juice from Florida. The reverse would have to be done to protect maple syrup producers in Florida. But Ricardo would think it a folly if Vermont's orange juice producers and Florida's maple syrup producers were kept in business. Protection would simply promote economic inefficiency and increase prices to consumers. Certainly some are harmed by free trade in the short term, most notably Vermont orange juice producers and Florida maple syrup producers. But from a larger, long-term perspective, everyone is better off as a result of the efficiency that comes from free trade.

From the standpoint of economic theory, tariffs and other barriers to imports are bad because they distort the market. In the free market, prices convey information to consumers about who is producing a commodity most efficiently. People then reward efficient producers by buying their lower-priced goods and punish the inefficient by not purchasing their products. When these purchasing decisions are aggregated, inefficient producers are driven out of business. When prices are artificially raised (or lowered) by government intervention, this information is not conveyed to consumers. As a result, inefficiency is not punished and efficiency is not rewarded. And in the long run the inefficient use of resources serves no one's interests.

Free Trade Within Nations, Free Trade Among Nations

Interestingly, virtually all nations practice free trade within their borders. In the United States one of the federal government functions under the Constitution is to prevent the adoption of restrictions on interstate trade. The government of Tennessee, for example, cannot impose taxes on cars imported from Michigan in order to protect the jobs of workers at a production plant located in that state. This would be an illegal restraint on interstate commerce. Everyone would probably agree that it would be a disaster if individual states within the United States could impose tariffs on goods coming from other states. The harm to the American economy if individual states pursued protectionism policies would be immense.

Advocates of free trade argue that the logic supporting free trade *within* nations applies to trade *among* nations. If it makes sense to practice free trade between Minneapolis and St. Paul or Vermont and Florida, it makes just as much sense to practice free trade between the United States and Germany or Japan and Botswana. The economic logic of free trade is not altered merely because a political boundary is crossed. As Jagdish Bhagwati explains, "If one applies the logic of efficiency to the allocation of activity among all trading nations, and not merely *within* one's own nation—that alone would ensure that goods and services would be produced where it could be done most cheaply."[10] We can refer to this argument as the "logic of extension"—extending the logic that justifies free trade within nations, which virtually no one questions, to trade among nations.

The Primacy of the Consumer

The interests of consumers are at the heart of the case for free trade. But it is important to realize that for Smith and Ricardo the distinction between producers and consumers is somewhat artificial—everyone is both a consumer and a producer. And as consumers, people are *always* better off buying what hey want and need for the lowest possible price regardless of where it is produced—across town, across the state, another state, or the other side of the world. It should not matter where an item is made. Consumers are better off because this leaves them with more money to buy other things we want and need. Consumers are never better off paying more.

This argument contains an implicit assumption about the compatibility of individual and collective interests. That is, if every individual consumer in a community is better off, it follows that the community as a whole is better off. In the case of free trade, this means that what serves the best interests of every American consumer, serves best interests of the United States as a whole. The individual and collective interest is in harmony. Ricardo makes this implicit assumption explicit: "Under a system of perfectly free commerce, each country naturally devotes its capital and labor to such employments as are most beneficial to each. The pursuit of individual advantage is admirably connected with the universal good of the whole."[11]

Here the liberal roots of free trade are most apparent. One of the key assumptions of liberalism is the existence of a harmony of interests. This is also the underlying assumption of free market capitalism in general and free trade in particular: Each individual and each nation pursuing their own economic interest results in a long-term situation where the interests of all are advanced. There is no conflict in terms of the economic interests of individuals and nations. In promoting economic efficiency, a system of free trade works to the benefit of all. To use some technical terminology, international trade is not a **zero-sum game** in which one consumer's or nation's gain is someone else's loss, but rather a **positive-sum game** in which all can benefit simultaneously. Economist and Nobel Laureate Paul Krugman, a leading advocate of free trade, emphasizes the harmony of interests in an essay with the telling title "The Illusion of Conflict in International Trade." If trade is treated as something involving conflicts of interests among nations, Krugman fears that "trade will be treated as war, and the current system of relatively open world markets will disintegrate.... And that will be a shame ... [because] the conflict among nations that so many policy intellectuals imagine prevails is an illusion; but is it an illusion that can destroy the reality of mutual gains from trade?"[12] It would be impossible to state the liberal argument more clearly: Conflict is an illusion.

Advocates of free trade view trade restrictions such as tariffs and quotas as policies that advance and protect special interests at the expense of the public interest. A tariff on imported automobiles, for example, serves the short-term interests of the domestic automobile industry. Although this may seem like a good idea to some, such policies merely protect a relatively inefficient industry from competition, remove incentives to become more efficient, and increase the price people pay for automobiles. This decreases the amount of money they have to spend on other things they want and need. The benefits of protectionism may be immediate and tangible to that sector of the economy, but the benefits are short-lived and illusory and come at the expense of consumers.

Contemporary Challenges to Free Trade

Even though free trade has been the cornerstone of the postwar order, the ideal of completely open trade has never been achieved. All nations continue to impose an array of tariffs and other restrictions. Even the United States, for example, imposes tariffs of 32 percent on acrylic sweaters, 17 percent on polyester bras, 16 percent on canvas handbags, and 28.5 percent on drinking glasses costing less than 30 cents a piece.[13] As Findlay and O'Rourke note, "it is safe to say that the majority of the world's population in 2000 lived in economies that had higher manufacturing tariffs than on the eve of the Great War."[14] Nations have also proven very ingenious in devising methods of protectionism. The most common alternatives are **nontariff barriers**, regulations on imported commodities that serve

zero-sum game A situation in which one actor's gain is another actor's loss (as opposed to a positive-sum game, in which actors can all gain simultaneously).

positive-sum game A "game" or situation in which the actors involved can all gain or benefit at the same time.

nontariff barriers Policies designed to inhibit trade and imports without imposing direct tariffs on imports. Safety regulations that make it nearly impossible for foreign producers to sell their goods are an example.

the same purpose as outright tariffs. Regulations requiring imported agricultural goods to meet certain quality and inspection requirements are a prime example. Although these safety requirements seem reasonable enough, if they result in imported goods sitting on docks for days to be inspected, this can be tantamount to an outright ban.

Government subsidies also violate the logic of free trade. If a government gives money to a company that enables it to sell its product for a price that does not accurately reflect the costs of production, this is as much a violation of the principle of comparative advantage as a tariff that raises prices. When politicians accuse other countries of **dumping**, this is what they mean—selling something on the world market for less than it costs to produce. Perhaps nowhere has this been a greater problem than in the area of agricultural subsidies. Developing nations complain bitterly that subsidies to farmers in the United States and Europe allow them sell their products on the world market at reduced prices, driving down the price of many commodities developing nations produce.

dumping Selling commodities to other nations for less than it costs to produce them, often made possible by government subsidies to industries and producers.

The persistence of agricultural subsidies illustrates why even when nations agree in principle that free trade is a good thing, it is difficult to maintain. The problem is that even if free trade is in everyone's long-term best interests, there are short-term losers: companies go out of business and workers lose their jobs. Such is the nature of economic competition and efficiency. These companies and workers are seldom comforted by the economic logic that they will be better off in the long run. As the chairman of the U.S. Federal Reserve, Ben Bernacke, explains, "the social and political opposition to openness can be strong … because changes in the patterns of production are likely to threaten the livelihoods of some workers and the profits of some firms, even when these changes lead to greater productivity." When this happens, as it inevitably will under free trade, "the natural reaction of those so affected is to resist change, for example, by seeking the passage of protectionist measure."[15] And politicians often cave into such pressures. President George W. Bush's decision to impose tariffs on imported steel during his first term, despite his commitment to free trade, is but one of many examples. That steel tariffs were favored by constituencies in Midwestern states with critical electoral votes, such as Ohio and Pennsylvania, was surely more than coincidence. The political temptation is sometimes to be a **free rider**—that is, let others practice free trade while you do not. The free rider enjoys all the benefits but pays none of the costs of free trade. The general problem is that political incentives do not always coincide with economic logic. What is good in terms of winning the next election is not always good for the economy in the long run.

free rider When an actor enjoys the benefits of policy without paying its share of the costs associated with that policy.

When we hear about disputes between the United States and its major trading partners in Western Europe and Japan, there are frequent accusations of unfair trade practices. These disputes largely usually involve accusation of free riding: We practice free trade while they do not. The charge of "cheating" embodies this dilemma. But many contemporary conflicts over trade go further and are more deeply rooted than this. It is not merely the difficulty of actually practicing free trade when everyone agrees it would be desirable. The problem is that there is disagreement about whether free trade is always the best policy and the circumstances under which free trade might be a bad idea. There are some compelling arguments

A protest against the North American Free Trade Agreement (NAFTA). Though the agreement passed, many were, and remain, concerned about the consequences of free trade with nations with lower wages and weaker regulations.

Source: Bob E. Daemmrich/Sygma/Corbis

against free trade, and these tend to be more widely accepted in Europe and Japan than in the United States. There are alternatives to the theory (some might say ideology) of free trade.

What's Wrong with Free Trade

Free trade is difficult enough to maintain even when policymakers believe it to be the right policy. This difficulty is, of course, magnified when free trade is viewed as detrimental. Though it borders on heresy in contemporary economics to suggest that free trade might be undesirable, some have voiced reservations ever since Ricardo first made his case. There are very few who believe that nations should never practice free trade or that foreign imports should always be subject to tariffs and quotas. No one seriously believes that economic autarky is possible or desirable. The argument against free trade really amounts to skepticism about whether free trade is always preferable. Even skeptics agree that much of the time, maybe most of the time, open trade is wise. But, they argue, there are times when, and very good reasons why, nations should not trade freely. The objection is that free trade has become an ideology, particularly in the United States, with critics being viewed as the equivalent of flat earthers. Paul Krugman, for example, suggests that anyone who does not see the wisdom of free trade is stupid and uniformed. The notion that there is any intellectually respectable argument against free trade is simply not entertained. But the fact is that Adam Smith and David Ricardo have not been alone in thinking about international trade, and not everyone who has thought seriously about the issue has reached the same conclusion.

After spending several years in Asia, columnist and author James Fallows was struck by how many there think about international trade compared to the United States. One symptom of this divergence is the popularity of the German economist **Friedrich List** (1789–1846). Most Americans can get an economics degree without ever having read List; one certainly hears a lot less about him in the United States than they do about Adam Smith and David Ricardo. Fewer still have actually read List's *The National System of Political Economy* (1841), probably the most powerful critique of Smith and Ricardo.[16] In Europe and Asia, however, List's work remains influential. List did not argue that nations should never practice free trade. He did not reject free trade in principle, and this point needs to be emphasized. Much of the time and for most commodities, List thought free trade was a good idea. Instead, List argued that Smith and Ricardo failed to recognize that there were also certain circumstances in which, for very legitimate reasons, states might be wise to depart from the logic of free trade.

List offered a decidedly conservative or realist critique of liberal trade doctrine. This will become evident as we deal with his major arguments. Yet, List's criticisms are not the only ones present; critics have looked at free trade from other perspectives as well. Marxist critiques analyze free trade within the general context of international capitalism. Feminists often worry about the impact of trade on women, an issue they think is usually ignored. Interestingly, these seemingly odd ideological bedfellows make many of the same arguments. This paradox is reflected in the somewhat unusual coalition that has emerged in opposition to the economic aspects of contemporary globalization in which many on the political right and left find themselves aligned.

Friedrich List (1789–1846) German economist critical of David Ricardo and free trade. Rejected the liberal notion that individuals advancing their own interests inevitably serve the interests of the larger community or nation. Argued that nations need to approach trade from the perspective of the national interest and the interests of the community as a whole.

More Efficient, But So What?

The first major justification for free trade is that it promotes economic efficiency. When production and trade are based on comparative advantage, efficient producers survive and inefficient ones go out of business. On purely economic grounds, critics of free trade concede the point: Free trade does promote economic efficiency. But so what? This does not automatically settle the matter. Merely because something is the most economically efficient thing to do, does this automatically imply that it should be done? Not necessarily. This would be the logical conclusion only if economic efficiency were the be-all and end-all of economic policy. In the real world, however, people and societies try to balance a variety of values and considerations.

Societies follow policies all the time that are inconsistent with strict standards of economic efficiency. For example, most societies spend the majority of their healthcare dollars on people in their last few years of life when they are no longer economically productive. If societies allocated resources based solely on economic efficiency, there would certainly be other areas where this money could be better spent. If we adopted policies simply on the grounds of economic efficiency, what sort of healthcare systems would we have? What would we do with people who were no longer economically productive? Why do we spend all this money on the economically unproductive elements of our society? We do so because other values influence our decisions. Economic efficiency is only one consideration. Demonstrating that a policy promotes economic efficiency is an important component of policy debates, but it does not end these debates. Thus, even if we concede the economic efficiency argument for free trade, this does not settle the policy debate.

Applying this point to international trade, we can easily imagine considerations that lead states to reject free trade, even if the result is less economic efficiency. Take, for example, the case of Japan and rice. Rice produced in Japan costs a lot more than rice grown in the United States. If the logic of free trade and comparative advantage was followed, Japan's rice farmers would almost certainly be chased out of business as Japanese consumers bought the cheaper foreign rice. But for the Japanese, rice is more than just another food; it is a deeply meaningful part of their history and culture. A Japan that did not grow its own rice would be like a Germany that produced no beer, a France that produced no wine or cheese, or a United States that produced no automobiles. To an economist, these are just commodities and it should not matter where they are made. But most people are not economists. If preserving this part of Japanese culture requires them to restrict foreign imports, can we say this is wrong?

Other countries have a similar problem with small family farms, which are almost never competitive with huge agricultural corporations or cheap foreign imports. Pure free trade would almost certainly spell death for these small farms. But what if people want to preserve a quaint countryside with small villages and cute farms they can return to on the weekends? If a government restricts cheaper imports in order to protect these farms and the rural way of life, is this necessarily a wrongheaded policy? Smith and Ricardo would think so, but others might not be so dismissive. If the people of a country have to pay a bit more for their peppers and tomatoes in order to protect a way of life they value, perhaps this is an acceptable trade-off in which strict considerations of economic efficiency lose out to broader cultural concerns.

The particulars of cases will vary, but the general point is to question the underlying assumption implicit in arguments for free trade that economic efficiency is *the* basis on which policies should be chosen. John Gray, a critic of free trade, concedes the economic argument: "There is not much doubt that the free market is the most *economically efficient* type of capitalism," and "for most economists that ends the matter."[17] For Gray and others, obviously, it does not. Instead, economic efficiency is merely *a* criterion, the beginning of the debate, not its end.

Free Trade Within Nations, Free Trade Among Nations

Friedrich List's most forceful criticism of free trade stemmed from what he saw as their failure to recognize the critical difference between domestic and international society. When this distinction is taken into account, it does not follow that free trade among nations makes as much sense free trade within nations Domestically people need not worry about becoming dependent on others for things they need because this dependence is unlikely to be used as leverage. For example, pro-choice shoppers do not worry that the grocery store will withhold food until they change their position. Floridians do not have to worry that Vermont will refuse to sell them maple syrup unless they vote the right way in the presidential election. Within nations, people do not have to be concerned about their dependence on one another. Nations, however, need to worry about the potential security consequences of dependence as well as about shifts in economic power resulting from growth in other countries. International economics cannot be divorced from considerations of international politics. As Mark Thirlwell explains, "some are now scared by the success of globalization in creating powerful new competitors in global markets, while others are spooked by the security implications of the consequent redistribution of economic power."[18] Economists are happy if everyone becomes more prosperous; international strategists are not.

Thus, List argued that if a nation can produce commodities that it really needs, it should do so rather than become dependent on others, even if these commodities can be purchased more cheaply from abroad. Take, for example, steel or computer chips, essential commodities for a modern industrial and technological economy. Let us assume that country A can manufacture steel for $20 a ton and chips for $50 each. If country B can produce steel for $18 and chips for $40, what should country A do? Ricardo's advice would be clear: Country A should buy steel and chips from country B and get out of the steel and chips business rather than impose a tariff or quota on steel and chip imports in order to protect its own industries. For List, however, this would be ludicrous because if A becomes dependent on B for vital commodities, B will have power and leverage over A. To avoid becoming dependent on others who might seek to convert economic dependence into political power, it may be advisable for A to impose tariffs in order to stay in the steel and chip businesses even though these commodities could be purchased more cheaply from abroad.

Sometimes nations have no option. Japan, for example, needs oil but has no reserves of it own to exploit. Japanese oil independence is not an option. Furthermore, for most things it really does not matter if a nation becomes dependent on others. Being dependent on others for honey or sneakers is not the same as being dependent for oil or steel. A threat to embargo sneakers is unlikely to produce much political leverage. So for most commodities, free trade is best. List would simply argue that there are some vital commodities that nations should retain the ability to produce if they can, even if it is economically inefficient.

Some take this argument a step further, arguing that nations should use trade policy not merely to protect their industries but also to undermine industries in

The movement to emphasize fair trade in place of free trade is reflected in product labels providing information to consumers about which products meet the criteria.

other countries. Assume, for example, that country A produces steel for $20 a ton and B for $18. Under free trade, country A would go out of the steel business and buy its steel from B. But country A could stay in the steel business by imposing a tariff of $2 or more to protect its domestic steel industry. But country A could also subsidize its domestic steel industry and sell its steel on the world market at a loss (maybe $17 a ton) in order to drive country B out of the steel business and make it dependent on A. The goal is not merely to avoid dependence on others but to make them dependent on you. This turns the logic of free trade and comparative advantage on its head. This sort of **predatory pricing** is an example of what is sometimes referred to as **strategic trade policy**, or consciously using trade policy to enhance national power and leverage over others.

Even economists supportive of free trade concede that "Ricardo's theory did not cover every circumstance." As Clive Crook notes, "exceptions to its general rule (potential benefits from protecting 'infant industries,' for instance) were recognized long ago."[19] List was among those who argued for the need to protect **infant industries** from foreign competition. When a nation first produces a commodity, it might be difficult to compete with established producers elsewhere in the world. If the logic of free trade were applied, these industries would "die in the cradle," so to

predatory pricing Setting the price of a commodity with the intention of driving others out of business, even if this requires selling the commodity for less than it costs to produce.

strategic trade policy Policies designed to enhance national power and encourage other nations to become dependent as a means of gaining leverage over them.

infant industries Industries at early stages of their development, particularly when the same industries are already well developed (i.e., mature) in other nations.

speak. List pointed out that many industries in the United States and Britain developed behind a wall of protection before the adoption of free trade. Even when free trade was desirable in the long run, List saw a need for "temporary protective measures in countries passing through a certain state of development to ensure that they could trade on equal terms with more advanced countries."[20] Foreshadowing some of List's themes, Alexander Hamilton made a very similar argument in the early years of the American republic: "to maintain, between recent establishments of one country, and the long-matured establishments of another, a competition upon equal terms … is in most cases, impracticable."[21] So there are times when some level of protection from more efficient foreign competition is seen as necessary for industrial development.[22]

These types of policies and concerns derive from List's conviction that trade policy cannot and should not be separated from national security policy. In an anarchic world, nations must worry about security in ways that people and groups within nations do not. This is why free trade might not make as much sense among nations as it does within. The economic logic may be the same, but the political context is very different. Nations have to consider the implications of trade policy in terms of their power over, and dependence upon, others. List criticizes "Adam Smith's doctrine … [because it] ignores the very nature of nationalities, seeks almost entirely to exclude politics and the State, presupposes the existence of a state of perpetual peace and of universal union, underrates the values of national manufacturing power, and the means of obtaining it, and demands absolute freedom of trade."[23]

In the final analysis a nation's power rests on its ability to produce, not consume. In this sense, List's criticisms of, and reservations about, free trade reflect a realist perspective. His emphasis on the different environments in which states operate, his focus on economic production as the foundation of national power, and his concern about the consequences of dependence embodies and is consistent with a realist view of the world. Whereas liberals tend to see international trade as a positive-sum game in which all can become better off at the same time, List and realists are more inclined to approach trade as a zero-sum affair in which the gains of one are the losses for others. Recall that List titled his treatise *The National System of Political Economy*. He chose his title purposefully. List thought that Smith and Ricardo provided a theory of *private* political economy that spoke to the interests of individuals. List thought it necessary to approach issues of trade in terms of the interests of nations as well.

Consumers and the Nation

The consumer lies at the heart of the case for free trade because consumers are better off when they can buy things for the lowest price regardless of where it is produced. This allows them to buy more of what they want and need. And because everyone is a consumer, everyone's interests are advanced by free trade. Furthermore, if each individual in a nation is better off, it follows that the nation as a whole is better off. For critics of free trade, this logic is deceptively attractive but wrong. When individuals do what is in their best interest, this does not "add up" to the best interests of that community. Understanding why not requires some explanation.

Every day consumers are faced with discrete purchasing decisions. Someone goes to the mall to buy a pair of jeans and finds two pairs to choose from: One made in the United States costing $40 and the other made in Malaysia for $20. The two pairs are pretty much identical. In this situation most consumers would buy the cheaper pair because it would leave them $20 to buy other things. In the world of Smith and Ricardo, this is as it should be. This one decision by the consumer is good for that person and has no wider social or economic consequences. But if we take this one decision and multiply it by thousands and millions of identical decisions, there are larger social and economic consequences. Perhaps the plant making jeans in the United States will go out of business or the workers will have to accept lower wages. If the workers are fired, they will be collecting unemployment insurance that has to be paid for through other people's taxes. If enough factories go out of business, maybe the entire local community's economy will collapse. As factories leave and unemployment goes up, tax revenues go down. Schools have less money. As schools decline, the community's downward spiral accelerates. Crime may increase and the quality of life erodes. The problem is that we cannot reasonably expect individual consumers to calculate and take into account these larger consequences for every purchasing decision. Emphasizing this point, List asks, "Can the individual ... take into consideration in promoting his private economy, the defense of the country, public security, and the thousand other objects which can only be attained by the aid of the whole community?"[24]

Contrary to the liberal assumption that individual and collective interests are in harmony, List explicitly rejects this conflation: "nor does the individual merely by understanding his own interests best, and by striving to further them, if left to his own devices, always further the interests of the community."[25] It does not necessarily follow that whatever serves the best short-term interests of each consumer also advances the long-term interests of the community. In such situations it is reasonable for the government to step in and protect the interests of the larger national community. This is what governments do. As James Fallows points out, people live in nations and communities and "in the real world happiness depends on more than how much money you take home. If the people around you are also comfortable ... you are happier and safer than if they are desperate."[26]

How do we deal with this problem? One option is trade restrictions. To continue with our jeans example, the national government might impose a tariff to make the foreign jeans less attractive. Again, Fallows explains that "the answer to this predicament is to pay explicit attention to the welfare of the nation. If a consumer has to pay 10 percent more for a product made by his neighbors than for one from overseas, it will be worse for him in the short run. But in the long run, and in the broadest definitions of well-being, he might be better off."[27] One can see these types of concerns when the European Union (EU) considers new nations for inclusion. The EU is an organization of European states that essentially practice free trade among themselves. They are wealthy and prosperous nations with high wages and generous welfare states. When poorer nations with lower wages seek admission, the current members are often hesitant. If poorer nations with much lower wages are allowed to compete on a free basis, the fear is that this will exert downward pressure on wages throughout the EU. Regulations that determine who may and may not join the EU are in part designed to protect European workers from the effects of competing with much cheaper labor.

Although it is primarily realists who express concerns about the impact of free trade on the economic bases of national power and security, others worry about the effects on workers and the general standard of living. Marxists, for example, see free trade (which is part and parcel of global capitalism) as potentially harmful to workers in developing as well as developed countries. Because capital (i.e., multinational corporations) is free to set up shop wherever wages are lowest, the net effect of free trade is to push and keep wages down. Part of the problem is that on a theoretical level completely free trade should allow labor to move as freely as capital and commodities do. In the real world, however, this is not possible. Thus, businesses can go in search of the lowest wages anywhere in the world, but workers cannot go in search of the highest wages. This fundamental difference in the mobility of capital and commodities compared to labor places workers at a great disadvantage.

Feminists are also often critical of free trade and its consequences. They tend to agree with Marxists that workers in all parts of the world are harmed by free trade. But feminists also point out that women in particular usually bear the brunt. Because women often find themselves as second-class economic citizens, occupying the lowest-paying and most expendable jobs, their interests are usually the first to be sacrificed. Even many liberals, who are generally predisposed to free trade, worry about the potential consequences, especially unrestricted trade between nations at very different levels of development. There are also issues that go well beyond those mentioned already, such as the impact on the environment when factories are moved to low-wage countries with fewer environmental protections in place. But an overall concern about the impact of free trade on workers and other vulnerable groups unites critics from a very broad range of viewpoints.

Fair Trade or Free Trade?

Concerns about the impact of free trade, particularly between developed and developing nations, have been central to the increasingly vocal and visible movement for "fair trade" rather than free trade. On college campuses this is often seen in anti-sweatshop movements pressuring universities and others not to buy collegiate apparel produced in developing nations where workers are paid very low wages and work in unsafe factories. There are, however, at least three different conceptualizations of what fair trade entails united only by a belief that some are being disadvantaged (i.e., being treated unfairly) in the current liberal trading order.[28]

The first vision of fair trade tries to deal with the problem of free riders who enjoy access to foreign markets but restrict access to their own. The unfairness here is differential market openness in which free trade is essentially a one-way street. To remedy this problem, some propose that countries with open markets should demand reciprocity—i.e., that others open theirs as well. If the offending nation does not comply, restrictions should be placed its exports. According to this analysis, allowing others to protect their industries as they challenge yours is tantamount to unilateral economic disarmament. The hope is that threatened retaliation would induce others to open their markets, thereby expanding and strengthening free trade. Critics worry, however, that in practice the result might be vicious cycles of retaliation leading to a collapse of the global trading system.

The second vision of fair trade focuses on what many see as an unlevel playing field in which wealthy nations with high wages and workplace safety regulations have to compete with nations with much lower prevailing wages and weak systems of worker protection. The proposed solution is to negotiate trade treaties with provisions that level the field by requiring certain wage levels and labor standards. If a potential trading partner is unwilling to accommodate these demands, then it would not enjoy open access to your markets. In this analysis, it is workers and business in developed countries that are disadvantaged (i.e.. being treated unfairly) by being forced to compete with workers paid a lot less and businesses whose regulatory costs are much lower.

The third approach to fair trade may be most familiar because it is evident every time you buy a latte at Starbucks and see "fair trade" coffee for sale. Coffee and other fair trade products are designated as such by various organizations verifying that producers received a "fair" price for the commodity, often substantially higher than the prevailing market price. The hope is that wealthier consumers are willing to pay slightly more if they know the money is going to poor producers rather than rich corporations. On one level this version of fair trade does not necessarily run counter to free trade in that it relies on voluntary consumer choices, not government restrictions, tariffs and quotas. Consumers still have the option of buying cheaper products that reflect market prices. Nonetheless, there is an underlying assumption that free trade as commonly practiced works to the disadvantage of many, particularly producers in developing nations.

Conclusion

Conflicts over issues of international trade are likely to continue both among the world's major trading partners and within them. One source of these conflicts is the political ramifications of free trade. Even those who support free trade concede that even if everyone benefits in the long run, in the short term there are winners and losers. Free trade, when it works as it is supposed to, drives comparatively inefficient producers out of business. Industries go under, investors and stockholders lose money, and workers lose jobs. We cannot expect these groups to be happy about their losses. In democratic societies, where the success of politicians depends on keeping people happy, there will continue to be strong political pressures to protect domestic interests from the inevitable consequences of free trade and competition. Even if the long-term benefits of greater efficiency work to the benefit of all, these benefits are often dispersed. The costs of free trade, however, are very concentrated. People who lose their job feel the costs more than people who save a dollar on a pair of jeans notice the benefits. Economic logic and political imperatives sometimes point in opposite directions. This is a dilemma even when there is agreement on an intellectual level that free trade would be desirable.

The problem goes beyond this because there is not a consensus, either within or among nations, that free trade is in fact always desirable. Among the advanced industrialized nations the belief in free trade is probably greatest in the United States. The Japanese and Europeans do not always share this country's enthusiasm. They see a greater scope for legitimate government intervention and are more inclined to recognize potential conflicts between the short-term interests of the consumer and the long-term well-being of the national community.

For many, it seems as though disagreements over trade issues are becoming more widespread and intense. Some cite declining American hegemony and the end of the Cold War as reasons for increasing conflicts over trade. The argument is that the decades immediately after World War II were characterized by American economic and military dominance over Japan and Western Europe. The United States was able to use its power to keep others in line with its policy preferences, and the common threat of the Soviet Union created a need for unity and desire to avoid conflict. Today the unifying threat of the Soviet Union is gone and the recovery and growth of other economies has eroded American hegemony. As a result, we are witnessing increasing conflict and tension over trade issues between the United States and its allies in Europe and Asia. Whether the liberal international order can be sustained in the face of declining American hegemony is subject of intense debate.[29] If the thesis about the importance of American hegemony is correct, we are likely to see more, not less, conflict over trade issues.

When we look at disagreements at the level of governments, we are largely in the realm of differences of degree. The Europeans and Japanese do not reject free trade in principle, but their commitment and attachment to free trade are weaker and more conditional. The same cannot be said of many of the social movements and groups protesting the move toward economic globalization. Many of these groups are animated by a much deeper and pervasive skepticism about the impact of free trade in the context of the contemporary global economy that approaches an outright rejection of the principle of free trade. Whether these movements and groups prove to be a powerful enough force to erode the liberal trading order remains to be seen.

CHAPTER SUMMARY

■ Debates over trade policy, both within the developed world as well as between the developed and developing worlds, have become increasingly intense in recent years. Occasional violent protests at global economic summits are among the more dramatic manifestations of this debate.

■ The Liberal International Economic Order (LIEO), which emphasizes the importance of free and open trade, was created in the aftermath of World War II under the auspices of the United States.

■ Free and open trade was deemed essential to the health of the U.S. economy, the preservation of democracy and peace, and the prospects for growth and prosperity around the world.

■ In terms of reducing barriers to trade, the General Agreement on Trade and Tariffs (GATT), created in 1947, was the most important element on the LIEO. GATT was replaced by the World Trade Organization in 1995.

■ The intellectual case for free trade was first made by liberal economists Adam Smith and, more important, David Ricardo, whose theory of comparative advantage remains the foundation of the case for free trade.

■ According to the theory of comparative advantage, nations should produce those commodities they produce more efficiently and trade these for those commodities that others produce more efficiently. Tariffs, quotas, and any other barriers to trade interfere with this process and promote economic inefficiency.

■ Supporters of free trade emphasize that consumers (and everyone is a consumer) are always better off when they can buy the things they want and need for the lowest possible price, no matter where in the world they are produced. And if every consumer in a nation is better off, the nation or community as a whole is better off.

■ One of the earliest critiques of Ricardo's case for free trade was provided by German economist Friedrich List.

■ Opponents of free trade usually concede that free trade promotes economic efficiency but argue that economic efficiency is not the only consideration that needs to be taken into account. There may be social, political, and strategic priorities that might outweigh purely economic considerations.

■ List argued that nations, unlike the individuals within them, need to be worried about becoming dependent on other nations for necessary commodities. He suggested that in such cases nations should maintain their industries, even if the commodities could be purchased more cheaply from other nations.

■ List also claimed that nations sometimes need to protect "infant" industries from foreign competition in the early stages of their development.

■ The idea that the pursuit of individual interests necessarily results in the common good, an essential element of the case for free trade, is, according to List, profoundly mistaken. Individual consumers cannot possibly know and evaluate the larger social consequences of their aggregated decisions. Thus, it is essential that the government regulate trade to protect the long-term interests of the nation as a whole.

CRITICAL QUESTIONS

1. If free trade really does benefit all in the long run, how might its supporters explain why it has been so difficult to achieve and sustain historically?

2. Are consumers always better off paying less for the goods they want and need regardless of where in the world they are produced?

3. How is possible for a nation without any import and export barriers such as quotas and tariffs to nonetheless violate the principles of free trade?

4. What is the significance of List's distinction between private economy and political economy in terms of evaluating free trade?

5. Why do some consider the distinction between *domestic* trade and *international* trade to be critical for evaluating the wisdom of free trade?

KEY TERMS

Adam Smith, 137
Autarky, 139
Corn Laws, 138
David Ricardo, 137
division of labor, 138
dumping, 142
economic nationalism, 137
free rider, 142

Friedrich List, 144
General Agreement on
  Tariffs and Trade
  (GATT), 136
infant industries, 147
International Monetary
  Fund (IMF), 136

Liberal International
  Economic Order (LIEO),
  136
mercantilism, 137
nontariff barriers, 141
positive-sum game, 141
predatory pricing, 147
Richard Cobden, 138

strategic trade policy, 147
theory of comparative
  advantage, 138
World Bank, 136
World Trade Organization
  (WTO), 137
zero-sum game, 141

FURTHER READINGS

A good place to start with the debate over free trade is the original sources, because the main outlines of the debate have not really changed very much. The case for free trade was first fully developed by David Ricardo in *On Protection to Agriculture* (London: J. Murray, 1822) and *On the Principles of Political Economy and Taxation* (London: J. Murray, 1819). Ricardo's most forceful critic was Friedrich List, whose ideas are best conveyed in his *The National System of Political Economy* (New York: August M. Kelley Publishers, 1966 [1885]). The best contemporary defenses of free trade are Jagdish Bhagwati's *Protectionism* (Cambridge, MA: MIT Press, 1988) and *Free Trade Today* (Princeton, NJ: Princeton University Press, 2003), and Douglas A. Irwin's *Free Trade Under Fire* (Princeton, NJ: Princeton University Press, 2002) and *Against the Tide: An Intellectual History of Free Trade* (Princeton, NJ: Princeton University Press, 1996). A good summary of the major arguments against free trade is presented by James Fallows's, "How the World Works," *The Atlantic* (December 1993), pp. 61–87. An interesting, though certainly opinionated, treatment of the debate over the North American Free Trade Agreement (NAFTA) is John R. MacArthur's, *The Selling of "Free Trade": NAFTA, Washington and the Subversion of American Democracy* (Berkeley: University of California Press, 2001).

FREE TRADE ON THE WEB

www.wto.org
Web site of the World Trade Organization, which has been at the center of attempts to promote and halt multi-lateral open trade.

www.cato.org/trade-immigration
A pro–free trade Web site, sponsored by the libertarian CATO Institute, which is intended to "increase public awareness of the benefits of free trade and the costs of protectionism."

www.usft.org
Site of United Students for Fair Trade. The focus is on how college students can work for "fair trade."

http://www.maketradefair.com
Another fair trade organization, focused on ensuring that the farmers and producers in Third World nations receive fair prices for the goods they produce.

www.wfto.com
Web site of the India-based World Fair Trade Organization.

NOTES

[1] Eduardo Poter, "Trade Bashing," *International Herald Tribune* (June 9, 2008). Accessed at: http://www.iht.com/articles/2008/06/09/opinion/edporter.php.

[2] See Manny Fernandez, "Diverse Foes: Wide Range of Protestors Unites Against IMF, World Bank," *Washington Post*, September 23, 2001, p. B1.

[3]Stephen Krasner, "United States Commercial and Monetary Policy: Unraveling the Paradox of External Strength and Internal Weakness," ed. Peter Katzenstein, *Between Power and Plenty: Foreign Economic Policies of Advanced Industrial States* (Madison: University of Wisconsin Press, 1978), p. 51.

[4]Roger Lowenstein. "Tariff to Nowhere," *New York Times Magazine*, June 15, 2008, pp. 15–16.

[5]Douglas A. Irwin, *Against the Tide: An Intellectual History of Free Trade* (Princeton: Princeton University Press, 1996), p. 217.

[6]An excellent account of the campaign to repeal the Corn Laws is William D. Grampp, *The Manchester School of Economics* (Stanford, CA: Stanford University Press, 1960). Oddly, even though Ricardo influenced those who favored repealing the Corn Laws, he actually opposed their repeal. Grampp explains the unusual reasoning behind Ricardo's opposition. See also Charles Kindleberger, "The Rise of Free Trade in Europe, 1820–1875," *Journal of Economic History* 35, no. 1 (1975): 20–55.

[7]Clive Crook, "Beyond Belief," *The Atlantic*, October 2007, p. 47.

[8]David Ricardo, *Principles of Political Economy and Taxation* (London: George Bell and Sons, 1908), pp. 115–116.

[9]Irwin, *Against the Tide*, p. 79.

[10]Jagdish Bhagwati, *Protectionism* (Cambridge, MA: MIT Press, 1988), p. 33.

[11]Ricardo, *Principles of Political Economy and Taxation*, p. 114.

[12]Paul Krugman, *Pop Internationalism* (Cambridge, MA: MIT Press, 1998), p. 84.

[13]Martha C. White, "Outdated Tariff System Means the Poor Pay More," *Washington Independent* (June 2, 2010). Accessed at: http://washingtonindependent.com/85893/outdated-tariff-systems-means-the-poor-pay-more.

[14]Ronald Findlay and Kevin H. O'Rourke, *Power and Plenty: Trade, War and the World Economy in the Second Millenium* (Princeton: Princeton University Press, 2007), p. 500.

[15]Ben Bernacke, "Global Economic Integration: What's New and What's Not." Accessed at http://www.federalreserve.gov/boarddocs/speeches/2006/20060825/default.htm # f4.

[16]Friedrich List, *The National System of Political Economy* (New York: Augustust M. Kelley Publishers, 1966 [reprint of 1885 edition]).

[17]John Gray, *False Dawn: The Delusions of Global Capitalism* (London: Granta, 1998), pp. 82–83.

[18]Mark Thirlwell, "Globalization was Good Then, Not Now," *YaleGlobal* (September 17, 2007). Accessed at: http://yaleglobal.yale.edu/display.article?id=9677

[19]Clive Crook, "Beyond Belief," p. 43.

[20]Irwin, *Against the Tide*, p. 127.

[21]Edward Earle Meade, "Adam Smith, Alexander Hamilton and Friedrich List: The Economic Foundations of Military Power," in *Makers of Modern Strategy: Military Thought from Machiavelli to Hitler*, ed. Edward Earle Meade (Princeton, NJ: Princeton University Press, 1971), p. 131.

[22]The argument that industrial development has usually included elements of protectionism is also made in William Lazonick, *Business Organization and the Myth of the Market Economy* (Cambridge: Cambridge University Press, 1991).

[23]List, *National System of Political Economy*, p. 347.

[24]Ibid., p. 165.

[25]Ibid., p. 166.

[26]James Fallows, "How the World Works," *The Atlantic* (December 1993), p. 70. See also James Fallows, *Looking at the Sun: The Rise of the New East Asian Economic and Political System* (New York: Pantheon, 1994).

[27]Fallows, "How the World Works," p. 70.

[28]These differentiations are drawn Jagdish Bhagwati comments in a online debate about fair trade conducted by the *Economist*. See: www.economist.com/debate/days/view/508/print.

[29]An influential examination of this issue is Robert Keohane, *After Hegemony* (Princeton, NJ: Princeton University Press, 1984).

Should Free Trade be Replaced with Fair Trade?

Unless one advocates complete economic self-sufficiency, some international trade is unavoidable. Because virtually no one favors autarky, the question is not whether to engage in international commerce but rather the principles guiding it and the rules under which nations trade. One of the problems for critics of the postwar economic order is articulating a competing vision that does not smack of the self-interested protectionism many hold at least partly responsible for the collapse of global trade and onset of the Great Depression in the 1920s. But what is the alternative to free trade? Is it merely a little less free trade, tinkering at the margins of the existing trading system? Or is there a different conceptual approach to international trade? These questions are central to the contemporary debate over "fair trade" reflected in the essays below. Echoing many of the familiar concerns about the impact of free trade, Devin Stewart makes the case for a "free *and* fair trade policy." In "redefining" fair trade Stewart argues that there is no inherent conflict between fair and free trade: Indeed, he suggests that increasing its fairness may be the only way to save the system of free trade. Jagdish Bhagwati and Arvind Pannagariya, on the other hand, see the movement for fair trade as threat to free trade, little more than protectionism with a nicer name that could do great damage to developing nations such as India.

PERSPECTIVE 1 — United States must Redefine "Fair Trade" (2010)

Devin T. Stewart[1]

Globalization is again under attack. Commentators from many perspectives have argued recently that globalization has reached a turning point and will never recover. Global inequities, failures of international institutions, and resentment of American power, they say, will usher in worldwide protectionism, threatening to end the current era of globalization.

An end to the current state of globalization doesn't have to lead to conflict, however, as did the pre-1914 era. Indeed, Washington's new political makeup provides an opportunity to shape a globalization that benefits all. In the realm of international trade, a starting point may be to reconcile free and fair trade.

After all, while the freest economies tend to be the richest, trade isn't an end in itself. Rather it is a tool to help increase living standards, lower poverty, and

[1] Source: Devin T. Stewart, "United States Must Redefine 'Fair Trade,'" Carnegie Council (January 29, 2007) © 2007 Carnegie Council, Reprinted with Permission.

advance political freedom and human rights. U.S. Congressman Sandy Levin, the new trade subcommittee chairman, recently issued a statement to this effect, adding that the terms of international competition must be shaped to achieve both growth and equity.

The concept of freedom seems pretty straightforward, but fairness means different things to different people. Fair trade is often depicted as antithetical to free trade, or as protectionism in disguise. Nevertheless, freedom and fairness are decent principles to guide an ethical U.S. economic policy, and reconciling the two would help restore American moral leadership. Fairness in economics is often concerned with offsetting "unfair" advantages created by lower wages in trading partners, but this notion incorrectly views the global economy as a zero-sum game.

A new, fairer U.S. trade policy would aim to give more people the opportunity to enjoy the benefits from world trade flows. Although Congress may attempt to use the term fairness to protect vulnerable domestic industries, doing so would be a mistake. As Treasury Secretary Henry Paulson recently said: "Giving in to protectionist sentiment would send a terrible signal. We would be telling developing nations that while we have benefited from increased trade, we aren't going to allow them the same opportunity to develop." He concluded that such a direction would be "morally wrong."

Adam Smith showed that economic freedom allows people to maximize their potential to the benefit of all society. But total freedom, as Thomas Hobbes argued, leads to a short and nasty life. The Aristotelian notion of moderation might help reconcile this paradox: Trade should be neither too free nor too regulated.

This is the puzzle a group of philosophers, economists, and practitioners tackled last month at the Carnegie Council. The question posed was, is it possible to fashion a free and fair trade policy that will build a more sustainable and equitable trading system? And, how can the principles of a more moral trade policy be applied to extractive industries? Three "freedoms" are worth examining here.

Freedom to trade anything

As philosopher Christian Barry has noted, some goods are unfit for trade. For example, it is widely maintained that some services, such as those offered by an assassin, should not be traded. Goods obtained through coercion may also be deemed unfit for trade. When it comes to the trade in natural resources, it is not always clear that the sellers are the rightful owners of the goods as they may have obtained them through bullying.

The issue of rightful ownership pertains also to trade in intellectual property. One question under debate is how to protect cultural intellectual property. For example, Ghana imports traditional African textile prints from China. Exacerbating tensions over Chinese textiles in Africa and the resulting loss of African jobs, some scholars have begun to question the fairness of trade in another country's cultural goods. The answer may lie in determining whether these vendors are the rightful owners of this property.

The process of producing goods traded should respect human rights and a country's labor and environmental laws. Slavery, poor working conditions, and environmental degradation are particularly problematic in illegal mining and logging operations. As a result, multinational corporations have started carefully scrutinizing their supply chains. Ford Motor and General Motors, for example, recently stopped using Latin American pig iron produced by slave labor. DaimlerChrysler, Ford, GM, and Honda joined together last month to train suppliers to avoid buying materials made by slaves.

Freedom to trade with anyone

Makers of a decent trade policy should remember the premise that trade is meant to improve peoples' lives, and they should deliberate when considering the use of trade barriers, sanctions, and embargos. The record shows that these tools are blunt and inaccurate in achieving broad security goals. Policy toward North Korea, for example, is often thought to be a choice between advancing human rights or a proliferation regime—or both. Instead, we have witnessed nuclear proliferation and mass famine on the Korean Peninsula despite a politically gratifying U.S. trade embargo.

The other side of the coin concerns trading partners that fail to enforce their own labor, human rights, and environmental standards, jeopardizing another kind of security. Part of the problem is simply keeping tabs on corporate behavior and publicizing the findings. Oxfam and the Business & Human Rights Resource Centre have excelled in this area. A country's human rights record may matter little if the trading partner feels that the exported good, for example oil, is vital to its national security. The United States must do its part to lower oil demand and invest in renewable energies, helping oil-exporting nations to shed the resource curse.

Freedom to trade with impunity

As the greatest beneficiary of globalization, the United States has a responsibility to give back to the system from which it benefits. In practical terms, this means the United States has an interest in working toward nurturing freedom and fairness not only at home but also in the global economy. It can do so by promoting fair and ethical trade practices, socially responsible business models, expanded stakeholder rights, and a stronger global civil society. The responsibility is great but fair for the biggest consumer of the world's resources.

These limits on free action can guide a fairer trade policy. Constructive policies are available to implement that vision. The U.S. Congress has made a promising start by passing bills to raise the minimum wage, make higher education more affordable, and eliminate subsidies for the U.S. oil industry, shifting resources toward developing clean energy technologies. It is also hopeful that Max Baucus, the new chairman of the Senate Finance Committee, would like to renew the Trade Adjustment Assistance program. He also supports a broader "Global Adjustment Assistance" that would offer benefits to workers displaced not just by trade, but by all aspects of globalization.

Enacting fair trade

To combat protectionist temptation and build on the ability of the country to cope with the tides of globalization, U.S. trade policy should also tailor its primary and secondary education system to equip graduates with the skills to compete in a global economy by emphasizing science, engineering, and foreign languages. The

United States will be forced to take a look at redirecting resources away from war and toward upgrading its own infrastructure. New York City's status as the preeminent financial center is threatened by cities like London and Tokyo.

To realize Baucus's goal of renewing fast track trade negotiation authority, the U.S. Congress must feel it has the capital to support trade agreements, otherwise fast track will be stuck in a pit stop. "Fair trade" agreements or comprehensive economic partnership agreements would continue the tradition of including labor and environmental provisions, like those with Jordan and Chile. A Washington trade journalist recently put it to me: "Labor and environmental enforcement is needed so that politicians feel comfortable enough to support FTAs without getting clobbered by labor groups. Then we can renew fast track. "

These comprehensive agreements commit partners to enforce their own environmental and labor laws, which in turn comply with the International Labour Organization. They could also offer deeper integration in the areas of labor movement and port screening, for example, to trading partners that honor the freedoms of speech, assembly, and religion. These three freedoms are good proxies for transparency, labor rights, and civil society, all necessary for the establishment of fair trade practices.

Other powerful approaches include fair trade and ethical trade initiatives. As clean energy consultant David Dell puts it: That which is truly profitable is also sustainable and that which is truly sustainable is profitable. Social entrepreneurs, local governments, and increasingly business gurus like Michael Porter have reached this axiom. To these ends, fair trade initiatives, such as HandCrafting Justice and Global Goods Partners, seek to cut out the middleman, pay producers fair wages, and reinvest in community health and education.

Ethically traded goods are those produced by companies that ensure labor standards are enforced within their own company and by their suppliers. Another idea is for companies to shoulder some of the burden of providing a safety net to those laid off when jobs are moved to take advantage of cheaper labor. Trade adjustment insurance and freer labor flows are part of the compact of free trade that is yet unfulfilled.

The above initiatives define corporate social responsibility: philanthropy and reinvestment, good labor practices, and business models that benefit people and the planet as a whole. They help sustain a healthy trading system and act as a de facto "trade Peace Corps," putting a human face to an American-led free market system. Given the services these initiatives provide to American leadership, the U.S. government should consider bolstering them by establishing a fund to support grassroots fair trade activities and giving tax breaks to socially responsible business models.

Notice that tariffs and competitive devaluations are not on the list. Although both of these approaches are advocated under the guise of protecting fairness and even human rights, history and economics tend to dispute those claims. Instead, openness—with the proper safety net—can help advance human rights.

For the United States to justify and prolong its international leadership, it must ensure that the rest of the world can access the benefits of globalization. It can start by promulgating a more thoughtful approach to trade—one that is neither protectionist nor free market fundamentalist. By finding a middle road between these extremes, the United States can realize its own dream of freedom and justice for all.

PERSPECTIVE 2   Protectionism's Other Names (2010)

Jagdish Bhagwati and Arvind Pannagariya[2]

Lagging employment recovery and continuing high levels of unemployment have marked the macroeconomic scenario in the United States. So, it is natural that the United States, which chaired the G-20 meeting in Pittsburgh, would use its privileged position as the host to invite the US secretary of labour, a well-known union activist, to convene a meeting of the employment and labour ministers on the jobs situation prior to the next G-20 heads of state meeting in Canada.

The macroeconomic aspects of the labour situation are indeed a proper focus of such a meeting. But the Pittsburgh declaration goes further and urges the G-20 countries not to "disregard or weaken internationally recognised labour standards" and to "implement policies consistent with ILO fundamental principles and rights at work".

Led by their federation, the AFL-CIO, the US labour unions have had a long history of pushing for a "social clause" into trade treaties at every forum. For international economists familiar with this history and the stranglehold the unions exercise on the Democratic Party and Congress today, the G-20 declaration constitutes a carefully designed trap. It is drafted in a way in which the US and the European Union can get developing-country employment and labour ministers unfamiliar with the agenda and influence of developed-country unions, to endorse measures that have a "feel good" but are, in fact, a protectionist dagger aimed at our jugulars. Indeed, the US undersecretary of labour, Sandra Polanski, who has been put in charge of the meeting, is well known to us as a long-standing proponent of such measures and a relentless activist on their behalf.

When the unions in the US and the EU insist on a set of labour standards in the developing countries with which they compete for markets at home and abroad, they take an altruistic line: we are doing this out of solidarity; we are doing it for your workers. But when you push them hard, they always say: it is "unfair" to have to compete with others who do not have our standards. Now, the latter is an argument about competition; it is about losing out in trade. So it is an argument motivated by self-interest, not altruism.

The traditional demand by the American unions has been that others should have the same standards as the US does. But this argument is comic, were it not tragic. Is the US a paragon of virtue on labour standards? After all, less than 10 per cent of its private workforce is now unionised. And this is because the main weapon that unions have, the right to strike, has been crippled by the Taft-Hartley legislation of over 50 years ago. Even liberal universities have refused to let their administrative employees organise. In consequence, Human Rights Watch, which

[2] Source: Jagdish Bhagwati & Arvind Panagariya, "Protectionism's Other Names," The Times of India (February 23, 2010) The Times of India. © Jagdish Bhagwati and Arvind Panagariya. Reprinted by permission of the authors.

has investigated the right to unionise, a central feature of the ILO principles, has found that this is far from being guaranteed in the US.

So, US unions have shifted to asking for ILO "core standards" instead. But this will not wash either. The US has not even ratified many of these core conventions. So, in effect, this version is also to be aimed at others, not themselves.

The truth of the matter is that, frightened by competition from our exports, the American and European unions seek relief. This can be obtained by conventional import protectionism. But, if this is constrained by WTO obligations, then it can be obtained by raising the cost of production of the foreign rivals. Raising their labour obligations is one way of doing this. Therefore, we have called it a form of "export protectionism", like the Voluntary Export Restraints, where the exporting country restrains its exports.

An alert must therefore be sounded and the matter discussed at the highest levels of the Indian government, with the labour minister fully briefed by trade experts and officials on the traps that await him at the impending meeting. We can also be sure that the US delegation will be assisted by Washington think-tank proponents of such protectionist proposals, many of them from the Carnegie Endowment (where Polanski sat during the Bush years), the Petersen Institute for International Economics (which has had a history of advocating trade-labour link), and the Centre for Global Development (which is captive to the protectionist notion of fair trade extending to labour standards in trade). Our best trade experts can effectively counter their arguments if only we use them.

But it is not enough to push back on proposals, which will harm us and the developing countries, more generally. India needs to be proactive and offer its own resolution that explicitly discourages the insertion of labour clauses into trade treaties and institutions. The intellectual argument is on our side on this issue. We should not be content to act as if we can eat at the banquet but have no say in the choice of the menu.

Bhagwati is university professor and Panagariya is professor of economics at Columbia University.

7

The IMF, Global Inequality, and Development

Key Controversy: What Are the Obstacles to Development?

Through the lens of the controversy surrounding the International Monetary Fund (IMF), this chapter explores the debate about the nature of the global economy and the obstacles to development. The immediate issue is the consequences of reforms enacted in many developing countries as a condition for receiving IMF loans. The purpose of these reforms was to promote economic development and reduce poverty. But as is often the case with disagreements on specific policies, there is a much deeper and more fundamental clash of worldviews informing this debate. The IMF's policies embody a liberal economic worldview in which pro-market policies and integration into the global economy are considered prerequisites for economic growth and development. From this perspective, the misguided policies of developing states have been the main obstacles to development. Critics of the IMF disagree. In their view, the primary obstacle to development is a global economic order that works systematically to the advantage of the wealthy and powerful at the expense of the poor and weak. Heavily influenced by a radical/Marxist analysis of global capitalism, this perspective portrays the IMF as an integral part of a global economic system that perpetuates poverty and inequality. ■

The post-World War II international economic order is based on the assumption that open markets and free trade benefit everyone in the long run—to reuse the cliché, a rising tide lifts all boats. This means that free trade is good not only for wealthy industrialized nations but also developing nations. Although trade issues often appear in the news in the context of disputes between the United States and China or other major trading partners, they are equally, if not more, important for understanding relations between developed and developing nations. The issues of trade, inequality, and development are inextricably intertwined. And these issues collide most vividly in the politically and intellectually charged controversy over the IMF and its role in promoting economic development.

International Monetary Fund
(IMF) One of the critical
institutions of the post-World
War II Liberal International
Economic Order. Initially
intended to help nations deal
with balance-of-payments
deficits, since the 1960s it has
played an increasing and
controversial role in assisting
developing nations.

At antiglobalization demonstrations the **International Monetary Fund (IMF)** is usually singled out for particularly harsh criticism, with a host of social and economic ills in the Third World laid at its doorstep. Conn Hallinan relates a riddle making the rounds among IMF critics: "What is the difference between Tony Soprano and the International Monetary Fund? Nothing, except that Tony and his Mafia pals, who extort and impoverish a handful of people in New Jersey, are television creations. The IMF, on the other hand, does this to hundreds of millions of people in the real world."[1] A harsh evaluation indeed.

Given the seemingly innocuous mission of the IMF, it might appear odd that it has become the object of such scorn. Founded in 1947, the IMF's original mandate was to help nations experiencing balance-of-payments problems and stabilize currency exchange rates, not exactly the sort of thing that leads people to take to the streets in protest. Criticism of the IMF today, however, has little to do with this mission. The contemporary controversy can be traced to the mid-1970s, when the IMF became increasingly involved in providing loans to developing countries. As a condition of assistance, however, developing nations agreed to implement policies and reforms the IMF thought were essential to promote economic development. At this point, the IMF jumped right into the middle of enduring debates about the reasons for the persistence of poverty and global economic inequality.

From Decolonization to Structural Adjustment

The wave of post–World War II decolonization transformed the political map of the world but had relatively little impact on its economic landscape. The optimistic expectation that economic development would follow rapidly on the heels of political independence was quickly dashed as sovereignty proved perfectly compatible with continuing economic inequality. Decolonization did nothing to alter the **international division of labor** that emerged over the previous century. Manufacturing was still concentrated in the industrialized economies of the North, whereas the newly independent countries of the South remained sources of primary products (e.g., unprocessed raw materials and agricultural goods). Not only were Third World economies still reliant on primary product exports, but also most depended on just one or two products for the bulk of their export earnings. They were highly-specialized compared to diversified economies such as the United States. It was (and still is) not unusual for a developing country to receive more than half of its export income from the sale of a single commodity. More than two decades after independence, for example, 96 percent of Uganda's export earnings came from coffee, 89 percent of Zambia's from copper, and 59 percent of Ghana's from cocoa.[2] A diversified economy can survive a slump in any single economic sector, but if the price of coffee falls by 50 percent in a given year, Uganda is in real trouble.

international division of
labor Refers to the division
between the core nations,
which have diversified
manufacturing based economies, and peripheral nations,
which have specialized economies that rely on raw material
exports.

By the late 1950s, this division of labor and specialization came to be viewed as an obstacle to development for two reasons. First, prices of many primary products often fluctuated wildly from year to year, and the resulting instability in income created difficulties for planning and development. Imagine, for example, individuals trying to borrow money or make investments if their incomes went up or down unpredictably by 50 percent from year to year. As Michael Latham explains with respect to Ghana and cocoa, "as prices for that commodity fluctuated on a volatile world market, the economy went through unpredictable cycles of boom and bust that made long-term development planning impossible."[3] Second, there was a general tendency for the price of primary products except oil to fall without any similar reduction in the price of manufactured goods. Economists refer to this as **declining terms of trade**—that is, the prices for those commodities developing nations sell are going down, whereas prices for the manufactured goods they buy are not. For example, when fiber optic cable began replacing copper wire in the 1980s, the price of copper on the world market fell by nearly 80 percent. Nations like Zambia were devastated. Focusing on Latin America, Latham notes that "as foreign exchange earnings in primary exports … continued to fall behind manufactured imports, Latin American nations accumulated little domestic savings to invest in development programs."[4] Left unchecked, this trend would inexorably lead to even greater poverty and inequality.

The logical solution to this dilemma was for developing nations to reduce their reliance on primary products and shift to manufacturing. As Dani Rodrik observes, "specialize in commodities and raw materials, and you will get stuck in the periphery of the world economy…hostage to fluctuations in world prices." But "if you can push your way into manufactures…you may pave a path to convergence with the world's rich countries."[5] Unfortunately, this is easier said than done. The problem was that in the initial stages manufactured goods from Third World countries would not be very competitive with those of established industries in North America, Europe, and Japan. How could developing nations create a manufacturing base in the face of competition from the already industrialized economies? The solution adopted in Third World countries, particularly in Latin America and Africa, was **import substitution**. That is, domestically manufactured goods would be substituted for previously imported manufactured goods. There were two components of this strategy. First, governments channeled investment into selected industries. Second, tariffs and quotas protected so-called infant industries from the international market until they could compete on their own.

Import substitution met with some initial success during the 1950s and 1960s, with many Latin American and African countries experiencing high rates of economic growth. During this period the focus was largely on low-tech, labor-intensive industries such as nondurable consumer goods (shoes, clothes, etc.). These industries did not require huge investments and were labor intensive, allowing Third World nations to take advantage of their large pools of low-wage labor. Making the transition to high-tech, capital-intensive manufacturing such as electronics and appliances proved more problematic. Poor countries lacked the domestic capital for investment because their poor populations had low rates of saving. Third World nations were forced to look abroad for investment capital. There were two potential sources—multinational corporations and northern financial institutions. Both options had drawbacks. Relying on corporations increased

declining terms of trade The tendency for the prices of raw material to decline relative to manufactured goods.

import substitution A policy designed to promote economic development by restricting foreign imports in order to replace them with domestically produced goods.

their power and influence, something viewed with great suspicion in recently-decolonized nations. Borrowed money, on the other hand, would have to be paid back, with interest. But because this investment was supposed to produce economic growth, paying back the loans a few years down the road was not expected to pose much of a problem.

By the 1970s, however, Third World economies began to stagnate. The situation was exacerbated when oil-producing nations, acting through the **Organization of Petroleum Exporting Countries (OPEC)** raised prices substantially, beginning in 1973 and again in 1979. Although higher oil prices inconvenienced wealthy industrial economies, they crippled many developing nations. Thus, by the mid- to late 1970s, many developing countries saw economic growth rates plummet and the costs of imported energy soar.

The cumulative result was the **debt crisis**. Several major developing countries, especially in Latin America, found themselves unable to pay back the money borrowed during the 1970s. The most significant of the early crises involved Mexico. Throughout the 1970s, Mexico's debt burden grew faster than its economy as a whole. By the early 1980s, it was clear that Mexico would be unable to pay back its loans on schedule. Fearing the consequences of a Mexican default, especially for major international banks, the IMF loaned Mexico money to makes it payments. The money did not come without strings, however. The IMF insisted that Mexico enact economic reforms. The IMF claimed the reforms were necessary to promote economic growth needed for Mexico to repay its loans. This set the precedent for subsequent IMF bailouts throughout Latin America, Africa, and Asia over the next two decades. The practice of requiring reforms in exchange for IMF assistance was known as **conditionality**. Though details differed, the same basic conditions were imposed on all nations seeking IMF assistance. Taken together, these were referred to as **structural adjustment policies**, and it is these policies that prompted the rising chorus of criticism directed against the IMF.

Organization of Petroleum Exporting Countries (OPEC) Founded in 1960, OPEC was and remains an attempt to create a cartel of major oil producers for the purpose of raising the global price of oil.

debt crisis The inability of many developing nations to pay back foreign debts, beginning in the early 1980s.

conditionality The IMF's policy of requiring certain economic policies and reforms in order to receive loans.

structural adjustment policies The bundle of market-oriented reforms required for developing nations to receive IMF loans.

Structural Adjustment: Cure and Diagnosis

IMF structural adjustment programs were designed to solve a problem. Mounting debts combined with slow growth left many Third World nations on the verge of bankruptcy. On this there is not much disagreement. But Jagdish Bhagwati reminds us that in economic policy as in medicine, "the cure is defined by the diagnosis."[6] To continue the medical metaphor, the debt crisis was the symptom and structural adjustment policies were the cure. But the nature of this cure depended upon the IMF's diagnosis of the problem. From the IMF's perspective, the immediate problem was the lack of economic growth, but this explanation begs the more basic question: What was the cause of poor growth? The IMF blamed the misguided economic policies of developing nations.

In blaming misguided policies for poor growth, the IMF stepped into the center of the most enduring debate in development studies: the relative importance of domestic versus international obstacles to development. For the last several decades, debates about the causes of underdevelopment have been defined by two basic positions. One perspective sees the capitalist global economic system as the primary obstacle to genuine development. The dynamics of global capitalism ensure that the rich get richer and the poor get poorer. From this perspective, it is the international economic order that needs to be reformed to achieve development. An alternative analysis locates the obstacles to development in the policies of developing states. The IMF sided with this position.

The IMF and Neoliberalism

The late 1970s and early 1980s were not only a period of emerging crisis in much of the developing world but also changing intellectual currents in the industrialized world. Since the end of World War II, economic thought in the United States and Europe was dominated by the ideas of British economist **John Maynard Keynes** (1883–1946). While supporting the essential features of capitalism, Keynes advocated a greater role for government in moderating the ups and downs of the capitalist business cycle. During recessions, for example, when growth is low and unemployment high, governments should spend at a deficit to inject money into the economy to encourage growth and employment. By the mid-1970s, Keynesianism came under attack by economists such as **Milton Friedman** (1912–2006), who favored a diminished role for government. The election of Ronald Reagan in the United States and Margaret Thatcher in Great Britain was an indication of these shifting intellectual currents. Domestically, both Thatcher and Reagan pursued similar agendas: tax cuts, lower government spending, fewer regulations, scaled-back social welfare programs, and privatization.

The growing influence of free market policies was bolstered by the total failure of state socialism and communism in the Soviet Union and Eastern Europe, where decades of state planning and government control produced economic stagnation and social malaise. Even though the Soviet model of development appeared attractive to some in the developing world during the 1950s and 1960s because it held out the promise of rapid development, by the 1980s its luster was gone. The political and intellectual triumph of liberal democratic capitalism appeared universal. This vision of smaller government and increased reliance on the market came to be known as **neoliberalism**.

The developing world's debt crisis coincided with the emergence of neoliberalism. The structural adjustment reforms imposed by the IMF and the policies Reagan and Thatcher tried to enact were cut from the same intellectual cloth. There were several key reforms in virtually every structural adjustment plan, including:

1. *Fiscal austerity*, or balancing government budgets. This usually entailed either increases in government revenues (usually new fees for government services) or, more commonly, reductions in government spending.

2. *Reductions in government subsidies to domestic industries*. These subsidies had often been part of import substitution strategies.

3. *Reduction of tariffs, quotas, and other barriers to imports*. This would subject domestic industries to international competition.

John Maynard Keynes (1883–1946) Influential British economist who advocated a substantial role for government in regulating the ups and downs of the business cycle through fiscal and monetary policy.

Milton Friedman (1912–2006) Nobel Prize–winning economist influential in the resurgence of liberal/neoliberal (i.e., pro-market) economic policies and thought in the 1970s and 1980s.

neoliberalism A contemporary version of economic liberalism, emphasizing the importance of limited government, reduced regulation, and the market economy.

Fiscal austerity Controlling government spending and taxation with a preference for balanced budgets. Demands for fiscal austerity were central elements of the IMF's structural adjustment programs.

Capital market liberalization
Removing barriers to foreign
investment, a key element of
IMF structural adjustment
programs.

4. *Capital market liberalization*. This is a technical term for reducing restrictions on foreign investment.

5. *Privatization*, or selling off government-owned industries to the private sector.

Taken together, these policies reflected the IMF's worldview "that market forces, liberalized trade and payments, and general freedom in economic matters are usually more efficient and promote greater prosperity and a better allocation of resources than a system characterized by controls and restrictions."[7] This bundle of policies and the underlying liberal/neoliberal economic philosophy became known as the **Washington consensus**, a description reflecting the United States' significant role in shaping these policies.

Washington consensus label
for the liberal ideas of free
trade and limited government
that guide many of the policies
of the IMF toward developing
nations, especially in the context of its structural adjustment
loans.

Growth Is Possible: The Market and Development

The IMF and its supporters reject the argument that a liberal international economic order is an obstacle to development. If all the development efforts of the past fifty years had met with failure, there might be good reason to blame the global economic system. But this has not been the case. The past fifty years have produced some abject failures, some modest development, and even some truly remarkable success stories. David Landes notes that "since independence, the heterogeneous nations that we know collectively as the South, or as the Third World ... have achieved a wide diversity of results. These have ranged from the spectacular successes of East Asia, to mixed results in Latin America to outright regression in such places as Burma and much of Africa."[8] This diversity of outcomes can be illustrated with some striking comparisons between Africa and East Asia. In the early 1950s, for example, Egypt had roughly the same average income as most East Asian nations, but today incomes in East Asia are between five and thirty times larger than Egypt's. Landes is struck particularly by the different trajectories of Nigeria and Indonesia: "In 1965, Nigeria (oil exporter) had higher GDP per capita than Indonesia (another oil exporter); twenty-five years later, Indonesia had three times the Nigerian level."[9] Even more dramatic is a comparison of Ghana and South Korea: In 1957, Ghana had a larger gross national product (GNP) than South Korea, but by 1996 Ghana's GNP stood at $7 billion whereas South Korea's GNP had soared to $485 billion, almost seventy times larger than Ghana's.[10] So any blanket assertion that development is impossible within the existing liberal economic order cannot be sustained.

What does this diversity tell us about the causes of development and underdevelopment? Can it help identify any answers to Keith Richburg's pointed question, "Why is Africa eating Asia's dust?"[11] The variance is not easily explained by histories of colonialism because some of the most successful East Asian nations had also been colonies. To many observers, the fact that some nations have achieved genuine development and others have not indicates that "the basic obstacles to economic development [can be found] within the less developed countries themselves." But what might these obstacles be? The list of possibilities is long indeed: war and frequent civil unrest, political instability, rampant government corruption, cultural and religious beliefs that inhibit initiative, and cumbersome bureaucracies, to identify just a few. One of the most commonly cited problems, however, is bad or misguided policies. From the IMF's perspective, one thing was clear: Excessive government control of the economy and attempts to cut off developing economies from foreign trade and investment are definitely *not* routes to development; instead, "market openness, fiscal discipline and noninterventionism constituted the route to economic development."[12]

The poster children for economic development are the so-called East Asian "tigers" or newly industrializing countries (NICs). As Robert Gilpin notes, "The most successful economies among the less developed countries are precisely those that have put their houses in order and that participate most aggressively in the world economy. They are the so-called Gang of Four: Hong Kong, Singapore, South Korea, and Taiwan."[13] Do these cases support the neoliberal view that free market policies and integration into the global economy lead to development? Is this what Gilpin means by "putting their houses in order"? This is a difficult question. On one hand, there is no denying that East Asian governments were often heavily involved in directing investment into targeted industries. This was development with a heavy dose of government guidance, which appears to contradict advice that such decisions are best left to the market. Nonetheless, their policies were more market and trade oriented than the import substitution policies of Latin America and many African nations. According to Stephen Haggard, "Intervention may have been extensive in the East Asian NICs .... but it has been less extensive than in

Urban slums like this one in Lagos, Nigeria are unfortunately still common in many developing nations decades after independence.

Source: William Campbell/Sygma/Corbis

Africa, South Asia, and Latin America."[14] In Gilpin's opinion, East Asian development policies "have worked with the market and not against it … They have demonstrated that the liberals are quite correct in their emphasis on the benefits of the price mechanism in the efficient allocation of resources."[15] Most important, the East Asian nations clearly embraced international trade as the engine of the economic growth even if governments played a more active role domestically.

India provides a somewhat more clear-cut example of successful market-oriented policies. In the two decades following independence, India's economic performance was disappointing. According to Jagdish Bhagwati, "The main elements of India's policy framework stifled growth until the 1970s." These elements included "extensive bureaucratic controls over production, investment and trade" as well as "inward looking trade and investment policies" and "a substantial public sector, going well beyond the conventional confines of public utilities and infrastructure."[16] Beginning in the 1980s (and especially after 1991), India undertook reforms to reduce government control and increase foreign trade and investment. The result has been consistently higher rates of economic growth and a substantial reduction in poverty. Though India's reforms were not the result of IMF pressure, its experience is seen as confirmation of the IMF's underlying market-oriented philosophy.

Recognizing the role of corruption in hindering economic development, anti-corruption campaigns have emerged in many developing countries.
Source: Per-Anders Pettersson/Getty Images

Chile provides a more controversial case. In the late 1970s, under the influence of economists trained by University of Chicago economists such as Milton Friedman, the Chilean government adopted a radical free market agenda, opening Chile's economy to imports and foreign investment while reducing government spending, going so far as to privatize Chile's version of social security. After some initial hardship, Chile enjoyed more than a decade of sustained economic growth unrivaled in Latin America. Chile's example remains controversial for two reasons. First, its market reforms were indeed radical, going well beyond anything the IMF demands. Second, the reforms were enacted by a military dictatorship that did not have to worry about its unpopularity.[17] The connection between military dictatorship and market reforms was not exactly a public relations success for advocates of similar reforms elsewhere in Latin America.

When these experiences are combined with the failure of state socialism in the Soviet bloc, the lessons seem clear. First, government interventions that work against the market are a recipe for economic inefficiency, stagnation, and perpetual underdevelopment. Second, those areas of the world that have prospered participate extensively in the global economy. P. T. Bauer, who advocated neoliberal policies before they became fashionable, saw this correlation: "The materially more advanced societies and regions of the Third World are those with which the West established the most numerous, diversified and extensive contacts." Conversely, "the level of material achievement usually diminishes as one moves away from the foci of Western impact … The poorest areas of the Third World have no external trade. Their condition shows that the causes of backwardness are domestic and that commercial contacts are beneficial."[18]

Recent evidence seems to support this position. In December 2001, the World Bank released a study of developing economies during the 1990s, focusing on the importance of trade as a measure of globalization. The most important indicator was a nation's ratio of international trade to overall national income (e.g., the significance of trade for its economy). The two dozen developing nations for whom trade was most significant saw their economies grow on average nearly 5 percent a year. Life expectancy and schooling levels increased as well. This was better than the 2 percent increase registered by developed nations. It was also much better than the rest of the developing world, for whom trade was less significant: Their GNP actually declined by 1 percent a year over the same period.[19] The conclusion: trade is good for the developing world and its people. Douglas Irwin reflects the consensus among neoliberal economists: "Recent experience suggests that developing countries can reap substantial benefits from adopting more open trade policies, but that such policies alone do guarantee development, particularly when corruption, civil conflicts and other institutional failings prevent local entrepreneurs from taking advantage of world markets."[20]

A Moral Hazard?

Criticism of the IMF comes from every part of the theoretical and political spectrum. Surprisingly, however, some of the strongest criticisms come from those who share the IMF's commitment to economic growth, free trade, and limited government intervention. According to this critique, IMF actions violate the very principles the organization supposedly stands for. Remember that IMF assistance is needed when nations can no longer meet their loan payments. If this were to happen to you or me, we would default on our loans and declare bankruptcy and the bank would lose its money (or at least most of it). This is why banks are usually careful to check an applicant's creditworthiness before lending. But even with these checks, banks still make mistakes. When a debtor goes bankrupt, the bank chalks it up as a loss, part of the inevitable costs of a business with some measure of risk. If we allowed the market to work at the international level, nations unable to pay would go bankrupt and banks would lose their money. Nations that default on loans would find it very difficult to borrow money again until they got their act in order, and banks would become more careful lenders. But this does not happen. Instead, the IMF steps in and saves nations and banks from the consequences of their unwise borrowing and lending. IMF actions, therefore, are themselves an interference in the operation of markets. This creates what critics refer to as a **moral hazard**—a policy that actually undermines efforts to enact needed reforms by relieving the parties of the consequences of their failures. Thus, banks and nations know that they can continue to make bad decisions because the IMF will be there to rescue them.

moral hazard Situation created when policies promote the very problems they were intended to solve. Many argue that IMF loans to debt-ridden developing nations serve to relieve them from the consequences of their mistakes and rescue banks that made bad loans. In doing so, these loans only encourage further irresponsibility.

The (Neo)Liberal Vision

It is important to understand how IMF policies are rooted in the fundamental assumptions of liberalism. The emphasis on the market prescriptions to spur development stems not only from a belief that it promotes economic efficiency, but also from a deeper assumption of a harmony of interests. When everyone pursues his own economic self-interest in the market, we are all better off in the long run. People and businesses prosper when they provide others with goods and services they want at prices they are willing to pay. In advancing their own interests, they are satisfying the needs and wants of others. Applying this assumption of the harmony of interests to the global economy, liberals reject any zero-sum analysis in which the wealth of the North is seen as coming at the expense of the South. Developing nations are not poor *because* others are rich. Egyptians did not become poorer as South Koreans grew richer, they simply failed to keep pace. There is no need to choose between Northern prosperity and Southern development. There is no need to choose between multinational profits and Southern development. The rising tide of global economic growth can lift all boats. Development and wealth are possible for all in a global capitalist economic system.

Neoliberalism as Neoimperialism

How can one argue with the apparent success of market policies and international trade in promoting development? Critics of the IMF, neoliberalism, and structural adjustment make three basic arguments. First, the neoliberal vision fails to recognize the fundamentally unequal terms on which developing nations participate in the global economy. Second, after twenty years there is little evidence that structural adjustment policies promote economic growth or reduce poverty. Third, developed nations are hypocritical in imposing a model of development that virtually none of them adopted during their growth.

The Political Economy of Dependence and Exploitation

Though criticisms of the IMF and neoliberalism come from many perspectives, the dominant critique is rooted in **dependency theory**, which emerged in Latin America during the 1950s and 1960s to explain the region's lack of development. Unlike neoliberals, "all dependency theorists maintain that underdevelopment is due primarily to external forces of the world capitalist system and is not due to the policies of LDCs [less developed countries] themselves."[21] Dependency theorists see a world divided between an industrial **core** and an underdeveloped **periphery** (a category of **semiperiphery** has also been included to account for the very few nations that have managed to move out of the periphery, such as the East Asian economies). Though the troops and governors of formal colonialism left long ago, a new form of economic imperialism, referred to as **neoimperialism** or **neocolonialism**, has taken its place. The primary agent of this new imperialism is the multinational corporation, "the embodiment of international capital."[22] Multinational corporations benefit from an impoverished periphery because it provides cheap commodities and inexpensive labor that allow them to reap windfall profits. This profiteering is done in conjunction with a domestic political-economic elite within Third World nations that has been bought off by, and serves the interests of, international capital. This **comprador class** collaborates with foreign capital in its domination of peripheral nations and forms an "anti-nation" within the nation. Even when developing nations experience high rates of economic growth, the benefits are not distributed evenly. The new wealth goes disproportionately to economic elites "who are able to enjoy the lifestyle and consumption patterns of developed countries of the North … [while] large segments of the population experience no significant improvement in their standard of living."[23] The benefits of growth do not "filter" or "trickle" down to the masses. So-called economic growth in many developing nations has not always resulted in the reduction of poverty or improved living standards. Growth and development are not one and the same. Impressive statistics about economic growth are misleading and all too often obscure the growing inequality within developing nations.

Increasing inequality within developing nations is accompanied by a growing gap between developed and developing nations in the global economy. The periphery is systematically impoverished or underdeveloped as multinationals earn substantial profits they send home to line the pockets of shareholders and corporate executives. Profits are not reinvested in the Third World nations where they were made. The result is a massive transfer of wealth from the periphery to the core. The contrast with the economic development of nations such as the United States is critical here. Although Andrew Carnegie and John D. Rockefeller raked in hundreds of millions in profits during the late 1800s and early 1900s, at least they reinvested most of their profits back into the American economy, producing genuine development. This is why even Marx agreed that capitalism was a "progressive"

dependency theory A theory of global economics influenced by a Marxist understanding of capitalism. The world is seen as divided between a wealthy and powerful core and a poor and impoverished periphery that are locked in an unequal and fundamentally exploitative relationship. From this perspective, it is the global economic system, not just bad policies pursued in developing nations, that perpetuate international inequality.

periphery The division of the world into classes somewhat analogous to Marx's bourgeoisie and proletariat. The **core** is the small group of wealthy and powerful states exploiting the larger group of weak and impoverished states (i.e., the **periphery**).

semiperiphery In dependency theory, the small number of developing nations that have developed to the point where they can no longer be considered part of the periphery.

neoimperialism or **neocolonialism** A pattern and a policy of economic inequality, exploitation, and domination that have persisted despite the end of formal colonialism.

comprador class From the perspective of dependency theory, the ruling elite in developing nations that collaborates with foreign capital in the exploitation of peripheral nations.

force: It is very good at developing a society's resources. But when corporations earn huge profits in the periphery today, these profits are *not* reinvested but rather siphoned away. This constitutes an exploitative process of unequal exchange that produces underdevelopment and exacerbates global inequality.

The fundamental difference between dependency theory and neoliberalism hinges on whether there is a harmony or a conflict of interests between North and South. As we have already noted, neoliberalism argues that Northern wealth does not require Southern underdevelopment. Brazil and Nigeria are not poor *because* the United States and Great Britain are rich. Northern and Southern nations can prosper simultaneously. Dependency theory makes the opposite assumption, seeing a basic conflict of interest in which Northern prosperity depends on the exploitation of an underdeveloped South. As Paul Baran explains, "Economic development in underdeveloped countries is profoundly inimical to the dominant interests in advanced capitalist countries. Supplying many important raw materials to the industrialized countries, providing their corporations with vast profits and investment outlets, the backward world has always represented the indispensable hinterland of the highly developed capitalist West."[24]

Although not all dependency theorists are Marxists, the parallels between them are clear. The distinction between core and periphery is roughly analogous to Marx's distinction between the bourgeoisie and proletariat. Just as the relationship between the bourgeoisie and proletariat was unequal and based on exploitation, so it is with the relationship between core and periphery.

According to this analysis, the IMF is a vehicle for advancing the interests of the dominant capitalist states. As an almost physical manifestation of its role in the global economy, the IMF is headquartered just a few blocks from the White House and the World Bank in Washington, DC. This alone is telling. Voting within the IMF is weighted according to a nation's contributions to the fund. Because it contributes 18 percent of IMF funds, the United States has an equivalent share of voting power; as a result, it is almost impossible for the IMF to do anything over the objections of the United States. Belgium and the Netherlands combined have more voting power than China, the world's most populous nation, and Canada has more voting power than India, the second most populous nation.[25] In what some found to be a moment of rare candor, U.S. Trade Representative Mickey Kantor once characterized the IMF as a "battering ram" for U.S. interests.[26]

There are also less direct sources of bias. Most IMF economists were trained at American universities, where they were inculcated into the dominant economic ideology of neoliberalism. They attend cocktail parties in Georgetown and dine in swanky Manhattan restaurants, discussing abstract economic theory without ever confronting the reality of global poverty. Many of the fund's top officials have close ties to investment banks and multinational corporations. Even though they may sincerely believe they have the best interests of the developing world at heart, they are deluding themselves. In the words of William Greider, the IMF and World Bank "serve as paternalistic agents of global capital—enforcing debt collection, supervising the financial accounts of poor nations, promoting wage suppression and other policy nostrums, preparing the poorer countries for eventual acceptance into the global trading system."[27]

The Failure of Structural Adjustment

The impact of structural adjustment programs is exhibit A in the brief against the IMF, because there is little evidence they have achieved their objectives. The IMF itself has been able to muster only cautious and lukewarm evaluations of its own programs. Withering critiques, on the other hand, are almost too numerous to count. The list of negative effects attributed to structural adjustment programs is long. It is difficult to think of any problem in the developing world that has not supposedly been exacerbated by IMF policies. Putting aside some of the more extreme critiques, the most common criticism is that structural adjustment policies have had a devastating impact on the poor and most vulnerable in developing nations.

Take, for example, the demand for fiscal discipline and balanced budgets. There are only two ways to balance a budget—bring in more revenues or reduce expenditures. In most instances the latter course is pursued, and reductions in government spending usually concentrate on social and welfare programs because cutting military spending runs the risk of angering powerful military establishments. As a result, "governments find it easier to trim their budgets by charging fees at rural clinics and schools than by firing soldiers or well-connected cronies."[28] These cuts usually fall most heavily on those already living on the edge. Even minor increases in fees could be crushing for people who live on the equivalent of one or two dollars a day.

Feminists have drawn particular attention to the impact of such cuts on women: "A measure which has an immediate impact on women is the reduction of state expenditures on social services, with women expected to expand their domestic responsibilities to compensate for decreasing state investment in children's education or health."[29] Increases in fees for government services such as health care and education can also have a perverse impact on girls from poor families in societies that have a gender bias in favor of male children. Faced with choosing which children get medical care or go to school, girls often lose out. And when government subsidies to industry are reduced, women workers are often the first to be laid off.

Trade liberalization and opening economies to unrestricted foreign investment also have a deleterious impact on the poor. Without government subsidies or protections from foreign competition, domestic industries are forced to reduce costs by lowering wages or laying off workers. Forced to compete with cheap labor elsewhere in the developing world, the result is downward pressure on wages. Multinational corporations, when they are willing to invest at all, are attracted by the lure of cheap labor. It is, after all, a large and inexpensive work force that provides developing nations with their primary competitive advantage.

Some of the most significant disagreements between the IMF and its critics concern foreign investment and its consequences. One of the goals of structural adjustment is to reduce barriers to foreign investment and create a stable economic environment that will attract investment. Building factories, hiring and training workers, and introducing new technologies all supposedly contribute to economic growth and development. Critics disagree. Foreign corporate investment tends to be limited to those things that contribute to the bottom line, profits. In the long run, genuine development requires a basic infrastructure—transportation systems, hospitals, and schools—that facilitates commerce and creates a healthy, educated work force. Foreign corporations, however, do not build roads, schools, and hospitals. Only governments can undertake these basic public investments. But saddled with huge debts, and under IMF pressure to balance budgets and reduce spending, most developing nations are unable to make these investments. Denied the resources to provide the infrastructure that only governments can, any escape from poverty and underdevelopment is unlikely. In this context, foreign investment will exploit underdevelopment, not reverse it. Foreign investment may contribute to economic growth in the sense that some people get richer, but this does not necessarily result in development or the alleviation of poverty.

Structural adjustment has even failed on its own terms. According to the IMF, the primary goal of structural adjustment was economic growth. The problem is that it does not appear to have created much growth. The IMF's own study concluded that growth rates in countries under structural adjustment increased from −1.5 percent in the 1980s to 0.3 percent in the early 1990s and 1 percent by the mid-1990s. This is certainly improvement, but nothing to get terribly excited about.[30] Other studies failed to find any improvement. A 2001 World Bank found "no evidence for a direct effect of structural adjustment on growth."[31] As Rodrik points out, "countries in Latin American and elsewhere that jettisoned ISI [import-substitution industrialization] in favor of the Washington Consensus ended up, for the most part, with considerably lower rates of growth."[32]

One can also make some fairly direct comparisons between countries that implemented IMF policies and others that refused. Faced with problems in paying back loans in 1997, several Southeast Asian countries, most notably Thailand and South Korea, approached the IMF for short-term loans. As elsewhere, the IMF insisted on liberalizing reforms to make the loans. Critics charged that the IMF unnecessarily turned a minor problem into an excuse to impose major restructuring. According to Harvard economist Jeffrey Sachs, IMF officials arrived in Thailand caught in the grips of their own ideology, "filled with ostentatious declarations that all was wrong and that fundamental and immediate surgery was needed."[33] The results proved disastrous (even the IMF admits its response "was not flawless")—gross domestic products actually declined and unemployment increased. In comparison, faced with a similar problem and IMF demands for wide-ranging reforms, Malaysia balked and declined the IMF loan. It was then able to resolve its loan-payment problem without the negative consequences experienced by Thailand and South Korea.[34]

The Hypocrisy of Neoliberalism: Do as We Say, Not as We Did

Developing nations also see a large measure of hypocrisy in demands for neoliberal reforms. Not only are neoliberal policies unlikely to produce development in the future, but also they have never done so in the past. The United States and other developed nations are caught in the grips of a mythology about their own history and development that bears little resemblance to reality. In his book *Business Organization and the Myth of the Market Economy*, economic historian William Lazonink examined the policies today's developed states followed during their development. The notion that free trade propelled their development is, as his title suggests, mythical. Every nation (except the first to develop, Great Britain) followed the same pattern, protecting industries from foreign imports until they were able to compete. In the United States, for example, basic industries were protected from European, especially British, competition in the latter part of the 1800s and early 1900s. As Rodrik explains, "The United States put up very steep tariffs on manufactured imports during the Civil War and kept them high throughout the century."[35] And contrary to the expectations of current neoliberal development orthodoxy, this was a period of tremendous economic growth during which the United States displaced Great Britain as the world's largest economy. Only after World War II, when it emerged as the world's only unscathed industrial economy, did the United States convert to free trade. It is almost comical to hear U.S. officials pontificate about the evils of tariffs and quotas, given their nation's development history. Rick Rowden explains that "the conditions attached to IMF and World Bank loans are nothing like the policies of industrialized countries over the past 150 years." In contrast to the mythical history of free market development, the growth of "Europe, the United States, Japan and the four tigers of Asia … involved several decades or more of government providing protective tariffs, large subsidies to domestic industry, … tax breaks and other incentives." The IMF, however, requires that developing nations eliminate subsidies and leave their industries open to foreign competition. But "since no country in history has ever industrialized under such a process, structural adjustment programs are essentially a massive, radical experiment foisted on the poorest two-third's of the world's population."[36] Harsher critics of the IMF find it both curious and telling that the developed world imposes policies that have not led to development in the past. This suggests that the IMF is not really interested in promoting genuine development. Perhaps the real purpose of these policies is to advance the economic interests of the developed states, Northern banks, and multinational corporations.

Conclusion

In 2008, the World Bank reported that the number of people in the world living on less than $1.25 a day declined from 1.9 billion to 1.4 billion between 1981 and 2005. This represents a decrease of 26 percent in 25 years.[37] "Thirty years ago," it notes, "half the developing world lived in extreme poverty – today, a quarter. Now a much smaller share of children are malnourished and at risk of early death. And access to modern infrastructure is more widespread."[38] A large amount of this improvement occurred in India and China, the two most populous nations of the developing world. Despite this good news, for the much of the remainder of the developing world there was little progress. The fact remains that a very large portion of the world's population lives under conditions that most people in the United States and Europe can barely imagine, never mind tolerate. Even if the

World Bank's figures are reliable, well over 1 billion people in the world live for an entire year on what many in the North spend on a single outfit. Even if the cost of living is lower, $1.25 a day is still very little money in any setting.

A United Nations study released a few years before the World Bank's put a slightly less optimistic spin on the data, highlighting what it labeled "grotesque" inequalities in the global distribution of wealth. It noted that "as of 1998, the three leading billionaires—Bill Gates, head of the Microsoft Corp., the Sultan of Brunei, and the Walton family who owns the Wal-Mart grocery store chain—had amassed at least $135 billion in combined assets, more than the total GNP of all 43 countries categorized by the United Nations as 'least developed'."[39] Though the fortunes of Bill Gates and the Walton family fluctuate with the value of their stock, even in a bad year for Wall Street their relative wealth is still striking. One need not be a radical egalitarian socialist in order to think there is something not quite right about a world in which one or two families possess more wealth than entire nations.

Though the debate over the IMF touches on many of the critical issues facing developing economies, it barely scratches the surface in other respects. For large parts of the Third World in which the prospects for development are bleakest, the bad news just keeps coming. The obstacles to development appear so numerous, intractable, and interrelated that it is hard to know where or how to begin addressing them. One feels trapped in an endless series of catch-22s. The interrelated problems of poverty, political instability, and investment provide one example. Extreme poverty often contributes to political instability as various segments of society compete over meager resources. As long as the political situation remains volatile, foreign companies are hesitant to risk investment (and because domestic savings are so low in poor countries, foreign investment is essential). But without this investment, it is hard to overcome the poverty that contributes to political instability in the first place. Societies end up caught on the horns of a dilemma: Without economic growth there will be no stability, but without stability there can be no economic growth. One can also look at the relationships among economic growth, education, and health care. Economic growth requires a decently educated and healthy work force, but without economic growth how do developing nations provide the education and health care their people need? The list goes on and on. Poverty and the lack of development seem *overdetermined*—that is, there are so many obstacles that the elimination of just one or two would barely make a dent in the larger scheme of things.

To make matters even worse, many of the most desperate nations in the developing world, particularly in sub-Saharan Africa, have been decimated by the AIDS crisis. As many as one in five Zambians is HIV positive, and between 1993 and 2003 the population of Botswana declined from approximately 1.4 million to under 1 million because of AIDS.[40] Demographically, the disease strikes the most vital and economically productive segments of society—young urban professionals. Healthcare systems, which have a hard enough time dealing with relatively easy-to-treat conditions, find it nearly impossible to cope with this complicated and very expensive illness. As a result, AIDS taxes health and social welfare systems that were already straining to meet people's most basic needs. And this does not even begin to take into account the psychological toll on a society that witnesses its young people dying in large numbers.[41]

The 1980s and 1990s are sometimes referred to as Africa's "lost decades," during which economic stagnation left the continent further behind the rest of the world. The first decade of the twenty first century has not been much better and prospects moving forward remain bleak in many places. Economic stagnation could easily be replaced by outright regression. Following the "right" economic policies might help bring development in some parts of the world, but in others the problems of poverty and underdevelopment resemble the proverbial Gordian knot in that we have no idea which string to pull to loosen the knot without fear of making it even tighter.

CHAPTER SUMMARY

■ Originally founded to help nations deal with balance of payments problems, since the late 1970s the IMF has played an increasingly controversial role in providing loans and policy advice to developing nations in response to the so-called debt crisis.

■ As a condition for granting these loans, the IMF required economic reforms reflecting a neoliberal view of the global economy and development. Convinced that previous development strategies failed because of excessive government interference in the economy and misguided attempts to limit foreign trade and investment, the IMF's structural adjustment programs called for reducing the role of government and opening developing economies to greater trade and investment.

■ By requiring these reforms to spur economic growth and development, the IMF implicitly assumes that the major obstacle to development has been the policies of developing nations themselves.

■ Pointing to the success of several East Asian nations, the IMF and its supporters reject the notion that development is impossible within the existing global economy. Only the differing policies of developing nations, not some fundamental feature of the global economy, can explain the diversity of outcomes.

■ From the IMF's perspective, the evidence of the past fifty years reveals one basic lesson: Market-oriented policies at home and integration into the global economy through trade and investment are the routes to growth and development, but socialism, state control, and isolation are a recipe for stagnation.

■ Though the IMF draws criticism from across the ideological spectrum, the harshest and most sustained critiques are informed by dependency theory, which sees poverty and inequality as inherent features of the global capitalist economic order.

■ From this perspective, IMF policies are designed to advance the interests of the wealthiest states and multinational corporations at the expense of the poorest and most vulnerable in developing countries.

■ As a result, critics are not surprised that structural adjustment policies have failed even on their own terms—they have not produced economic growth or reductions in poverty.

■ More important, critics reject the underlying assumption that limited government interference and opening the domestic economy to foreign competition and investment are the path to development. This is not the model successful nations have followed in the past, and it will not work in the future. Such a development strategy is actually a recipe for inequality, poverty, dependence, and exploitation.

■ Concerns about the IMF and structural adjustment aside, it is important to recognize the magnitude of global inequality and the multitude of obstacles to development that many Third World nations confront. Even the "right" policies, whatever those are, might not be enough in some of the most problematic areas.

CRITICAL QUESTIONS

1. What are the main elements and criticisms of the "Washington consensus"?

2. In what sense did debates about IMF structural adjustment policies raise the central controversy in development studies?

3. Why do the East Asian economies such as Taiwan, South Korea, and Singapore play such a controversial role in debates over the causes of underdevelopment?

4. What developments contributed to the debt crisis?

5. Why do some charge the IMF and others in the developed world with hypocrisy in their prescriptions for developing nations?

KEY TERMS

Capital market liberalization, 168
comprador class, 173
conditionality, 166
core, 173
debt crisis, 166
declining terms of trade,
  165

dependency theory, 173
Fiscal austerity, 167
import substitution, 165
international division of
  labor, 164
International Monetary
  Fund (IMF), 164
John Maynard Keynes, 167

Milton Friedman, 167
moral hazard, 172
neocolonialism, 173
neoimperialism, 173
neoliberalism, 167
Organization of Petroleum
  Exporting Countries
  (OPEC), 166

periphery, 173
semiperiphery, 173
structural adjustment
  policies, 166
Washington consensus,
  168

FURTHER READINGS

For those interested in the IMF and structural adjustment policies, the most recent and comprehensive account is James R. Vreeland's *The IMF and Economic Development* (Cambridge: Cambridge University Press, 2003). In terms of the larger debate about the global economy and development, it might be useful to begin with two influential statements of dependency theory: Fernando Enrique Cardoso and Enzo Faletto, *Dependency and Development in Latin America* (Berkeley: University of California Press, 1979) and Peter Evans, *Dependent Development: The Alliance of Multinational, State, and Local Capital in Brazil* (Princeton, NJ: Princeton University Press, 1979). One of the few attempts to subject dependency theory to empirical testing is Vincent Mahler, *Dependency Approaches to International Political Economy* (New York: Columbia University Press, 1980). Perhaps the most forceful (and quite harsh) critique of dependency theory is Robert Packenham, *The Dependency Movement: Scholarship and Politics in Development Studies* (Cambridge, MA: Harvard University Press, 1992). Though not explicitly intended as critiques of dependency

theory, two works that reject its underlying assumptions are David Landes, *The Wealth and Poverty of Nations: Why Some Are So Rich and Some Are So Poor* (New York: W. W. Norton, 1998), and Nathan Rosenberg and L. E. Bridzell Jr., *How the West Grew Rich: The Economic Transformation of the Industrial World* (New York: Basic Books, 1987). An effort to explain the success and failure of development in terms of cultural values is Lawrence E. Harrison and Samuel Huntington, *Culture Matters: How Values Shape Human Progress* (New York: Basic Books, 2001). And an excellent overall survey of international economics is Robert Gilpin, *Global Political Economy: Understanding the International Economic Order* (Princeton, NJ: Princeton University Press, 2001). Two recent works by the authors included in the POV section are Jeffrey Sachs, *The End of Poverty: Economic Possibilities of Our Time* (New York: Penguin, 2005) and William Easterly, *The White Man's Burden: Why the West's Efforts to Aid the Rest Have Done So Much Ill and So Little Good* (New York: Penguin, 2006).

THE IMF, GLOBAL INEQUALITY, AND DEVELOPMENT ON THE WEB

www.imf.org
The official Web site of the International Monetary Fund.

www.worldbank.org
Web site of the World Bank with a lot of data on economic development and links to the organization's annual *World Development Report*

www.unicef.org
Web site of a United Nations organization that deals extensively with the developing world. Its yearly "Progress of Nations" reports can be found on this site.

www.cedpa.org
Web site of the Center for Development and Population Activities, an organization that emphasizes the role and status of women in developing countries.

www.jubileeusa.org
Organization dedicated to relieving developing nations of crippling foreign debts.

www.oxfam.org.uk
One of the oldest and most influential organizations interested in assistance to developing nations.

NOTES

[1]Conn Hallinan, "The Global Goodfellas at the IMF," *San Francisco Examiner* (January 11, 2002), p. 23.

[2]Peter Korner, Gero Maass, Thomas Siebold, and Rainer Tetzlaff, *The IMF and the Debt Crisis: A Guide to the Third World's Dilemma* (London: Zed Books, 1986), p. 35.

[3]Michael E. Latham, *The Right Kind of Revolution: Modernization, Development, and U.S. Foreign Policy from the Cold War to the Present* (Ithaca: Cornell University Press, 2011), p. 85.

[4]Ibid., p. 124.

[5]Dani Rodrik, *The Globalization Paradox: Democracy and the Future of the World Economy* (New York: W. W. Norton, 2011), p. 156.

[6]Jagdish Bhagwati, *India in Transition: Freeing the Economy* (Oxford: Clarendon Press, 1993), p. 71.

[7]Bahram Nowzad, *The IMF and Its Critics, Essays in International Finance, no. 146* (Princeton, NJ: Princeton University Department of Economics, 1981), p. 8.

[8]David Landes, *The Wealth and Poverty of Nations: Why Some Nations Are So Rich and Some Are So Poor* (New York: W. W. Norton, 1998), p. 433.

[9]Ibid., p. 499.

[10]This comparison is drawn from Keith R. Richburg, "Why Is Africa Eating Asia's Dust?" *Washington Post National Weekly Edition*, July 20–26, 1992, p. 11.

[11]Ibid.

[12]Robert Gilpin, *Global Political Economy: Understanding the International Economic Order* (Princeton, NJ: Princeton University Press, 2001), p. 312.

[13]Robert Gilpin, *The Political Economy of International Relations* (Princeton, NJ: Princeton University Press, 1987), p. 268.

[14]Stephan Haggard, *Pathways from the Periphery: The Politics of Growth in Newly Industrializing Countries* (Ithaca, NY: Cornell University Press, 1990), p. 14.

[15]Gilpin, *Political Economy of International Relations*, p. 302.

[16]Bhagwati, p. 46.

[17]See Juan Gabriel Valdes, *Pinochet's Economists: The Chicago School in Chile* (Cambridge: Cambridge University Press, 1995), and Daniel Yergin and Joseph Stanislaw, *The Commanding Heights: The Battle Between Government and the Marketplace That Is Remaking the Modern World* (New York: Simon & Schuster, 1998), pp. 238–240.

[18]P. T. Bauer, *Equality, the Third World, and Economic Delusion* (Cambridge, MA: Harvard University Press, 1981), pp. 70, 76.

[19]"Going Global: Globalisation and Prosperity," *The Economist* (December 8, 2001), p. 67.

[20]Douglas A. Irwin, *Free Trade Under Fire* (Princeton: Princeton University Press, 2005), p. 160.

[21]Gilpin, *Political Economy of International Relations*, p. 286.

[22]Peter Evans, *Dependent Development: The Alliance of Multinational, State and Local Capital in Brazil* (Princeton, NJ: Princeton University Press, 1979), p. 34.

[23]The Report of the South Commission, *The Challenge to the South* (Oxford: Oxford University Press, 1990), p. 38.

[24]Paul A. Baran, *The Political Economy of Growth* (New York: Monthly Review Press, 1962), pp. 11–12.

[25]David Crane, "Global State No Longer a Reflection of Reality," *Toronto Star* (January 29, 2007). Accessed at http://www.thestar.com/article/175804 on February 14, 2007.

[26]Cited in Michael Camdessus, "A Talk with Michael Camdessus about God, Globalization and His Years Running the IMF," *Foreign Policy* (September/October 2000): 34.

[27]William Greider, *One World, Ready or Not: The Manic Logic of Global Capitalism* (New York: Touchstone Books, 1997), p. 281.

[28]"Nothing to Lose But Your Chains: Aid for Africa," *The Economist* (May 1, 1993), p. 44.

[29]Robert O'Brien, Anne Marie Goetz, Jan Aart Scholte, and Marc Williams, *Contesting Global Governance: Multinational Economic Institutions and Global Social Movements* (Cambridge: Cambridge University Press, 2000), p. 37.

[30]IMF Policy Development and Review Group, "Experience Under the IMF's Enhanced Structural Adjustment Facility," *Finance and Development* (September 1997): 32–35. Another study that departs from conventional wisdom and offers a modestly positive assessment of the effect of structural adjustment is David E. Sahn, Paul A. Dorosh, and Stephen D. Younger, *Structural Adjustment Reconsidered* (Cambridge: Cambridge University Press, 1997).

[31]William Easterly, "IMF and World Bank Structural Adjustment Programs and Poverty," paper prepared for the World Bank, February 2001.

[32]Rodrik, *The Globalization Paradox*, p. 171.

[33]Cited in Joseph M. Grieco and G. John Ikenberry, *State Power and World Markets: The International Political Economy* (New York: W. W. Norton, 2003), p. 280.

[34]See Joseph Stiglitz, *Globalization and Its Discontents* (New York: W. W. Norton, 2002), p. 132.

[35]Rodrik, *The Globalization Paradox*, p. 26.

[36]Rick Rowden, "A World of Debt," *The American Prospect* (Summer 2001). Accessed at www.prospect.org/print-friendly/print/V12/12/rowden-r.html.

[37]See http://econ.worldbank.org/WBSITE/EXTERNAL/EXTDEC/EXTRESEARCH/0,,contentMDK:21882162~pagePK:64165401~piPK:64165026~theSitePK:469382,00.html.

[38]World Bank, *World Development Report 2010: Climate Change and Development* (Washington D.C. : The World Bank, 2010), p. 1.

[39]Colum Lynch, "U.N. Cites Disparities in Wealth," *Washington Post* (July 13, 1999).

[40]Hugh Russell, "It's Worse Than You Imagined," *Spectator* (March 1, 2003), p. 22.

[41]See also "AIDS in the Third World: A Global Disaster," *Economist* (January 2, 1999), pp. 42–44.

Does Foreign Aid Promote Development?

Whether or not foreign aid helps developing nations is one of those arguments that just never seem to go away. Whenever an international organization or NGO urges developed nations to increase their aid budgets, development economists renew their debate about the benefits and pitfalls of aid. As with most debates about which policies will promote development, debates about aid are often rooted in unstated assumptions about the causes of underdevelopment in the first place. Opponents of such aid see no evidence that past efforts have helped much at all, sometimes going so far as to argue that aid inhibits development by promoting dependency and enriching powerful and corrupt elites who care little for their people's well-being. Supporters acknowledge that previous efforts were often poorly administered but claim that well-conceived aid programs can help deal with some of the major obstacles to development. Two of the more prominent figures in the contemporary debate are William Easterly, an economist who spent more than fifteen years with the World Bank, and Jeffrey Sachs, an Economics professor at Columbia University. Why, according to Easterly, does foreign aid usually accomplish so little? In what way does Sachs think aid programs can make valuable contributions? To what extent does their disagreement about aid reflect differing views about the causes of underdevelopment?

The Handouts That Feed Poverty (2006)

PERSPECTIVE 1

William Easterly

Foreign aid today perpetrates a cruel hoax on those who wish the world's poor well. There is all the appearance of energetic action—a doubling of foreign aid to Africa promised at the G-8 summit ... [in July 2005], grand United Nations and World Bank plans to cut world poverty in half by 2015 and visionary statements about prosperity and democracy by George W. Bush, Tony Blair, and Bono. The economist Jeffrey Sachs even announced the "end of poverty" altogether by 2025, which he says will be "much easier than it appears."

No doubt such promises satisfy the urgent desires of altruistic people in rich countries that something be done to alleviate the grinding misery of the billions who live in poverty around the world. Alas, upon closer inspection, it turns out to be one big *Potemkin* village [facade]. These grandiose but unreal visions sadly crowd out better alternatives to give real help to real poor people.

Source: "The Handouts that Feed Poverty" by William Easterly, World Hunger Notes, April 30, 2006 from www.worldhunger.org/articles/06/editorials/easterly.htm. Reprinted by permission of the author.

The new proposals to end world poverty are, for one thing, not new. They are recycled ideas from earlier decades that have already failed. There was, for instance, the idea of the 1950s and 1960s that aid is necessary to finance a "Big Push" to allow poor countries to escape a "poverty trap" and climb the ladder toward prosperity.

This push has been underway for four decades now—and has resulted in the movement of $568 billion in foreign aid from the rich countries to Africa. The result: zero growth in per capita income, leaving Africa in the same abysmal straits in which it began. Meanwhile, a number of poor countries that got next to no aid had no trouble escaping the "poverty trap."

Hence, it is a little surprising to see Sachs, who is director of the Earth Institute at Columbia University and an influential advisor to U.N. Secretary-General Kofi Annan, announcing once again that aid is necessary to finance a "Big Push" to allow poor countries to escape a "poverty trap" and climb the ladder toward prosperity.

Where did all the aid money go? The $2.3 trillion, that is, that has been sent to all the world's poor countries over the last five decades. Well, for one thing, it was stuck (and remains stuck) in a "bureaucracy-to-bureaucracy" aid model in which money gets lost all along the way.

The way it works is that a large aid bureaucracy such as the World Bank (with its 10,000 employees) or the United Nations designs a complicated bureaucratic plan to try to solve all the problems of the poor at once (for example, the U.N. Millennium Project announced … [in 2005] laid out 449 steps that had to be implemented to end world poverty). The aid money is then turned over to another bureaucracy in the poor country, which is asked to implement the complicated plan drawn up by out-of-country Westerners. (How complicated? Tanzania—and it's not an unusual case—is required to issue 2,400 different reports annually to aid donors.)

In the best case, the bureaucracy in the poor country is desperately short of skilled administrators to implement complex top-down plans that are not feasible anyway—and report on their failure to do so. In the worst, but all too common, case—such as that of the corrupt dictator Paul Biya of Cameroon, who will get 55 percent of his government revenue from aid after the doubling of aid to Africa—the poor country's bureaucrats are corrupt or unmotivated political appointees.

It shouldn't be too surprising, then, that aid money doesn't reach the poor and instead goes to such dubious projects as the $5-billion Ajaokuta steel mill in Nigeria, which was begun in 1979 and has yet to produce a bar of steel (thanks to the corruption and incompetence of local bureaucrats).

Nor is it surprising that the poor of Cambodia have trouble benefiting from aid-financed education when corrupt schoolteachers "supplement their income by soliciting bribes from students, including the sale of examination questions and answers." (The quote comes from the U.N. Millennium Project, which nevertheless concluded that corruption was not a significant hindrance to aid.)

A new initiative by Sachs calls for aid-financed "Millennium Villages" (moving the Potemkin village out of the realm of metaphor into reality). It envisions a whole package of quick fixes, ranging widely from fertilizer, grain storage, rainwater harvesting and windmills to Internet connections—which would, supposedly, alleviate poverty in a handful of specifically targeted rural villages around Africa.

This much-trumpeted idea once again shows the amazing recycling ability of the aid industry—because a similar package of fixes called "Integrated Rural Development" was already tried in the 1970s (minus the Internet connections). It failed.

Flying in foreign experts to create a miniature village utopia has little to do with the complex roots of poverty, such as corrupt, autocratic and ethnically polarized politics; absent institutions for efficient markets, and dysfunctional bureaucracy. Millennium Villages are to world poverty what Disney World is to urban blight.

Bureaucrats have never achieved the end of poverty and never will; poverty ends (and is already ending, such as in East and South Asia) by the efforts of individuals operating in free markets, and by the efforts of homegrown political and economic reformers.

What are the better alternatives? If the aid agencies passed up the glitzy but unrealistic campaign to end world poverty, perhaps they would spend more time devising specific, definable tasks that could actually help people and for which the public could hold them accountable.

Such tasks include getting 12-cent doses of malaria medicines to malaria victims; distributing ten-cent doses of oral rehydration therapy to reduce the 1.8 million infant deaths from dehydration due to diarrheal diseases last year; getting poor people clean water and bed nets to prevent diarrheal diseases and malaria; getting textbooks to schoolchildren, or encouraging gradual changes to business regulations to make it easier to start a business, enforce contracts and create jobs for the poor.

True, some of the grand plans include some of these tasks—but to say they have the same goals is like saying that Soviet central planning and American free markets both aimed to produce consumer goods. These tasks cannot be achieved as part of the bureaucratically unaccountable morass we have now, in which dozens of aid agencies are collectively responsible for trying to simultaneously implement 449 separate "interventions" designed in New York and Washington to achieve the overall "end of poverty." That's just nuts.

The end of poverty will come as a result of homegrown political and economic reforms (which are already happening in many poor countries), not through outside aid. The biggest hope for the world's poor nations is not Bono, it is the citizens of poor nations themselves.

Foreign Aid Is in Everyone's Interest (2006)

PERSPECTIVE 2

Jeffrey D. Sachs

The developing world often seems like highway traffic. Countries such as China, India, and Chile are in a slipstream of rapid economic growth, closing the technological gap with the industrialized countries, while nations such as Nepal, Niger, and Sudan are rushing in the reverse direction, with rising unrest, confrontation, drought, and disease.

Source: Jeffrey D. Sachs, "Foreign Aid Is in Everyone's Interest," May 10, 2006. The Christian Science Monitor by Christian Science Publishing Society. Copyright 2006. Reproduced with permission of Christian Science Monitor in the format Textbook via Copyright Clearance Center.

The costs of the economic failures are enormous for the whole world because conflicts, terrorism, the drug trade, and refugees spill across national borders.

But drivers can change direction, and so can countries. India, China, and Chile were hardly success stories in the 1960s and 1970s. All were in turmoil, beset by poverty, hunger, and political instability. Their economic transformations show that today's "basket cases" can be tomorrow's emerging markets.

Those who contend that foreign aid does not work—and cannot work—are mistaken. These skeptics make a career of promoting pessimism by pointing to the many undoubted failures of past aid efforts. But the fact remains that we can help ensure the successful economic development of the poorest countries. We can help them escape from poverty. It's in our national interest to do so.

The first step out of rural poverty almost always involves a boost in food production to end cycles of famine. Asia's ascent from poverty in the last 40 years began with a "green revolution." Food yields doubled or tripled. The Rockefeller Foundation helped with the development and propagation of high-yield seeds, and US aid enabled India and other countries to provide subsidized fertilizer and seeds to impoverished farmers. Once farmers could earn an income, they could move on to small-business development.

A second step out of poverty is an improvement in health conditions, led by improved nutrition, cleaner drinking water, and more basic health services. In the Asian success stories, child mortality dropped sharply, which, in turn, led to smaller families because poor parents gained confidence that their children would survive to adulthood.

The third step is the move from economic isolation to international trade. Chile, for instance, has become the chief source of off-season fruit in the US during the past 20 years by creating highly efficient supply chains. China and India have boomed as exporters of manufacturing goods and services, respectively. In all three, trade linkages were a matter of improved connectivity—roads, power, telecommunications, the Internet, and transport containerization.

Today, the skeptics like to claim that Africa is too far behind, too corrupt, to become a China or India. They are mistaken. An African green revolution, health revolution, and connectivity revolution are all within reach. Engineers and scientists have already developed the needed tools. The Millennium Villages project, which a group of colleagues and I developed, is now rapidly expanding in ten countries in Africa and is showing that this triple transformation—in improved agriculture, health, and connectivity—is feasible.

Improved seed varieties, fertilizers, irrigation, and trucks have all helped convert famine into bumper crops in just one or two productive growing seasons.

Malaria is under control. Farmers have access to capital to make the change from subsistence to cash crops. Children are being treated for worms and receive a midday meal to help keep them healthy and in school.

Skeptics said that African peasants would not grow more food, that fertilizers would go missing, that bed nets would be cut up to make wedding veils, and that local officials would block progress.

The truth is the opposite. In any part of the world, the poorest of the poor want a chance for a better future, especially for their children. Give them the tools, and they will grasp the chance.

Aid skeptics such as professor William Easterly, author of the recent book *The White Man's Burden*, are legion. Instead of pointing to failures, we need to amplify the successes—including the green revolution, the global eradication of smallpox, the spread of literacy, and, now, the promise of the Millennium Villages.

The standards for successful aid are clear. They should be targeted, specific, measurable, accountable, and scalable. They should support the triple transformation in agriculture, health, and infrastructure. We should provide direct assistance to villages in ways that can be measured and monitored.

The Millennium Villages project relies on community participation and accountability to ensure that fertilizers, medicines, and the like are properly used.

Millennium Promise, an organization I co-founded, champions and furthers the development of the Millennium Villages project. It has partnered with the Red Cross, UNICEF, the UN Foundation, Centers for Disease Control, and the World Health Organization to get antimalaria bed nets to the children of Africa.

In this fragile and conflict-laden world, we must value life everywhere by stopping needless disease and deaths, promoting economic growth, and helping ensure that our children's lives will be treasured in the years ahead.

8

Globalization and Sovereignty

Key Controversy: Is Globalization a Threat to National Sovereignty?

This chapter explores a central aspect of the larger debate over what has become known as *globalization*—whether national societies and governments are becoming part of a single global society. The question is whether globalization is robbing nations of their ability to shape their own policies and destinies. Some believe that economic and technological trends are taking critical decisions out of the hands of national governments, placing them at the mercy of supranational forces, actors, and institutions. Economic actors such as multinational corporations are increasingly able to escape the power of national governments. Observers from a variety of perspectives—liberal, Marxist, and feminist—agree that globalization is occurring, though they disagree on whether this process is essentially beneficial or harmful. Others, particularly realists, believe these arguments are wildly exaggerated: National boundaries, communities, and governments are still paramount and the world remains fundamentally a collection of national communities rather than a truly global society or economy. ■

A walk down the KurfÜstendam, Berlin's major shopping street, would come as something of a disappointment to a first-time visitor hoping to be overwhelmed by the sights and sounds of a different culture and society. Were it not for the fact that most people were speaking German, one might just as well be walking down Fifth Avenue in New York or Michigan Avenue in Chicago. The clothes would look familiar—Levi jeans and Nike sneakers abound. The food would taste familiar—it takes little effort to find a McDonald's, Pizza Hut, or Starbucks. The music would sound familiar, and larger-than-life posters of pop stars known to any American teenager grace the windows of Virgin Records. Automatic teller machines make access to one's checking account no more difficult than at home. After a long day buying items you could just as easily have purchased in the

United States, you could duck into an Internet café to check the day's e-mail messages. Back at the hotel, an episode of *Lost* is likely to be on television and you could catch the news on CNN before falling asleep. This would not have been the experience of someone making the same transatlantic journey thirty years ago, when traveling to another country was, well, like traveling to another country

The sense that Berlin is no longer much different from Chicago are manifestations of something we call **globalization**, a term more widely used than defined. When people refer to globalization, they generally mean that traditional divisions and boundaries that used to mark global society are no longer what they once were. In clichéd terms, the world is becoming a smaller place. Anthony Giddens sees globalization as "the intensification of worldwide social relations which link distant localities in such a way that local happenings are shaped by events occurring many miles away and vice versa." But Martin Albrow provides the most succinct and general definition of globalization as "all those processes by which the people of the world are incorporated into a single world society."[1]

globalization The multifaceted process by which the nations and societies of the world are increasingly being merged into a single global society and economy.

Starbucks in Beijing's Forbidden City. Many Chinese objected when the Seattle based coffee company began peddling lattes in this place where only their emperors used to walk. The spread of such international brands is only the most vivid symbol of globalization.

Source: Macduff Everton/Terra/Corbis

Globalization is, of course, a multifaceted phenomenon. Though many focus on its economic aspects, and perhaps rightly so, this is not the be-all and end-all of globalization. There are important environmental, cultural, and even medical aspects of globalization. It is no understatement, for example, to note that "the globalization of trade is inextricably linked to the globalization of disease…. With globalization, widespread diseases are literally a plane ride away."[2] The worldwide spread of AIDS and fears of bird flu are dramatic examples of the globalization of disease. And the same technologies that allow us to move consumer goods and legitimate investments around the world with ease can be utilized to traffic in illegal narcotics and funnel money to terrorist organizations. The Internet might undermine totalitarian governments by making it easier for people to access ideas and information, but it is also "emerging as the critical dimension of twenty-first century global terrorism, with Web sites and electronic bulletin boards spreading ideological messages, perpetuating terrorist networks, [and] providing links between operatives in cyberspace."[3] The technology and process of globalization are neutral and can be used for good or ill.

What Is at Stake

Beneath the very general observations about our shrinking world lie tremendous debate and unease about the nature and consequences of globalization, ranging from seemingly petty concerns that English is corrupting the French language to worries about increasing global economic inequality. The debates are both empirical and normative. Empirically, the disagreement is about the extent of globalization—are nations, economies, and cultures really as interconnected as some believe, or is such talk exaggerated "globaloney"? Normatively, the issue is whether globalization is a progressive force to be welcomed and encouraged or a malignant process to be condemned and resisted.

Obviously, it is not possible to do justice to all aspects of the globalization debate in a single chapter. Fortunately, many of the issues associated with globalization are dealt with in other chapters. We have already looked at the debates over free trade and development, both central elements of the larger globalization controversy. Later, we will examine global environmental issues. This chapter focuses on another issue that lies at the heart of debates about globalization—whether it is undermining national sovereignty. The fear is that nations are gradually losing the ability to determine their own fate as the forces of globalization shift power and decision making to other entities. According to this **constrained state thesis**, "changes in the international political economy have radically restricted policy choice and forced policy shifts that play to the preferences of global investors and mobile corporations, rather than to the needs of the domestic political economy and its citizenry."[4] Dani Rodrik frames the stakes in the globalization debate most succinctly and dramatically, arguing that "we cannot have hyperglobaliztion, democracy, and national self-determination all at once."[5] If this is the case, which of the three should we be prepared to sacrifice?

constrained state thesis The idea that the forces driving globalization are profoundly weakening or limiting the ability of national states to shape their own policies and destinies.

The Vision of a Borderless World

Interdependence was the buzzword of the 1970s. Middle East crises, oil embargoes, and long gas lines brought home how interdependent the economies of the world had become. *Globalization* appears to have entered the lexicon of international relations in the early 1980s and reflected a sense that *interdependence* no longer captured the full magnitude of how much our world was changing. Interdependence suggested that increasing levels of international trade and investment were creating mutual dependencies among different national economies. Globalization conveys something more—not merely increasing interdependence but the emergence of single global economy. To use an analogy, we usually do not describe the economy of Minneapolis as being dependent on the economy of St. Paul. These are not two separate economies dependent on each other but rather part of a single economy. This is what globalization implies—not just greater interdependence, but something well beyond that.

No one has been more articulate in presenting a vision of globalization as eroding national sovereignty than Kenichi Ohmae. In his boldly-titled books *The Borderless World* and *The End of the Nation State*, Ohmae argues that economic and technological trends are rendering the nation-state increasingly irrelevant and impotent. This effect can be seen most vividly in the global economy: "On the political map, the boundaries between countries are as clear as ever. But on the competitive map, a map showing the real flows of financial and industrial activity, those boundaries have largely disappeared."[6] If we remove the political borders from a map and look only at the patterns of economic activity, we would no longer be able to redraw the world's political boundaries.

This disconnect between economic and political realities, however, cannot last forever. Ohmae thinks a readjustment is already well under way: "the modern nation-state itself—the artifact of the eighteenth and nineteenth centuries—has begun to crumble."[7] Nicholas Negroponte outdoes even Ohmae in consigning the nation-state to the dustbin of history: "Like a mothball, which goes from solid to gas directly, I expect the nation-state to evaporate."[8] And Anthony Giddens joins the funeral chorus: "Nations have lost the sovereignty they once had, and politicians have lost their capability to influence events.... The era of the nation-state is over."[9] But why? Why might globalization be eroding the nation-state's sovereignty, or even threatening its extinction? The answer is to be found in technological and political changes that have made it easier to move, communicate, and trade without regard to location and national borders.

Ending the Tyranny of Location

Throughout most of human history people lived in local economies. They either grew their own food or bought it from local producers, and most of their possessions were made nearby. Today, hardly anything on our supermarket shelves is grown locally—the tomatoes are from New Jersey, the pineapples from the Philippines, and the broccoli from Chile. Virtually nothing in our homes was produced within even a hundred miles of where we live. We no longer live in localized economies. Certainly global trade is nothing new—the Dutch East India Company was global in scope back in the 1500s and 1600s and people in Europe enjoyed spices from Asia. But in the larger scheme of things, the volume of such trade was miniscule and unimportant in the lives of most people.

The process of moving from local to national economies and from national economies to an international economy has taken several centuries and involves developments allowing people to overcome previous obstacles to long-distance commerce. Before the industrial revolution, transporting goods across great distances was either extremely expensive or impossible (e.g., one could hardly transport fresh produce from Brazil to France without refrigeration). The advent of the internal combustion engine, the railroad, the steamship, and the telegraph helped overcome many of these obstacles. Advances in transportation drove the first wave of globalization in the 1800s and early 1900s. The current wave of globalization rests more on revolutions in communications (though easy and cheap air transportation is part of contemporary globalization). As Thomas Friedman explains, "Today's era of globalization is built around falling telecommunications costs—thanks to microchips, satellites, fiber optics and the Internet.... technologies now allow companies to locate different parts of their production, research and marketing in different countries, but still tie them together ... as though they were in one place."[10] The head of Levi-Strauss provides an illustration: "Our company buys denim in North Carolina, ships it to France where it is sewn into jeans, launders these jeans in Belgium, and markets them in Germany using TV commercials developed in England."[11]

Limited technology, however, was not the only obstacle to the emergence of a genuinely international economy. Except for relatively rare and brief periods of free trade, tariffs, quotas, and other barriers made international commerce difficult. In order for a truly global economy to emerge, the technological *and* political obstacles had to be overcome. The creation of a liberal trading order after World War II provided the political foundation for the emergence of a global economy. As Martin Wolf explains, "before markets, modems and manufacturers could do their work, political changes had to take place ... the foundations of the globalized business world are political."[12]

Thus, until the industrial revolution economic production and exchange suffered from the **tyranny of location**—that is, a business's prospects depended to a significant degree on its physical location. In the contemporary world, however, this no longer matters very much. A company producing cars in my hometown enjoys no significant competitive advantage over one on the other side of the globe, though this may not remain the case indefinitely. Given dramatic increases in the price of oil in 2007–2008 and 2011, some suggest that rising transportation costs might reverse this trend. Jeff Rubin and Benjamin Taj warn that "Globalization is reversible. Higher energy prices are impacting transport costs at an unprecedented rate. So much so, that the cost of moving goods, not the cost of tariffs, is the largest barrier to global trade today."[13] Until recently, however, the conjuncture of free trade policies and technological advances liberated commerce from the shackles of geography, permitting the emergence of national and, now, international economies. This declining relevance of physical location underpins the threat to national sovereignty.

tyranny of location
Conditions in which a producer's geographical proximity to sources of supply or markets is a critical determinant of its ability to compete effectively.

The Mobility of Capital

When location mattered a great deal, businesses often had no alternative but to locate in certain places. Take the hypothetical example of a tire company. If it wants to sell tires in Cleveland and the U.S. government imposes a tax on imported tires, companies producing in the United States enjoy a price advantage because they avoid the import tax. Similarly, if it costs a lot of money to ship tires 1,000 miles, then the company should probably locate its factory close to Cleveland. But if transporting products is cheap, the company can locate anywhere within the United States. And if there are no import taxes, it can locate anywhere in the world. Diminishing technological and political obstacles to trade increases what we call the **mobility of capital**, allowing our tire company to locate in Cleveland, Georgia, or Indonesia.

mobility of capital The ease with which businesses and investment can move from one part of the world to another. Potential obstacles might include costs associated with commerce over long distances or government policies that make trade difficult.

When corporations enjoy such freedom, the relative power between governments and business shifts. This is the critical point. If a business needs to locate in a certain place, the government controlling that territory has leverage allowing it to tax and regulate. The stronger the shackles of location, the stronger are the powers of governments to control and regulate business. But as businesses enjoy greater mobility, they can simply relocate if governments enact policies they do not like.

We can see this on a small scale when companies shop around for places to build plants. The scenario is familiar. Company X announces that it has narrowed its choice for a new factory to three cities. City leaders then engage in a feverish competition to see who can offer the best deal, usually involving exemptions from local taxes. In such cases, one has to wonder who is really in charge: Are governments regulating businesses, or are businesses regulating governments? Martin and Schumann frame the problem in stark terms: "It is no longer democratically elected governments which decide the level of taxes; rather, the people who direct the flow of capital and goods themselves establish what contribution they wish to make to state expenditure."[14] The fear of "capital flight" allows businesses to dictate what policies, regulations, and tax levels governments can impose: Give us what we want, or we (and our jobs) move elsewhere. This shifting of power from governments to mobile capital is one of the developments threatening the sovereignty of states.

The Race to the Bottom

race to the bottom The proposition that globalization is exerting downward pressure on wages, regulations, taxes, and social welfare benefits as corporations relocate in search of lower wages, fewer regulations, and lower taxes.

The ability of capital to dictate policies is most clearly seen in what critics of globalization refer to as the **race to the bottom**. If corporations are no longer tied to any particular location, what determines where they will set up shop? There are, of course, a host of considerations that businesses take into account. But surely the costs of doing business are paramount. All other things being equal, businesses prefer to locate where the costs of production are lowest, because this maximizes profits. The story of Nike, the familiar American sports apparel company, provides an illustration:

> All but 1 percent of the 90 million shoes Nike makes each year are manufactured in Asia. If the costs in a particular country or factory move too far out of line, productivity will have to rise to compensate, or Nike will take its business elsewhere.... Until

recently, almost all of Nike's shoes were made in South Korea and Taiwan, but as labor costs there have soared, the firm's contractors in these two countries have moved much of their production to cheaper sites in China, Indonesia, and Thailand. Now, Vietnam looks like the next country on the list.[15]

But there is no need to look to the other side of the world for examples. Immediately south of the U.S.–Mexican border a host of U.S. companies manufacture everything from auto parts to kitchen appliances. Why not locate a few miles away in Texas instead? A large part of the answer has to be the lower costs of production—lower wages, fewer benefits, and less regulation. Because the final product can be imported into the United States without barriers thanks to free trade agreements, it would make little economic sense to locate in the United States, where the costs of production are higher.

This ability to move around in search of lower costs is what propels the race to the bottom. In a globalized free market economy, workers everywhere compete as companies like Nike go shopping for the best deal. If the workers in Taiwan ask for too much, Vietnam awaits. The problem is exacerbated by the fact that labor does not share the same level of mobility. Because restrictions on immigration remain in force throughout the world, workers are not free to move around in search of the highest wages. This imbalance of mobility puts workers at a tremendous disadvantage. There is nothing new about fears that trade with poorer countries will depress wages at home. As early as the seventeenth century John Pollexfen worried about the impact of British trade with India: "This [goods] from India must otherwise be the cheapest, and all people will go to the cheapest markets, which will affect the rents of land and bring our working people to poverty."[16]

Declining wages are only part of the race to the bottom. Complying with government regulations is also part of the cost of doing business. In a globalized economy, states imposing the fewest regulations will be most attractive to corporations. This pressures states to reduce regulations to attract business. In terms of environmental regulations, John Gray explains the result: "The countries that require businesses to be environmentally accountable will be at a systematic disadvantage…. Over time, either enterprises operating in environmentally accountable regimes will be driven out of business, or the regulatory frameworks of such regimes will drift down to a common denominator in which their competitive advantage is reduced."[17]

The problems continue. Globalization also poses a danger to social welfare programs that protect the poor. Businesses, like individuals, generally prefer lower taxes to higher taxes. Though celebrities can escape to tax havens or hide their money in foreign banks, the average person is stuck paying whatever taxes the government imposes. In a globalized economy, corporations can move to places where taxes are minimal. This freedom places national governments with generous welfare programs in a bind. If they impose high taxes on business to finance social welfare spending, they run the risk that the businesses will pick up and move. This leaves two unpalatable options. First, governments can raise taxes on people and businesses that cannot move. Rodrik explains how the ability of firms to move around the globe "puts downward pressure on corporate tax rates and shifts the tax burden from capital, which is internationally mobile, to labor, which is much less so."[18] Second, governments can simply cut the social welfare programs financed through taxation. Thus, the race to the bottom in corporate taxes can also become a race to bottom in social welfare programs, further harming those already vulnerable to the pressures of globalization.

Thus, the mobility of capital creates a race to the bottom on many levels—wages, environmental and safety regulations, corporate taxes, and social welfare benefits. Jeremy Brecher and Tim Costello summarize the problem in their vividly titled *Global Village or Global Pillage*: "Corporations can now outflank the controls governments and organized citizens once placed on them by relocating.... So each [government] tries to reduce labor, social, and environmental costs below the others. The result is a 'downward leveling'—a disastrous 'race to the bottom' in which conditions for all tend to fall toward those of the poorest and most desperate."[19] And to the extent that individual states must respond to these pressures or risk the flight of capital, they have been robbed of their effective sovereignty. Corporations tell governments what they can and cannot do rather than the other way around. Governments that do not toe the line are "disciplined" by the global market and capital. National governments either conform to the dictates of the global market or suffer the consequences.

It is not only business and the global market that threaten national sovereignty. Nations also have to deal with increasingly powerful international organizations, such as the International Monetary Fund (IMF) and the World Bank. As discussed in Chapter 7, many Third World nations borrowed money during the 1970s and found themselves unable to pay back these loans in the 1980s. The IMF and the World Bank stepped in to deal with the crisis. As a condition for rescheduling debt payments or granting new loans, the IMF required nations to adopt structural adjustment programs, which included reductions in social spending, the elimination of deficit spending, privatization, and opening markets to international competition. The IMF deemed these policies essential for attracting foreign investment and thus for promoting economic growth. Not coincidentally, critics are quick to point out, these policies also "neatly coincide with the agenda of mobile capital."[20] Such is the power of the IMF that noted economist Jeffrey Sachs describes it as "an all-too constant presence, almost a surrogate government in financial matters.... These governments rarely move without consulting the IMF staff, and when they do they risk their lifelines to capital markets, foreign aid and international respectability."[21] The characterization of the IMF as a surrogate government highlights the issue of lost sovereignty.

Taken as a whole, the race to the bottom thesis embodies three key fears about globalization. First, the possible erosion of national sovereignty and ability of governments to pursue independently determined policies. Second, the further immiseration of poor, working class, and marginalized people around the world as wages are depressed, environments degraded, and social welfare benefits slashed. Third, the erosion of democratic governance as international markets, corporations, and organizations shape, influence, or even dictate policies to national governments. When the corporations and the unelected leaders of the IMF and World Bank can tell elected leaders what to do, both sovereignty and democracy are compromised. As a result of globalization, national policies are increasingly determined by forces, people, and institutions that no one ever voted for. This results in a **democratic deficit**. "The fear is that the global economy is undermining democracy by shifting power

democratic deficit Problem created when critical decisions are taken out of the hands of democratic and representative institutions.

from elected national governments to faceless global bureaucracies.... Power is going global but democracy, like politics, still stops at frontiers."[22]

The Myth(s) of Globalization

In our overview of international history (Chapter 1), we noted that one of the recurring difficulties in analyzing world politics is trying to look simultaneously at changes and continuities while evaluating the significance of that which is new relative to what is enduring. This is problematic because there is always a tendency to focus on those things that are changing, if only because novelty is more interesting than continuity. The problem can be seen in debates about extent and magnitude of globalization. The question is not whether international trade, investment, and cultural diffusion are increasing. It would be silly to contend otherwise. The issue is whether patterns of international interactions are changing in ways and to a degree so that it makes sense to talk about a borderless world or demise of the nation-state. For globalization skeptics, such talk is wildly premature at best and rests on a persistent pattern of exaggeration and selective evidence.

Location Still Matters

There is no denying that advances in transportation and communications have helped overcome the obstacles of distance. Skeptics caution, however, to confuse this with an "end" of geography. Is location less important for commerce today than two hundred years ago? Certainly. Is geography even close to becoming irrelevant? Certainly not. Most accounts of globalization focus on companies and plants that relocate production in order to illustrate the irrelevance of location. But do these examples tell the full story? Skeptics charge that there is a tendency to focus on examples (often derided as "anecdotes") that conform to the thesis of globalization. The technical term for this problem is *selection bias*. That is, focusing on firms that relocate while ignoring those that stay put inevitably biases analysis in favor of the declining significance of location. Local papers tend not to report on the factories that remain, only those that relocate. But a full and fair evaluation requires that we look at both. Only then will we have an accurate picture of how much location matters.

Somewhat tongue in cheek, Micklethwait and Wooldridge wonder what Bill Gates and Microsoft's legal troubles tell us about the mobility of business. Though the object of some extremely expensive antitrust lawsuits by the U.S. Department of Justice, Gates has not moved his company from the comfortable confines of Seattle in order to escape the long arm of the law. Why not? If companies can move for cheaper labor and/or discipline governments by threatening to relocate, why hasn't Bill Gates moved and why has the U.S. government not been disciplined? The answer is that "Bill Gates could not have threatened to move his operation to the Bahamas, even though Microsoft has relatively few fixed assets. Microsoft depends not just on a supply of educated workers (who would have refused to move) but also on its close relationship with American universities."[23] Focusing on the same case,

Thomas Friedman reminds us "even when a U.S. firm becomes a much-envied world-class gem, like Microsoft, it still has to answer to a Justice Department anti-trust lawyer making $75,000 a year."[24] The news that national governments are impotent would come as something of a surprise to Microsoft's lawyers.

Microsoft, however, is a high-tech firm. Would the same apply to a company making t-shirts or notepads? There are also plenty of examples of low-tech firms staying put. "Wander around Los Angeles, America's main manufacturing center, and you will find squadrons of low-tech factories turning out toys, furniture, and clothes, all of which could probably be made cheaper elsewhere." Why do they remain in Los Angeles? Micklethwait and Wooldridge explain that "they stay partly for personal reasons (many are family owned), partly because they can compensate for high labor costs by using more machines, but mostly because Los Angeles is a hub of all three industries—a place where designers, suppliers and distributors are just around the corner."[25] That is, in many respects it does still matter where businesses are located. These examples are also just anecdotes. But for skeptics, they at least indicate that proclamations of the end of the tyranny of location and the consequent erosion of government power are at best premature.

The Myth of a Borderless World

Kenichi Ohmae proposes that if we look at a map of the world indicating flows of trade, investment, and production, we would not be able to redraw the political map because economic flows no longer conform to political boundaries. Interestingly, Ohmae does not actually provide a map that allows us to test his neat idea. For globalization skeptics there is a very good reason he does not—instead of supporting his position, such a map would actually prove him wrong.

In his book *How Much Do National Borders Matter?* John Helliwell takes up Ohmae's challenge focusing on the United States and Canada—two of the world's closest trading partners who share one of its most porous borders. If Ohmae is correct, the political border separating these two countries should be nearly unnoticeable if we look at trade statistics. Given the specifics of the U.S.–Canada case, this should be a relatively easy test of the borderless-world thesis. Helliwell's findings are not good news for Ohmae. Even though the importance of trade between the United States and Canada has been increasing, the significance of trade *within* both nations still dwarfs trade *between* them. He compares patterns of trade between Ontario and British Columbia (Canadian provinces) with trade between Ontario and Washington State. If Ohmae is correct about the borderless world, there should be little difference in the patterns of intra-Canadian trade compared to its trade with the United States. In fact, there is a marked difference: "Ontario's exports to British Columbia were more than twelve times larger than those to Washington."[26] On a map showing trade flows there would be twelve arrows pointing from Ontario to British Columbia for every one connecting Ontario and Washington. On this basis, most would assume that British Columbia and Ontario were part of the same political unit but Washington and Ontario were not. And, of course, they would be correct. The same pattern is found elsewhere. Despite the creation of a single market in the European Union, people in Europe are still six times more likely to trade within their own national boundaries than across them. Again, there is no denying that the relative importance of trade across national borders is on the rise, but skeptics see this as a far cry from a borderless world.

The continuing significance of national borders is even more evident in other areas. Timothy Taylor points out that investors still behave as if national borders mattered. Within the confines of the United States, investors do not let location shape their decisions: Investors residing in Los Angeles exhibit no greater preference for companies located in their city as opposed to New York or Chicago. In a truly borderless world economy, we would see the same pattern internationally: Investors in the United States or Japan would display a similar lack of concern about the nationality of companies they invest in. But the evidence reveals a striking correlation between nationality and investments: "U.S. investors [hold] 88 percent of their stock portfolios in U.S. stocks. Canadian investors [hold] 90 percent of their equity in Canadian stocks. Ninety-four percent of stock owned by Japanese investors is in Japanese stocks."[27] Thus, if we had a map of the world showing where investors send their money, national borders would stand out like sore thumbs. Thus, even though "international flows of goods, services and financial capital have increased dramatically, … we are still a long way from a single global market."[28]

The Myth of a Race to the Bottom

The race to the bottom is usually presented as an integral element of globalization. The argument makes intuitive sense. Even Jagdish Bhagwati, an enthusiastic supporter of globalization, concedes that "it is certainly possible that closer integration by richer nations with the poor countries, with a more abundant supply of unskilled labor, will depress the wages of richer countries' workers."[29] Daniel Drezner agrees that "the race-to-the-bottom hypothesis appears logical, "but ultimately concludes that" it is wrong. Indeed, the lack of supporting evidence is startling."[30] No doubt there are examples of companies moving plants to reduce costs. But the race-to-the-bottom thesis suggests more than that. This movement of capital is portrayed as a significant, if not dominant, feature of the global economy, occurring on a scale sufficient to depress wages and reduce regulations worldwide. It is not just a handful of companies or even a few economic sectors; it is a fundamental feature of the new global economy.

What sort of evidence beyond specific examples of plant relocation would validate the race-to-the-bottom thesis? If there is a race to the bottom, we should see an inverse relationship between overseas investment and wage/regulation levels. That is, countries with relatively high wages and greater regulation should attract a declining share of investment, whereas countries with low wages and few regulations should attract an increasing share. Bhagwati explains that economists examining the race-to-the-bottom thesis "have asked if there is evidence that multinationals are partial to investing in poor countries that have weak protection of worker's rights to unionize and to enjoy a safe workplace."[31] Wages and regulations are generally highest in North America, Europe, and Japan and lowest throughout the developing world. Thus, if there is a race to the bottom, investment should be pouring into the developing world as corporations shop the world and relocate to lower their production costs.

FIGURE 8.1

Share of net FDI inflows to low-income and least developed countries, 1990-2004

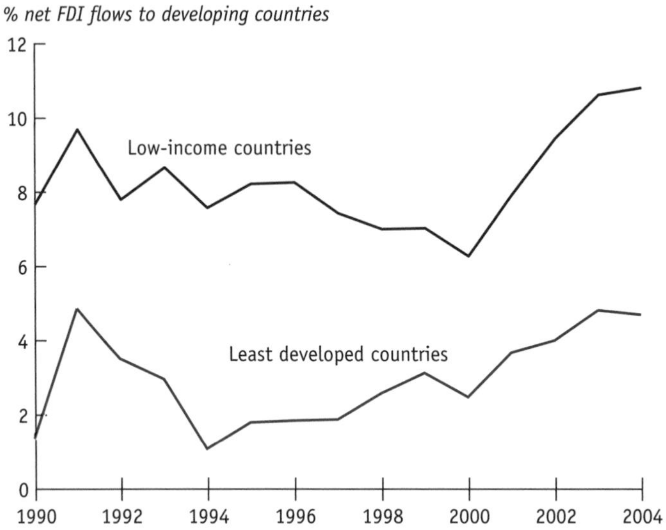

% net FDI flows to developing countries

Source: World Bank, *Global Development Finance* 2005. Used with permission.

The evidence on this front is less than compelling. As an example, Figure 8.1 presents World Bank data on the share of overall foreign investment in developing nations. We see that between 1990 and 2004 the least developed countries attracted between 2 percent and slightly more than 4 percent of foreign investment. For low-income countries the fluctuation is between 8 percent and slightly more than 10 percent. There certainly does not appear to be any clear trend in favor of developing nations. As of 2004 they attracted roughly the same percent of overseas investment as in 1990. The vast majority of foreign investment (more than 80 percent) continues to go to developed, higher-income countries. Hirst and Thompson reach the same conclusion: "Capital mobility is not producing a massive shift of investment and employment to the developing countries. Rather, foreign direct investment (FDI) is highly concentrated among the advanced industrial economies."[32] Bhagwati agrees: "the evidence suggests that multinationals, generally speaking, do not go streaking to where labor rights are ignored or flouted."[33]

Anecdotal examples also illustrate the trend. In the spring of 2002, for example, the company producing LifeSavers candies in Michigan announced it was relocating its factory. Interestingly, the factory was moved to Canada, another high-wage, high-regulation economy, not Mexico. The company was not looking for lower wages or fewer regulations but cheaper sugar. Because tariffs on sugar imported into the United States nearly double its price, a number of candy manufacturers have made similar moves. The critical point is that it did not relocate to a developing country where sugar *and* wages were cheaper. Recall also the description provided by the head of Levi-Strauss. Where were the jeans assembled? France. Where were they laundered? Belgium. France and Belgium can hardly be considered low-wage, low-regulation economies. Because assembling and washing jeans require low-skilled labor, these are precisely the jobs that should be moving to low-wage areas. Although plant relocations to other high-wage, high-regulation economies rarely receive the same attention as those that flee to Mexico, the aggregate data suggest that the former are more representative than the latter.

Why aren't companies flocking to places where they can take advantage of lower costs? According to Micklethwait and Wooldridge, fears of a race to the bottom rest on a simplistic misconception that reducing costs is the only way for companies to improve their bottom line. This misconception fails to distinguish the *cost of labor*, which is not terribly important, from the *value of labor*, which is critical. Although "some companies will undoubtedly move routine tasks to parts of the world where hourly wages are lower, … what employers want is not cheap workers but productive ones. And the most productive workers are usually those with the best education, access to the best machinery, and a support system that includes things like a good infrastructure."[34] All other things being equal, businesses prefer to pay lower wages. But in the real world all other things are rarely equal. In addition to lower wages, businesses also want political stability, low levels of corruption, and effective legal systems, all of which are in much greater supply in countries with high wages and more regulations. This is why most transnational corporations continue to invest overwhelmingly in Europe, the United States, and Japan despite the option of places where wages and regulations are much lower.

None implies that wages for unskilled workers in developed countries are not declining. In fact, many supporters of globalization agree that wages for these workers have stagnated or declined since the mid-1980s. And because this also happened to be a period of accelerating globalization, it is easy to see why many would connect the two trends. Bhagwati and other economists, however, trace the problem to labor-saving technologies that are increasingly replacing unskilled workers.[35] Wages are being depressed as a result of competition from technology and machines, not lower paid workers overseas. If this is the case, halting or reversing globalization would do little to address the problem. The only solution is education and training that transforms unskilled workers into skilled workers.

Conclusion

Is a single global society emerging in which traditional national divisions are increasingly meaningless? Is the sovereign state on its way to the dustbin of history? Is this process beneficial or detrimental? These questions lie at the heart of debates over globalization. This chapter has tried to focus on the first two questions, but it is extremely difficult to separate the empirical and normative controversies. In the most general sense, answers to these questions combine to provide three general perspectives on globalization. The skeptics, often realists, answer "no" to the first two questions, believing that the case for globalization relies on selective trends and statistics rather then more substantial evidence pointing to the continuing centrality of nations and national communities. Since skeptics answer the first two questions in the negative, the third becomes moot. Liberals and Marxists generally answer the first two questions in the affirmative but part company on the third. Liberals, despite some reservations, are essentially optimistic in their assessment of globalization, whereas Marxists, who see globalization in the context of their analysis of capitalism, offer a more pessimistic analysis.

Realist Skepticism

Realists typically focus on the enduring features of world politics; as a result, they are usually skeptical of claims of fundamental transformation. Realists see globalization, which Kenneth Waltz referred to as "the fad of the 1990s," as either wildly exaggerated or mythical. Realists remind us that many of the same arguments associated with contemporary globalization were made a hundred years ago, another period in which national boundaries appeared to be increasingly porous. International trade exploded in the second half of the nineteenth century and by the eve of World War I reached levels comparable to what we see today. Unfortunately, two world wars and the Great Depression brought this earlier globalization to a screeching halt. It took the peace of the post-World War II period to sustain what Findlay and O'Rourke refer to as the "reglobalization" of the world.[36] In 1999, for example, U.S. exports were 20.5 percent of GDP, more than double the 9.5 percent of 1960. Advocates of globalization frequently point to such statistics while failing to note that 20.5 percent is roughly the same as it was in 1900. So even though trade as a percentage of GDP has doubled since 1960, it is unchanged since 1900. Kal Raustiala points out that "for many historians this early wave of globalization differs not that greatly in magnitude from the current wave; some even think we have just begun to surpass the achievements of the late 19th century."[37] On the issue of overseas investment, Robert Wade points out that "today the stock of U.S. capital invested abroad represents less than 7 percent of the U.S. GNP. That figure is, if anything, a little less than the figure for 1900."[38] Robert Gilpin summarizes the basic argument: "Trade, investment, and financial flows were actually greater in the late 1800s, at least relative to the size of national economies and the international economy, than they are today."[39] Furthermore, in at least one respect the world was even more globalized in 1900: People moved with greater ease, with large-scale immigration to the United States being the most prominent example. At the time there were also optimists who saw an emerging world of trade, prosperity, and peace, at least until World War I and the Great Depression put a damper on things.

In terms of contemporary globalization, realists do not reject the evidence of globalization. Most of the facts are not in dispute. But facts do not speak for themselves; they need to be selected and interpreted. In 1986, for example, exports accounted for 7 percent of U.S. GDP. By 2008 this had risen to 13 percent.[40] There is no significant disagreement about this. Those who see a process of globalization under way find it remarkable that the importance of exports almost doubled in just two decades. But even after this large increase, 87 percent of all goods and services produced in the United States were consumed domestically. Realists and globalization skeptics wonder which figure tells us more about the extent of globalization, 13 percent or 87 percent?

Realists also reject the view of globalization as an irreversible process threatening state sovereignty. On the contrary, realists see globalization as a process promoted and enabled by states. Whether it be free trade policies, rules and regulations conducive to foreign investment, or the adoption of a common currency in Europe, states have advanced globalization as a political project. Globalization will again come to a screeching halt if the major states reverse the policies that sustain it. Martin Wolf, for example, worries what will happen if globalization comes to be viewed in negative terms. "Political elites in the U.S., Asia and Europe are struggling to convince citizens that globalization is not just a game that benefits the rich." "If the argument is lost in any of the major world economies," Wolf fears "the political consensus that underpins globalization could unravel."[41] But there would be nothing to fear if governments were powerless to halt or reverse globalization. As is the case today, in the early twentieth century many argued that the economic and technological forces bringing the world together were irreversible. They proved to be woefully wrong. Realists argue that those enamored of contemporary globalization (both pro and con) may be equally wrong. After observing that "the world has seen globalization collapse once already....in 1914," Dani Rodrik asks, "could we witness a similar global economic breakdown in the years to come?" "The question," in his view, " is not fanciful."[42]

Liberal Optimism

Whenever asked what he thinks about globalization, Thomas Friedman answers that he "feel[s] about globalization a lot like I feel about the dawn. Generally speaking, I think it's a good thing that the sun comes up every morning. It does more good than harm. But even if I didn't much care for the dawn there isn't much I could do about it."[43] This observation embodies two typical liberal reactions to globalization—that it is largely an irreversible and beneficial process. The growth of trade and the elimination of barriers are embraced for the same reasons liberals have always favored free trade. The belief that globalization works to the advantage of all reflects the underlying liberal assumption of the harmony of interests. But there is more to the liberal vision of globalization than economics. Globalization is as much about the spread of ideas as commerce, particularly notions of human rights and political democracy. As we have observed elsewhere, the world has witnessed a dramatic expansion of democracy over the past two or three decades, and this is just as much a part of globalization as the spread of McDonald's and Starbucks. Globalization, trade, and democratization are part of the same process. When all the various elements are brought together, liberals view globalization "as the latest in a series of Enlightenment grand narratives purporting to outline a universal civilization and a common destiny for mankind: in this sense it simply incorporates and resurrects the belief in progress and becomes its current embodiment."[44]

Even though Thomas Friedman thinks globalization does more good than harm, this still implies that it does some harm. There are forces in the world that have reacted negatively to the modernizing dynamics of globalization, such as fundamentalist religious movements that feel threatened by what they see as the secular and amoral values that are part of the emerging global culture. For these movements, opposition to globalization is easily converted into hostility toward the United States because for many globalization is tantamount to Americanization.

Perhaps the most troubling aspect of globalization, however, is the widening gap between the haves and have-nots of the world. Whereas some critics see this widening gap as an integral and unavoidable consequence of globalization, liberals are more inclined to see insufficient globalization as the primary culprit. The problem is not that people and nations are being impoverished by globalization, but rather that some are being left behind, excluded from the process of globalization. The poorest of the poor among and within nations lack the basic resources—technology, infrastructure, and education—to take advantage of the opportunities that globalization presents. This holds for large sections of the Third World, particularly Africa, and the former Soviet Union, as well as some groups within wealthy nations. For liberals, the solution is to find ways to include these people and nations in the process of globalization: We need more, not less, globalization.

Marxist Resistance

For Marxists, globalization is inseparable from global capitalism. According to Bertell Ollman, " 'Globalization' is but another name for capitalism, but it's capitalism with the gloves off and on a world scale. It is capitalism at a time when all the

A television factory in China. The relocation of such manufacturing to low wage countries is one of the prominent manifestations of globalization.

Source: AP Images/Imaginechina

old restrictions and inhibitions have been or are in the process of being put aside."[45] And since the current global(izing) order is at its core a capitalist system, it suffers from all the shortcomings of capitalism that Marx identified more than a century and a half ago: the concentration of capital, the increasing misery of the working class, the widening of economic inequalities, and the sacrifice of all values to the imperatives of the market. Although Marx might not have foreseen globalization in all its details, he would not be surprised by it, either. William Greider believes that "the ghost of Marx hovers over [today's] global landscape, perhaps with a knowing smile" because "the gross conditions that inspired Karl Marx's original critique of capitalism in the nineteenth century are present and flourish again." In Greider's view, "the world has reached ... the next great conflict over the nature of capitalism. The fundamental struggle, then as now, is between capital and labor ... and capital is winning big again ... and the inequalities of wealth and power that Marx decried are marching wider almost everywhere in the world."[46]

Hopes and Fears

For critics, globalization conjures up images of tacky fast-food joints, escapist Hollywood entertainment, rampaging multinational corporations, the loss of cultural identities, and faceless, unelected international bureaucrats telling national governments what they can and cannot do. For its supporters, globalization means increased trade, prosperity, the spread of liberal values of democracy and human rights, the sharing of cultures and traditions, and the erosion of the artificial boundaries that have divided human societies. Following the debate over globalization, one is reminded of the famous inkblot (Rorschach) tests psychologists use to gain insight into their patients' mental state. Because the images are so nebulous, they are open to numerous interpretations. The assumption is that the patients' interpretation will reveal more about them than the image. It is tempting to see the Rorschach test as an especially good metaphor for the globalization debate. Because globalization is such a multifaceted phenomenon encompassing social, cultural, economic, and political trends, there are many places we might look for evidence, much of which remains vague, preliminary, and contradictory. It is not surprising that observers from different perspectives can find evidence that allows them to see wildly divergent realities.

Though in this sense no different from other debates we examine, the controversy over globalization appears more intellectually and politically charged. Perhaps this is because very few debates touch upon so many of the basic issues that divide competing perspectives—for example, the nature of the state system, the dynamics of international conflict, and the nature of international capitalism. But there is more to it than that. If globalization is occurring, it portends a fundamental transformation of international relations and global society on a scale we might not have witnessed since the rise of the modern state system. Because the ambiguities of globalization combine with the possibility of a historic transformation, it engages not only divergent beliefs about how the world works today, but also hopes and fears about the future of global society.

CHAPTER SUMMARY

■ Over the past twenty years, the concept of globalization has gradually made its way from academic to popular thinking about international relations. In general terms, globalization refers to the multifaceted social, cultural, technological, economic, and political processes that are gradually merging the world's nations and societies into a single larger global society.

■ Although references to globalization are common, there is an intense debate about the reality and consequences of this process. One of the major points of disagreement is the effect of globalization on the ability of national governments and communities to shape their own destinies in the face of multi-and supranational actors, forces, and institutions.

■ Those convinced that globalization is real claim that technological trends and economic policies are reducing the importance of geographic location, particularly in terms of economic production and commerce. The economic map of the world is increasingly becoming "borderless."

■ The declining significance of location is seen as shifting power away from nations and governments to forces and actors that are able to transcend national boundaries, including multinational corporations, mobile capital, and more amorphous global "market forces."

■ This shift in power is most vividly demonstrated in the notion of a "race to the bottom" in which wages, regulations, and social welfare programs are reduced as corporations and mobile capital move freely about the world in search of low wages, few regulations, and low taxes.

■ Skeptics question the evidence supporting dramatic claims of a "borderless" global economy and society. The data on economic production, trade, and investment demonstrate the continued relevance, not disappearance, of national boundaries.

■ Globalization skeptics also point out that contrary to the predictions of those who see a race to the bottom, the overwhelming majority of corporate investment occurs in those nations with high wages, numerous regulations, and high taxes.

■ The debate over globalization involves at least two basic questions. First, are we seeing the emergence of a single global society? Second, if so, is this development beneficial or harmful? Realists tend to answer the first question in the negative, which makes the second irrelevant. Others, including liberals and Marxists, answer the first question in the affirmative but disagree on the second. On balance, liberals are inclined to see globalization as a positive force. But largely because globalization is synonymous with global capitalism, Marxists view it as a harmful process.

CRITICAL QUESTIONS

1. Why is it so important to recognize both the technological and political forces driving the current wave of globalization?

2. To some extent the debate over globalization and sovereignty is also a debate about globalization's "inevitability." Explain.

3. In a recent analysis of globalization Dani Rodrik points to what he sees as "one of the central truths of the global economy: National democracy and deep globalization are incompatible."[47] What is the source of this compatibility?

4. What do we mean by a "borderless world" in the context of debates over globalization?

5. How might globalization look different for people in other societies than it does for Americans?

KEY TERMS

constrained state thesis, 191

democratic deficit, 196

globalization, 190

mobility of capital, 194

race to the bottom, 194

tyranny of location, 193

FURTHER READINGS

For those interested in globalization, there are few better places to start than Thomas Friedman's popular *The Lexus and the Olive Tree* (New York: Farrar, Straus and Giroux, 1999), an enjoyable yet informative analysis of globalization in terms that laypersons can easily understand. The borderless world thesis is advanced most forcefully in Kenichi Ohmae's two works, *The End of the Nation-State* (New York: Free Press, 1995) and *The Borderless World* (New York: Harper Business, 1999). One of the more favorable and enthusiastic analyses of globalization is John Micklethwait and Adrian Wooldridge, *A Future Perfect:* The Challenge and Promise of Globalization (New York: Random House, 2002). A very critical and influential critique of globalization is Naomi Klein, *No Logo: No Space, No Choice, No Jobs* (New York: Picador, 2002). Another interesting and more eclectic critique is John Gray, *False Dawn: The Delusions of Global Capitalism* (London: Granta Books, 1998). Paul Hirst and Grahame Thompson's *Globalization in Question* (Cambridge: Polity, 1999) casts doubt on the extent of globalization. A recent work skeptical of claims of the constrained state thesis is Linda Weiss, ed., *States in the Global Economy: Bringing Domestic Institutions Back In* (Cambridge: Cambridge University Press, 2003). For a spirited defense of globalization, particularly in terms of its benefits for the world's poor, see Jagdish Bhagwati, *In Defense of Globalization* (New York: Oxford University Press, 2004) and Martin Wolf, *Why Globalization Works* (New Haven, CT: Yale University Press, 2004). A much more critical perspective is provided by William K. Tabb, *Economic Governance in the Age of Globalization* (New York: Columbia University Press, 2004). For an even-handed evaluation of globalization's impact on the poor, see Jay R. Mandle, *Globalization and the Poor* (Cambridge: Cambridge University Press, 2002). The most recent indispensible analysis of globalization is Dani Rodrik's *The Globalization Paradox: Democracy and the Future of the World Economy* (New York: W.W. Norton Company, 2011).

GLOBALIZATION ON THE WEB

http://yaleglobal.yale.edu/
An interesting and constantly updated collection of articles and studies on all aspects of globalization, with a tendency to challenge simplistic and widely held assumptions (e.g., "cultural globalization" is synonymous with "Americanization").

www.globalpolicy.org/globaliz/index.htm
Web site with information on many aspects of globalization.

www.fantasyworldorder.com
Contains a questionnaire that allows people to determine their stand on globalization debates.

www.globalization101.org
A self-described "student's guide to globalization."

NOTES

[1] Both the Giddens and Albrow quotations are found in Jan Aart Scholte, "The Globalization of World Politics," in *The Globalization of World Politics*, ed. John Baylis and Steven Smith (Oxford: Oxford University Press, 2001), p. 15.

[2] Richard Ernst, "Globalization of Disease Is Overlooked," *Gazette* (Montreal, Quebec) (March 6, 2001), p. B2.

[3] Audrey Kurth Cronin, "How al-Qaida Ends," *International Security* 31, no. 1 (Summer 2006): 12.

[4] Linda Weiss, "Introduction: Bringing the State Back In," in *States in the Global Economy*, ed. Linda Weiss (Cambridge: Cambridge University Press), p. 3.

[5] Dani Rodrik, *The Globalization Paradox: Democracy and the Future of the World Economy* (New York: W.W. Norton, 2011), p. 200.

[6] Kenichi Ohmae, *The End of the Nation-Sate* (New York: Free Press, 1995), p. 7.

[7] Kenichi Ohmae, *The Borderless World* (New York: Harper Business, 1999), p. 18.

[8] Quoted in John Gray, *False Dawn: The Delusions of Global Capitalism* (London: Granta Books, 1998), p. 68.

[9] Anthony Giddens, *Runaway World: How Globalization Is Reshaping Our Lives* (New York: Routledge, 2000), p. 26.

[10]Thomas Friedman, *The Lexus and the Olive Tree* (New York: Farrar, Straus and Giroux, 1999), pp. xv–xvi.

[11]Quoted in Jan Aart Scholte, "Global Trade and Finance," in Baylis and Smith, *Globalization of World Politics*, p. 526.

[12]Martin Wolf, "The Political Threats to Globalization," *Financial Times* (April 7, 2008), p. 24

[13]Jeff Rubin and Benjamin Taj, "Will Soaring Transportation Costs Reverse Globalization?" *StrategEcon* (May 27, 2008), p. 4. Accessed at: http://yaleglobal.yale.edu/about/pdfs/oil.pdf.

[14]Hans-Peter Martin and Harald Schumann, *The Global Trap: Globalization and the Assault on Democracy and Prosperity* (New York: Zed Books, 1996), p. 201.

[15]James C. Abegglen, *Sea Change: Pacific Asia as the New World Industrial Center* (New York: Free Press, 1994), pp. 26–27.

[16]Douglas A. Irwin, *Against the Tide: An Intellectual History of Free Trade* (Princeton: Princeton University Press, 1996), p. 53.

[17]Gray, *False Dawn*, p. 5.

[18]Rodrik, *The Globalization Paradox*, p. 193.

[19]Jeremy Brecher and Tim Costello, *Global Village or Global Pillage: Economic Reconstruction from the Bottom Up* (Boston: South End Press, 1994), pp. 20, 24.

[20]David Ranney quoted in ibid., p. 56.

[21]Quoted in William K. Tabb, *The Amoral Elephant: Globalization and the Struggle for Social Justice in the Twenty-first Century* (New York: Monthly Review Press, 2001), pp. 79–80.

[22]R. C. Longworth, "Resisting Globalization's 'Democratic Deficit'," *Chicago Tribune* (October 15, 2000), pp. 1, 6.

[23]John Micklethwait and Adrian Wooldridge, "The Globalization Backlash," *Foreign Policy* (September/October 2001): 22.

[24]Friedman, *Lexus and the Olive Tree*, p. 301.

[25]Micklethwait and Wooldridge, "Globalization Backlash," p. 20

[26]John Helliwell, *How Much Do National Borders Matter?* (Washington, DC: The Brookings Institution Press, 1998), p. 17.

[27]Timothy Taylor, "The Truth About Globalization," *The Public Interest* (Spring 2002): 27.

[28]Ibid.

[29]Jagdish Bhagwati, *In Defense of Globalization* (Oxford: Oxford University Press, 2004), p. 123.

[30]Daniel Drezner, "Bottom Feeders," *Foreign Policy* (November/December 2000): 64.

[31]Bhagwati, *In Defense of Globalization*, p. 129.

[32]Paul Hirst and Grahame Thompson, *Globalization in Question* (Cambridge: Polity, 1999), p. 2.

[33]Bhagwati, *In Defense of Globalization*, p. 130.

[34]Micklethwait and Wooldridge, "Globalization Backlash," p. 22.

[35]Bhagwati, *In Defense of Globalization*, p. 127.

[36]Ronald Findlay and Kevin H. O'Rourke, *Power and Plenty: Trade, War and the World Economy in the Second Millenium* (Princeton: Princeton University Press, 2007), p. 473.

[37]Kal Rautstiala, "Globalization and Global Governance." Accessed at: http://www.cato-unbound.org/2007/06/13/kal-raustiala/globalization-and-global-governance/

[38]Robert Wade, "Globalization and Its Limits: Reports of the Death of the National Economy Are Greatly Exaggerated," in *National Diversity and Global Capitalism*, ed. Suzanne Berger and Ronald Dore (Ithaca, NY: Cornell University Press, 1996), p. 72.

[39]Robert Gilpin, *Global Political Economy: Understanding the International Economic Order* (Princeton, NJ: Princeton University Press, 2001), p. 364.

[40]Figures on trade and GNP are from the World Bank and can be accessed at: http://data.worldbank.org/indicator/NE.EXP.GNFS.ZS

[41]Martin Wolf, "The Political Threats to Globalization," p. 24.

[42]Rodrik, *The Globalization Paradox*, p. xvi.

[43]Friedman, *Lexus and the Olive Tree*, p. xviii.

[44]Clark, *Globalization and International Relations Theory*, pp. 41, 35.

[45]Bertell Ollman, "Bertell Ollman on Globalization." Accessed at http://www.pipeline.com/~rgibson/OllmanGlobalism.htm.

[46]William Greider, *One World, Ready or Not* (New York: Touchstone Books, 1997), p. 39.

[47]Rodrik, *The Globalization Paradox*, p. 188.

What to Do About the Race to the Bottom?

A race looks very different depending on one's position in it. The frontrunner follows one strategy in attempting to maintain the lead, while those at the back of the pack pursue another strategy in trying to makeup some ground. The same could be said of the race to the bottom that many associate with globalization. In wealthy nations with high wages and stringent regulations we tend to think about the race from the perspective of the leader who fears falling behind. But in countries where wages are already low and regulations lax workers view the race from the back/bottom, wondering if there is any possibility of gaining ground. The two essays below approach the race to the bottom from these differing perspectives, the top and the bottom.

In an article from Gemany's leading news magazine *Der Speigel,* Alexander Jung and Wieland Wagner illustrate the race's dynamics from the perspective of China, which is, or at least was, at the bottom. With pool of labor larger than the population of the United States willing to work for a fraction of the wages enjoyed by American and European workers, China was often seen a major force driving the race to the bottom. The fear of losing jobs to China fueled concerns about a race to the bottom beginning in the mid-1980s when it began to reform and open its socialist economy. Interestingly, Jung and Wagner explain that China no longer finds itself at the bottom. The same companies that came in search of low wage labor a decade or two ago are now fleeing to Vietnam and elsewhere. Rather than attracting business with its low wages, China is losing factories due to increasing wages and regulations. Rather than fret, however, the Chinese see this as a good thing. While movement to places like Vietnam is consistent with the dynamics of the race to the bottom, it raises several critical questions. First, how and why has China managed to improve its position in the race and move out of the bottom position? And second, does the ability of countries like China to raise wages and increase regulations undermine the validity of the race to the bottom thesis?

While Chinese workers are interested in moving out of the bottom, American workers worry about sliding into the bottom. A supporter of free trade and globalization, Lawrence Summers nonetheless sees a problem in a "decoupling of the interests of businesses and nations," arguing that the costs of globalization are increasingly borne by labor. He fears that unless something is done to address the problem, political support for policies that sustain globalization will erode. Because Summers sees globalization as an essentially positive phenomenon with some negative side-effects, he proposes policies to prevent a race to the bottom harmful to American workers in order to promote a "healthy globalization." What does Summers mean by a decoupling of business and interests? What does he suggest be done at the domestic and international levels to deal with the consequences of this decoupling? From what you know about the dynamics of international politics in general, what are the potential obstacles for implementing his policies? And do you see any conflict between policies to keep workers in high wage countries out of the bottom and policies allowing low wage countries to move out of the bottom?

PERSPECTIVE 1

Vietnam is the New China: Globalization's Victors Hunt for the Next Low-Wage Country (2008)

Alexander Jung and Wieland Wagner[1]

What can Western companies do when China's factory workers start demanding better wages and conditions? Easy—just transfer production to a cheaper country. China's loss is Vietnam's gain.

The world's manufacturing powerhouse needs new low-wage workers, which is why the man in the dark suit is talking himself hoarse. "Do not delay," he calls out to the people gathered around him, pressing his mouth to the microphone. "We will handle everything in minutes, and you'll have work right away."

The man, whose name is Zhou Liang, works for a private employment agency, which has its office in a bus terminal in Shenzhen, the southern Chinese industrial center. Buses are constantly arriving at the terminal from all across China, bringing in fresh supplies of young migrant workers.

But Zhou, the employment agent, sounds desperate, like someone trying to hawk a product no one wants. Posters on the wall advertise some of the lowest-paid jobs in the world. A wide range of factories are seeking workers, but they pay only the minimum monthly wage of 750 yuan, or about €70 ($107), and that for an eight-hour day, five days a week. But by working overtime and on weekends, Zhou calls out, hoping for takers, workers can easily earn twice as much.

He has finally managed to drum up 40 applicants, and he asks them to line up in three rows. One of them is 20-year-old Zhong Xia from Sichuan province. Her luggage consists of a suitcase and a plastic bucket. The bucket is so she can wash her clothes in the factory dormitory where she is likely to be living soon, sharing a room with several other women.

The young woman is given a job assembling electric components, including cables and plugs. It's a start, and better than nothing, she says quickly before her group is led away to a waiting row of minibuses that will take the workers to factories. The entire process is designed to happen as quickly as possible, to deter workers from changing their minds at the last minute. Labor has become a scarce commodity in China these days.

There is a shortage of 2 million workers in the Pearl River Delta alone, China's industrial zone abutting Hong Kong, where companies from Adidas to Mattel have their products manufactured. The manufacturers there compete relentlessly for labor, fighting desperately for each worker. This struggle marks a new chapter in the history of globalization.

---

[1] Source: Alexander Jung and Wieland Wagner, Translated from German by Christopher Sultan. "Vietnam is the New China: Globalizations's Hunt fo the Next Low-Wage Country," Spiegel Online (May 18, 2008) © Spiegel 2008, Reprinted with Permission.

For a long time, it seemed as if China, with its 1.3 billion people, offered the world an inexhaustible reservoir of low-wage workers. It was the basis of the recipe for success that reformer Deng Xiaoping prescribed for the country 30 years ago. Foreign companies would outsource the production of simple products to China. And the communists would provide them with the workers they needed.

Everyone benefited from the arrangement. About 300 million Chinese were liberated from deep poverty, and China transformed itself into a principal supplier for the industrialized countries. Consumers in the West were pleased they could buy cheap T-shirts and sneakers.

But now this symbiotic system is no longer working as smoothly as it did in the past. A booming economy in the country's poorer western provinces has caused the influx of migrant workers to subside, as many Chinese prefer to look for work closer to home. This in turn has forced businesses to completely revise their assumptions.

Costs are on the rise everywhere. The labor shortage has made production more expensive, as workers can now command higher wages. A more stringent labor law, more expensive raw materials and the revaluation of the Chinese yuan against the dollar have also contributed to rising costs. Inflation recently climbed to 8 percent. China's role as the ultimate low-cost production location is fast becoming history.

German investors, once lured to the Far East by low costs, have recently begun to realize that the financial advantages of outsourcing production to China have all but vanished. "Turning a profit is becoming increasingly rare," reports consultant Wilfried Krokowski, who specializes in helping German companies enter the Chinese market.

As result, production regions like the Pearl River Delta are experiencing a veritable exodus. According to a survey by the US Chamber of Commerce in Shanghai, one in five companies are already considering pulling out of China. Many are taking their factories to places where wages are now lower, like Vietnam, Bangladesh or India.

Or they shut down completely, like the Boji Company. Until recently, Boji was one of the world's largest producers of artificial Christmas trees, employing 20,000 people. Now its complex of buildings in Shenzhen is abandoned and its factory stores closed. "We want our money," angry suppliers have scrawled on the walls.

In December and January alone, more than 1,000 companies left the Pearl River Delta. Most were from Taiwan or neighboring Hong Kong. But they are merely the tip of the iceberg. According to Stanley Lau, the deputy head of a Hong Kong federation of businesses, 10 percent of the up to 70,000 small and mid-sized manufacturers in the area will likely close up shop this year. About 4,000 companies in the shoe industry, says Lau, have already shut down.

What is most surprising about this exodus is that no one in China is concerned about the departure of these sweatshops. There have been no major protests or desperate appeals from politicians. On the contrary, the change is intended.

China's planners know that their country has no future as a low-cost producer. Following in the footsteps of Japan and South Korea, they are converting their industrial base, hoping to catapult Chinese industry to the high-tech level. It is a change that Beijing's communist strategists are promoting as energetically as only dictatorships can.

Beijing recently eliminated some incentives for foreign investors, including exemptions from corporate income tax and tax discounts for many export goods. As a result, it has become nearly impossible to turn a profit exporting certain products, like shoe leather.

At the same time, Beijing seeks to promote the social "harmony" that Communist Party leader and President Hu Jintao constantly touts. It is a campaign meant to counteract growing dissatisfaction in the People's Republic. Beijing's subjects are becoming aware of their rights and are no longer willing to be exploited.

Every few days, workers at Clever Metal & Electroplating in Shenzhen suddenly stop working. Wearing blue uniforms with yellow numbers attached to them, they squat on the side of the road, looking harmless enough—almost as if they were having a picnic. But the mood is tense.

The workers say that they have been waiting for their pay for two weeks. They speculate that the company's managers are running out of money, just as they are gradually losing patience. "I spray-paint metal frames for up to 12 hours a day," complains one worker, "and even the thin mask I wear doesn't keep out the stench."

Conditions still haven't improved significantly in many Chinese factories. The employers pay starvation wages, neglect to give credit for overtime hours and ruin the health of their employees. A worker with Taiway, a supplier to the sporting goods industry, describes how rough life is behind the scenes in a Chinese factory.

Using a device only slightly larger than a toothbrush, she spends up to 10 hours a day applying glue to shoe soles. The stench is terrible and she often suffers from headaches. Although the company has distributed face masks, the worker says, they are so ineffective that hardly anyone wears them—except when the inspectors visit.

Every night, she falls into bed, exhausted. She shares a room with six other women in the company-owned dormitory. There are no showers for the workers, who must carry hot water in buckets to wash themselves.

In the past, the Chinese would have quietly tolerated such conditions. But now they are no longer willing to accept them, and they can even expect support from the very top. The new labor law, introduced at the beginning of the year, provides employees with improved protections against dismissal and higher settlement payments. It also drives up costs for companies, especially low-wage producers.

PERSPECTIVE 2   A Strategy to Promote Healthy Globalization (2008)

Lawrence Summers[2]

Last week, in this column, I **argued** that making the case that trade agreements improve economic welfare might no longer be sufficient to maintain political support for economic internationalism in the US and other countries. Instead, I suggested that opposition to trade agreements, and economic internationalism more

---

[2] Source: Lawrence Summers, "A Strategy to Promote Healthy Globalization," Financial Times (May 5, 2008) © Financial Times, 2008. Reprinted with Permission.

generally, reflected a growing recognition by workers that what is good for the global economy and its business champions was not necessarily good for them, and that there were reasonable grounds for this belief.

The most important reason for doubting that an increasingly successful, integrated global economy will benefit US workers (and those in other industrial countries) is the weakening of the link between the success of a nation's workers and the success of both its trading partners and its companies. This phenomenon was first emphasised years ago by Robert Reich, the former US labour secretary. The normal argument is that a more rapidly growing global economy benefits workers and companies in an individual country by expanding the market for exports. This is a valid consideration. But it is also true that the success of other countries, and greater global integration, places more competitive pressure on an individual economy. Workers are likely disproportionately to bear the brunt of this pressure.

Part of the reason why US workers (or those in Europe and Japan) enjoy high wages is that they are more highly skilled than most workers in the developing world. Yet they also earn higher wages because they can be more productive – their effort is complemented by capital, broadly defined to include equipment, managerial expertise, corporate culture, infrastructure and the capacity for innovation. In a closed economy anything that promotes investment in productive capital necessarily raises workers' wages. In a closed economy, corporations have a huge stake in the quality of the national workforce and infrastructure.

The situation is very different in an open economy where investments in innovation, brands, a strong corporate culture or even in certain kinds of equipment can be combined with labour from anywhere in the world. Workers no longer have the same stake in productive investment by companies as it becomes easier for corporations to combine their capital with lower priced labour overseas. Companies, in turn, come to have less of a stake in the quality of the workforce and infrastructure in their home country when they can produce anywhere. Moreover businesses can use the threat of relocating as a lever to extract concessions regarding tax policy, regulations and specific subsidies. Inevitably the cost of these concessions is borne by labour.

The public policy response of withdrawing from the global economy, or reducing the pace of integration, is ultimately untenable. It would generate resentment abroad on a dangerous scale, hurt the economy as other countries retaliated, and make us less competitive as companies in rival countries continue to integrate their production lines with developing countries. As Bill Clinton said in his first major international economic speech as president, "the United States must compete not retreat."

The domestic component of a strategy to promote healthy globalisation must rely on strengthening efforts to reduce inequality and insecurity. The international component must focus on the interests of working people in all countries, in addition to the current emphasis on the priorities of global corporations.

First, the US should take the lead in promoting global co-operation in the international tax arena. There has been a race to the bottom in the taxation of corporate income as nations lower their rates to entice business to issue more debt and invest in their jurisdictions. Closely related is the problem of tax havens that seek to lure wealthy citizens with promises that they can avoid paying taxes altogether on large parts of their fortunes. It might be inevitable that globalisation leads to some increases in inequality; it is not necessary that it also compromise the possibility of progressive taxation.

Second, an increased focus of international economic diplomacy should be to prevent harmful regulatory competition. In many areas it is appropriate that regulations differ between countries in response to local circumstances. But there is a reason why progressives in the early part of the 20th century sought to have the federal government take over many kinds of regulatory responsibility. They were concerned that competition for business across states, and their ease of being able to move, would lead to a race to the bottom. Financial regulation is only one example of where the mantra of needing to be "internationally competitive" has been invoked too often as a reason to cut back on regulation. There has not been enough serious consideration of the alternative – global co-operation to raise standards. While labour standards arguments have at times been invoked as a cover for protectionism, and this must be avoided, it is entirely appropriate that US policymakers seek to ensure that greater global integration does not become an excuse for eroding labour rights.

To benefit the interests of US citizens and command broad political support, US international economic policy will need to focus on the issues in which the largest number of Americans have the greatest stake. A decoupling of the interests of businesses and nations may be inevitable; a decoupling of international economic policies and the interests of American workers is not.

Lawrence Summers is the Charles W. Eliot university professor at Harvard University.

9

International Law

Key Controversy: Does International Law Matter?

Discussions of international law are often framed by the extremes—those who dismiss international law as a meaningless sham versus those who see it as a tool for dramatically improving international order. Those who question the value of international law argue that because it is so diverse, vague, and contradictory, nations can find a legal basis or justification for just about anything they do. And given the absence of an effective international legal system, it is easy for states to ignore international law when it serves their interests. Although realists usually do not dismiss international law completely, they are inclined to see its role as extremely limited, especially when it conflicts with the interests of powerful states. Liberals have historically offered a more favorable assessment. Although few contemporary liberals suggest that we can eradicate war or other problems simply by making them illegal, they believe that international law embodies norms widely shared in international society. The existence of these laws does influence states in the same ways that domestic laws influence individuals. Constructivists share this more robust view of international law: International law may not prevent states from pursuing their national interests, but it does influence how states define their national interests and what behaviors are considered appropriate in pursuit of national interests. ∎

States are always eager to claim they are acting in accordance with international law. Teams of lawyers in foreign ministries the world over provide detailed legal justifications for almost everything their nations do. Supposed violations of international law are even cited as grounds for using force against other states. But at some levels the whole concept of international law might appear puzzling. International society is anarchic, lacking a central political authority. Unlike domestic politics, there is no higher authority that states feel obligated to obey. This raises the obvious question: How can we have international law without any international government to make and enforce it? The absence of government would seem to imply the absence of law. In the famous passage from his *Leviathan*, Thomas Hobbes expressed this point of view: "Where there is no common power, there is no law."[1] This skepticism is never far from the surface in debates about international law: As Goldsmith and Posner note, "international law has long been burdened with the charge that is it not really law."[2]

Despite the "no law without government" argument, most agree that international law does indeed exist. Modern international law is usually traced to the early seventeenth century when the modern sovereign state began to emerge from the maelstrom of the Thirty Years War and the Peace of Westphalia (1648). Reacting in part to the horrors of that conflict, **Hugo Grotius** (1583–1645), sometimes referred to as the father of international law, devised a system of rules specifying acceptable and unacceptable behavior in war. Though there was no overarching government, he argued that sovereign states still formed a society or community in which regular interactions took place within the framework of rules and norms of behavior. Some of these rules could be found in formal agreements while others were reflected in customary behavior. More ambitiously, Grotius argued that states were bound to obey a higher moral code even in the absence of higher political authority. But where did this code come from? One possible source was God (or religious texts). Perhaps because he lived through the Thirty Years War and the devastation of religious conflict, Grotius preferred a more secular foundation. He argued that human reason allows us to devise a code of moral conduct necessary for the preservation of a civilized community of states. Though he accepted the existence and legitimacy of sovereign states, Grotius provided a vision of a more humane international order in which shared moral values could tame the excesses witnessed during the Thirty Years War. For Grotius there was no necessary contradiction between state sovereignty and international law.[3]

The debate over international law focuses primarily on its impact and significance, not on its existence. Some remain skeptical that international law offers much of a constraint on state behavior. At the margins and on some relatively insignificant issues international law may influence states, but power and interests usually trump law and justice in international politics on the big issues. Others have a more favorable view, claiming that international law provides not only direct constraints on state behavior, but shapes and embodies the norms that influence how states think about the world and their role in it.

Hugo Grotius (1583–1645)
Dutch philosopher often considered the founder of international law. Even without a world government, he argued that nations still formed a community and were bound to obey a higher moral code.

What Is International Law and Where Does It Come From?

Though definitions of international law vary, most characterize it as "the customs, norms, principles, rules and other legal relations among states and other international personalities that establish binding obligations"[4] or the "body of rules which binds states and other agents in world politics with one another."[5] This is, admittedly, a messy way of thinking about law. Domestic (or *municipal*) law has the virtue of centralization—it usually originates from easily identifiable government institutions and is enforced by agents of the state. International law is decentralized both in its origins and enforcement.

Historically, international law has focused on states—that is, how states were supposed to behave vis-à-vis other states. The preceding definitions of international law make some allowance for "other" agents, largely because international law has gradually moved beyond a sole focus on states. Human rights, for example, are increasingly part of international law. This area of international law involves rules about how states should behave vis-à-vis their own citizens. We will have more to say about this new role for individual rights in international law in a later chapter. At this point it is enough to note that the general strengths and weaknesses of international law are relevant in this area as well.

If there is no international government to enact laws, where do they come from? Article 38 of the Statute of the International Court of Justice identifies four (or five, depending on how one counts) sources of international law. In order of declining significance these are:

1. International conventions, whether general or particular, establishing rules expressly recognized by consenting parties.

2. International custom, as evidence of a general practice accepted as law.

3. The general principles of law recognized by civilized nations.

4. Judicial decisions and the teachings of the most highly qualified publicists of the various nations.[6]

Treaties and *conventions* are formal documents specifying behaviors that states agree to engage in or refrain from. Some treaties, such as nuclear arms control agreements signed by the United States and Soviet Union during the Cold War, are bilateral (i.e., involving only two nations), whereas others, such as the Nuclear Non-Proliferation Treaty (1968) involve virtually all nations. But whether a treaty involves two or two hundred nations, it obligates signatories to abide by its terms. Treaties in international law are the equivalent of *contracts* in domestic law. Thus, when we say that a state has violated international law, this assertion is usually accompanied by a reference to the specific treaty or convention whose terms have been violated.

The fact that most international legal obligations derive from treaties and conventions automatically indicates one of the major differences between domestic and international law. Domestic laws are usually binding on everyone. If a state legislature decides to impose a speed limit, it applies to all regardless of any individual's approval. Laws are not circulated among citizens for signatures. We do not get to choose which laws apply to us. In international law, nations are only obligated to abide by those treaties and conventions they consent to. E. H. Carr explains that "a treaty, whatever its scope and content, lacks the essential quality of law: it is not automatically and unconditionally applicable to all members of the community whether they assent to it or not."[7] Thus, international law relies on voluntary consent to a much greater degree than domestic law.

Not all international law is codified in written documents. Practices and norms that states have come to adopt and routinely abide by form an unwritten body of

customary law One of the major sources of international law. The fact that states routinely and consistently abide by a particular norm is often considered sufficient for that norm to attain the status of law, even if it is not codified in any actual agreements or treaties.

customary law that does not require explicit consent like treaties: Consent is inferred from behavior. Sometimes customary rules find their way into actual agreements, but not always. Many laws regarding the conduct of diplomacy, such as diplomatic immunity (about which there will be more to say later), began as customs that evolved gradually over time. It was only with the Vienna Conventions on Diplomatic (1961) and Consular Relations (1963) that these norms acquired the status of written law. Similarly, the prohibition on slavery and the slave trade was part of international customary law before the formal Slavery Convention of 1926. Until recently, the issue of how far off shore a nation's sovereignty extended was also a matter of customary law. The limit used to be three miles because this was about as far as a cannon could reach, though it was eventually extended to twelve miles and was codified in the UN Convention on the Law of the Sea (1982). The same convention contained another example of the codifying of custom. In the early 1950s, several South American countries claimed exclusive fishing rights out to 200 miles, which was viewed at the time as violating freedom of the seas beyond the 12-mile limit. In subsequent years, other nations, including the United States, followed suit. The 1982 convention recognized this new norm by specifying a 200-mile exclusive economic zone (EEC).

Interestingly, though customary international law is often more difficult to identify than treaty-based law, in exceptional cases it can be more powerful because it may apply universally, irrespective of state consent. David Bederman provides the example of genocide. Though there is an international convention against genocide, it is possible to argue that genocide is also a violation of customary law. As a result, "two states may not conclude a treaty reciprocally granting themselves the right to commit genocide against a selected group." The rule against genocide may be one of those "rules of custom that are so significant ... that the international community will not suffer States to 'contract' out of them by treaty."[8] Even those not party to the genocide convention are bound by the customary prohibition.

Though custom should not be overlooked as a source of international law, it remains very difficult to know when a norm has entered the realm of customary international law. How many states, one might wonder, must abide by the norm and for how long before it can confidently be classified as a law? It is even harder to gauge when an international custom has reached a level where it becomes binding on all states even if they claim not to accept it, as would be the case with genocide and slavery. Even experts in international law have no clear answer: "How these particular rules of 'super-custom' are designated and achieve the exceptionally high level of international consensus they require is a bit of mystery."[9]

The Weakness of International Law

As we have already noted, the harshest rejections of international law simply dismiss it by definition: because there is no international government, international law does not exist. This argument might be a clever debating strategy, but it does not really help us understand how most people, critics and supporters alike, think about international law. Most critics concede that international law exists. What remains uncertain is its influence. Those who question the value of international law make several basic arguments. First, international law is a contradictory and vague mass of agreements and norms that offers few clear guidelines. Second, even if we could specify the contents of international law, the absence of an effective legal system severely limits its impact. Third, to the extent that international law does influence state behavior, it is on issues of relatively minor importance: When it comes to the most pressing issues of international politics involving the great powers, security and war and peace, international law gives way to power and national interests.

Vague and Conflicting Obligations

What exactly is the content of international law? Which behaviors are condoned or condemned? Even when we rely on written agreements, answers to these questions are not always easy. The first problem is that most nations are parties to literally thousands of treaties, conventions, and other international agreements entered into over decades, if not centuries. Since 1945 more than 40,000 international treaties, agreements, and conventions have been signed throughout the world. It would be unrealistic to expect all of these agreements to be perfectly consistent with one another (indeed, it is not unheard of for the same treaty to contain seemingly contradictory provisions). This lack of consistency sometimes makes it very difficult to even know what a nation's treaty obligations are. Of course, this is also a problem domestically—legislatures pass laws that contradict other laws already on the books and states might pass laws that are inconsistent with federal law. But on the domestic level there are mechanisms for dealing with conflicts of laws, particularly courts that decide which laws take precedence. The problem is much greater at the international level for two reasons: first, the decentralized nature of laws (not only treaties but also nebulous customary law) increases the likelihood of conflicts; and second, the lack of an authoritative legal system makes the resolution of these conflicts problematic.

Treaties create not only problems of conflicts of laws but also vagueness. This is particularly the case when it comes to treaties and conventions signed by many nations. Hans Morgenthau explains what frequently happens when negotiating international agreements: "In order to find a common basis on which all those different national interests can meet in harmony, rules of international law embodied in general treaties must often be vague and ambiguous, allowing all the signatories to read the recognition of their own national interests into the legal text agreed upon."[10] As with conflicts of laws, vagueness and ambiguity are not unknown in domestic laws. Lawmakers often adopt vague wording to get the votes needed to pass legislation. This is one of the reasons that courts frequently have to interpret laws—if the laws were crystal clear in the first place, interpretation would not be necessary. And to repeat a point that should not need repeating, there is no judiciary to do the same at the international level.

Contradictory and vague laws create dilemmas for even the disinterested observer. For those with a vested interest, there is much room for self-serving uses (or abuses) of international law. With references to the right treaties and a generous interpretation of ambiguous wording, critics charge, almost any action can be supported with a plausible legal justification. Foreign ministries in all countries, including the U.S. State Department, employ staffs of very smart lawyers to do just that. The number of times they have been unable to do so can be counted on a few fingers. Nations rarely alter their behavior to conform to international law. It is more likely that nations will twist international law so that it conforms to their behavior.

No Effective Legal System

To be meaningful and effective, laws must be implemented. It is not enough that laws exist; there must be a legal system with the tools and powers to enforce them. And in order for a legal system to work properly, it must enjoy **compulsory jurisdiction**. Carr explains that domestic legal systems are effective because "the jurisdiction of national courts is compulsory. Any person cited before a court must enter an appearance or lose his case by default; and the decision of the court is binding on all concerned."[11] Individuals charged with crimes cannot opt out of the process. Imagine the state of domestic law if people were free not to appear in court and ignore verdicts they disliked. But this is precisely the state of the international legal system.

Among existing international courts, the **International Court of Justice (ICJ)**, also known as the World Court, headquartered in The Hague, Netherlands, is the most important. The ICJ is the judicial branch of the United Nations. Any state can bring a case when it feels its rights under international law have been violated. The ICJ, however, is not a terribly busy court—between 1946 through the end of the 1980s, the court heard fewer than ten cases in each decade. The U.S. Supreme Court hears more cases in just two or three years than the ICJ has heard in almost fifty. Nonetheless, it provides something that at least gives the appearance of an international legal system.

The problem is that nothing compels states to attend trials or abide by the court's verdict. The Statute of the International Court of Justice (the treaty creating the ICJ) contains an **optional clause** allowing states to choose whether to be subject to the compulsory jurisdiction of the ICJ. Less than one-third of states have accepted the compulsory jurisdiction of the ICJ by signing the optional clause. Even nations that sign the optional clause can specify conditions under which they will not automatically recognize the court's jurisdiction. When the United States signed the optional clause in 1946, it stipulated reservations so broad as to totally negate the principle of compulsory jurisdiction.

This lack of compulsory jurisdiction can be illustrated with a case involving the United States. During the 1980s, the Reagan administration pursued a controversial policy of aiding anticommunist rebels fighting to overthrow the Marxist Sandinista government of Nicaragua. In addition to providing money and arms to the "contra" rebels, the United States also mined harbors within Nicaragua's territorial waters. In 1984, Nicaragua asked the ICJ to determine whether U.S. actions violated international law. The United States first challenged the ICJ's jurisdiction over the matter. The ICJ rejected this challenge and heard the case, issuing a

compulsory jurisdiction
When legal bodies can force parties to appear before them and be bound by their final decisions. Domestic legal systems usually enjoy compulsory jurisdiction, whereas international legal bodies do not.

International Court of Justice (ICJ) Also known as the World Court, the legal judicial branch of the United Nations. Any state that feels its rights under international law have been violated is free to bring suit in the ICJ against the offending parties.

optional clause A critical component of the treaty that created the International Court of Justice, this clause gives states the option of agreeing or not agreeing in advance to be bound by the decisions of the ICJ.

preliminary opinion ordering the United States to cease its mining of Nicaraguan harbors. The United States ignored the order and removed itself from the entire process in January 1985. In 1986, the ICJ ruled in support of Nicaragua, declaring the United States in violation of international law. The United States ignored the court's ruling. When Nicaragua brought the matter before the United Nations Security Council to have sanctions imposed, the United States exercised its veto. That was pretty much the end of the matter.[12] The United States is not unique in this respect. In September 2008 Georgia requested an emergency ruling from the ICJ against Russia's military actions in disputed Georgian territory. In April 2011 the court dismissed Georgia's complaint. But even if Georgia had prevailed, any sanctions would have had to be imposed by the UN Security Council. Because Russia enjoys a veto, the likelihood that this would have happened is minimal. To those skeptical of the value of international law, this is perhaps its most critical weakness, because "no legal system can be effective in limiting the activities of its subjects without compulsory jurisdiction over their disputes."[13]

The International Court of Justice (ICJ) prepares to hear a case. Though it remains the preeminent international legal body, the ICJ's powers are severely restricted by the decentralized nature of the international system.

The general problem and inherent weakness of the ICJ is the enduring principle of state sovereignty. As Ian Hurd notes in his discussion of ICJ, "it is unavoidable in the very definition of a court that it should have power to impose its decision on the losing party, and yet the rules of state sovereignty have been developed over the centuries precisely to insulate countries from such outside and overarching influence." Even though Hurd describes the court's decisions as "final and binding on all states," he admits that "its authority is sharply limited by the fact that it only has jurisdiction over disputes in which all parties consent to its involvement."[14]

judicial hierarchy The chain of command in legal systems in which the decisions of higher courts possessing greater authority are binding on lower courts.

In addition to compulsory jurisdiction, a clear **judicial hierarchy** is another essential element of an effective legal system. Such a hierarchy requires the existence of lower and higher courts with a definite line of authority. Higher courts fulfill several functions. First, parties unsatisfied with lower court decisions can sometimes appeal to higher courts. Second, when lower courts issue contradictory rulings, higher courts decide which ruling prevails. Third, the highest courts, such as the Supreme Court in the United States, establish precedents, or interpretations of laws that lower courts are bound to obey. The international legal system does not have an effective legal hierarchy. The ICJ does not stand over national courts in the same way that the U.S. Supreme Court does over district or state courts. Although treaties signed and ratified by the United States become the law of the land and acquire the status of domestic law, the U.S. Supreme Court does not have to abide by the decisions of the ICJ. Indeed, in conflicts between the U.S. Constitution and international law, the Constitution prevails: "It is now a well-established principle that neither a rule of customary international law nor a provision of a treaty can abrogate a right granted by the Constitution."[15] The U.S. Supreme Court might take the ICJ's decisions and interpretations into account in its own deliberations, but it does not recognize the ICJ as a superior authority.

Law and Power

Historically, realists have been most skeptical about the value of international law. It is easy to understand why. Realists typically emphasize the fundamental difference between domestic and international politics, namely the absence of a central political authority on the global level. This is the "first fact" of international politics for realists. To the extent that criticisms of international law stress the absence of institutions to create and enforce laws, they reflect this basic realist tendency to see the international realm as distinct from the domestic realm. Realists would also agree with James Brierly's conclusion that "the fundamental difficulty of subjecting states to the rule of law is the fact that states possess power."[16]

On the rather mundane day-to-day issues that nations deal with, they may indeed abide by thousands of international laws. But this is not the point. The real test of international law is not whether it constrains relatively weak states on issues of lesser importance. The test is whether it has any impact on the actions of great powers on the pivotal issues of international politics, war and peace, and the use of force. When national power and interests come into conflict with international law, which prevails? Is there any chance that law trumps power and interests in such cases? For realists, the answer is "no." And some realists take the argument even further. It is not just that international law *will be* pushed aside when critical national interests are at stake, but that international law *should be* ignored if it conflicts with fundamental national interests.

At an even deeper level, realists (and, interestingly, Marxists) argue that international laws and norms are themselves reflections of power. International law does not just appear out of nowhere. It originates in concrete social-political settings in which power and resources are unequally distributed. The norms and rules that prevail in any society are likely to be consistent with the interests of those with the power to create and enforce them. Most contemporary international law originated in Europe beginning in the 1600s and developed over the course of the last four hundred years. As Peter Malanczuk points out, "most developing countries were under alien rule during the formative period of international law, and therefore played no part in shaping that law."[17] As a result, it would be naïve to assume that international law has not been influenced by the particular values and interests of European societies: "Law has the inclination to serve primarily the interests of the powerful. 'European' international law, the traditional law of nations, is no exception to this rule."[18] Such principles as freedom of the seas and the protection of private property no doubt serve the interests of those with the power to use the seas and possess the property. According to Lenin, law (domestic and international) is but the "formulation, the registration of power relations ... and expression of the will of the ruling class."[19] On this issue at least, realists would agree with Lenin.

The Enduring Value of International Law

Defenders of international law appear to have a fairly steep uphill battle to make their case. Most of its weaknesses need to be conceded at the outset: "International law has no legislature ... there is no system of courts ... and there is no executive governing authority ... there is no identifiable institution either to establish rules, or clarify them or see that those who break them are punished."[20] How, then, does one make a case for international law? There are essentially three arguments advanced by those who see international law as a powerful constraint on state behavior. First, critics of international law tend to exaggerate its shortcomings by focusing on a handful of spectacular failures and attacking an unrealistic, almost straw-man, vision of what international law can accomplish. Second, nations almost always abide by international law for many of the same reasons people abide by domestic laws even in the absence of a government. Third, critics tend to underestimate how powerful international laws and norms can be in altering and shaping state behavior.

The False Lessons of Spectacular Failures

Extreme criticisms of international law as a worthless sham often highlight some of its more spectacular failures, and there are plenty to choose from. A favorite example from the 1920s is the **Kellogg-Briand Pact** (1928), or the "General Treaty for the Renunciation of War," which was signed by sixty-five states, including Italy and

Kellogg-Briand Pact (1928)
Formally known as the General Treaty for the Renunciation of War, the agreement obliged signatories to renounce war as an instrument of policy and to settle their disputes peacefully.

Japan. The pact obliged signatories to renounce war as an instrument of policy and to settle their disputes peacefully. Though many at the time realized the treaty for what it was—an unenforceable statement of moral aspirations—others actually believed that it could transform international politics. Although the attempt to abolish war by treaty appears silly in retrospect, the failure of the Kellogg-Briand Pact provides a good basis to begin understanding what international law realistically can and cannot accomplish. Even those who think international law is generally effective and worthwhile recognize that it has limits, as does domestic law (after all, laws prohibiting the production, sale, and consumption of alcohol in the United States during the 1920s and 1930s fared about as well as the attempt to outlaw war).

In thinking about the promise and limits of international law, we need to understand two very different approaches to go about deciding what actions should and should not be illegal. Over the past several centuries, the **natural law tradition** and the **positive law tradition** have shaped thinking about the sources and functions of law, domestic and international.[21] A natural law approach is driven by a moral analysis, whereas a positivist approach rests on a behavioral analysis. A natural law approach begins by identifying an abstract standard of moral absolutes—the delineation of what behaviors are morally right or wrong—and then translates these absolutes into law. "Natural lawyers," according to Lea Brilmayer, "suggested that international law followed from the basic universal principles of morality."[22] These moral principles are derived without reference to the actual behavior of people. Morality, after all, is not a popularity contest. If people are already behaving in accordance with these absolutes, so much the better. But what if they are not? In this case, the law becomes a tool for changing the way people behave, sometimes dramatically.

Positivist legal theory adopts a very different approach: "Applied to international law, positivism … regard[s] the actual behavior of states as the basis of international law."[23] Positivists try to identify those norms of behavior that states generally adhere to. These norms then become the basis for law. In many cases, these behavioral norms are also consistent with moral absolutes. We are fortunate, for example, that laws against murder are consistent with both moral absolutes and actual behavior. But there are also many instances in which behavior and abstract principles diverge. In these cases, the law needs to be reconciled to prevailing behavior. Laws that dictate behaviors at great variance with actual behavior are doomed to failure. Brierly explains that "the real contribution of positivist theory to international law has been its insistence that the rules of the system are to be ascertained from observation of the practice of states and not from *a priori* deductions."[24] One of the earliest positivists, Niccolo Machiavelli (1469–1527) warned of the dangers of excessive moralism: "The gulf between how one should live and one does live is so wide that a man who neglects what is actually done for what should be done learns the hard way to self-destruction."[25] From a positivist perspective, the purpose of law is not to radically alter most people's behavior, but rather to punish and alter the behavior of the handful of people who are inclined not to follow these norms.

The problem with treaties such as the Kellogg-Briand Pact is that they attempted to apply a moral standard that bore little resemblance to the way statesmen actually thought and behaved. Although the signatories of the treaty certainly

natural law tradition
A tradition that holds that universal moral principles should form the basis for laws. Usually contrasted with the positive law tradition.

positive law tradition
A tradition that holds that laws need to take into account the ways in which people (and states) actually behave. Attempts to rigidly translate moral principles into law without regard for the realities of human behavior are unlikely to be very successful.

consented to its terms, there was an almost surreal disconnection between the treaty's lofty sentiments and the depressing realities of world politics. The logic of Kellogg-Briand was simple: if war was wrong, it should be illegal, case closed. Its goal was to fundamentally transform international politics. It tried to alter political reality rather than work within it. The pact was the international equivalent of domestic laws against alcohol consumption. But it is easy to overlearn the lessons of such failures. It would be a wild exaggeration to use these examples such as Kellogg-Briand to support any sweeping denunciation of international law as a worthless collection of rules, just as the failure of Prohibition cannot be used to support a blanket condemnation of domestic law in general. The point here is simple: We need to have a reasonable expectation of what international law can accomplish. Criticizing international law for failing to achieve the unattainable is a decidedly pointless endeavor.

States Usually Abide by International Law

It is easy to produce a long list of violations of international law. But this proves little. It would be just as easy to compile a similarly long list of violations of domestic laws. If laws were never violated, there would not be much of a need for them in the first place. The value of international law does not depend on universal compliance. Occasional violations of law should not be allowed to obscure the frequency with which it is obeyed. Unfortunately, compliance never draws much attention: There are never headlines announcing the millions of people who are not robbed or murdered every day. But an accurate evaluation of international law requires an assessment of both compliance and violation. And virtually everyone agrees with Stanley Michalak's assessment that "most of the time states do obey international law; most of the time they do get along with their neighbors; and most of the time, they do cooperate on countless issues and problems."[26] And even Hans Morgenthau, a realist who spends a lot of time discussing the weaknesses of international law, concedes "that during the four hundred years of its existence international law has in most instances been scrupulously observed."[27]

Why Do States Abide by International Law?

If there is no central enforcement mechanism, why do states abide by international law, even when they might derive some immediate benefits from ignoring it? As with individuals and domestic law, states typically have a variety of motives for abiding by international law. The first set of reasons fall under the rubric of **identitive compliance**. When we think about why we usually abide by domestic laws, the most prominent reason is that they embody norms of behavior we agree (i.e., identify) with. How many of us would engage in rape, murder, or theft even if we were certain of never being caught or punished? Fortunately, not many. For the vast majority of laws, especially those that seek to protect people from direct harm, the threat of punishment is not the primary reason people comply. Undoubtedly, "some people do in fact obey laws because law-breaking will bring them into unwelcome contact with the police and courts ... but no community could survive only through an ever-present fear of punishment."[28] The threat of punishment deters the relatively

identitive compliance The fact that people and nations usually abide with laws not out of fear of punishment but because the laws embody norms that are viewed as right.

small number of people who would not be restrained by their own conscience. Similarly, most nations refrain from attacking their weaker neighbors and committing genocide or kidnapping foreign diplomats simply because such actions are considered wrong. The importance of good conscience should not be underestimated, even in the supposedly cutthroat world of international politics.

States also abide by international law because it is in their interests to do so, which we refer to as **utilitarian compliance**. Even when some benefit may be gained by violating a law in specific instances, nations recognize that in the long run they benefit from upholding the law. Take an example that sometimes infuriates people—international laws that prohibit trying and punishing foreign diplomats who commit crimes, or **diplomatic immunity**. Typically, these are relatively harmless but nonetheless annoying violations, such as UN diplomats who rack up tens of thousands of dollars in unpaid parking tickets. But occasionally there are more egregious examples: Foreign diplomats have abused children and killed people in drunk driving accidents without being prosecuted or arrested. In these cases, the host government has two options: First, it can ask the diplomat's government to waive their diplomatic immunity; or second, the diplomat can be declared a *persona non-grata* and expelled. Despite these (admittedly rare) horror stories, it remains in the interest of the United States, and of other countries, to respect the norm of diplomatic immunity. But why? Because U.S. diplomats are stationed all over the world in nations whose laws and legal systems might not be to our liking. Without diplomatic immunity, a U.S. diplomat caught with alcohol or a *Playboy* magazine in some countries might be subject to draconian punishments and might be tried in corrupt courts. Thus, the overall benefits of abiding by diplomatic immunity vastly outweigh the occasional costs.

A related motivation for state compliance with international law is a *fear of chaos*. There is a value to international law as a whole that transcends such narrow calculations regarding individual laws. States benefit from the preservation of a certain measure of international order and stability. Even if immediate benefit might be gained by violating a given law, states recognize that they have a more fundamental, long-term interest in upholding the general system of international law. "The ultimate explanation of the binding force of all law," explains Brierly, "is that man, whether he is a single individual or whether he is associated with other men in a state, is constrained, in so far as he is a reasonable being, to believe that order and not chaos is the governing principle of the world in which he has to live."[29] The preservation of order depends on reciprocity—if you expect others to abide by the rules, you need to abide by them yourself. If states begin violating some laws in order to gain an advantage, this encourages other states to do likewise. If the entire system begins to unravel, the costs are almost certain to outweigh the gains from the initial violation.

States also abide by international law because they fear punishment. This might seem odd given the absence of a central political authority to enforce laws and carry out the punishment. The mere fact that there is no centrally imposed punishment does not mean there is no punishment; it simply requires that punishment be imposed in a decentralized fashion by other states. International law recognizes a right of **reprisal** or retaliation—that is, the right of states to take actions that would otherwise be impermissible in response to another state's violation of international

utilitarian compliance When people or states abide by laws because they think it is in their interests to do so.

diplomatic immunity The principle that nations cannot try and punish diplomats of other nations who violate their domestic laws. This is an example of an international law that emerged first through custom but was eventually codified in treaties.

reprisal An act that is normally a violation of international law but that is permitted as a response to another nation's violation of international law.

law. For example, when Iranian radicals took U.S. diplomats hostage in 1979 with the approval and support of the Iranian government, this was universally recognized as a violation of the longstanding international law. As a result, the United States had the right to take actions that would normally not be allowed in reprisal, such as seizing Iranian assets in the United States. Furthermore, international law recognizes a right of **collective reprisal**. Even though it was U.S. diplomats who were taken hostage, all nations had a right to punish Iran. The right to punish is not restricted to the state whose rights were violated because it is the obligation of all states to uphold international law.

> **collective reprisal** Under international law, the ability or obligation for all states to punish those who violate international law (as opposed to only those states whose rights were violated).

The Iranian hostage case provides an example of yet another reason states usually abide by international law: In the event that a state's rights are violated in the future, other nations are less likely to come to its aid if that state has violated international law in the past. States need to care about their reputations, something Iran would soon find out. Several years after the hostage crisis, Iran found itself embroiled in a bitter war with Iraq during which chemical weapons were used against Iranian targets in clear violation of international law. When Iran protested that its rights were being violated, it got little sympathy or support. Nations cannot violate the rights of others and then expect others to care very much when their rights are violated. Thus, nations are usually unwilling to be saddled with the reputation of violating international law for fear that their ability to call on the international community for help in the future will be diminished.

Liberalism and the Promise of International Law

Liberals have traditionally seen a greater scope for common interests in international relations than realists. But like realists, liberals recognize that the uncertainties and insecurities of anarchy make it difficult for states to cooperate to achieve their common interests. This is one of the valuable functions of international law. Because nations usually do comply, international law gives states some reasonable assurance, if not a guarantee, about how other states will behave. International law lessens some of the uncertainties of anarchy. As Hedley Bull explains, "international law provides a means by which states can advertise their intentions with regard to the matter in question [and] provide one another with a reassurance about their future policies in relation to it."[30] Thus, it is not that states abide by international law only when it is in their interests to do so, but rather that a system of law makes it possible for states to achieve common interests that would be unattainable without international law.

Though they agree that self-interest is a powerful motive for state compliance with international law, liberals are more likely to interpret state behavior as resulting from ethical and moral considerations, what we have termed identitive compliance. When we look at the reasons people and states usually abide by laws, motives other than self-interest are paramount. Is it self-interest that stops people from assaulting, killing, and robbing each other? No. People refrain from such activities because they believe that such acts are wrong. Similarly, is it self-interest that stops nations from attacking each other more often? Probably not. For liberals, the emphasis on self-interest and/or fear of punishment is an unduly pessimistic

The United States' Representative to the United Nations casts a veto in the Security Council. A no vote from a permanent member can kill any motion, making it difficult for the United Nations to act against their interests and wishes.

Source: AP Photo/Mary Altaffer

assessment of state motivations. Remember that liberals view people as essentially rational, reasonable, ethical, and moral beings. Because states are collections of people, state behavior reflects many of the same traits. This perspective provides a much more optimistic vision of the potential of international law.

There are limits to liberal optimism, however. Most liberals have long since abandoned the utopian view of international law that informed the Kellogg-Briand Pact and other attempts to transform international politics through legalistic fiats. There is a realization that international law cannot completely ignore the realities of power politics. But utopian idealism does not have to be replaced with dismissive cynicism. Even if international law cannot bring world peace, it can significantly ameliorate the imperatives of power politics. The realist inclination to reduce all aspects of international politics to relations of power provides a caricature of how the world works. There has always been more to international politics than narrow national interests—there is also restraint, common interests, enlightened self-interest, and, yes, even morality and a commitment to do what is right.

Constructivism, Law, Norms, and the National Interest

For constructivists, the relationship between international law and national interests is a bit more complicated than realists (or liberals) suggest. To say that states abide by international law primarily (and perhaps only) when it is in their national interest to do so ignores the critical issue of how and why nations arrive at their definitions of the national interest. National interest is not something nations discover like scientists discovering the laws of physics. It is not an objective fact; *national interest* is a subjective and variable social construction. Nations think about their national interests today very differently than in centuries past. They also reject as unacceptable, even unthinkable, practices that used to be routine for advancing national interests. David Lumsdaine cites a few examples: "Two centuries ago it was acceptable to wage war with hired foreign mercenaries; now it is not. Killing and enslaving the inhabitants of conquered countries, a common if brutal practice in Thucydides' day, would make a state a total outlaw today. Wars to acquire territory, normal enough in the seventeenth century, are increasingly regarded as unacceptable."[31] Most states today would not dream of doing certain things that were once perfectly legitimate. Why not? Because we adhere to very different notions about what states should be allowed to do; state behavior has changed along with our evolving moral standards.

Realists ask whether international law constrains nations in the pursuit of their national interests, and generally they conclude that it does not. For constructivists, this is not only the wrong answer but also a very simple-minded way of thinking about the relationship between international law and national interests. Once we accept the idea that definitions of the national interest evolve over time, a whole new set of possibilities opens up. Is it possible, for example, that prevailing conceptions of morality and rules of law help shape the way nations define their interests? Not only is it possible, but it also seems self-evidently to be the case. Thus, the relationship among national interests, state behavior, and international law is more complicated than is often believed. "Norms are not simply an ethical alternative to or constraint on self-interest," Audie Klotz tells us, "rather, in the constructivist view … norms play an explanatory role…. Thus international actors—even great powers such as the United States—inherently are socially constructed; that is, prevailing global norms … partially define their interests."[32] We noted earlier that laws, domestic and international, are typically obeyed because people identify with the norms of behavior they embody. This is consistent with the constructivist view that states behave on the basis of shared understandings (i.e., norms) of appropriate behavior. So merely looking for instances where international legal norms constrained state behavior underestimates their importance; we also need to appreciate how legal norms influence definitions of national interest in the first place.

Conclusion

Discussions of international law used to be defined by the extremes: at one end of the spectrum, international law was dismissed as a nonexistent or worthless sham; at the other, international law was presented as an alternative to power politics and the use of force. Contemporary thinking about international law generally rejects both positions in favor of a more nuanced view. There is, in fact, a substantial amount of agreement in the debate over the value of international law. At a general level, Peter Malanczuk comes closest to summarizing prevailing opinion: "The role of international law in international relations has always been limited, but it is rarely insignificant."[33] There is also a consensus that the vast majority of states abide by international law the vast majority of the time. But there are still differences, particularly concerning the motives for compliance, that reflect underlying disagreements about the forces that shape state behavior.

Realists argue that states are primarily motivated by concerns about power and national interest. International anarchy requires that states prioritize power and interests because those that do not will suffer at the hands of those who do. The scope for moral behavior is severely limited in the competitive arena of international politics. The fact that states usually comply with international law is seen as perfectly consistent with this view. For realists, this compliance is driven largely by considerations of national interest, and when there is a conflict between international law and national interests, the latter will certainly prevail. States do not obey international law out of moral commitment. Sometimes the moral and legal course of action is also in the national interest, but this is merely a happy coincidence.

Liberals and constructivists are united in rejecting realist attempts to explain everything in terms of power and national interest. Although morality may or may not be the predominant reason for compliance with international law, it is certainly not the insignificant factor that realists would have us believe. The realist argument, however, is very difficult to counter, largely because the concept of national interest is so vague and elastic that it can account for almost anything states do. Those convinced that calculations of national interest dictate how states behave will always be able to explain their actions in these terms. The "national interest" is like inkblot tests psychologists show patients and ask them to tell what they see. You can usually see pretty much anything you want—if you want to see a tiger, there it is; if you want to see your mother, there she is. If a state abides by international law, you can show that it was in its national interest to do so; if it violated the same law, you could show how that, too, was in its national interest. The realist position is almost impossible to disprove. But even if we accept the realist position that national interests determine state behavior, this only leads to the more fundamental question of how states arrive at their definitions of national interests. Conceptions of national interest do not exist independent of international laws and norms. Certainly, definitions of national interest are reflected in laws and norms, but these laws and norms also influence how states think about their national interests.

CHAPTER SUMMARY

■ Despite the absence of a world government, most agree that there is a body of rules and norms of behavior that make up international law.

■ International law has often been viewed from two different (and extreme) positions. Skeptics see international law either as nonexistent or as a worthless sham that can be easily ignored when it clashes with power and interests. Its more enthusiastic supporters have sometimes seen international law as a powerful tool to shape and change the behavior of states for the better.

■ There are several major sources of international law, the most important being customs and treaties or conventions. Decisions of international legal bodies and writings of widely recognized legal authorities are secondary sources of international law.

■ The major weakness or limitation of international law is the conflicting and often vague provisions in international treaties and conventions as well as a legal system that lacks compulsory jurisdiction and an accepted hierarchy.

■ The ability of nations, particularly the most powerful, to ignore and escape the restrictions of international law provides the most vivid illustration of the weakness of international law.

■ Supporters point out that in the vast majority of instances, nations scrupulously abide by international law for a variety of reasons (e.g., they agree with the laws, it is in their self-interest, and they fear punishment by other states). This fact is often obscured by some of the more dramatic failures of international law, such as the attempt to "outlaw war" in the 1920s.

■ Even supporters realize that international law has its limits, as does domestic law. An effective legal code needs to reconcile itself to actual behavior of individuals and/or states and not try to radically remake them according to abstract moral principles.

■ International law also has profound impact on how states define their national interest and what types of actions they consider acceptable in pursuit of these national interests.

In general, realists are most skeptical of the value of international law, whereas liberals and constructivists believe it is, and can be, an important force shaping the behavior of states.

CRITICAL QUESTIONS

1. How can there be international law without a world government?

2. How do liberal, constructivist, and realist perspectives on international law differ?

3. Why do states usually abide by international law?

4. Critics are able to point to frequent violations of international law to illustrate its impotence, especially when it comes to limiting the actions of great powers. How might supporters of international law respond to this line of criticism?

5. How is international law different from and similar to domestic law?

KEY TERMS

collective reprisal, 227
compulsory jurisdiction, 220
customary law, 218
diplomatic immunity, 226

Hugo Grotius (1583–1645), 216
identitive compliance, 225
International Court of Justice (ICJ), 220

judicial hierarchy, 222
Kellogg-Briand Pact, 223
natural law tradition, 224
optional clause, 220
positive law tradition, 224

reprisal, 226
utilitarian compliance, 226

FURTHER READINGS

The essential reference work in international law that provides the texts of most important treaties is Burns H. Weston, Richard A. Falk, and Hilary Charlesworth (eds.), *Supplement of Basic Documents to International Law and World Order* (St. Paul, MN: West, 1997). Excellent overviews of the sources, content, strengths, and weaknesses of international law are J. R. Brierly, *The Law of Nations: An Introduction to the International Law of Peace* (Oxford: Oxford University Press, 1963), and Peter Malanczuk, *Akehurst's Modern Introduction to International Law* (New York: Routledge, 1997). For conflicting views on the role of international law, see Lewis Henkin, Stanley Hoffman, and Jeanne Kirkpatrick, *Right vs. Might: International Law and the Use of Force* (New York: Council on Foreign Relations, 1991). A theoretically challenging discussion of international law from a constructivist perspective is Friedrich V. Kratochwil, *Rules, Norms and Decisions: On the Conditions of Practical and Legal Reasoning in International Relations and Domestic Affairs* (Cambridge: Cambridge University Press, 1989). A more recent discussion on the merits of international law is Jack L. Goldsmith and Eric A. Posner, *The Limits of International Law* (Oxford: Oxford University Press, 2005).

INTERNATIONAL LAW ON THE WEB

www.icj-cij.org
The Web site of the International Court of Justice provides information on current and past cases before the court as well as international law more generally.

www.un.org/law
The United Nation's international law Web site offers a wealth of information on international legal bodies as well as treaties.

www.asil.org
The Web site of the American Society of International Law provides information on all aspects of international law, including how it relates to current events.

http://avalon.law.yale.edu/default.asp
Maintained by the Yale Law School, this Web site posts texts of almost every significant treaty and legal document of the last five hundred years.

www.law.nyu.edu/library/foreign_intl/
A Web site containing links to a wide variety of sources on all aspects of international law.

www.icc-cpi.int/Menus/ICC
Web site of the International Criminal Court with information on procedures as well as past and pending cases.

NOTES

[1]Cited in Mark V. Kauppi and Paul R. Viotti, *The Global Philosophers: World Politics in Western Thought* (New York: Lexington Books, 1992), p. 165.
[2]Jack L. Goldsmith and Eric A. Posner, *The Limits of International Law* (Oxford: Oxford University Press, 2005), p. 3.
[3]Kauppi and Viotti, *The Global Philosophers*, pp. 172–174.
[4]Catha Nolan, *The Longman Guide to World Affairs* (New York: Longman, 1995), p. 177.
[5]Hedley Bull, *The Anarchical Society: A Study of Order in International Politics* (New York: Columbia University Press, 1977), p. 127.
[6]See J. L. Brierly, *The Law of Nations: An Introduction to the International Law of Peace* (Oxford: Oxford University Press, 1963), p. 56.
[7]E. H. Carr, *The Twenty Years' Crisis, 1919–1939* (New York: Harper & Row, 1964), p. 171.
[8]David J. Bederman, *International Legal Frameworks* (New York: Foundation Press, 2001), p. 23.

[9]Ibid., pp. 23–24.
[10]Hans Morgenthau, *Politics Among Nations* (New York: Alfred A. Knopf, 1968), p. 269.
[11]Ibid., p. 193.
[12]See Robert Pastor, *Condemned to Repetition: The United States and Nicaragua* (Princeton, NJ: Princeton University Press, 1987), p. 257; and David P. Forsythe, *The Politics of International Law: U.S. Foreign Policy Reconsidered* (Boulder, CO: Lynne Rienner Publishers, 1990), pp. 31–63.
[13]Morgenthau, *Politics Among Nations*, p. 277.
[14]Ian Hurd, *International Organizations: Politics, Law and Practice* (Cambridge: Cambridge University Press, 2011), p. 187 and 206.
[15]Bederman, *International Legal Frameworks*, p. 153.
[16]Brierly, *Law of Nations*, p. 48.
[17]Peter Malanczuk, *Akehurst's Modern Introduction to International Law* (New York: Routledge, 1997), p. 29.
[18]B. V. A. Roling cited in ibid., p. 33.

[19]Cited in Carr, *Twenty Years' Crisis*, p. 176.

[20]Malcolm N. Shaw, *International Law* (Cambridge: Cambridge University Press, 1997), p. 3

[21]See Bederman, *International Legal Frameworks*, pp. 4–5.

[22]Lea Brilmayer, *American Hegemony: Political Morality in a One-Superpower World* (New Haven, CT: Yale University Press, 1994), p. 98.

[23]Malanczuk, *Akehurst's Modern Introduction to International Law*, p. 16.

[24]Brierly, *Law of Nations*, p. 54.

[25]In Kauppi and Viotti, *Global Philosophers*, p. 151.

[26]Stanley Michalak, *A Primer in Power Politics* (Wilmington, DE: Scholarly Resources, 2001), p. 3.

[27]Morgenthau, *Politics Among Nations*, p. 265.

[28]Carr, *Twenty Years' Crisis*, p. 176.

[29]Brierly, *Law of Nations*, p. 56.

[30]Bull, *The Anarchical Society*, p. 142.

[31]David Lumsdaine, *Moral Vision in International Politics: The Foreign Aid Regime* (Princeton, NJ: Princeton University Press, 1993), p. 26.

[32]Audie Klotz, "Norms Reconstituting Interests: Global Racial Equality and U.S. Sanctions Against South Africa," *International Organization* 49, no. 2 (Summer 1995): 460.

[33]Malanczuk, *Akehurst's Modern Introduction to International Law*, p. 6.

Should the United States Accept the International Criminal Court?

Since the end of World War II, several treaties and conventions have outlawed particularly egregious violations of human rights—crimes against humanity, genocide, and other war crimes. Until recently, however, there was no international judicial body designed to prosecute *individuals* suspected of engaging in these proscribed behaviors. The International Court of Justice hears cases against *states*, not individuals. Typically, the ICJ has created ad hoc courts to hear cases against individuals, such as the one trying those suspected of mass killings in the former Yugoslavia. During the 1990s, there was a movement to establish a permanent court to deal with such cases. These efforts were successful, and on July 17, 1998, 120 nations voted in favor of the Rome Statute of the International Criminal Court (ICC). Only seven nations voted against the establishment of this court, including China, Israel, Iraq, and the United States. As of September 2002, 81 countries had ratified the statute; the United States was not among them. The Clinton administration claimed to support the idea of the ICC but opposed some provisions of the actual treaty. In 2002, the Bush administration announced its opposition and its decision not to seek ratification of the Rome Statute. Though the Obama administration has rejected the "hostility" of the previous administration in favor of a policy of "principled engagement," it has not sought ratification of the Rome Statute. Still, the administration insists that the ICC is part of the solution for dealing with human rights abuses.

The following documents deal with the controversy over the ICC. Brett D. Shaefer, though claiming to support the concept of a credible international court, echoes most of the themes of the ICC's opponents, particularly those voiced by conservatives in the United States. Law professor Joanne Mariner offers a defense of the ICC as an essential element of holding major human rights abusers accountable for their crimes. What are the main points of disagreement in terms of the specifics of the ICC? More important, how does their disagreement about the ICC reflect a more fundamental difference about the role and value of international law versus the importance of national sovereignty?

PERSPECTIVE 1 The United States and the International Criminal Court (2009)

Brett D. Shaefer[1]

The International Criminal Court (ICC)—which was formally established in 2003 to prosecute war crimes, crimes against humanity, genocide, and the as-of-yet-undefined

[1] Source: Brett D. Schaefer, "Crimes Need To Be Punished, But Is ICC the Right Means?" Radio Free Europe/Radio Liberty (February 12, 2009) © Radio Free Europe/Radio Liberty 2009. Reprinted with Permission.

crime of aggression—has long held a special place in the hearts of human rights activists and those hoping to hold perpetrators of terrible crimes to account.

Although supporters of the court have a noble purpose, there are a number of reasons to be cautious and concerned about the effect the ICC could have on national sovereignty and politically precarious situations the world over.

One of the most basic principles of international law is that a state cannot be bound by a treaty to which it is not a party. Further, long-standing international legal norms hold that a state cannot be bound to legal assertions that it has specifically rejected. The ICC, however, directly contravenes these norms and precedents of international law; it claims jurisdiction to prosecute and imprison citizens of countries that are not party to the Rome Statute and, more shockingly, over those who have specifically rejected the court's jurisdiction.

Seeking to impose international legal requirements and jurisdiction on unwilling sovereign states is unsupportable, and a clear contravention of international law. It also has significant implications for states that are unable or unwilling to ratify the Rome Statue establishing the ICC.

U.S. Opt-Out

For instance, both the Clinton administration and the Bush administration concluded that the ICC is a seriously flawed institution that the United States should not join. However, because of the ICC's unprecedented claims of jurisdiction, the United States has had to take unusual steps to protect its citizens and military personnel, including negotiating a network of nonsurrender agreements (or Article 98 agreements, after the section of the Rome Statute that permits such arrangements) with as many countries as possible. Countries that sign such agreements with the United States promise, in effect, not to surrender U.S. nationals to the ICC without the consent of the U.S. government.

America pursued Article 98 agreements out of concern that the ICC could be used as a tool by those opposed to its foreign policy to make political statements through ICC prosecutions. Supporters of the ICC disparage this as unnecessary. They claim there are protections in the ICC treaty to prevent abuse of the court—after all, the court can only intervene in cases committed within the territory or involving a citizen of an ICC party, and then only if that country proves unwilling or unable, in the judgment of the court, to investigate and prosecute alleged crimes.

This is cold comfort. Unscrupulous individuals and groups will seek to misuse the ICC for politically motivated attacks, as demonstrated by those urging the court to indict Bush administration officials for alleged crimes in Iraq and Afghanistan. In the first two years of the ICC, more than 100 charges against U.S. citizens were submitted to the court. While the ICC chief prosecutor declined to pursue these cases, there is no assurance that future cases will be similarly resolved.

Because of its relative lack of checks to prevent it from being misused, the ICC represents a dangerous temptation for those with political axes to grind. This is a lesson currently being learned by Israel. Despite the fact that Israel is not a party to the Rome Statute, the ICC prosecutor is reportedly exploring ways to prosecute Israeli commanders for alleged war crimes committed during the recent actions in Gaza.

Palestinian lawyers argue that Palestine can request ICC jurisdiction as the de facto sovereign even though it is not an internationally recognized state. This is a political twofer for the Palestinians: Pressure is applied to Israel over alleged war crimes while excluding Hamas's incitement of the military action (as well as its war crimes against Israeli civilians) and, at the same time, momentum is increased for Palestinian statehood without the need to make compromises with Israel.

Uncompromising Prosecution

The current situation in Sudan raises other issues. Although the UN Security Council has been largely deadlocked on possible sanctions against the government of Sudan for its role in supporting Janjaweed militia groups that have committed terrible crimes in Darfur, it did pass a resolution in 2005 referring the situation in Darfur to the ICC. This past summer, the ICC announced that it would seek an indictment against Sudanese President Omar al-Bashir for his alleged involvement in crimes committed in Darfur.

Indicting the sitting head of state of Sudan, no matter how awful his role in the Darfur atrocities may have been, could aggravate the situation in Darfur and put more people at risk. Al-Bashir may decide he has nothing to lose, increase his support of the Janjaweed, and encourage an escalation of their attacks to, possibly, include aid workers and UN and African Union peacekeepers serving in UN mission in Darfur.

If it destabilizes the government, it could also rekindle the north-south conflict that saw roughly 2 million people killed in a 22-year civil war ended by a 2005 peace agreement. These dangers spurred African countries, which would bear the most immediate consequences of a more chaotic Sudan, to call on the UN Security Council to defer the al-Bashir prosecution.

Moreover, since the Office of the Prosecutor is largely autonomous, once a case is brought to the ICC, there is little opportunity to resolve disputes, conflicts, or sensitive political issues diplomatically. For instance, Sudan's neighbors may be faced with the choice of arresting al-Bashir, which could spark conflict with Sudan, or ignoring the court's warrant. If Uganda could resolve its long-festering conflict with the Lord's Resistance Army by agreeing not to prosecute its leader, it would have no ability to call off the ICC prosecution.

It is unlikely the ICC prosecutor or its judges will be held to account if its decisions lead to greater carnage in Darfur, or advancing politically motivated charges in Gaza, or prolonging the conflict in Uganda. They are free to act without considering the potential consequences. Those having to deal with the consequences are not so lucky.

A Credible Court

For these reasons and others, the United States has declined to join the ICC. It is not alone in its concerns as demonstrated by the many states that are not ICC parties. Major countries like China, India, and Russia have refused to ratify the Rome Statute out of concern that it unduly infringes on their foreign- and security-policy decisions—issues rightly reserved to sovereign governments.

Even the Obama administration has expressed the need to make sure U.S. troops have "maximum protection" from politically motivated indictments by the ICC and has not rushed to support ratification of the treaty. Do not look for the

United States to abandon the Article 98 agreements Washington has signed with some 100 countries around the world anytime soon.

While the ICC embodies an admirable desire to hold criminals accountable for their crimes, the court is flawed notionally and operationally. The more ICC advocates seek to use the court to press political agendas and supersede the prerogatives of government in foreign policy, the more they undermine the credibility of the court and threaten its future as a useful tool for justice.

To protect its own interests and to advance the overarching intent of building a credible international criminal court, the United States should continue to insist that it: is not bound by the Rome Statute because it has not ratified the treaty; will not recognize the authority of the ICC over U.S. citizens or consider joining the court without significant changes to the treaty; and will exercise great care over decisions that support actions of the court in cases like Darfur.

Brett D. Schaefer is Jay Kingham Fellow in international regulatory affairs in the Margaret Thatcher Center for Freedom at the Heritage Foundation. The views expressed in this commentary are the author's own and do not necessarily reflect those of RFE/RL

The Case for the International Criminal Court (2002)   PERSPECTIVE 2

Joanne Mariner[2]

In stepping up its campaign against the International Criminal Court, the United States is now threatening an array of drastic measures. Endangering the international presence in Bosnia, warning of a possible boycott of United Nations peacekeeping missions, and pledging a policy of total noncooperation with the court's prosecutions, Washington's stubborn enmity toward the court has led it to take actions that anger even its closest allies.

So what is the nature of this "threat" to American interests, as Secretary of Defense Donald Rumsfeld recently described it? Does the ICC undermine American sovereignty and jeopardize our national security? Is the United States justified in seeking full immunity from the court's activities because of the serious dangers inherent in any assertion of the court's jurisdiction, even over U.N. peacekeepers?

Washington's actions presuppose that the answers to these questions is yes. It would be foolish and ill-advised to alienate so many of our allies, particularly at a time when our national security depends on international cooperation, if the stakes were not extremely high.

But a review of the ICC's history, rules, and structure presents a very different picture than that understood by Washington. Rather than a court that wrongly threatens U.S. interests, the evidence suggests that the United States is wrongly damaging an international tribunal, thoughtlessly undermining international legal standards, and unwisely subverting the development of international justice.

[2] Source: "The Case for the International Criminal Court," by Joanne Mariner, Find Law's, July 8, 2002. Copyright © 2002. Reprinted by permission of the author.

A Court for the World's Worst Criminals

The International Criminal Court, whose underlying treaty came into force this past July 1, has jurisdiction over the world's worst criminals: those who have committed genocide, crimes against humanity and war crimes. It will also have jurisdiction over the crime of aggression, if and when a definition is decided upon in the future.

Most of the definitions of crimes in the court's treaty were already well established in international law when the treaty was drafted. In addition, there is now a substantial body of case law from existing international war crimes tribunals to flesh out their meanings. Finally, the Elements of Crimes, drafted subsequent to the court's underlying treaty, further specifies the breadth of the ICC's subject matter jurisdiction.

In terms of the temporal limitations, the court will only have jurisdiction over crimes committed after the treaty's entry into force. In other words, there is no possibility that the court will be used to right all the wrongs of the past. It is not a court for Idi Amin, but instead for the Idi Amins of the future.

Developments in the U.S. Position

There is nothing preordained about the current U.S. hostility toward the ICC. Indeed, it was not always so: the U.S. was an early and enthusiastic supporter of the idea of an international criminal court. In the early 1990s, the U.S. Congress passed resolutions in favor of the court's establishment, and high-level Clinton Administration officials were active participants in the process of drafting the court's treaty.

What finally turned the United States against the court was other countries' refusal to allow the U.N. Security Council to be the court's gatekeeper. Under the rules proposed by the United States, the Security Council was to have a veto over the court's docket. Because of the U.S. power on the Security Council, Washington was assured that a Security Council–controlled court would pose no threat to its interests.

Although such a court would, in principle, target those responsible for human rights crimes the world over, in practice, it could never prosecute an American citizen in the face of U.S. opposition, or, indeed, prosecute the citizen of any member of the Security Council in the face of the member's opposition. In this way, a handful of countries would have been exempted from norms applicable to all the rest.

Although this proposal was rejected at the 1998 Rome Conference where the ICC treaty was negotiated, the treaty did include the "Singapore compromise," by which the Security Council may delay a prosecution for twelve months if it believes the ICC would interfere with the Council's efforts to further international peace and security. Under this compromise provision, the Security Council must pass a resolution requesting the court not to proceed; an individual permanent member cannot block an investigation by exercising its veto.

In refusing to sign the ICC treaty at the Rome Conference, the U.S. found itself quite isolated. Only China, Iraq, Libya, Qatar, Yemen and Israel joined in boycotting the court, while 120 nations voted in its favor. Although the outgoing Clinton Administration did finally sign the ICC treaty in late December 2001, it continued to insist that the court was flawed. By signing the treaty, however, the U.S. would be able to remain engaged in shaping the new institution.

In other countries, ratification efforts have proceeded at a rapid pace, beyond the hopes of the court's most optimistic supporters. To date, seventy-four countries, including every country in the European Union, have ratified the ICC treaty.

U.S. Unilateralism

The U.S. may have failed to undermine the court's universality at the Rome Conference, but it has not given up in its quest to be totally exempt from the court's jurisdiction. Moreover, the U.S. position with regard to the court is symptomatic of a broader unwillingness to be subject to the same international legal norms that bind other countries.

Although in the wake of the September 11 atrocities U.S. officials called for global coalition-building and multilateral cooperation, Washington's actions belie this approach. Now, perhaps more than ever in the past, the United States seems to be willing to force its agenda on the rest of the world—to substitute unilateral power for global consensus.

Those who portray the ICC as a rogue court should wonder instead whether, in persisting in its efforts to sabotage the court, the U.S. is acting more and more like a rogue state.

10

The United Nations and Humanitarian Intervention

Key Controversy: Are Humanitarian Interventions Justified?

This chapter explores the complex moral and political issues raised by the debate over humanitarian intervention. Advocates of humanitarian intervention come mainly from a liberal perspective, arguing that states forfeit their sovereignty rights when they violate or fail to protect the basic rights of their citizens. Though willing to make rare exceptions, they strongly prefer that interventions take place under the auspices of international organizations such as the United Nations because this framework increases legitimacy and reduces opportunities for abuse. Opponents of humanitarian intervention, often reflecting a realist perspective, believe that sovereignty should remain a principle of international order. The primary obligation of states is to the interests and well-being of their own citizens, not that of the citizens of other states. Furthermore, no matter how noble the ideal of humanitarian intervention is in theory, in practice it will become another tool for the powerful to impose their will and values. Because the United Nations is merely another arena, rather than an alternative, for power politics, its participation will not solve the problem of abuse. ■

On March 19, 2011 French warplanes attacked targets in Libya, marking the beginning of the most recent chapter in the controversial history of humanitarian intervention. A response to Colonel Muammar Qaddafi's promise to show "no mercy" in suppressing the rebellion against his brutal decades-long dictatorship, this use of military force enjoyed the sanction of the United Nations, which authorized "all necessary measures" to protect Libyan civilians from impending slaughter.[1] The United Nations sanction and multilateral nature of the intervention, however, did not prevent debate about the wisdom of the Libyan intervention in particular or humanitarian intervention generally. Those supporting military action, including President Obama, argued that the international community could not stand idly by as Qaddafi bombed his own people into submission. Advocates of intervention invoked a "responsibility to protect" the innocent victims of egregious human rights abuses. Critics, on the other hand, wondered about the international community's inconsistency, asking why no similar intervention was undertaken when protesters in Bahrain (which hosts a critical United States air force base) were brutally suppressed. As one skeptic noted, "If R2P [the responsibility to protect] justifies intervention in Libya, then it certainly obligates us to overthrow the governments of Sudan and North Korea."[2] The specifics of the Libyan debate may be new but the themes on both sides are as old as the doctrine of humanitarian intervention itself.

Debates over specific interventions such as the one in Libya raised a number of general questions. How effective can international organizations be in an anarchic world of independent states? When, if at all, is it acceptable to interfere in the domestic affairs of another state? What role should moral considerations, as opposed to calculations of national interest, play in international affairs? These are some of the most enduring questions in international relations. Stated in such general terms, however, these issues often become unwieldy and abstract. It is sometimes more useful to approach these questions through the lens of more concrete policy debates. Because most advocates of humanitarian intervention favor a critical role for the United Nations, it addresses the capabilities and limits of international organizations. Intervention of any sort involves outside interference in the domestic affairs of states. And the suggestion that states should intervene in defense of human rights brings questions of morality and international politics into focus. Thus, the problems of international organizations, sovereignty, and morality are all thrown into sharp relief by debates over humanitarian intervention.

When the United Nations was founded in the immediate aftermath of World War II, memories of two devastating total wars and the League of Nations' failure were still fresh. An effective international organization was considered essential to avoiding another global war. Unfortunately, the United Nations fell victim to the superpower Cold War rivalry. Nowhere was the impact of the Cold War more evident than on the UN Security Council, whose five permanent members—the United States, the Soviet Union, China, France, and Britain—each possessed a veto that could block any action. The ten nonpermanent members of the Council, elected for two-year terms by the UN General Assembly, have one vote each but no veto. During the Cold War, geopolitics combined with veto power produced paralysis. With the end of the Cold War, many hoped that the United Nations, freed from its geopolitical shackles, would finally fulfill its promise. As Michael Barnett notes, "the atmosphere at the UN during the early 1990s was positively triumphant."[3]

Perhaps no event did more to shatter this optimism than the Rwandan genocide in 1994. Like many African states, Rwanda is characterized by a division between ethnic groups—the majority Hutus and minority Tutsis. The animosity and suspicion between them is largely a legacy of colonialism. The Germans and Belgians had imposed this ethnic classification, encouraging the notion that Tutsis were somehow superior to Hutus. Dividing the native population this way facilitated external domination. After independence, the Hutu-controlled government treated Tutsis as second-class citizens. This simmering conflict eventually erupted into a civil war lasting from 1990 until the signing of a ceasefire in February 1993. At this point the United Nations became involved, sending a small force of 2,500 peacekeepers. Things began to unravel on April 6, 1994, when a plane carrying the Hutu president was shot down as it approached Kigali airport. Hutu extremists exploited the attack to incite violence against the minority Tutsis. Within days, it was clear to UN officials in Rwanda that a systematic campaign, not merely spasmodic violence, was under way. The head of UN peacekeeping forces "understood that Hutu extremists were carrying out ethnic cleansing … [and] emphasized to headquarters the magnitude and scale of the crimes."[4] Over the course of the next few weeks, between 500,000 and 1,000,000 Tutsis were slaughtered in a horrific orgy of violence.

The tale of how officials in New York, Washington, and elsewhere failed to recognize and/or admit what was going on in Rwanda is both complicated and depressing. Suffice it to say that no significant action was taken to halt the genocide. The post–Cold War optimism concerning the United Nations' ability and willingness to act was replaced by doubt and soul searching. If humanitarian action

The Nuremberg Trials of Nazi leaders marked a critical turning point in weakening the principle of sovereignty when governments commit egregious violations of human rights.

was not forthcoming in one of the most egregious violations of human rights since the Holocaust, it was hard to hold out much hope for an effective response to the next such catastrophe. But before we debate the wisdom and prospects for humanitarian intervention, it is useful to understand the origins of the notion that nations should intervene to protect the rights of people in other nations. Not so long ago, this would have been considered a very odd notion indeed.

Sovereignty and Human Rights

The idea of national sovereignty was codified in the Peace of Westphalia (1648) as the only feasible solution to the religious conflict that gave rise to the bloody Thirty Years War (1618–1648). By making each ruler the sole authority on questions of religion over the territory they controlled, the monarchs of Europe devised a formula they could live with. But sovereignty did not entail religious tolerance. Monarchs frequently repressed subjects who did not share their faith, and this was deemed to be nobody else's business. Because rulers did not recognize the rights of their own subjects, they could hardly be expected to care about the rights of another monarch's subjects. Sovereignty was intended to restore international order, not protect individual rights. All of this began to change with the Enlightenment and the emergence of liberalism, which introduced notions of individual rights into political discourse. Liberalism established the principle that governments needed to respect the rights of their own subjects. The result was the gradual erosion of absolutist monarchism. But even though individuals increasingly gained rights in the domestic realm, they still lacked rights under international law. If a government refused to respect the rights of its people, this was still no justification for violating its sovereignty.

Nuremberg war crimes trials Post-World War II trials in which top officials of Nazi Germany were tried for violations of international law, including massive violations of human rights.

It took the horrors of the Holocaust and World War II to finally shake the bedrock principle of national sovereignty. As advancing allied armies liberated the concentration camps, they uncovered Nazi atrocities beyond anyone's wildest imagination. When those responsible were prosecuted at the **Nuremberg war crimes trials**, their defenses were predictable. Some claimed the charges were all lies, whereas others said they were just following orders. Those at the top who issued the orders needed a different defense. Confronted with the evidence, one of Hitler's deputies, Hermann Goering, shouted, "But that was our right! We were a sovereign state and that was strictly our business."[5] There were two problems with this defense. First, many of these crimes took place on non-German territory acquired through aggression. Second, even claims of sovereignty proved unacceptable in the face of such barbarism. The limits of sovereignty had finally been exceeded. The Nuremberg trials (and similar trials in Tokyo for Japanese leaders) represented the first time that "a legal proceeding attempted to make government leaders internationally responsible as individuals for crimes against humanity covering so much time, so many nations, or so many people, *including their own citizens* [emphasis added]."[6] Goering was convicted of crimes against humanity but cheated the executioner by taking his own life.

After Nuremberg, sovereignty was no longer absolute. Some actions were now beyond legitimate claims of sovereignty. The exact limits of sovereignty were less clear. Since World War II, the tension between individual rights and national sovereignty has remained unresolved. This can be seen in the **United Nations Charter** (1945), which obliges "all members [to] refrain in their international relations from the threat or use of force against the territorial integrity or political independence of any state." The organization as a whole faces the same restriction as member states: "Nothing contained in the present Charter shall authorize the United Nations to intervene in matters which are essentially within the domestic jurisdiction of any state."[7] Prohibitions against intervention are even more explicit in the Charter of the Organization of American States (OAS): "No state or group of states has the right to intervene, directly or indirectly, *for any reason whatever*, in the internal or external affairs of any other state [emphasis added]."[8] The only instance in which the United Nations, acting through the Security Council, can authorize forceful intervention in a state's domestic affairs is when "international peace and security" are threatened. The real dilemma, however, concerns large-scale human rights abuses that do not pose any wider threat to peace and security.

While seeming to strengthen norms of national sovereignty, the UN Charter also "reaffirm[s] faith in fundamental human rights, in the dignity and worth of the human person, in the equal rights of men and women." In addition to the UN Charter, the "non-binding" **Universal Declaration of Human Rights** (1948) specifies an almost comically long and detailed list of rights, including the right to "rest and leisure." But this raises the obvious question: What good are treaties guaranteeing human rights if outside forces are prohibited from intervening to protect those rights?

The Growth of Human Rights Activism

Treaties and past human rights abuses alone cannot account for the increased recognition of human rights and acceptance of humanitarian intervention. For ideas to have consequences there must usually be a political movement working on their behalf. The Universal Declaration of Human Rights may date to 1948, but as Margaret Keck and Kathryn Sikkink note, "as recently as 1970, the idea that the human rights of citizens of any country are legitimately the concern of people and governments everywhere was considered radical."[9] How did such a radical notion become mainstream? Its acceptance was encouraged by international activists and organizations dedicated to the promotion and protection of human rights. The growth of these human rights organizations is part of a much larger explosion of **nongovernmental organizations** (**NGOs**)—private and voluntary advocacy groups and networks that seek to influence the policies of states, international organizations, and even nonstate actors such as multinational corporations across a whole range of economic, political, environmental, cultural, and humanitarian issues. Although NGOs have been around for some time (the International Committee of the Red Cross was founded in 1863), the last few decades have seen a sharp rise in their numbers. As of 2000 there were almost 40,000 such organizations, and they continue to proliferate at a rapid pace.[10] By one count there are well over 300 NGOs focused on the issue of human rights alone.[11]

United Nations Charter (1945) The founding document of the United Nations that appears to enshrine the principle of state sovereignty by prohibiting forceful external intervention unless the Security Council finds a threat to international peace sufficient to authorize intervention.

Universal Declaration of Human Rights (1948) A nonbinding United Nations declaration that recognizes a long list of basic human rights. Combined with the United Nations Charter, it revealed an emerging tension between the principles of state sovereignty and human rights.

nongovernmental organizations (NGOs) Voluntary and private advocacy organizations that try to influence the behavior and policies of states, intergovernmental organization and nonstate actors.

The most well-known international human rights NGO is probably **Amnesty International**. Founded in 1961 as a neutral, impartial organization proclaiming to defend to the rights of all as embodied in the Universal Declaration of Human Rights, Amnesty has been involved in numerous high-profile campaigns on behalf of prisoners of conscience in countries of all political persuasions. Though these campaigns may be its most visible activities, Amnesty has employed a wide array of tactics on a host of human rights issues, including abolition of the death penalty and torture, the humane treatment of prisoners of war, the end of extra-judicial executions and disappearances, and the provision of fair and prompt trials. Widely-praised for most of its actions, Amnesty was awarded the Nobel Peace Prize in 1977. Nonetheless, Amnesty has not been without its critics. Governments that routinely find themselves the object criticism, such as China, bristle at what they see as interference in their domestic affairs. Even in the United States many are unhappy with Amnesty's blanket opposition to the death penalty and criticism of some post–September 11 policies (e.g., the treatment of prisoners at Guantanamo Bay detainment camp).

NGOs often have difficulty advancing their agendas in the international arena because they frequently lack the resources available to states and intergovernmental organizations. Nonetheless, NGOs such as Amnesty have often been quite successful in advancing their objectives through a combination of lobbying, persuasion, and direct action. Amnesty and other groups have been particularly effective in raising public awareness of human rights abuses. As Ann Marie Clark explains, "marshalling public opinion is correctly seen as a major role of NGOs, and Amnesty International has been uniquely able to do so over time."[12] Amnesty's well-organized letter-writing campaigns on behalf of prominent political prisoners, for example, were aimed at bringing the pressure of international opinion to bear on target states. Even states that routinely violated human rights often exercised restraint when they became the object of international attention. But it is important to realize that these direct actions to influence governments in particular cases were part of a larger long-term strategy of altering public discourse about human rights issues. This may be the most important legacy of human rights NGOs. In publicizing human rights violations and holding governments to account, Amnesty contributed to the emergence and acceptance of norms of behavior that simply did not exist a few decades ago.

The Case for Humanitarian Intervention

To its supporters, the case for humanitarian intervention is clear. When Pol Pot's Khmer Rouge kill 2 million of their fellow Cambodians and 800,000 Rwandans are slaughtered in a span of few weeks, what possible logic can excuse or condone the inaction of those who had the power to prevent and/or end these tragedies, yet sat on the sidelines? By some estimates, as few as 5,000 troops deployed to Rwanda in 1994 could have saved a few hundred thousand lives.[13] In retrospect, what cold calculus could possibly justify nonintervention?

Humanitarian intervention is defined as the uninvited interference by a state, states, or international organization in the domestic affairs of another state to prevent and/or end human rights abuses. The *humanitarian* part of the equation speaks to the motivation, and *intervention* implies the absence of the target state's consent. This is not to be confused with peacekeeping operations, which generally occur with the consent of the relevant parties in order to preserve a peace that has already been achieved. It is also different from interventions that happen to produce collateral humanitarian benefits. U.S. intervention in Afghanistan in the wake of the 2001 terrorist attacks, for example, may have "liberated the Afghan people from the Taliban and impending starvation, but that was just frosting on the cake. They were never what this war was about."[14]

Three questions are central to the debate over humanitarian intervention. First, should states forfeit their right to sovereignty if they engage in massive human rights violations? Second, if intervention is justified, who has the right to intervene? Can states act on their own (**unilateral intervention**), or must intervention be sanctioned by an international organization, namely the United Nations (**multilateral intervention**)? Finally, if such interventions need to be endorsed by the UN, and the Security Council in particular, is the organization equipped to carry out this mission effectively?

The Limits of Sovereignty

Like most controversial issues, humanitarian intervention requires a choice between competing values: The rights of individuals and the sovereignty of states. Advocates of humanitarian intervention realize the existence of a trade-off. Former UN Secretary-General Kofi Annan implicitly recognizes as much in asking, "If humanitarian intervention is, indeed, an unacceptable assault on sovereignty … how should we respond to a Rwanda … to gross and systematic violations of human rights that offend every precept of our common humanity?"[15] Note Annan's formulation: He concedes that humanitarian intervention *is* an "assault on sovereignty"; the question is whether it is an *acceptable* or *unacceptable* assault on sovereignty.

Advocates of humanitarian intervention see no reason why sovereignty should be absolute. In the first place, the idea that states have consistently respected each other's sovereignty since the Peace of Westphalia is a fantasy. Over the past four hundred years, states have routinely meddled in each other's domestic affairs. Some of these interventions were even "humanitarian" in nature, such as those to protect Christian minorities from mistreatment in the Ottoman Empire during the 1800s.[16] Most interventions were motivated by less admirable concerns, such as undermining strategic rivals, exacerbating ethnic conflicts, or crushing revolutionary governments.[17] Given this huge gap between rhetoric and practice, the newfound reverence for the principle of sovereignty when it comes to saving people from outrageous assaults on their basic human rights seems like little more than a convenient and hypocritical evasion of moral responsibility.

But even if the principle of sovereignty had been scrupulously adhered to, the mere fact that we have done something for four hundred years is a fairly lame

Humanitarian intervention
Uninvited intervention by external actors into the domestic affairs of a state with the primary motive of ending or preventing violations of human rights.

unilateral intervention
Uninvited intervention by a state or small group of states into the affairs of another state without the approval or sanction of some larger international organization such as the United Nations.

multilateral intervention
Uninvited interference in the domestic affairs of another state carried out by many nations with the approval or sanction of a legitimate international organization such as the United Nations.

reason to continue to do so. Sovereignty is not a law of physics; it is a social custom or practice that can (and perhaps should) be changed if it is inconsistent with contemporary mores and norms. As David Forsythe explains, "State sovereignty is not some immutable principle decreed in fixed form once and for all time.... It is an idea devised by social beings. It can change along with changing circumstances."[18]

In fact, we long ago discarded the idea that states possessed some automatic right to have their sovereignty respected. Sovereignty is no longer seen as a divine gift as it was in the age of Louis XIV. Monarchical absolutism has been replaced by **popular sovereignty**, the principle that governments must derive their legitimacy from their citizens. Because it is the people who grant legitimacy, any state that denies basic rights to its citizens can hardly claim legitimacy. And if a state becomes illegitimate in the eyes of its own citizens, why should other states be obligated to respect its sovereignty? As David Rieff argues, "a state that engages in criminal behavior toward its own people had forfeited not just its moral but also its legal right to sovereignty."[19]

popular sovereignty The principle that governments must derive their legitimacy from the people over whom they rule. Embodied in the French and American revolutions, this assertion challenged the principle of the divine right of kings.

A Right or Obligation to Intervene?

Does one state's forfeiture of its sovereign right necessarily give others a right to intervene? Not directly. The right of intervention derives not from the target state's loss of sovereignty but from the rights of those who are being abused. Lea Brilmayer is certainly correct when she notes, "the victims themselves have a right of resistance to crimes perpetrated against them ... [and] other groups in the same society have a good claim (if not in fact an obligation) to come to the aid of the victims." Who could disagree? But if we accept the proposition that "victims within states, and locals who would assist them, have a right of resistance, then it is hard to imagine why they should not be able to summon outside help."[20] And if the victims have a right to ask for outside help, it would be downright perverse if outsiders lacked the right to come to their assistance. Thus, the right to intervene is a natural extension of a principle that virtually no one rejects—that people and groups within nations are entitled to resist when their rights are violated, even when the perpetrator is their own government.

The trickier question is whether outsiders have a positive *obligation* to help. To use Brilmayer's terminology, if intervention is only a right, it becomes tantamount to an act of *charity*, but if intervention is obligatory, it is a *duty*. Nicholas Wheeler is among those who see a moral obligation to intervene: "Once it is accepted that there is nothing natural or given about sovereignty as the outer limits of our moral responsibilities, it becomes possible to argue for a change in moral horizons ... [in which case] governments are responsible not only for protecting the human rights at home but also for defending them abroad."[21] In recent years this sentiment has been reflected in calls to accept a **responsibility to protect**, or "a duty to react to situations in which there is a compelling need for humanitarian protection."[22] The desire was to change "the discretionary 'right to intervene' into a more muscular 'responsibility to protect'."[23] This doctrine was endorsed at the 2005 World Summit whose final document declared that "the international community, through the United Nations, also has the responsibility to use the appropriate diplomatic, humanitarian and other peaceful means .... to protect populations from

responsibility to protect The emerging doctrine that humanitarian intervention should be viewed as a responsibility or obligation as opposed to merely a right.

genocide, war crimes, ethnic cleansing and crimes against humanity." The same language was adopted by the Security Council in 2006.[24] Two aspects of these statements stand out: first, the requirement for UN involvement, and second, the absence of any endorsement of forceful or military intervention. It is not altogether clear, however, why if there is sometimes a moral *right* to intervene forcefully, there is not also sometimes a moral *responsibility* to intervene forcefully.[25]

Who Should Intervene?

If outsiders have a right or obligation to intervene in defense of human rights, which outsiders have the right? Can any external actor intervene whenever it thinks a state is violating its citizens' rights, or does intervention need to be directed by the international community as a whole (or at least with its sanction)? Advocates of humanitarian intervention lean toward opposing a right of unilateral intervention. And even those who concede that in some very rare instances (which we will discuss shortly) unilateral intervention may be acceptable, it is always seen as preferable that intervention be multilateral.

The reasons for requiring multilateral intervention are not immediately obvious. If violations of rights are occurring, why should it matter whether one nation, five nations, one hundred nations, or Microsoft, for that matter, intervene to stop them? The moral imperative would seem to dictate that human rights be defended, with the issue of exactly who defends them being of little moral consequence. Why the almost reflexive preference for multilateral action? The commitment to multilateralism has more to do with practical and political, not moral, considerations. Supporters worry that individual nations will only intervene in defense of human rights when abuses occur in areas of strategic interest (e.g., in Yugoslavia but not Rwanda), that humanitarian rationales will be little more than cynical fig leafs offered by great powers for interventions motivated by more narrow and selfish concerns, and that selective and opportunistic intervention will breed skepticism and erode international legitimacy.

If decisions about humanitarian intervention are left to individual states, there is likely to be tremendous variation (that is to say, inconsistency) in the standards and criteria guiding these interventions. Placing the decisions in the hands of a single, centralized international body increases the likelihood that a consistent standard can be developed and applied. The requirement for some authorization from an international body would also act as a check on those states inclined to abuse a right of intervention. This requirement is particularly critical for reassuring the weaker, more vulnerable states that a right of intervention will not become license for great power meddling. This is why Bernard Kouchner, a co-founder of the Nobel Peace Prize–winning humanitarian organization Doctors Without Borders and who currently serves as France's Foreign Minister, insists that "humanitarian intervention will never be the action of a single country or national army playing policeman to the world.... Humanitarian intervention will be carried out by an impartial, multinational force acting under the authority of international organizations and controlled by them."[26] Gareth Evans and Mohamed Sahnoun make it clear the requirement for multilateral sanction is political, not moral: "As a matter of *political reality* … it would be impossible to build a consensus around any set of proposals for military intervention that acknowledged the validity of any intervention not authorized by the Security Council or General Assembly [emphasis added]."[27]

rule of law The principle that laws need to be applied to all in an equal fashion.

The desire is to establish an international equivalent of the domestic **rule of law**, or the principle that rules need to be applied even-handedly. Consistency is important because in the realm of moral principles "selectivity is prima facie morally suspect."[28] Principles applied inconsistently are not really principles at all. As George Kennan notes, "a lack of consistency implies a lack of principle in the eyes of much of the world."[29] Thus, in order to provide consistent implementation, minimize opportunities for abuse, and sustain international legitimacy, humanitarian interventions need to be conducted by, or at least with the sanction of, the world's most inclusive organization, the United Nations.

Even its defenders realize, however, that the United Nations is not perfect, as its failure in Rwanda made clear. There is no way to guarantee consistent UN action in defense of human rights. It would seem odd if the requirement for organizational sanction became so absolute that it trumped the defense of human rights. After all, if it is impermissible to sacrifice people because of a commitment to an abstract principle of sovereignty, it would appear equally impermissible to sacrifice them because of a commitment to multilateralism. Faced with the choice between human rights and a requirement for multilateral action or sanction, which should prevail? Given the moral case for humanitarian intervention, the answer seems clear: Human rights win every time. But does this mean we should explicitly recognize the legitimacy of intervention without international sanction? Jim Whitman expresses typical hesitance in taking the argument that far: "It is a reasonable expectation that the international legal system should be sufficiently flexible to accommodate specific instances of law-breaking which clearly serve the interests of justice, particularly those which address serious and large-scale humanitarian emergencies."[30] That is, unilateral intervention could be morally justifiable even if it remained a violation of international law. Former UN Secretary-General Kofi Annan himself confessed that he would have been hard pressed to object to an unsanctioned intervention that stopped the Rwandan genocide. This position appears to concede a moral right to unilateral humanitarian intervention but unwillingness to codify such a legal right. Unilateral intervention should generally be discouraged and prohibited, but in rare cases it may need to be met with a "wink and a nod."

Liberalism and Humanitarian Intervention

Calls for recognizing a right of humanitarian intervention resonate mostly with a liberal perspective on international politics. As with individual rights and popular sovereignty at the domestic level, "the international law of human rights is based on liberalism."[31] The move for a more humane and moral international politics is in many respects a continuation of the liberal revolutions that have remade domestic political orders over the past few centuries. The primacy of individual rights and the view that governments receive their legitimacy from their citizens both strike deep cords with liberal social and political philosophy. Without liberal assumptions of individual rights and popular sovereignty, it is difficult to imagine a case for humanitarian intervention. Arguments for humanitarian intervention rest on a profoundly liberal vision of a common humanity, a world in which the moral obligations and people and states are not limited by artificial and transitory lines on a map.

The growing salience of human rights and proposals for humanitarian intervention not only give hope to liberals, but also provide constructivists with some confirmation that international politics is shaped, and can be changed, by prevailing and evolving norms. As long as citizens and leaders believed in absolute sovereignty, the possibility of humanitarian intervention was precluded. The acceptance of norms of human rights and popular sovereignty provides a foundation for changing state practices. One sees elements of this conviction in Forsythe's observation that sovereignty is a social construction, an idea that limits the actions states are willing to consider. Social constructions, however, can be replaced with other constructions. We may be in the middle of a process in which some fundamental ideas or norms about international politics are being transformed, and the increasing willingness to consider humanitarian intervention may be part of this evolution. As Daniel Thomas argues, "International human rights norms affect the behavior, the interests, and the identity of states by specifying which practices are (or are not) considered appropriate by international society."[32] Altered norms can change how nations define themselves, their identities, and their interests, from exclusive national communities to a universal human community.

The Case Against Humanitarian Intervention

Negatives can usually be rephrased as positives; thus, the case *against* humanitarian intervention is also an argument in *favor* of the principle of sovereignty. In many respects, the case for sovereignty remains what it was in 1648. At that time, religious diversity in Europe necessitated acceptance of sovereignty and nonintervention to preserve international order. Today, with respect to humanitarian intervention versus sovereignty, the problem is diverse conceptions of human rights. But even if it were possible to reach nearly universal agreement on some minimal definition of basic rights, there are reasons to doubt whether the United Nations or any other organization can possibly implement a consistent and impartial doctrine of humanitarian intervention. The critique of humanitarian intervention is both moral and political.

The Problem of Moral Diversity

Though supporting a limited right of intervention, Bhikhu Parekh is honest enough to concede that "since views about [human rights] are culturally conditioned, *no definition of humanitarian intervention can be culturally neutral.*"[33] As a result, any doctrine of humanitarian intervention will necessarily be based on a certain vision of human rights that might not be shared by those upon whom it is imposed. This harsh reality is often avoided because it smacks of an extreme moral relativism in which there is no such thing as right and wrong. Actually, it is just a realization that people and cultures do not always agree on what is right and wrong. Though there may be a natural tendency to assume that others do (or should) adhere to our moral standards, in fact "there is no universal morality … rules about morality vary from place to place."[34] As long as this is the case, the norm of sovereignty serves the same purpose today that it did for the authors of the Peace of Westphalia: It provides a basis for order in a diverse world.

One test of the legitimacy of humanitarian intervention is whether its advocates are willing to accept restrictions on their nation's sovereignty. This is a touchy point because nations have always been more protective of their own sovereignty than that of others. But if a consensus actually exists on the moral principles guiding intervention, there should be little concern about intervention in your own nation's affairs. Frank Ching touches on this issue when he asks, "If the same doctrine [of humanitarian intervention] had been enunciated in an earlier era, would today's proponents have been in favor? Would the U.S. agree that other countries had the right to punish it for practicing slavery? Would Britain, France, Italy, Belgium, and other European countries agree that others had the right to bomb them to protect the human rights of their colonial subjects?"[35]

Ching's rhetorical questions highlight several problems that inevitably arise with the practice of humanitarian intervention. One is the issue of double standards—the strongest advocates of intervention are often unwilling to concede that others have a right to intervene in their affairs. Second, in raising the issue of how moral norms change over time, Ching touches on the problem of cultural relativism. If notions of morality vary from one era to another, they can also vary from one culture to another. The magnitude of this problem becomes evident once we move beyond the easy but fortunately rare example of outright genocide. Apart from this exception, it becomes very difficult to delineate a list of basic human rights that merit intervention. Bernard Kouchner adopts an extreme form of moral universalism: "everywhere, human rights are human rights … if a Muslim woman in Sudan opposes painful clitoral excision, or if a Chinese woman opposes the binding of her feet, her rights are being violated." In the face of such abuses, he proposes that we "establish a forward-looking right of the world community to actively interfere in the affairs of sovereign states to prevent the explosion of human rights violations."[36] This sort of universalism denies the culturally specific nature of rights and gives critics of humanitarian intervention the chills. The application of a single moral code in which "human rights are human rights everywhere," leading to a norm of "active interference" in the domestic affairs of states, could provide a license for endless intervention and meddling.

Frank Ching's questions also reflect a sentiment shared by many non-Western governments that "there is something not quite right when the same countries that perpetrated unspeakable offences against human rights should now set themselves up as the arbiters of human rights, in some cases condemning countries that they had previously oppressed."[37] Many in the Third World detect an element of ethnocentrism and fear that humanitarian intervention will be nothing more than imperialism with a happy face. Notice the examples Kouchner cites—clitoral excision in Somalia and foot binding in China. Humanitarian intervention always seems to be suggested outside the confines of Western Europe and North America and directed against weaker powers. Are there never any violations of human rights in Paris,

Connecticut, Russia, or China that the world needs to worry about? Many nations and societies have long been on the receiving end of outside intervention, which was often accompanied by noble rhetoric of spreading the virtues of civilization and Christianity. These nations had to fight long and hard to achieve their independence. Having finally achieved the sovereignty they were denied for so long, they are now told that the time has come to give it up. It is easy to understand why they are hesitant to surrender their hard-won sovereignty to nations whose motives they have good reason to doubt.

To be fair, supporters of humanitarian intervention have a fairly good response to concerns about moral diversity and imperialism. Lea Brilmayer admits that "the cultural relativity argument is hard to rebut directly.... There is no denying that some moral norms vary from one culture to another." Nonetheless, "the philosophical power of the argument is vastly overrated." A doctrine of humanitarian intervention does not require that all societies have precisely the same conception of morality on every issue. Merely because cultures differ in their evaluations of *some* behaviors does not mean that they differ in their evaluation of *all* behaviors.

Brilmayer uses the conflict in the former Yugoslavia to illustrate her point: "If the United States [or anyone else] were to intervene, its actions could hardly be criticized on cultural relativism grounds. For it would be hard to argue that the murder of civilians, gang rape, and deliberate starvation are considered innocent activities in the Balkans." Those charged with crimes against humanity in the former Yugoslavia have not defended themselves by claiming that their culture accepts the actions they are charged with. Their defense is that they did not commit the acts attributed to them: The disagreement is about the facts, not the morality of the alleged acts. Under close scrutiny, the cultural relativism objection is revealed to be a disingenuous debating trick in which moral consensus is ignored by references to trivial and meaningless moral differences. Thus Brilmayer is able to dispose of the problem quite easily: "For relativism to be an objection, it is not enough that morality may *in theory* differ from culture to culture; morality must *in fact* differ.... Most human rights abuses involve the perpetration of harms that are undeniably wrong in the eyes of all parties to the dispute."[38]

From Abstraction to Action

The dilemmas, however, become somewhat more severe when we move to implementing a policy of humanitarian intervention. We may agree that it is a violation of basic rights for a government to kill its political opponents, but does this mean that ten assassinations should trigger intervention? Exactly how great must the violation of rights be? Some draw the line at genocide, which is precisely defined in international treaties and conventions. But few are willing to restrict the right of intervention to the handful of cases that meet the strict definition of genocide. David Gibbs notes that "the issue of deciding which conflicts merit intervention has been a difficult one for advocates of intervention." Those who deal with the problem usually call for "a form of triage, according to which intervening powers will decide...based on a number of criteria (such as the severity of the humanitarian emergency, the potential expense of such intervention, or the logistical problem

Calls for the United States and NATO to enforce a no-fly in Libya marked the beginning of a humanitarian intervention that contributed to the ouster of Muammar Qadaffi after 42 years of dictatorial rule.
Source: Francois Lenoir /REUTER

of dispatching troops)."[39] The right of intervention is most usually restricted to such cases that involve "gross," "egregious," and "massive" violations of human rights or, to use Michael Walzer's famous formulation, acts that "shock the conscience of humanity." The devil, as usual, is in the details.

Stephen Solarz and Michael O'Hanlon provide a commendable attempt to confront this thorny issue, arguing that humanitarian intervention should be considered "only to stop extreme violence when the death rate reaches or threatens to reach at least tens of thousands a year." They cite the usual examples of Rwanda and Cambodia but eliminate virtually every other case because they "were simply not bloody enough to justify outside military intervention."[40] If the Rwandan and Cambodian genocides are the standard, it is difficult to see anything close to a persuasive case for intervention in Libya in March 2011. Critics pounce on such apparently crass head counting. What moral calculus requires us to protect someone being killed with 100,000 of his fellow citizens but not someone being killed with only 5,000 others? There are answers to this uncomfortable question, but they are messy ones that dull the moral luster of humanitarian intervention. But there is no avoiding the problems of moving beyond the tidy moral plane in which words such as "gross" and "massive" need not be defined with any precision. Thus, even with agreement in principle, there is still a lot of leeway for inconsistency and selectivity in practice.

The Problem of Power

The more fundamental dilemma is a familiar one in the history of international relations, which provides many examples of noble moral projects (such as treaties outlawing war in the 1920s) that proved to be miserable failures. The general problem is "the antagonistic relationship between an ideal system of norms and the reality of power politics."[41] The dilemmas pile up as we move beyond the purely normative analysis and "take into consideration the unequal constellation of power under which humanitarian intervention [will be] practiced."[42] The fact is that nations with the power to conduct and resist interventions will surrender much less of their sovereignty than nations lacking equivalent power. As a result, "any right of state intervention, however clearly delineated, would in fact and perception empower the already powerful."[43] *In theory*, accepting the principle of humanitarian intervention erodes every nation's sovereignty. *In practice*, however, there is no danger that foreign troops will land in the United States to stop the death penalty or in China to save the Tibetans.

On one level, advocates of humanitarian intervention are aware of the difficulties resulting from the "reality of power politics." Taking decisions about intervention away from individual states and placing them under the authority of the United Nations is designed to deal with this problem. Recall Bernard Kouchner's assurance that humanitarian intervention would be "impartial." The unstated assumption is that individual states are "partial" and the United Nations is "impartial," which means untainted by national interests and differences in power. Skeptics find this untenable. They view the United Nations as merely another arena for, rather than an escape from, power politics. As an organization of independent states, it cannot help but be influenced by the relative power of its members. Hans Kochler gets to the heart of the matter: "We have to admit that the step from *idealistic vision* to the *realization* of an international policy of intervention cannot be responsibly made … An implementation of the doctrine outside the realm of power politics … is impossible. Any act of humanitarian intervention, *whether exercised on a unilateral, regional or multilateral level*, will be determined by the interests of the power(s) initiating it."[44] It is with good reason that the president of Algeria asks, "Is interference valid for only weak states or for all states without distinction?"[45] Can anyone but the hopelessly naïve believe that all states will be equally liable to intervention, regardless of their power?

We need not even look very deeply to see the impact of power politics because it is built into the basic structure of the Security Council in which any of the five permanent members can scuttle an intervention with a simple "no" vote. As Stanley Michalak explains, "The United Nations was explicitly designed so that it would be unable to act against any of the permanent members or even against their pleasure."[46] This is one reason that NATO intervention in the former Yugoslavia was conducted without the authorization of the Security Council. Everyone knew that Russia or China would have vetoed any intervention because "each has ethnic minorities whose treatment might be used by other countries as an excuse for military intervention."[47] Power can be abused for political reasons not only by conducting interventions but also by preventing them. Stanley Hoffman states the problem bluntly: "Too many states among UN members have bloody domestic records, and they can be expected to block any proposal for collective intervention."[48] Many see this as an argument for reforming the United Nations and the Security Council. The obstacle, of course, is that the United States, Russia, and China are not likely to look kindly on reforms that erode their power. The difficulty of altering rules and procedures that give some nations greater influence is itself a reflection of the United Nations' lack of immunity from the very power politics that advocates of humanitarian intervention hope it will transcend.

In the final analysis, the United Nations is an organization of imperfect independent states. It is not a world government; it does not have its own armed forces; and it relies on voluntary contributions from members to fund and implement its operations. Nations can refuse to provide troops for humanitarian intervention and they can withhold their financial support. The United Nations is a political organization, not a council of moral philosophers. The United Nations can act consistently and impartially only if its members, particularly those with the wealth and resources to conduct interventions, are willing to act consistently and impartially.

The Limits of Moral Action

Debates about humanitarian intervention focus on two basic issues. First, do states have the right or obligation to intervene in the affairs of other states in order to defend human rights? Second, can we devise mechanisms for implementing a policy of humanitarian intervention that lives up to its moral impulses? Though realists will disagree on some specific issues, they have generally been skeptical of humanitarian intervention on both counts.

George Kennan provides a typical realist response to the suggestion that states should risk their citizens' interests and even lives to defend the rights of others. He draws a distinction between how we should think about individual versus state morality. If individuals chose to barge into homes to defend people being attacked, that is their right because they are placing only their own safety at risk. But if the president sends troops into Rwanda to halt a genocide, this is more problematic because he is risking the lives of people whose interests he is supposed to protect. As a result, the "commitments and moral obligations of governments are not the same as those of the individual. Government is an agent, not a principal. Its primary obligation is to the interests of the national society it represents." Kennan draws an analogy between governments and lawyers: "No more than the attorney vis-à-vis the client, nor the doctor vis-à-vis the patient, can government attempt to insert itself into the consciences of those whose interests it represents."[49] Samuel Huntington reflected this sentiment when he argued that "it is morally unjustifiable and politically indefensible that members of the [U.S.] armed forces should be killed to prevent Somalis from killing each other."[50]

Rather than relying on the proposition that states *should not* act for moral reasons, most realists (and many Marxists and feminists interestingly) prefer to emphasize that they *will not*. Though perhaps regrettable, states are simply unwilling to incur substantial costs to defend the rights of others when their own national interest is not involved. John Mearsheimer notes that "despite claims that American foreign policy is infused with moralism, Somalia (1992–93) is the only instance during the past one hundred years in which U.S. soldiers were killed in action on a humanitarian mission." And in this case the public's reaction to a small number of American casualties was so great "that they immediately pulled all U.S. troops out of Somalia and then refused to intervene in Rwanda in the Spring of 1994, when ethnic Hutu went on a genocidal rampage against their Tutsi neighbors."[51] Making a similar point about the former Yugoslavia, Henry Kissinger observes a "vast gap between the rhetoric and the means with which to back it up. Allies' pronouncements have ritually compared Milosevic to Hitler. But the transparent reluctance to accept casualties signaled that the Alliance would not make the commitment necessary to overthrow the accused tyrants."[52] Realists see in calls for humanitarian intervention something we have witnessed before: Moral pronouncements and empty slogans readily abandoned the moment they clash with national interests or threaten to actually cost anything.

Though liberals are generally predisposed to support a right of humanitarian intervention and realists are inclined to be skeptical or opposed, other perspectives display less unity. Feminists certainly welcome an international discourse that elevates human rights to a central place, though they are quick to stress that prevailing notions of rights tend to ignore the deprivations that women are routinely subjected to around the world. Why, feminists wonder, did the plight of women under Afghanistan's Taliban regime become a justification for intervention only after September 11, 2001? And now that women in Afghanistan may have been liberated to some degree, what about the women in Saudi Arabia, a U.S. ally, whose status is only slightly better? Indeed, feminists were deeply divided on the question of whether the use of force in Afghanistan was justifiable.[53] Many feminists are also uncomfortable with using military intervention or force to protect human rights, because militarism is seen as an integral part of domestic and international systems of oppression. This is not to say that feminists would never see military force as justified (except for those who combine feminism with pacifism), but there is a strong presumption against it in most feminist analysis.

A definitive Marxist position is also difficult to identify. In general, however, Marxists find it hard to imagine that a doctrine of humanitarian intervention can be applied consistently and impartially in the current international system. Such a policy is almost certainly going to be used by the dominant powers to pursue their interests vis-à-vis the poor, weak, and vulnerable of the world. David Gibbs suggests that in the contemporary world "perhaps the doctrine of humanitarian intervention is merely a way of excusing US aggression."[54] And Walden Bello urges people to "forcefully delegitimize this dangerous doctrine of humanitarian intervention to prevent its being employed again in the future against candidates for great power intervention like Iran and Venezuela. Like its counterpart concept of 'liberal imperialism,' there is only one thing to do with the concept of humanitarian intervention: dump it."[55]

Conclusion

Though we cannot turn back the clock and bring to life the victims of genocide in Rwanda and the Khmer Rouge in Cambodia, we are almost certainly going to be faced with similar human catastrophes in the future. Evans and Sahnoun offer a prediction and ask a question: "It is only a matter of time before reports emerge again from somewhere of massacres, mass starvation, rape, and ethnic cleansing. And the question will arise again in the Security Council: What do we do? This time the international community must have answers." Reflecting the sober soul-searching that followed the Rwandan genocide, they claim that "few things have done more harm to its shared ideal that people are all equal in worth and dignity than the inability of the community of states to prevent these horrors. In the new century, there must be no more Rwandas."[56]

Unfortunately, it did not take long in this new century for another Rwanda to emerge. The world may have witnessed its next Rwanda in the Darfur region of the Sudan in Africa, where government-supported militias are widely believed to have killed tens if not hundreds of thousands and displaced many more. There were, of course, some differences with Rwanda. Whereas that Rwandan genocide took place in just a few weeks, the crisis in Darfur dragged on for years, leading some to describe it as slow-motion genocide. Most of the international community, including the U.S. government, classified the Darfur crisis as "genocide," a term most governments scrupulously avoided in Rwanda. Rallies and concerts designed to highlight the crisis were commonplace. Nonetheless, "the stubborn fact is that despite this extraordinary mobilization, no effective intervention has actually been mounted to prevent the genocide in Darfur."[57] And skeptics of the entire doctrine of humanitarian intervention as well as supporters frustrated by its haphazard and inconsistent implementation wonder why the much lesser humanitarian tragedy in Libya, which resulted in a few thousand deaths at most, elicited a much greater international response than Dafur where as many as a quarter million may have perished.

Cases such as Libya, Darfur, and Rwanda test the limits of human compassion. But it is not only in our time that people have wondered whether there are limits. More than two centuries ago, in *The Theory of Moral Sentiments*, Adam Smith pondered the same question that still haunts us today. He wondered how a perfectly decent and moral European would react to two hypothetical events: first, tragedy in China that resulted in the deaths of millions; and second, an accident that cut off his own finger. With regard to the death of millions on the other side of the world, Smith speculated that the average person would feel sorry and utter all the appropriate sympathies about the tragic loss of life. Nonetheless, he would soon go on with his life "as if no such accident happened." Upon losing a finger, however, this same person would obsess endlessly about his comparatively "paltry misfortune." This juxtaposition led Smith to ask a pointed question: "To prevent, therefore, this paltry misfortune to himself, would a man of humanity be willing to sacrifice the lives of millions of his brethren, provided he had never to see them?"[58] Merely to ask the question suggests a harsh judgment. Perhaps it is a sign of how little has changed that this same question comes to mind as we witness contemporary human tragedies that the world does nothing to stop. But maybe the growing acceptance of humanitarian intervention suggests how far we have come. Either way, the fundamental question today remains what it was for Adam Smith: Are there limits to human compassion? The answer is still in doubt.

CHAPTER SUMMARY

■ The current debate over the wisdom of humanitarian intervention touches three of the most enduring issues in international politics: (1) the importance of state sovereignty, (2) the utility of international organizations, and (3) the relative importance of morality versus power and national interest in foreign policy.

■ Though state sovereignty has been a central element of international order since the Peace of Westphalia (1648), the horrors of World War II led many to argue that massive human rights violations could not be ignored or excused by assertions of sovereignty.

■ Since the end of World War II, a series of international agreements has established the principle that there are limits to sovereignty, though the line between acceptable and unacceptable violations of sovereignty has remained unclear.

■ Building on liberal principles of popular sovereignty and human rights, supporters of humanitarian intervention argue that states that violate or fail to protect their citizens' basic rights forfeit their right to sovereignty. In these cases, outside actors have a legitimate right to intervene in defense of basic human rights. The right of outsiders to intervene is a logical extension of the right of domestic actors to defend their own rights.

■ Those who favor humanitarian interventions generally prefer that they be undertaken within the framework of the United Nations. This is preferable for two reasons.

First, it reduces the chances that individual nations will use or abuse a reasoned humanitarian intervention as a cover for more selfish objectives. Second, it will assure the weak nations of the world that the strong will not be allowed to intervene at will.

■ Drawing on realist assumptions about the inevitability of power politics, critics argue that any doctrine of humanitarian intervention will necessarily reflect the power and values of the strong. Implementing a policy of humanitarian intervention untainted by power and national interest is impossible.

■ The requirement for United Nations action is often based on the naïve assumption that the organization is an alternative to power politics when it is actually just another venue for power politics.

■ Opponents of humanitarian intervention reject the idea that the governments of some states are required to intervene to protect the rights of citizens of other states. The primary obligation of a government is to protect the interests of its citizens, not the citizens of other states. States are not justified in risking the lives of their citizens to defend the rights of citizens of other states.

■ The legal, political, and moral issues raised by the debate over humanitarian intervention have been with us for centuries. The end of the Cold War and recent tragedies such as the ethnic genocide in Rwanda have merely increased their salience.

CRITICAL QUESTIONS

1. What is the moral basis for humanitarian intervention in the eyes of those who support the doctrine?

2. Why is selective humanitarian intervention often considered problematic? Which would be preferable, selective humanitarian intervention or consistent nonintervention?

3. Is humanitarian intervention inevitably a form of cultural and moral imperialism?

4. Would other nations ever be justified intervening in U.S. domestic affairs to prevent what they perceive as violations of human rights?

5. How does the doctrine of a "responsibility to protect" reflect and extend traditional arguments for humanitarian intervention?

KEY TERMS

Amnesty International, 246

Humanitarian intervention, 247

multilateral intervention, 247

nongovernmental organizations (NGOs), 245

Nuremberg war crimes trials, 244

popular sovereignty, 248

responsibility to protect, 248

rule of law, 250

unilateral intervention, 247

United Nations Charter (1945), 245

Universal Declaration of Human Rights (1948), 245

FURTHER READINGS

A good place to begin considering the role of morality in international politics is Stanley Hoffman's, *Duties Beyond Borders: On the Limits and Possibilities of Ethical International Politics* (Syracuse, NY: Syracuse University Press, 1981), and Lea Brilmayer's *American Hegemony: Political Morality in a One-Superpower World* (New Haven, CT: Yale University Press, 1994) is particularly useful for thinking about humanitarian intervention in the post-Cold War world. An excellent introduction to the topic of human rights in international politics is David P. Forsythe's *Human Rights in International Relations* (Cambridge: Cambridge University Press, 2000). On the more specific question of humanitarian intervention, Nicholas Wheeler provides one of the best discussions in *Saving Strangers: Humanitarian Intervention in International Society* (Oxford: Oxford University Press,

2001). Gary Bass traces the surprisingly long history of humanitarian intervention in *Freedom's Battle: The History of Humanitarian Intervention* (New York: Vintage, 2009). Samantha Power (who serves in the Obama administration and was a strong advocate in intervention in Libya) looks at failures to intervene, even in the face of obvious genocide, in her hugely influential *A Problem from Hell: America and the Age of Genocide* (New York: Harper, 2007). Ann Clark's *Diplomacy of Conscience: Amnesty International and Changing Human Rights Norms* (Princeton, NJ: Princeton University Press, 2001) focuses on the origins and influence of Amnesty International. An excellent history of the United Nations can be found in Paul Kennedy, *The Parliament of Man: The Past, Present and Future of the United Nations* (New York: Random House, 2006).

HUMANITARIAN INTERVENTION ON THE WEB

www.hrw.org
Web site of Human Rights Watch, which monitors and publicizes human rights abuses worldwide.

www.amnesty.org
Web site of Amnesty International, perhaps the most famous and influential international human rights organization.

www.dfait-maeci.gc.ca/iciss-ciise/menu-en.asp
Web site of the International Commission on Intervention and State Sovereignty, maintained by the Canadian Department of Foreign Affairs.

http://www.responsibilitytoprotect.org
Web site with resources on the emerging doctrine of the responsibility to protect, including the history of the

doctrine, and documents and information on current humanitarian crises.

www.pbs.org/wgbh/pages/frontline/shows/evil
Based on *Frontline*'s documentary about the Rwandan genocide, this site discusses its historical background as well as the international response.

www.ictr.org
Details the proceedings of the International Criminal Tribunal for Rwanda, which is trying to bring those responsible for the genocide to justice.

NOTES

[1] See "Into the Unknown," *Economist* vol. 398, no. 8726 (March 26, 2011), pp. 29–31.

[2] Paul D. Millar, "Libya is Not Rwanda," *Foreign Policy online* (March 30, 2011). Accessed at: http://shadow.foreignpolicy.com/posts/2011/03/30/libya_is_not_rwanda

[3] Michael Barnett, *Eyewitness to a Genocide: The United Nations and Rwanda* (Ithaca, NY: Cornell University Press, 2002), pp. 22–23.

[4] Ibid., p. 109.

[5] Paul Lauren Gordon, *The Evolution of International Human Rights* (Philadelphia: University of Pennsylvania Press, 1998), p. 210.

[6] Ibid., p. 209.

[7] A text of the United Nations Charter can be found at www.un.org.

[8] Cited in Lea Brilmayer, *Justifying International Acts* (Ithaca, NY: Cornell University Press, 1989), p. 105.

[9] Margaret E. Keck and Kathryn Sikkink, *Activists Beyond Borders* (Ithaca, NY: Cornell University Press, 1998), p. 79.

[10] Helmut Anheier, Marlies Glasius and Mary Kaldor (eds.), *Global Civil Society 2001* (Oxford: Oxford University Press, 2002), p. 300.

[11] Margaret Karns and Karen Mingst, *International Organizations: The Politics and Processes of Global Governance* (Boulder, CO: Lynne Rienner, 2004), p. 420.

[12] Ann Clark, *Diplomacy of Conscience: Amnesty International and Changing Human Rights Norms* (Princeton, NJ: Princeton University Press, 2001), p. 128.

[13] Scott R. Feil, *Preventing Genocide: How the Early Use of Force Might Have Succeeded in Rwanda* (Washington, DC: Carnegie Commission on Preventing Deadly Conflict, 1998).

[14] Clifford Owen, "Humanitarian Wars Are a Past Luxury," *National Post* (February 15, 2002), p. A22.

[15] Cited in Olivia Ward, "In Defense of Human Rights—Debate Rages Over When, If Ever, International Intervention in a Sovereign Nation Is Justified," *Toronto Star* (February 18, 2001), p. 1.

[16] See Martha Finnemore, "Constructing Norms of Humanitarian Intervention," in *The Culture of National Security: Norms and Identity in World Politics*, ed. Peter Katzenstein (New York: Columbia University Press, 1996), pp. 161–165. Also see Steven Krasner, *Sovereignty: Organized Hypocrisy* (Princeton, NJ: Princeton University Press, 1999), pp. 73–126.

[17] See Cynthia Weber, *Simulating Sovereignty* (Cambridge: Cambridge University Press, 1995), pp. 61–91.

[18] David P. Forsythe, *Human Rights in International Relations* (Cambridge: Cambridge University Press, 2000), p. 20.

[19] David Rieff, "Humanitarian Vanities," *New York Times Magazine* (June 1, 2008), p. 13.

[20] Lea Brilmayer, *American Hegemony: Political Morality in a One-Superpower World* (New Haven, CT: Yale University Press, 1994), p. 152.

[21] Nicholas Wheeler, *Saving Strangers: Humanitarian Intervention in International Society* (Oxford: Oxford University Press, 2000), p. 294.

[22] Gareth Evans and Mohamed Sahnoun, "The Responsibility to Protect," *Foreign Affairs* 81 (November/December 2002). p. 107.

[23] "To protect sovereignty, or to protect lives," *Economist* (May 17, 2008), p. 73.

[24] See: http://domino.un.org/UNISPAl.NSF/361eea1cc08301c485256c f600606959/e529762befa456f8852571610045ebef!OpenDocument

[25] A recent overivew of the emergence of the responsibility to protect is Anne Orford, *International Authority and the Right to Protect* (Cambridge: Cambridge University Press, 2011).

[26] Bernard Kouchner, "Humanitarian Intervention—A New Global Moral Code Must Emerge," *Toronto Star* (October 20, 1999), p. 1.

[27] Evans and Sahnoun, "The Responsibility to Protect," p.107.

[28] Brilmayer, *American Hegemony*, pp. 161–162.

[29] George Kennan, "Morality and Foreign Policy," *Foreign Affairs* 64 (Winter 1985/86): 45.

[30] Jim Whitman, "A Cautionary on Humanitarian Intervention," *GeoJournal* 34 (October 1994): 170.

[31] Forsythe, *Human Rights in International Relations*, p. 217.

[32] Daniel C. Thomas, The Helsinki Effect: International Norms, Human Rights and the Demise of Communism (Princeton, NJ: Princeton University Press, 2001), p. 281.

[33] Bhikhu Parekhh, "Rethinking Humanitarian Intervention," *International Political Science Review* 18 (1997): 54–55, emphasis added.

[34] R. J. Vincent, *Human Rights and International Relations* (Cambridge: Cambridge University Press, 1986), p. 37.

[35] Frank Ching, "UN: Sovereignty or Rights?" *Far Eastern, Economic Review* (October 21, 1999), p. 40.

[36] Kouchner, "Humanitarian Intervention," p. 1.

[37] Ching, "UN: Sovereignty or Rights?" p. 40.

[38] All quotes in these two paragraphs are from Brilmayer, *American Hegemony*, pp. 148–149.

[39] David N. Gibbs, *First Do No Harm: Humanitarian Intervention and the Destruction of Yugoslavia* (Nashville, TN: Vanderbilt University Press, 2009), p. 7.

[40] Stephen Solarz and Michael E. O'Hanlon, "Humanitarian Intervention: When Is Force Justified?" *The Washington Quarterly* 20 (Fall 1997): 8.

[41] Hans Kochler, *Humanitarian Intervention in the Context of Modern Power Politics* (Vienna: International Progress Organization, 2001), p. 17.

[42] Ibid., p. 7.

[43] Whitman, "Cautionary on Humanitarian Intervention," p. 171.

[44] Kochler, *Humanitarian Intervention*, p. 17.

[45] In Ching, "UN: Sovereignty or Rights?" p. 40.

[46] Stanley Michalak, *A Primer in Power Politics* (Wilmington, DE: Scholarly Resources, 2001), p. 29.

[47] Ching, "UN: Sovereignty or Rights?" p. 40.

[48] Stanley Hoffman, "America Goes Backward," *New York Review of Books* 50 (June 12, 2003). Accessed at www.nybooks.com/articles/16350.

[49] Ibid.

[50] Michael J. Smith, "Humanitarian Intervention: An Overview of Ethical Issues," *Ethics and International Affairs* 12(1998): 63.

[51] John Mearsheimer, *The Tragedy of Great Power Politics* (New York: W. W. Norton, 2001), p. 47.

[52] Henry Kissinger, "A New World Disorder," *Newsweek* (May 31, 1999), p. 41.

[53] See Sharon Lerner, "Feminists Agonize Over War in Afghanistan," *Village Voice* (October 31–November 6, 2001). Accessed at www .villagevoice.com/issues/1044/lerner.php.

[54] Gibbs, *First Do No Harm*, p. 8.

[55] Walden Bello, "Humanitarian Intervention: Evolution of a Dangerous Doctrine," *Focus on the Global South* (January 19, 2006). Accessed at: http://www.globalpolicy.org/empire/humanint/2006/0119humintbello.htm.

[56] Evans and Sahnoun, "The Responsibility to Protect," p. 99.

[57] David Rieff, "Humanitarian Vanities," p. 16.

[58] Adam Smith, *The Theory of Moral Sentiments* (1759). Full text containing this passage can be accessed at www.adamsmith.org/smith/tms/tms-p3-c3a.htm.

Humanitarian Intervention in Libya?

In 2011 uprisings in parts of the Arab world, particularly Egypt, Yemen, Bahrain, Syria, Tunisia and Libya, presented a series of crises that appeared to merit humanitarian intervention, especially in those cases where desperate authoritarian rulers resorted to brutal suppression to put down protests that threatened their regimes. Although each case involved its own unique combination humanitarian, strategic and practical considerations, the questions that shape any discussion of humanitarian intervention inevitably came into play: How great must the violation of rights be to warrant intervention? Who has the right to intervene? What organizations need to sanction intervention? Why intervene in one country but not another? Are moral motivations really paramount or are there other agendas at work in decisions for intervention?

It was the crisis in Libya that brought the loudest and most sustained calls for intervention. This was in part because of Colonel Qaddafi, who was seen as somewhat unstable and disconnected from reality in addition to being brutal. Qaddafi's incoherent ramblings in televised speeches early in the crisis led many to wonder about his grip on reality. His determination to hold on to power led him to turn the Libyan military on protestors, something that fortunately did not happen in neighboring Egypt. Given his history and apparent instability, Qaddafi's promise to show no mercy to his opponents was a believable threat of a humanitarian catastrophe in the making. Many saw this as the last straw, a chance to take action before the situation took a turn for the worse. In the address below President Obama lays out the rationale for his decision to involve the United States in Libya as part of a multilateral effort, articulating many of themes associated with humanitarian intervention and the doctrine of a responsibility to protect. He takes pains, however, to limit the scope of intervention, placing almost as much emphasis on what the intervention will *not* entail as what it will. Rejecting the description "humanitarian intervention" in favor of "humanitarian war," David Rieff portrays Libya as the liberals' Iraq in the sense of being a moral quest almost doomed to disappoint. What basic themes in the debate about humanitarian intervention in general are evident in Obama and Rieff's disagreement about the wisdom of intervention in Libya? In what ways do they see the conflict and intervention in Libya differently? Is there a difference between humanitarian intervention and humanitarian war? Is Rieff's comparison of Libya to Iraq persuasive?

U.S. Policy in Libya (2011)

President Barack Obama[1]

Good afternoon, everybody. I want to take this opportunity to update the American people about the situation in Libya. Over the last several weeks, the world has watched events unfold in Libya with hope and alarm. Last month, protesters took to the streets across the country to demand their universal rights, and a government that is accountable to them and responsive to their aspirations. But they were met with an iron fist.

Within days, whole parts of the country declared their independence from a brutal regime, and members of the government serving in Libya and abroad chose to align themselves with the forces of change. Moammar Qaddafi clearly lost the confidence of his own people and the legitimacy to lead.

Instead of respecting the rights of his own people, Qaddafi chose the path of brutal suppression. Innocent civilians were beaten, imprisoned, and in some cases killed. Peaceful protests were forcefully put down. Hospitals were attacked and patients disappeared. A campaign of intimidation and repression began.

In the face of this injustice, the United States and the international community moved swiftly. Sanctions were put in place by the United States and our allies and partners. The U.N. Security Council imposed further sanctions, an arms embargo, and the specter of international accountability for Qaddafi and those around him. Humanitarian assistance was positioned on Libya's borders, and those displaced by the violence received our help. Ample warning was given that Qaddafi needed to stop his campaign of repression, or be held accountable. The Arab League and the European Union joined us in calling for an end to violence.

Once again, Qaddafi chose to ignore the will of his people and the international community. Instead, he launched a military campaign against his own people. And there should be no doubt about his intentions, because he himself has made them clear.

For decades, he has demonstrated a willingness to use brute force through his sponsorship of terrorism against the American people as well as others, and through the killings that he has carried out within his own borders. And just yesterday, speaking of the city of Benghazi—a city of roughly 700,000 people—he threatened, and I quote: "We will have no mercy and no pity"—no mercy on his own citizens.

Now, here is why this matters to us. Left unchecked, we have every reason to believe that Qaddafi would commit atrocities against his people. Many thousands could die. A humanitarian crisis would ensue. The entire region could be destabilized, endangering many of our allies and partners. The calls of the Libyan people for help would go unanswered. The democratic values that we stand for would be overrun. Moreover, the words of the international community would be rendered hollow.

[1] Source: President Barack Obama, "U.S. Policy in Libya (2011)," www.whitehouse.gov/blog/2011/03/18/presidentlibya-our-goal-focused-our-cause-just-and-our-coalition-strong.

And that's why the United States has worked with our allies and partners to shape a strong international response at the United Nations. Our focus has been clear: protecting innocent civilians within Libya, and holding the Qaddafi regime accountable.

Yesterday, in response to a call for action by the Libyan people and the Arab League, the U.N. Security Council passed a strong resolution that demands an end to the violence against citizens. It authorizes the use of force with an explicit commitment to pursue all necessary measures to stop the killing, to include the enforcement of a no-fly zone over Libya. It also strengthens our sanctions and the enforcement of an arms embargo against the Qaddafi regime.

Now, once more, Moammar Qaddafi has a choice. The resolution that passed lays out very clear conditions that must be met. The United States, the United Kingdom, France, and Arab states agree that a cease-fire must be implemented immediately. That means all attacks against civilians must stop. Qaddafi must stop his troops from advancing on Benghazi, pull them back from Ajdabiya, Misrata, and Zawiya, and establish water, electricity and gas supplies to all areas. Humanitarian assistance must be allowed to reach the people of Libya.

Let me be clear, these terms are not negotiable. These terms are not subject to negotiation. If Qaddafi does not comply with the resolution, the international community will impose consequences, and the resolution will be enforced through military action.

In this effort, the United States is prepared to act as part of an international coalition. American leadership is essential, but that does not mean acting alone—it means shaping the conditions for the international community to act together.

That's why I have directed Secretary Gates and our military to coordinate their planning, and tomorrow Secretary Clinton will travel to Paris for a meeting with our European allies and Arab partners about the enforcement of Resolution 1973. We will provide the unique capabilities that we can bring to bear to stop the violence against civilians, including enabling our European allies and Arab partners to effectively enforce a no fly zone. I have no doubt that the men and women of our military are capable of carrying out this mission. Once more, they have the thanks of a grateful nation and the admiration of the world.

I also want to be clear about what we will not be doing. The United States is not going to deploy ground troops into Libya. And we are not going to use force to go beyond a well-defined goal—specifically, the protection of civilians in Libya. In the coming weeks, we will continue to help the Libyan people with humanitarian and economic assistance so that they can fulfill their aspirations peacefully.

Now, the United States did not seek this outcome. Our decisions have been driven by Qaddafi's refusal to respect the rights of his people, and the potential for mass murder of innocent civilians. It is not an action that we will pursue alone. Indeed, our British and French allies, and members of the Arab League, have already committed to take a leadership role in the enforcement of this resolution, just as they were instrumental in pursuing it. We are coordinating closely with them. And this is precisely how the international community should work, as more nations bear both the responsibility and the cost of enforcing international law.

This is just one more chapter in the change that is unfolding across the Middle East and North Africa. From the beginning of these protests, we have made it clear that we are opposed to violence. We have made clear our support for a set of universal values, and our support for the political and economic change that the people of the region deserve. But I want to be clear: the change in the region will not and cannot be imposed by the United States or any foreign power; ultimately, it will be driven by the people of the Arab World. It is their right and their responsibility to determine their own destiny.

Let me close by saying that there is no decision I face as your Commander in Chief that I consider as carefully as the decision to ask our men and women to use military force. Particularly at a time when our military is fighting in Afghanistan and winding down our activities in Iraq, that decision is only made more difficult. But the United States of America will not stand idly by in the face of actions that undermine global peace and security. So I have taken this decision with the confidence that action is necessary, and that we will not be acting alone. Our goal is focused, our cause is just, and our coalition is strong. Thank you very much.

The Road to Hell (2011)

PERSPECTIVE 2

David Rieff[2]

Had the purpose of an air exclusion zone over Libya been solely to protect the people of Benghazi and of other insurgent-controlled areas in the east from being massacred by Colonel Qaddafi's advancing forces, opposing it might still have made intellectual sense, but it would not have made moral sense, which is what should count most. Qaddafi had promised a slaughter in the evening before the United Nations authorized the Western intervention, and there was no sane reason not to take him at his word. It is one thing to be a principled anti-interventionist, or, for that matter, anti-imperialist (however much liberal interventionists in the United States, besotted as they still are with fantasies of America's inherent goodness, may resent and reject the term). But to apply such principles mechanically to the Libyan case would have exemplified Emerson's famous remark that a foolish consistency was the hobgoblin of small minds.

But from the beginning it has been clear that while this intervention has been couched in the language of humanitarianism and of the global good deed, invoking the so-called Responsibility to Protect (R2P), the U.N.'s new doctrine that is supposed to govern those instances when outside powers must step in militarily to prevent tyrants from killing their own people, the more important goal has been to support the insurgency, which is to say, to bring about regime change. Had it been otherwise, the bombing could have been halted once the Libyan government attack on Benghazi had been halted. Instead, it goes on, with various French, British, and American politicians and military officials at odds mainly about how

---

[2] Source: "The Road to Hell" by David Rieff, originally published by The New Republic. Copyright © 2011 by David Rieff, used by permission of The Wylie Agency LLC.

much (not whether) the bombing campaign should be widened, and whether Colonel Qaddafi is himself a legitimate target for assassination from the air.

So much for the hope that Iraq and Afghanistan might actually have taught the West anything lasting about trying to impose democracy at the point of a gun. Instead, it is as if Iraq, which, in the United States, was initially welcomed by most liberal internationalists and neoconservatives alike as a war of liberation, had never happened, and, instead, we have traveled backward in time. Remember those halcyon days of the late 1990s when Tony Blair was promising the world that in the future the West would fight wars in the name of its values, not just of its interests, in effect promising that the wars of the twenty-first century would be noble wars of altruism? If you don't, well, don't worry: If the war in Libya is any indication, you'll have the chance to live them all over again. Of course, the catastrophe in Iraq was supposed to have sobered us, and made even the most ardent liberal interventionists realize that Pascal's great phrase, "He who would act the angel, acts the beast," expresses the stark truth about what we self-flatteringly call humanitarian interventions. But instead, here we go again.

It is tempting to say that what is taking place here is some sort of Freudian "return of the repressed." But in reality, the infatuation of liberal elites in the West with humanitarian war was barely shaken by Iraq. Many of the same activists who either opposed the Iraq invasion from the beginning, or soon recanted their support for it, campaigned ardently for a military intervention in Darfur. The problem, it seemed, was not with the idea of regime change, which to be successful would have required regime change in Khartoum, even if most of the leaders of Save Darfur in the United States and SOS Darfour in Western Europe denied it, but with regime change when practiced by George W. Bush, Dick Cheney, and Paul Wolfowitz. And now, some of those liberal interventionists are in positions of power, whether formal or informal. Two of the most prominent among those who called for Western military action in Darfur played crucial roles in persuading their respective governments to start bombing in Libya. Grotesque as it may sound, though he held no government appointment, Bernard-Henri Levy played a greater role in France's decision to spearhead the bombing campaign, which involved at least one instance of French aircraft flying close air support for a rebel column, than did the foreign minister, Alain Juppe. Samantha Power, whose book, *A Problem From Hell*, about the failure of the United States to prevent or halt genocide in the twentieth century, has been the touchstone for American liberal interventionists since its publication (it was a favorite of the late Richard Holbrooke), is in government, where, to give her her due, she will finally be in position to help put these ideas into practice.

This war—let us call it by its right name, for once—will be remembered to a considerable extent as a war made by intellectuals, and cheered on by intellectuals. The main difference this time is that, particularly in the United States, these intellectuals largely come from the liberal rather than the conservative side. Presumably, when the war goes wrong, they will disown it, blaming the Obama administration for having botched it, in much the same way that many neoconservatives blamed Secretary of Defense Rumsfeld for his strategic errors, rather than blaming themselves for urging a war that never had a chance of transforming Iraq in the way that they hoped. The judgment of history will almost certainly be that it was Iran, not the United States, which won that war. And Libya? Anything is possible, of course, but the odds of this war, so grandiose in terms of the moral claims made for its necessity and so incoherent in its tactics, turning out in the way its advocates are promising seem remarkably small.

But in humanitarian war, which its supporters nonetheless continue self-servingly to refuse to think of as being war, that is, as something that invariably involves the slaughter of innocents even when this slaughter takes place in a just cause (and for all the talk of "smart" weapons, war from the air is particularly prone to kill civilians), the moral good intentions of those who would wage it is somehow thought to trump all other considerations. Again, this war is no longer about protecting the people of Benghazi, if it ever was. That goal was accomplished on the first day and NATO planes could have continued to protect it as they did in Kurdistan between the end of the First Gulf War in 1991 and the beginning of the Second in 2003. Rather, it is about overthrowing Muammar Qaddafi and installing the insurgent leadership in Benghazi in his place.

Why Barack Obama, Nicolas Sarkozy, or David Cameron feel that who rules Libya is any of their affair, and why they were more intent on securing the (grudging) assent of the Arab League than the assent of their own legislatures, shows just how misguided the doctrine of humanitarian intervention really is. These leaders are more intent on imposing democracy by force than in honoring the democratic judgment of their parliaments at home. As a result, what we are left with is the angelic Caesarism of the "empire of the good"! And all with the *nihil obstat* of an intellectual class whose good intentions are not the solution to Power's "problem from hell," but rather the problem itself. Humanitarian savagery from 15,000 feet or from a missile-bearing submarine is still savagery. And the road to hell is still paved with good intentions.

David Rieff is a contributing editor for the New Republic.

11

Nuclear Proliferation

Key Controversy: How Dangerous Is Nuclear Proliferation?

This chapter focuses on the debate over the consequences and the desirability of nuclear proliferation. In its simplest form, the essential issue is whether nuclear weapons have been, and will be, a force for peace and stability. Those who favor (or at least do not fear) nuclear proliferation claim that because nuclear weapons substantially increase the potential costs of war, they also tend to reduce the likelihood of war. Realists in particular are attracted to this logic of peace through nuclear deterrence. But there is disagreement on how much proliferation is desirable. Advocates of limited proliferation argue that nuclear deterrence contributes to stability only under certain conditions. More extreme proliferation proponents see nuclear weapons as stabilizing in almost any setting. These two versions of the pro-proliferation position remain minority stances. More common is opposition to any further spread of nuclear weapons. Nuclear weapons cannot eliminate the chances for war (purposeful or accidental) even if they do reduce them. Because the consequences of nuclear war would be so devastating, it is not a gamble worth taking. But even in the face of these disagreements, there is one point of consensus: The spread of nuclear weapons to nonstate actors would be a disaster because deterrence ceases to be an option in facing an enemy lacking any identifiable territory or assets that can be targeted or destroyed. ■

In the fall of 2010 some observers began to speculate that Israel might be within a few months of an attack on facilities in Iran associated with its suspected nuclear weapons program. Short of a direct attack, there were also reports of clandestine assassinations of Iranian nuclear scientists and elaborate computer viruses designed to attack and disable critical components of Iran's nuclear infrastructure.[1] All of this reflects a concern on the part many Israelis and others that Iran's leaders are, in the words of Israeli Prime Minister Benjamin Netanyahu, "a messianic apocalyptic cult" representing the greatest threat to the Jewish people since Adolph

Hitler that cannot be trusted with nuclear weapons.[2] The fear is that the normal dynamics of nuclear deterrence that have prevented other nuclear powers from using their weapons might not restrain the fanatical Iranian regime bent on destroying the Jewish state. Even if Iran did not attack Israel, a nuclear Iran might embolden the Islamic regime and its proxies in the region to make life difficult for Israel, forcing its citizens to live with the permanent threat of annihilation by a regime whose leadership has expressed a desire to see it wiped it off the face of the map.

These concerns, however, are only the most recent manifestation of fears that have marked the nuclear age since the first atomic bombs were dropped on Japan in 1945. In previous decades people worried whether Joseph Stalin and Mao Tse Tung could be deterred. No one could be certain. Fortunately, the world managed to avoid the catastrophe of nuclear war. But is past success a harbinger of the future, or is there a real possibility that our nuclear luck is about to run out? One analysis offers the following framing of the most recent nuclear dilemma: "if Iran is simply a new example of the 60 year-old problem, then classic containment should work in 2016 the way it worked in 1956. But traditional deterrence strategy will not work if Iran is the first nightmare of the nuclear age."[3] The problem is that we may not have an answer to such questions until is it too late to do much about it.

Contemporary fears of nuclear proliferation have become great enough to produce a fundamental shift in U.S. strategic doctrine. In the months leading up to the 2003 invasion of Iraq, the Bush administration claimed that the consequences of nuclear and other weapons of mass destruction falling into the hands of undeterrable rogue nations were so dire that the United States reserved the right to use military force to prevent that possibility. The idea of preemptive military action to prevent nations from acquiring nuclear weapons has been controversial. When Israel destroyed an Iraqi nuclear reactor in 1981 on the grounds that Iraqi nuclear weapons posed an immediate threat to its security, the United States and most other nations condemned the attack. Although there were several rationales for the 2003 invasion of Iraq, the possibility that Saddam Hussein's regime might acquire nuclear weapons was high on the list. The new U.S. doctrine, driven largely by concerns about weapons of mass destruction, represents one of the more stunning strategic turnarounds in recent memory.[4]

The Reality of Proliferation and Nonproliferation

Although many worry about nuclear proliferation, it is important to remind ourselves that there is good news, too: The problem could be much worse than it is. As of 2008, only eight countries definitely possessed nuclear weapons: the United States, Russia, Britain, France, China, Israel, Pakistan, and India (see Map 11.1). North Korea claims to have tested a nuclear device in October, 2006, but data regarding the test remain a subject of intense debate among experts. South Africa, which had a small nuclear arsenal in the 1980s, is the only nation to develop nuclear weapons and abandon them later, though a few former Soviet republics inherited nuclear weapons upon the Soviet Union's breakup and later returned the weapons to Russia. In many respects, it is remarkable that only nine or ten nations have demonstrated the ability and desire to build nuclear weapons. As James Carroll notes, "We could just as easily be living in a world with nuclear weapons as common, say, as high-tech fighter aircraft—with countries like Egypt, Indonesia, Australia and numerous others armed with nukes."[5] Why we do not live in such a world is an interesting question.

"Nuclear proliferation," explains Mitchell Riess, "is a function of two variables: technological capability *and* political motivation … capability without motivation is innocuous … [and] motivation without capability is futile [emphasis added]."[6]

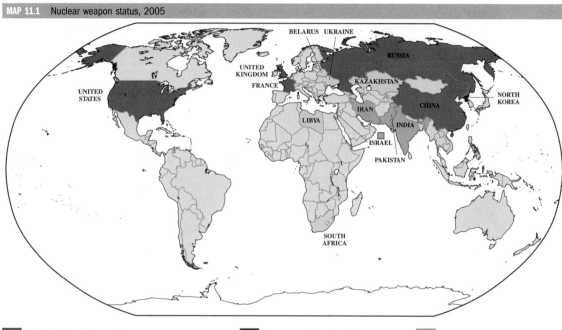

MAP 11.1 Nuclear weapon status, 2005

NPT Nuclear Weapon States

Non-NPT Nuclear Weapon States

1. India is thought to have produced enough weapons-grade plutonium to produce between 75 and 110 nuclear weapons. The number of actual weapons assembled or capable of being assembled is unknown. No weapons are known to be deployed among active military units or on missiles.

2. Israel is thought to possess enough nuclear material for between 100 and 170 nuclear weapons. The number of weapons assembled or capable of being assembled is unknown, but likely to be on the lower end of this range.

3. Pakistan may have produced enough weapons-grade uranium to produce up to 110 nuclear weapons. The number of actual weapons assembled or capable of being assembled is unknown. Pakistan's nuclear weapons are reportedly stored in component form, with the fissile core separated from the non-nuclear explosives.

Suspected Nuclear Weapon State

Suspected Clandestine Program

Abstaining Countries

These countries have the potential ability to develop nuclear weapons, but have chosen not to do so. Some have installations under international inspection that could produce weapons-grade nuclear material.

Recent Renunciations

South Africa produced six complete nuclear bombs during the 1980s, but renounced such activities and joined the NPT in 1991. Belarus, Kazakhstan, and Ukraine acceded to the NPT as non-nuclear weapon states and returned all remaining nuclear weapons to Russia in the early 1990s.

Egypt and Sweden both had active nuclear weapon programs but terminated them prior to the founding of the NPT in 1970. After 1970, Argentina, Brazil, Libya, Iraq, Romania, South Korea, Spain, Taiwan, and Yugoslavia all had active programs researching nuclear weapons options. All of these programs were terminated by the early 1990s, except for Libya, which was renounced in December 2003.

Source: Reprinted by permission of the publisher from Deadly Arsenals: Nuclear, Biological, and Chemical Threats (Washington, DC; Carnegie Endowment for International Peace, 2005), www.carnegieendowment.org

Pakistanis celebrate their nation's successful test of nuclear weapons. Because of the long-standing conflict between nuclear armed India and Pakistan, the Indian subcontinent remains a focus of concern for those worried about nuclear proliferation.

Source: Zahid Hussain/Corbis Wire/Reuters/Corbis

Early predictions of two or three dozen nuclear powers were based on the assumption that any nation capable of building nuclear weapons would do so. It was difficult to imagine nations able to build nuclear weapons exercising voluntary restraint. As one observer asks, "When in history ... [have] so many nations had the capability to produce a powerful weapon, and chosen not to exercise it?"[7]

Fortunately, these predictions have not come to pass. The list of **nuclear abstainers**—that is, nations that have the ability to build nuclear weapons but have chosen not to—is a long one. A 2002 Carnegie Foundation report pointed to forty such abstainers.[8] What accounts for this restraint? For many abstainers, such as Germany and Japan, the American **nuclear umbrella** might provide an explanation. As allies of the United States, it is understood that any attack on them would be treated as an attack on the United States, requiring the appropriate response. Thanks to the United States, most Western European nations and some Asian nations, particularly Japan and South Korea, have had no reason to build their

nuclear abstainers Nations with the economic and technological ability to build and maintain nuclear weapons who have chosen not to acquire them.

nuclear umbrella When one nation promises to employ its nuclear arsenal in order to defend another nation from attack.

Many have embraced the goal of "global zero," or the elimination of all nuclear weapons.
Source: Alex Wong/Getty Images

own weapons. But this cannot account for all the abstainers, because others (e.g., Sweden and Switzerland) do not enjoy the benefits of U.S. protection.

Perhaps part of the explanation can be found in the **Nuclear Non-Proliferation Treaty (NPT)**.[9] Signed in 1968 by forty-eight nations, including the United States and the Soviet Union, the NPT was designed to prevent what many feared most—a world with dozens of nuclear powers. Since 1968, the list of signatories of NPT has grown to 189 nations. Parties to the treaty agree not to provide technological or material assistance that would allow other nations to build nuclear weapons. Nations not already possessing nuclear weapons agree to forgo them in the future. Nations possessing nuclear weapons promise to work toward reducing their levels, with the ultimate objective of eliminating nuclear weapons entirely. However, in its specific provisions, the NPT essentially tried to preserve the nuclear status quo as it existed in 1968.

How successful has the NPT been? The answer depends on how we measure success. On one level, it can be seen as a great success: only a handful of nations

Nuclear Non-Proliferation Treaty (NPT) Agreement designed to prevent the spread of nuclear weapons. Existing nuclear powers promised not to aid others in acquiring nuclear weapons, and those without nuclear weapons agreed not to build them. Only three nations have not signed the NPT—Israel, India, and Pakistan.

have joined the nuclear club since 1968. And if we judge international treaties by the number of nations that sign on, the NPT would have to be considered a smashing success. Only three nations have refused to sign—Israel, India, and Pakistan. But it is unclear whether the treaty prevented any nation from getting nuclear weapons. Though "Egypt, Sweden, Italy, and Switzerland gave up serious nuclear weapons program upon signing,"[10] the most comprehensive study of nuclear nonproliferation concludes that all potential nuclear powers "had chosen to give up their nuclear options prior to joining the Nuclear Non-Proliferation Treaty."[11] It is possible that the treaty merely formalized decisions that had already been made.

Evaluating the success of the NPT also raises the question of enforcement—what are the consequences of violation? The **International Atomic Energy Agency (IAEA)** monitors compliance with the NPT. It was the IAEA that conducted inspections for evidence of an Iraqi nuclear weapons program during the winter of 2002–2003 (the inspections for chemical and biological weapons were carried out by a separate team assembled by the United Nations). The IAEA has also been active in assessing Iran's compliance with the NPT. The IAEA, however, has no powers to enforce the treaty and must approach the UN Security Council to impose sanctions for violations. This difficulty of enforcement is compounded by a provision allowing any signatory to withdraw from the treaty "if it decides that extraordinary events … have jeopardized the supreme interests of its country." Who decides what constitutes an extraordinary event or supreme interest? Each state decides for itself. In January 2003 North Korea exercised its right to withdraw from the NPT, citing this provision. Subsequently, in October 2006 North Korea claimed to have tested its first nuclear weapon. In response, the UN Security Council imposed sanctions, citing the threat posed to international peace and security. In 2007, North Korea agreed to suspend its nuclear program in exchange for financial aid and the removal of sanctions. In the summer of 2008, North Korea even destroyed one of its nuclear reactors before a Western audience (video of which can be found on youtube.com), yet suspicions about North Korean intentions linger.

In the final analysis, however, the problem of nuclear proliferation is not really *how many* nations possess nuclear weapons, but rather *which* nations. Headlines announcing a Norwegian nuclear weapon would not exactly leave the world in a state of fear. The spread of nuclear weapons into the hands of certain nations provokes more anxiety than the spread of weapons to others. But before we get into details of why some nations might provide cause for greater concern, we might ask an even more basic question: Do we need to be worried about nuclear proliferation at all? Some might think the answer is so obvious that the question need not even be asked. After all, are there people who actually view nuclear proliferation as desirable? Many would be surprised to find that in fact there are serious analysts who consider nuclear weapons a good thing, a powerful force for peace and stability. For **proliferation optimists,** more nuclear powers may indeed be good, though there is disagreement about how much proliferation is desirable. This perspective contrasts with the more common argument of **proliferation pessimists** that the consequences of using nuclear weapons are potentially so disastrous that any proliferation should be prevented. This is the basic debate addressed in this chapter: Whether, and under what circumstances, nuclear weapons might be a force for peace and stability.

International Atomic Energy Agency (IAEA) Organization charged with monitoring compliance with the Nuclear Non Proliferation Treaty.

proliferation optimists Those who believe that the spread of nuclear weapons can contribute to international peace and stability.

proliferation pessimists Those who believe that any spread of nuclear weapons is undesirable and should be prevented.

Three basic positions are presented: the case for limited proliferation, the argument for nearly unlimited proliferation, and the case against any further proliferation.

The Case for Limited Proliferation

Debates about the consequences of nuclear proliferation derive in part from disagreements about the impact of nuclear weapons during the Cold War. John Mearsheimer has been particularly influential in setting the terms of the debate. In 1990, just as the Cold War was coming to an end, he claimed that the United States would soon miss the good old days of Cold War stability.[12] As the United States basked in the glory of victory, Cold War nostalgia seemed odd. But Mearsheimer's position was quite simple. In retrospect, the Cold War was a period of almost unprecedented great power peace, particularly in Europe, where two total wars had been waged in the three decades preceding 1945. Tens of millions of battlefield and civilian deaths were a testament to the instability of the pre–Cold War world. Despite the intensity of the Cold War superpower rivalry, there was never any direct military engagement between the United States and the Soviet Union. What accounted for this enduring peace in the face of intense rivalry? Mearsheimer thought nuclear weapons had a lot to do with it.

How did nuclear weapons help keep the peace? Mearsheimer assumes that nations start wars because they expect to win. Only in rare instances do nations start wars they anticipate losing. Winning means that the expected benefits of war exceed the costs. Historically, however, nations frequently miscalculated, losing wars they initiated and expected to win. Before the nuclear era, decision makers confronted two major problems that contributed to the "fog" of war (mis)calculations. First, it was easy to misjudge the likely effects of using conventional weapons. Second, it was also easy to imagine that conventional weapons might be used in ways that would allow a nation to "win." This is where the benefits of nuclear weapons come into play. With weapons of such incredibly destructive potential, there is no doubt that their use would result in such tremendous destruction that it would be impossible to conclude that war would bring greater benefits than costs. Nuclear weapons impose a clarity on strategic calculations that conventional weapons do not. By so obviously raising the potential costs of war relative to any conceivable benefits, nuclear weapons dramatically reduced the chances that either the United States or the Soviet Union would risk their use. As Charles Krauthammer concludes, "Deterrence has a track record. For the entire postwar period it has maintained the peace between the two superpowers, preventing not only nuclear but conventional war as well."[13]

Mearsheimer worried that the post–Cold War world would resemble Europe on the eve of World War I. No longer would there be only two major powers—a new, multipolar order would emerge. There was no assurance that a balance of power would be achieved among the major powers. Perhaps worst of all, many of these powers would not have nuclear weapons. That is, the post–Cold War world was reverting to a world like the one that produced World War I and World War II. Though he did not predict another world war, Mearsheimer saw trouble coming.

In order to deal with this situation, Mearsheimer advocated a "managed proliferation" of nuclear weapons, especially to Germany. When he was writing in 1990, the Soviet Union still existed as a unified nation. It seemed clear to Mearsheimer that Germany and the Soviet Union would emerge as the dominant powers in Europe. Like all great powers, Germany and the Soviet Union would eventually find themselves in conflict. Because Germany could not rely forever on the American nuclear deterrent, stability in Europe required a German nuclear arsenal. Mearsheimer believed this was desirable and inevitable. And if it was going to happen, it should preferably occur in a "managed" and orderly fashion during a period of relative international calm.

The Soviet Union's demise in 1991 did not alter Mearsheimer's opinion about the wisdom of a German nuclear arsenal, but it did create a new dilemma. The Soviet Union's collapse left a sizable number of its nuclear weapons on the territory of some newly independent states, most notably Ukraine. What should be done with these weapons? Consistently applying his logic, Mearsheimer advised Ukraine to keep them. Russia, after all, would continue to maintain a nuclear arsenal well into the future. Ukraine and Russia were bound to come into conflict at some point. If both had nuclear weapons, the chances they would go to war would be greatly diminished. Mearsheimer was nothing if not consistent.[14]

Mearsheimer's focus was on the future of Europe, and he did not address fully the question of nuclear proliferation elsewhere. But how far can his logic extend? As Jonathan Schell (an opponent of proliferation) asks, "If, as many analysts say, [nuclear] deterrence was a successful solution to the dangers of the Cold War, then why should it not be accepted by all nations prone to conflict?"[15] Mearsheimer was unwilling to carry his argument to this logical extreme. His concern that German nuclear weapons be acquired in a managed fashion in tranquil times hinted that other times and settings may be too volatile. While advocating a Ukrainian nuclear deterrent, he warned that "nuclear proliferation does not axiomatically promote peace and can in some cases even cause war." He worried that "smaller European powers might lack the resources to make their nuclear force survivable, and vulnerable nuclear forces would invite a first strike in the event of a crisis."[16] If there are reasons to fear that some smaller European powers may be ill prepared to build and maintain the necessary nuclear forces, one might conclude that few countries outside of Europe possess the requisite resources.

The Case for Widespread Proliferation

Mearsheimer was not the first to see virtues in nuclear proliferation. Long before the end of the Cold War, Kenneth Waltz had made a very similar argument but did not see the benefits of nuclear proliferation as limited to the handful of states. In arguing that more nuclear weapons may be better even in the most dangerous of places, Waltz provides an extreme case in favor of nuclear proliferation.[17]

Waltz, like Mearsheimer, views nuclear weapons as good because they increase the potential costs of war, thereby decreasing the chances for war. Waltz is as succinct as possible: "War becomes less likely as the costs of war rise in relation to the possible gains."[18] As long as each side knows that any use of nuclear weapons would result in its own destruction, such weapons will not be used, and situations that might entail their use will be mostly avoided. This is the situation that existed between the United States and the Soviet Union and became known as **mutual assured destruction (MAD)**. In order for MAD to exist, both powers need to have the ability to absorb an attack by the other side with enough nuclear weapons left over to inflict unacceptable destruction in retaliation. This requires an **invulnerable second-strike** capability—that is, nuclear weapons that the other side cannot eliminate in the first strike. The United States and the Soviet Union accomplished this by putting a lot of nuclear weapons in places where the other side could not attack them (e.g., underground in missile silos and underwater in submarines). Mearsheimer's concern that lesser powers may not be able to build and maintain invulnerable forces focuses on this issue.

Waltz agrees that invulnerable nuclear forces are the key to stable nuclear deterrence. But he thinks it is relatively easy to build and maintain an invulnerable second-strike capability. Take the case of Pakistan and India. Waltz claims that they do not need to do what the United States and Soviet Union did. A handful of weapons will suffice because "once a country has a small number of deliverable warheads of uncertain location, it has a second strike force."[19] Pakistan needs only ten or twenty nuclear weapons, not thousands, to inflict incredible damage and casualties on India. Nuclear weapons landing in Delhi and Calcutta alone could kill millions. This would certainly raise the potential costs of war to an unacceptable level. So in order for stable nuclear deterrence (MAD) to exist, all a nation needs is a few nuclear weapons the other side cannot locate and target. A handful of well-concealed or mobile missiles would do the trick. This is where Mearsheimer and Waltz part company: Mearsheimer views nuclear deterrence as a good thing, but he thinks it is expensive and difficult. Waltz agrees that nuclear deterrence is a good thing, but thinks it is relatively cheap and easy: any nation with the resources to get nuclear weapons in the first place is almost certainly capable of acquiring enough invulnerable weapons to create stable deterrence.

Fears that countries like Iran or North Korea might get nuclear weapons, however, are not always based solely on assessments of their ability to build stable deterrents. Even with the necessary weapons, some measure of rationality is essential for deterrence to hold. Decision makers must understand the futility of using nuclear weapons. This is where the specter of irrational rogue states enters the equation. Andrew Sullivan expresses the fear in many discussions of proliferation: "The problem with deterrence and Iran's current regime, I think, lies in its religious orientation…. We are dealing with a religious movement in which suicide bombing is a virtue. How do we deter suicide bombers? We cannot."[20] This echoes Israeli fears that Iran's regime is an irrational cult bent on destroying the Jewish state.

Waltz, however, sees no reason to assume that today's so-called rogue leaders will prove less rational than predecessors like Joseph Stalin or Mao Zedong. In fact, one of the best things about nuclear deterrence is that it does not require an incredible level of rationality to understand the harsh realities. It is useful to recall the reaction to China going nuclear in 1964. At the time Mao Zedong was viewed as

mutual assured destruction (MAD) A strategic reality and doctrine in which any use of nuclear weapons would inevitably entail one's own destruction. Achieved when each party possesses an invulnerable second-strike (retaliatory) capability.

invulnerable second-strike Nuclear weapons that cannot be destroyed in a preemptive attack, providing the ability to respond to any attack with a second (retaliatory) strike.

a rogue leader: bellicose, unpredictable, brutal, ideological, and fanatical. Certainly this was not someone to trust with nuclear weapons. There was even consideration of a preemptive attack on China's small arsenal. We tend to forget this today because Mao and his successors proved perfectly responsive to the realities of deterrence. Comparing some supposedly "crazy" leaders to recent U.S. presidents, Waltz wondered why "we continually worry about the leaders of 'rogue' states—the likes of Qaddafi, Saddam and Kim Il Sung." Though supposedly irrational, "they have survived for many years, despite great internal and external dangers." He doubts that "hardy political survivors in the Third World [are] likely to run the greatest of all risks by drawing the wrath of the world down on them by accidentally or in anger exploding nuclear weapons they may have."[21] In response to Sullivan's worries about suicide bombers, Waltz would observe that there is a world of difference between sending a few poor souls off to their deaths and courting national annihilation. Nothing promotes sober reflection like a few hundred or thousand nuclear weapons staring you in the face.

Exactly What Are We Worried About?

There is sometimes a lack of clarity about what exactly worries opponents of proliferation. Is the danger that new nuclear powers will use their weapons against the United States or against each other? These are two distinct problems. Waltz is least worried about the prospect of an attack on the United States due to the overwhelming power of its nuclear deterrent. Any nation attacking the the United States could rest assured that it would be on the receiving end of a devastating response. Whatever one thinks about some of the world's more unsavory leaders, it is probably safe to assume they have no desire to rule over a radioactive parking lot. This, presumably, is why the United States keeps several thousand nuclear weapons: to deter those who need to be deterred, not France and Great Britain.

But even if nuclear weapons are not used against the United States, might new nuclear powers use them against each other? Again, Waltz thinks it will be easy for stable deterrence to emerge as nuclear weapons proliferate. There is some evidence supporting this position. Examining the India–Pakistan crisis of 1990, Devin Haggerty concludes that "New Delhi and Islamabad were deterred from war by their recognition of each other's nuclear capabilities … [which] lends further support to the already impressive evidence that the chief impact of nuclear weapons is to deter war between their possessors."[22] Nonetheless, even Waltz concedes that "no one can say that nuclear weapons will never be used." Though confident that new powers are extremely unlikely to attack major nuclear powers, Waltz grants a somewhat greater possibility that they might use them against each other. What then? In what some might consider a callous and/or cavalier response, Waltz answers that "if such states use nuclear weapons, the world will not end. The use of nuclear weapons by lesser powers would hardly trigger them elsewhere."[23] For opponents of proliferation, the mere fact that the "world will not end" offers little comfort.

The Case Against Nuclear Proliferation

Much of the case in favor of nuclear proliferation relies on the argument that nuclear weapons stabilized U.S.–Soviet relations during the Cold War. Those with a less benign view of nuclear proliferation usually reject this analysis. The problem is a familiar one: We cannot assume that because we had nuclear weapons and peace that we had peace *because* of nuclear weapons. To use the familiar cliché, correlation does not prove causation.

Alternative interpretations of the Cold War peace relegate nuclear weapons to a much less important, and perhaps completely irrelevant, role. Historian John Lewis Gaddis, who first characterized the Cold War as the "long peace," lists nuclear weapons as only one of many factors that helped the superpowers avoid war. He accords much greater weight to the simplicity of bipolarity, the conservative nature of political leadership in both societies, the emergence of norms of peaceful competition, and geographical distance.[24] Others go one step further, arguing that nuclear weapons were completely irrelevant. For John Mueller, the two world wars were enough to convince U.S. and Soviet leaders that even a conventional war would have imposed costs exceeding any potential gains. Using a colorful metaphor to illustrate the comparative destructiveness of conventional and nuclear war, Mueller observes that "a jump from the fiftieth floor is probably quite a bit more horrible to think about than a jump from the fifth floor, but anyone who finds life even minimally satisfying is extremely unlikely to do either."[25]

Of course, as Robert Malcolmson explains, it is impossible to offer any final, definitive answer to the question of whether nuclear weapons kept the Cold War peace: "perhaps the nuclear threat played a major role in deterring war, perhaps it did not: the fact is, we do not know and never will." Though Malcolmson believes it likely that "the fear of nuclear catastrophe probably did impose some restraint on the actions of the superpowers," he wonders whether "it is possible to establish the relative importance of this restraining fear." Because we cannot provide firm answers to these questions, the supposedly pacifying impact of nuclear weapons is a rather shaky basis for increasing the number of nations with their fingers on the nuclear trigger. No matter how compelling the argument might seem, "the proposition that nuclear deterrence kept the peace is not a matter of knowledge, it is a matter of belief and often rather dogmatic belief."[26]

The Gamble of Proliferation

One of the most effective strategies in any debate is to take your opponent's best argument and turn it against them. Proliferation optimists rest much of their case on the commonsensical notion that because nuclear weapons increase the potential costs of war, they reduce the chances for war. Even if this fundamental point is granted, opponents of proliferation see a weakness. Proliferation optimists cannot argue that nuclear weapons *eliminate* the chances for war. As Waltz is honest enough to admit, "No one can say that nuclear weapons will never be used."[27] At best, nuclear weapons only reduce the chances for war. But by how much? Do nuclear weapons lower the odds of another India–Pakistan war by 10 percent, 50 percent, or 90 percent? No one can know. This uncertainty inidcates that advocates of proliferation are willing to make a trade-off. They admit that an India–Pakistan war with nuclear weapons would be much more destructive than one without them—indeed, this is the very crux of their argument—but in their view the reduced chances of war are worth taking the risk of a much more destructive war. Proliferation proponents, to put it crudely, are willing to "play the odds," though without knowing exactly what these odds are. But, critics wonder, do nuclear weapons reduce the chances for war enough, given the potentially horrific consequences of their use? As Steven Miller concludes, "Even a small risk of war despite nuclear weapons makes nuclear proliferation too dangerous to contemplate…. When one considers the stakes and risks involved, the gamble is too great."[28]

Why Worry About Iran But Not Germany?

Why would proliferation of nuclear weapons to some states elicit greater anxiety than proliferation to others? Many within the Third World see a mildly racist double standard: As long as nuclear weapons remain in the hands of Northern nations, there is no problem; it is only when all those different-looking people in Asia and the Middle East get them that Westerners need to worry. Ahmed Hashim suggests that such fears are based on "hoary clichés about the irrationality and callousness of leaders and peoples in the Middle East."[29] From this perspective, the insistence on preventing any further proliferation reinforces a **nuclear apartheid** giving current nuclear powers an enduring strategic advantage. Most opponents of proliferation, of course, would reject such charges, insisting that there are good reasons to be concerned.

nuclear apartheid A term used by critics of attempts to create two classes of nations—those allowed to possess nuclear weapons and those who cannot be trusted with them. The term apartheid has unavoidable racial connotations because of its association with the white supremacist regime that used to exist in South Africa.

From the perspective of the United States at least, Germany or Israel with nuclear weapons is less troubling than Iran or North Korea former are allies. The nuclear weapons of friends are less worrisome than those of enemies. But concerns about proliferation to developing countries go beyond considerations of their political allegiances. The fact that all nations currently pursuing nuclear weapons are relatively poor causes the most concern. This is because their relative poverty will influence how many nuclear weapons they are likely to build as well as what kind. The fear is that poor nations will be able to afford only a small number of the most basic and worst types of nuclear weapons. This will bring all the drawbacks and risks of nuclear weapons without the benefits.

Mutual assured destruction in the U.S.–Soviet context came about because each nation had thousands of nuclear weapons located in places that the other could not get to, such as underground silos and underwater submarines. This meant that any attack would be met with a devastating counterattack. Consequently, there was never any incentive to use nuclear weapons first. The two powers spent billions and billions of dollars and rubles building these arsenals. Proliferation pessimists worry that new nuclear powers will never be able to do likewise. Iran, North Korea, Pakistan, and India are likely to have arsenals measured in the dozens or hundreds, not thousands. These weapons will be based above ground rather than in invulnerable silos or submarines. This being the case, the argument goes, we cannot assume that the pacifying effects of nuclear weapons during the Cold War will be replicated in new contexts.

So what if two opponents have only a few nuclear weapons? Wouldn't a few nuclear explosions create enough damage to increase costs of war beyond any possible gains? On an objective level, the answer is probably yes. But what matters is whether those making decisions believe it. Deterrence is ultimately a psychological process that relies on decision makers' beliefs and expectations about the likely consequences of certain actions. One nation's fifty or a hundred nuclear weapons will deter only if potential aggressors are convinced those weapons will be used and the damage inflicted will be unacceptable. When a nation has 25,000 nuclear weapons, it is almost impossible to reach any other conclusion. Things may be very different with only a few dozen weapons. Proliferation opponents worry that with only a handful of weapons, nuclear powers might come to believe, however incorrectly, that a limited nuclear war might be winnable.

History is replete with examples of leaders who were unable to recognize what in hindsight appears obvious. The leaders of Europe on the eve of World War I failed to grasp the potential horrors of the war they unleashed, even though they were aware of each other's huge armies with massive quantities of weapons. In 1914, deterrence failed miserably. During the crisis between India and Pakistan in the spring and summer of 2002, some observers were disturbed by what they saw as "nuclear denial." Among the general population there was little awareness of what nuclear weapons could actually do. Even among some in the military there was a disturbingly cavalier attitude toward the possible consequences of nuclear war. One Pakistani general, when asked about fears of nuclear war, responded, "I don't know what you're worried about. You can die crossing the street, hit by a car, or you could die in a nuclear war. You've got to die someday anyway."[30] Though we should not exaggerate the significance a single general's off-the-cuff remark, such comments certainly do not reveal an appreciation of the devastation nuclear weapons could bring. Kenneth Waltz may be correct about the futility of using even a few weapons, but unfortunately he will not be making the decisions. We need not assume rampant irrationality in order to worry that miscalculations, misperceptions, and wishful thinking might lead to the failure of deterrence. It has happened before.

A Very Delicate Balance of Terror[31]

Even for basically rational decision makers, nuclear arsenals consisting of a few weapons in vulnerable positions create problems. In addition to the possibility that a nuclear war with only a few weapons might be viewed as winnable, there are serious dilemmas relating to what strategists call **crisis stability**, or the likelihood that a crisis will escalate to war. One fear is that nations with relatively small nuclear arsenals may be tempted to launch a **preemptive strike** crisis—that is, an initial attack to eliminate the nuclear forces of the other side before it has a chance to use them. If two enemies have thousands of weapons in many different places, as was the case with the United States and the Soviet Union, such an attack would be futile. There would be no possibility of eliminating all the other side's weapons, and whatever weapons remained would surely be launched in retaliation. With only a small number of weapons in vulnerable places, a preemptive attack becomes a feasible, even attractive, option.

crisis stability The presence or absence of incentives to initiate military action in the event of crisis.

preemptive strike An attack intended to disarm a nation before it has the chance to use (or maybe even develop) its nuclear weapons.

launch on warning When a
nation launches its own
nuclear weapons on indications that it is under attack (as
opposed to waiting for the
attack to be completed).

To make matters even worse, there will also be strong pressures to adopt a policy of **launch on warning**—that is, to launch weapons the moment one suspects an attack is under way. The danger is that if one side waits for an attack to be completed before responding, they may find themselves with few or no weapons for retaliation. They could be placed in a "use them or lose them" situation. And because there may be only four or five minutes of warning time for nations close to each other, time pressures on decision makers will be intense. And when the warning time is so short that decisions need to be almost instantaneous, the danger of inadvertent nuclear war increases dramatically. During the Cold War the superpowers would have had thirty to forty minutes to determine if an attack was real. Even though thirty minutes might not be a lot of time to make a decision on which the future of humanity rests, it was sufficient to allow mistaken indications that an attack was under way (and there were several such incidents during the Cold War) to be detected before rash decisions regarding retaliation.[32]

As a result of these crucial differences, critics of nuclear proliferation believe that we cannot extrapolate the U.S.–Soviet experience into the most likely scenarios for future nuclear proliferation. Even if nuclear weapons did produce, or at least contribute to, the superpower peace, it was only because the United States and the Soviet Union had the money and technology to build a lot of the right kinds of weapons. They also had the technology and time that allowed them to avoid rash, impulsive decisions that might have led to war by mistake. It was a balance of terror, to be sure, but it was a stable balance of terror. Nuclear proliferation will produce more balances of terror in the world, but these may be delicate, fragile, and unstable.

Terrorists, Black Markets, and Nuclear Handoffs

There is one aspect of nuclear proliferation on which everyone agrees: the acquisition of nuclear weapons by nonstate actors (a euphemism for terrorist groups in this context) would be disastrous. Even those who do not worry much about so-called rogue states concede that this would be a problem of a different order. It is not hard to understand why. When dealing with states, there is always the possibility of deterrence. Even leaders we despise and whose rationality might be questioned have assets that can be targeted and threatened in order to prevent them from using their weapons. The threat of utter annihilation is plausible and easily understood. With nonstate actors the problem, as Carl Builder explains, is that "an opponent cannot be deterred by the threat of nuclear weapons if that opponent has no definable society to threaten."[33] Presumably, these groups would not go to the trouble of getting nuclear weapons unless they are willing to use them, and because the option of deterrence would not exist, nothing would prevent them from doing so.

Opponents of proliferation argue that we cannot treat proliferation to states and nonstate actors as if they were separate, unrelated problems. The proliferation of nuclear weapons to other states increases the likelihood of proliferation to nonstate actors. How so? We need to remember that building nuclear weapons is no easy feat. States with a lot of resources at their disposal often require decades before they are finally successful. The problem is not the knowledge of how to build a bomb—a few hours on the Internet will yield the necessary plans. The big obstacle is getting one's hands on the *fissile material*—that is, the fuel that feeds the explosion, plutonium or highly enriched uranium (HEU). These are not naturally occurring substances. They very difficult and expensive to produce. It is extremely unlikely that a nonstate actor could manufacture either on its own. If a terrorist group does get nuclear weapons, there are two likely routes—acquiring either the fissile material or a completed weapon from a state. This could occur either voluntarily, as a so-called handoff from a sympathetic regime or some faction within it, or through a black market. Thus, there is a potential link between nuclear proliferation to states and the likelihood that terrorist organizations might get them. It only stands to reason that more nuclear powers, more nuclear weapons, and more nuclear fuel in the world will only increase the chances that weapons will wind up in the wrong hands. And because the dangers of nuclear weapons in the hands of nondeterrable actors are so immense, the argument goes, we need to prevent anything that increases this risk, including proliferation to other states.

Other Weapons of Mass Destruction

Concern about nuclear weapons proliferation is often expressed in the context of **weapons of mass destruction (WMD)** more generally, a category that includes chemical and biological weapons as well as radiological weapons or "dirty bombs." Chemical weapons include such things as nerve gas or other substances that disable or kill people exposed to them. Biological weapons involve the release of bacteria or viruses that cause disease. Radiological weapons are conventional bombs that would spread radioactive material. In the lead up to the 2003 Iraq War, for example, the Bush administration emphasized the possible presence of chemical and biological weapons in Iraq. Though Iraq was suspected of having a nuclear weapons program, most thought it would be some time before it could have them.

weapons of mass destruction (WMD) A general category of unconventional weapons including nuclear, chemical, biological, and radiological weapons.

On one level there are good reasons to be more worried about these other WMDs. One good thing about nuclear weapons is that they are both difficult and expensive to build. But because chemical and biological weapons are easier and cheaper, other states and organizations are more likely to acquire them. This is why biological weapons are often referred to as the "poor man's nuke." This is not to say that it is easy to make usable biological weapons—there are still many obstacles to growing and weaponizing biological agents. Chemical weapons, the easiest to manufacture, were used almost a century ago when soldiers in World War I confronted a variety of gasses on the battlefield. Though certainly frightening, it would be difficult for chemical weapons to achieve nuclear-like destructiveness. For this reason, it might be a mistake to classify them as genuine weapons of mass destruction. On the other hand, a successful biological attack with a highly infectious and lethal agent could produce casualties of nuclear proportions.

Unlike nuclear weapons, however, there is no real debate about the merits of chemical and biological weapons proliferation. No one seriously argues that the world would be a better place with more biological weapons. One reason is that although a nuclear bomb would produce great damage, its effects can be contained and calculated. But once an infectious biological agent is released into the human population, its eventual course cannot be controlled. It is almost impossible to know where the agent will travel, whom it will kill, or how many. Because these weapons are so inherently unpredictable, it is difficult to imagine how they would fit into any rational policy of deterrence.

Conclusion

The debate over whether the spread of nuclear weapons contributes to peace and stability is largely an in-house discussion among realists. Kenneth Waltz, who advocates widespread proliferation, and John Mearsheimer, who favors more limited proliferation, are both self-described realists. Other realists oppose any further proliferation. This divergence among realists illustrates something we have seen already: Debates exist not only between and among different perspectives, but also within them. Despite shared assumptions, people can arrive at different conclusions.

Both Mearsheimer and Waltz agree that nuclear deterrence can be a powerful force for peace. They also agree that nuclear deterrence works because it increases the costs of war, making it less likely that war will be initiated. The connections between this argument for nuclear deterrence and the realist worldview are easy to discern. Realists have always emphasized the inevitability of conflict among nations. International conflict, like social conflict in general, can never be entirely eliminated. Politics is about the management of conflict, not its elimination. In the absence of a central government to deal with disputes among nations, the distribution of power becomes a critical factor influencing whether conflicts lead to war. Realists have generally seen a balance of power between antagonists as the most stable situation. When a balance of power exists, neither side can be confident of prevailing in a war, which decreases the likelihood that war would be initiated. States are deterred from going to war because of the fear that they might lose. The argument that nuclear weapons are a stabilizing force is an understandable extension of this basic logic. Conflicts are prevented from escalating to war not by eliminating their underlying causes but by convincing both sides they have much more to lose than to gain. Thus, nuclear weapons deter war in much the same way as the balance of power. The logic is quintessentially realist.

Acceptance of the general argument, however, does not always lead to agreement on specific issues. This is because additional questions need to be answered before general principles can be translated into policy: What constitutes an adequate deterrent? Which nations have the capacity to build a sufficient deterrent? The basic assumptions of realism do not provide answers to these questions. Because realists make different judgments on these issues, they do not agree on whether nuclear weapons decrease or increase the danger of war between Ukraine and Russia or between India and Pakistan. An essentially realist argument can be made either way. The basic principles of realism (or any other perspective) provide a general framework, not a detailed road map, for thinking about international problems.

Even though realists have dominated discussions about the consequences of nuclear proliferation, they have not monopolized it. Liberals have also weighed in on the question, generally opposing proliferation in favor of strengthening the NPT and other international efforts to control the spread of nuclear weapons. But liberal opposition to proliferation usually does not focus on the ability or inability of nations to build an adequate deterrent. Liberal opposition to proliferation derives from a deeper unease with nuclear deterrence itself. Stripped to its barest essentials, the case for nuclear deterrence is an argument for peace based on fear. Peace prevails because nuclear weapons make war too horrible to contemplate. For realists, who view some measure of international conflict as inevitable, the logic of peace through deterrence or fear makes sense. But liberals have always been uncomfortable with the notion that peace is preserved by making war ever more horrific. Liberals would rather bring about peace by finding a way to resolve the issue(s) that create hostility. A peace based on the mutual threat of total destruction is not a long-term solution to anything. For liberals, the debate over proliferation raises issues that go well beyond worries about crisis stability. As Jonathan Schell explains, "The principle strategic question is whether the doctrine of deterrence, having been framed during the cold war, will now be discredited as logically absurd and morally bankrupt or, on the contrary, recommended to nations all over the world."[34] For Schell, the narrow focus on the consequences of proliferation obscures the more important question. The most pressing issue is not whether *any more* nations should get nuclear weapons, but whether *any* nation should have them in the first place.

CHAPTER SUMMARY

- Despite current fears about nuclear proliferation, the past few decades are remarkable for the number of nations that have refrained from developing nuclear weapons, even when they have the financial and technological ability to do so. The reasons for this restraint are many—the U.S. "nuclear umbrella," the Nuclear Non-Proliferation Treaty, and the absence of any compelling strategic rationale being important factors.

- The fact that relatively few nations have pursued nuclear weapons is of little comfort if these are the ones we need to worry most about. The debate over the consequences of nuclear proliferation raises the question of whether we really need to be that fearful. Some even argue that a world with more nuclear weapons might be more peaceful and stable.

- There are essentially three major positions in the debate over nuclear proliferation: the case for limited spread of nuclear weapons, a more extreme argument for virtually unlimited proliferation, and the more common opposition to any further proliferation.

- Those who favor proliferation claim that nuclear weapons were a force for stability during the Cold War and can be in other settings. By increasing the potential costs of war, nuclear weapons have the effect of reducing the chances for war. In this sense, nuclear deterrence "works."

- Those who favor only limited proliferation argue that although nuclear deterrence works, it is difficult and expensive. Very few nations have the ability to build and maintain an adequate nuclear deterrent. The case for more widespread proliferation rests on the assumption that only a few nuclear weapons would be sufficient, making nuclear deterrence relatively easy and cheap.

- The debate about how much proliferation is desirable usually pits realists against other realists. Though attracted to the logic of deterrence, realists disagree among themselves about exactly what is needed for deterrence to work.

- Opponents of proliferation point out that even if nuclear weapons reduce the chances for war, they do not eliminate them. And because war with nuclear weapons would be so horrible, this is not a risk worth taking. Proliferation pessimists also worry more about the "rationality" of the leaders of rogue states and the danger of accidental launches from countries with primitive command and control systems.

- Whatever the disagreements concerning the spread of nuclear weapons to other states, there is consensus that it would be a disaster if nonstate actors acquired nuclear weapons. When an actor lacks any territory or assets that can be easily targeted and destroyed, deterrence is not an option.

CRITICAL QUESTIONS

1. Why does the prospect of an Iranian nuclear arsenal elicit so much more concern than India's?

2. Are there legitimate reasons to worry about a handful of Indian and Pakistani nuclear weapons but not thousands of American nuclear weapons?

3. Why do states and nonstate actors pose fundamentally different problems in terms of nuclear proliferation?

4. Why might so many nations with the ability to acquire nuclear weapons refrain from doing so?

5. Can the arguments in favor of nuclear proliferation be applied to other weapons of mass destruction?

KEY TERMS

crisis stability, 281
International Atomic Energy Agency (IAEA), 274

invulnerable second-strike, 277
launch on warning, 282

mutual assured destruction (MAD), 277
nuclear abstainers, 272
nuclear apartheid, 280

Nuclear Non-Proliferation Treaty (NPT), 273
nuclear umbrella, 272
preemptive strike, 281

FURTHER READINGS

Because much of the debate about nuclear proliferation relies on assessments about the impact of nuclear weapons during the Cold War, it is useful to begin by looking at the U.S.–Soviet experience. Two excellent surveys are Richard Smoke, *National Security and the Nuclear Dilemma, 1945–1991* (New York: McGraw-Hill, 1992), and Ronald Powaski, *Return to Armageddon: The United States and the Nuclear Arms Race, 1981–1999* (Oxford: Oxford University Press, 2000). In terms of the debate over proliferation, Kenneth Waltz's essay, "The Spread of Nuclear Weapons: More May Be Better," *Adelphi Papers*, vol. 17 (Oxford: Oxford University Press, 1981), is the best place to begin because this seminal article set the terms for the entire debate. Differing views of the impact of nuclear weapons on the "peace" of the Cold War are presented by John Mearsheimer, "Back to the Future: Political Instability in Europe After the Cold War," *International Security* 15 (Summer 1990): 5–56, and John Mueller, "The Essential Irrelevance of Nuclear Weapons," *International Security* 13 (Fall 1988): 55–79. The best overall presentation of the debate is Scott D. Sagan and Kenneth N. Waltz, *The Spread of Nuclear Weapons: A Debate Renewed* (New York: W. W. Norton, 2003). An excellent collection of essays dealing with individual countries is Peter R. Lavoy, Scott D. Sagan, and James Wirtz, eds., *Planning the Unthinkable: How New Powers Will Use Nuclear, Chemical and Biological Weapons* (Ithaca, NY: Cornell University Press, 2001). On the dynamics of nuclear proliferation the most recent and study is Matthew Kroenig's *Exporting the Bomb: Technology Transfer and the Spread of Nuclear Weapons* (Ithaca: Cornell University Press, 2010).

NUCLEAR PROLIFERATION ON THE WEB

www.armscontrol.org
Web site of the Arms Control Association provides information and news on all aspects of nuclear weapons, including nuclear proliferation.

www.nuclearfiles.org
Provides the test of the Nuclear Non-Proliferation Treaty as well as other information about nuclear weapons, including the history of the nuclear arms race.

www.ceip.org/files/nonprolif
Web site maintained by the Carnegie Endowment for International Peace provides the latest news on nuclear, chemical, and biological weapons proliferation.

www.globalzero.org
Information about the most prominent contemporary movement to create "a world without nuclear weapons."

www.nci.org
Perhaps the best source for up-to-date information on nuclear proliferation, this is the Web site of the Nuclear Control Institute.

www.iaea.org
Web site of the International Atomic Energy Agency. Provides up-to-date information, for example, regarding its inspections and activities in Iran.

NOTES

[1]"The Sabotaging of Iran," *Financial Times* (February 13, 2011): 1 and 21.

[2]See Jeffrey Goldberg, "Point of No Return," *Atlantic* vol. 306, no. 2 (September 2010): 56–69.

[3]David E. Sanger, "Suppose We Just Let Iran Have the Bomb," *New York Times* (March 19, 2006): 4:1.

[4]See Louis Rene Beres and Yoash Tsiddon-Chatto, "Reconsidering Israel's Destruction of Iraq's Osiraq Nuclear Reactor," *Temple International and Comparative Law Journal* 9, no. 2(1995): 437–440; and by the same authors, "Sorry Seems to Be the Hardest Word," *Jerusalem Post* (June 5, 2003), p. 37A.

[5]James Carroll, "The President's Nuclear Threat," *Boston Globe* (October 1, 2002), p. A15.

[6]Mitchell Reiss, *Without the Bomb: The Politics of Nuclear Nonproliferation* (New York: Columbia University Press, 1988), p. 247.

[7]Quoted in Jim Walsh, "Understanding the Nuclear Puzzle," *International Studies Review* 13, no. 1 (Fall 2001): 177.

[8]Drake Bennett, "Critical Mess: How the Neocons Are Promoting Nuclear Proliferation," *American Prospect* (July/August 2003): 50.

[9]The full text of the treaty can be found at www.state.gov/www/global/arms/treaties/npt1.html. A list of signatories is available at the same site.

[10]Bennett, "Critical Mess," p. 50.

[11]T. V. Paul, *Power versus Prudence: Why Nations Forgo Nuclear Weapons* (Montreal: McGill–Queens University Press, 2000), p. 151.

[12]John Mearsheimer, "Why We Will Soon Miss the Cold War," *Atlantic* (August 1990): 35–50. A more detailed and scholarly version of the argument is presented in John Mearsheimer, "Back to the Future: Political Instability in Europe After the Cold War," *International Security* 15, no. 1 (Summer 1990): 5–56.

[13]Charles Krauthammer, "On Nuclear Morality," in *Nuclear Arms: Ethics, Strategy, Politics,* ed. R. James Woolsey (San Francisco: Institute for Contemporary Studies, 1984), p. 15.

[14]Mearsheimer's advice was not followed and Ukraine did return its inherited weapons to Russia.

[15]Jonathan Schell, "The Gift of Time: The Case for Abolishing Nuclear Weapons," *Nation* (February 9, 1998): 21.

[16]John Mearsheimer, "The Case for a Ukrainian Nuclear Deterrent," *Foreign Affairs* 72, no. 3 (Summer 1993): 51.

[17]Kenneth Waltz, "The Spread of Nuclear Weapons: More May Be Better," *Adelphi Papers*, vol. 17 (Oxford: Oxford University Press, 1981). The argument contained here was later refined and incorporated into Scott Sagan and Kenneth Waltz, *The Spread of Nuclear Weapons: A Debate* (New York: W. W. Norton, 1995).

[18]Sagan and Waltz, *The Spread of Nuclear Weapons*, p. 3.

[19]Ibid., p. 109.

[20]"Iran and Deterrence," accessed at http://time.blogs.com/daily_dish/2006/05/iran_and_deterr.html (July 31, 2006).

[21]Sagan and Waltz, *The Spread of Nuclear Weapons*, p. 97.

[22]Devin T. Haggerty, "Nuclear Deterrence in South Asia: The 1990 Indo-Pakistani Crisis," *International Security* 20, no. 3 (Winter 1995/1996): 82, 114.

[23]Sagan and Waltz, *Spread of Nuclear Weapons*, pp. 16–17.

[24]John Lewis Gaddis, *The Long Peace: Inquiries into the History of the Cold War* (New York: Oxford University Press, 1987), pp. 215–245.

[25]John Mueller, *Retreat from Doomsday: The Obsolescence of Major Power War* (New York: Basic Books, 1988), p. 116.

[26]Robert W. Malcolmson, *Beyond Nuclear Thinking* (Montreal: McGill–Queens University Press, 1990), p. 89.

[27]Sagan and Waltz, *The Spread of Nuclear Weapons*, p. 17.

[28]Steven Miller, "The Case Against a Ukrainian Nuclear Deterrent," *Foreign Affairs* 72, no. 3 (Summer 1993): 80.

[29]Ahmed Hashim, "The State, Society and the Evolution of Warfare in the Middle East: The Rise of Strategic Deterrence?" *Washington Quarterly* 18, no. 4 (Autumn 1995): 69.

[30]Cecilia Dugger, "Eyeball to Eyeball, and Blinking in Denial," *New York Times* (June 2, 2002), Section 4, p. 1.

[31]This section subtitle is, of course, taken from Albert Wohlstetter's seminal article, "The Delicate Balance of Terror," *Foreign Affairs* 37 (1959): 211–234.

[32]Scott Sagan discusses some of the scarier near-misses in *The Limits of Safety: Organizations, Accidents and Nuclear Weapons* (Princeton, NJ: Princeton University Press, 1993).

[33]Quoted in Alvin and Heidi Toffler, *War and Anti-War* (New York: Warner Books, 1995), p. 198.

[34]Schell, "Gift of Time," p. 22.

Can a Nuclear Iran Be Deterred?

For the last half century nuclear deterrence has worked, or at least it has not failed. Nuclear weapons have never been used (other than in tests) since the United States dropped the atomic bomb. Whether this was the result of the compelling logic of nuclear deterrence or sheer luck is a matter of debate, as we saw in this chapter. This debate gets renewed whenever a new nation appears ready to join the nuclear club. In the summer of 2006, attention in this regard focused on Iran. Despite protestations that Iran's nuclear program was peaceful and designed to produce energy, most observers believed that the country's goal was to develop nuclear weapons. Diplomats from Europe, the United States, Russia, and China spent much of the summer trying to find a way to stop Iran from going nuclear. But beyond the debate over how to prevent a nuclear Iran is the more fundamental question of why a nuclear Iran would be so dangerous. The basic issue is whether a nuclear Iran could be dealt with using the normal dynamics of nuclear deterrence. Many assume that it could not be. But why? In his essay below, Graham Allison expresses the commonly held view that Iran differs from past nuclear powers and might not be deterrable. Christopher Layne, however, sees no reason why deterrence would not be effective. With whom do you agree and why?

The Nightmare This Time: A Nuclear Showdown Could Be This Generation's Cuban Missile Crisis (2006)

PERSPECTIVE 1

Graham Allison[1]

According to a recent Gallup poll, most Americans now view Iran as our country's greatest national enemy. Indeed, a *Washington Post*–ABC News survey reports that 42 percent of Americans support a military strike to prevent Iran from developing nuclear technology. Online betting sites make the odds of a U.S. or Israeli airstrike against Iran … as 1 in 3.

As Senator John McCain has summed up the hard-line position, "There is only one thing worse than the U.S. exercising a military option, and that is a nuclear armed Iran."

On the other hand, some commentators, even in the administration, now suggest that a nuclear-armed Iran is inevitable. "Look, the Pakistanis and the North

[1] Source: Graham Allison, "The Nightmare This Time: A Nuclear Showdown with Iran Could Be This Generation's Cuban Missile Crisis; Here Are the Reasons We Must Not Let It Come to That," *Boston Globe*, March 12, 2006. Reprinted by permission of the author.

Koreans got the bomb," a "senior official" told the *New York Times*, "and they didn't have Iran's money or engineering expertise."

As citizens, we are watching a slow-mo Cuban missile crisis in which events are moving, seemingly inexorably, toward a crossroads at which President Bush will have to decide between McCain's options. Before we get there, however, Americans should vigorously debate the bottom-line question: Can we live with a nuclear Iran?

Barry Posen, professor of political science at MIT, has presented the most cogent argument for the proposition that "we could readily manage a nuclear Iran." Writing recently on the *New York Times* op-ed page, he identified and refuted the two most commonly cited reasons for opposing a nuclear Iran: that it would attempt to destroy Israel or strike the United States. Such an action, he rightly argues, would be suicidal for the Iranian regime. In either case, a nuclear attack would trigger overwhelming retaliation that could end life in Persia for a century to come.

Yet Posen's attempt to deal with a third concern—namely, Iran's transfer of nuclear weapons to terrorists who might use them—is less satisfactory. Relying on the Cold War logic of deterrence, he asserts that "Iran would have to worry that the victim would discover the weapon's origin and visit a terrible revenge on Iran." Worry, yes. But Israel and the U.S. have to worry even more about an Iranian president who denies the Holocaust and asserts that "Israel must be wiped off the map." Might he not also believe that he could sneak a weapon to Al-Qaeda, Hamas, or Hezbollah with no fingerprints?

Tehran might not be overly concerned about getting caught—and with good reason. If a terrorist exploded a nuclear bomb in Tel Aviv or Boston, Iran would not be the only suspected source. The bomb could have come from Pakistan, Russia, or elsewhere in the former Soviet Union, where thousands of potential nuclear weapons are vulnerable to theft.

The U.S. government is actively pursuing improvements in its nuclear forensic capability to increase the likelihood that it could identify the fissile material that powered a terrorist's bomb. But it's worth noting that more than two years after Libya's Khadafy disclosed his nuclear activities, the U.S. has yet to conclude which nation provided him with enough uranium hexafluoride to make a nuclear bomb.

Before accepting the answer that the U.S. can deal with an Iranian nuclear bomb, four further risks must be weighed: the threat of proliferation, the danger of an accidental or unauthorized nuclear launch, the risk of theft of an Iranian weapon or materials, and the prospect of a preemptive Israeli attack.

"A Cascade of Proliferation"

The current nonproliferation regime is a set of agreements between the nuclear "haves" and "have-nots," including the Nuclear Nonproliferation Treaty, in which 184 nations agreed to eschew nuclear weapons and existing nuclear weapons states pledged to sharply diminish the role of such weapons in international politics. Since 1970, the treaty has stopped the spread of nuclear weapons with only two exceptions (India and Pakistan).

UN Secretary General Kofi Annan's High Level Panel on Threats, Challenges, and Change warned in December 2004 that current developments in Iran and North Korea threatened to erode the entire nonproliferation regime to a point of "irreversibility" that could trigger a "cascade of proliferation." If Iran crosses its nuclear finish line, a Middle Eastern cascade of new nuclear weapons states could produce the first multiparty nuclear arms race, far more volatile than the Cold War competition between the U.S. and USSR.

Given Egypt's historic role as the leader of the Arab Middle East, the prospects of it living unarmed alongside a nuclear Persia are very low. The International Atomic Energy Agency's reports of clandestine nuclear experiments hint that Cairo may have considered this possibility. Were Saudi Arabia to buy a dozen nuclear warheads that could be mated to the Chinese medium-range ballistic missiles it purchased secretly in the 1980s, few in the American intelligence community would be surprised. Given its role as the major financier of Pakistan's clandestine nuclear program in the 1980s, it is not out of the question that Riyadh and Islamabad have made secret arrangements for this contingency.

In 1962, bilateral competition between the U.S. and the Soviet Union led to the Cuban missile crisis, which historians now call "the most dangerous moment in human history." After the crisis, President Kennedy estimated the likelihood of nuclear war as "between 1 in 3 and even." A multiparty nuclear arms race in the Middle East would be like playing Russian roulette with five bullets in a six-chamber revolver—dramatically increasing the likelihood of a regional nuclear war.

Accidental or Unauthorized Nuclear Launch

A new nuclear state goes through a period of "nuclear adolescence" that poses special dangers of accidental or unauthorized use—and Iran would be no different. When a state first acquires a small number of nuclear weapons, those weapons become a tempting target: Successful attack would disarm any capacity to retaliate with nuclear weapons. Fearing preemption, new nuclear weapons states rationally adopt loose command and control arrangements. But control arrangements loose enough to guard against decapitation inherently mean more fingers on more triggers and consequently more prospects of a nuclear weapons launch.

Theft from an Uncertain Iranian Regime

For outsiders, Iran appears to be a black box. Beneath this exterior, however, there are multiple centers of power and competing security structures. The supreme leader, Ayatollah Ali Khamenei, who commands the armed forces, appears to have the last word on nuclear policy. But three other groups share constitutional authority over foreign policy with the leader: President Mahmoud Ahmadinejad; former president Ali Akbar Hashemi Rafsanjani as head of the Expediency Council, which resolves conflicts among government branches; and the Foreign Ministry. Sharp differences among these groups reveal themselves in contradictory statements.

Could rogue elements within Iran's nuclear or security establishment divert nuclear weapons or nuclear materials to other nations or to terrorists? Stop and think about what we have learned recently about the father of Pakistan's nuclear bomb, A. Q. Khan. Over the decade of the 1990s, he became the first global nuclear black marketer, running what Mohamed ElBaradei, the director of the International Atomic Energy Agency, has called a "Wal-Mart of private-sector proliferation." His network sold to Libya, North Korea, Iran, and others nuclear warhead designs, technologies for producing nuclear weapons, and even the uranium hexafluoride precursor of nuclear bomb fuel.

An Israeli Attack on Iran's Nuclear Facilities

Lieutenant General Dan Halutz, the Israeli military's chief of staff, has called an Iranian nuclear bomb "Israel's sole existential threat." ... Prime Minister Ehud Olmert has warned unambiguously: "Under no circumstances, and at no point, can Israel allow anyone with these kinds of malicious designs against us to have control of weapons of destruction that can threaten our existence."

The Israeli national security establishment has focused anxiously on a red line that Iran will cross when it achieves "technical independence"—sufficient knowledge about how to construct and operate a limited cascade of centrifuges that could produce enough highly enriched uranium for its own nuclear bombs. The head of Mossad, Israel's secret service, states publicly that Iran could cross that red line by July [2006]. In contrast, Washington talks about a different, and much later, red line: when Iran achieves industrial-level production of enriched uranium, or even operates an industrial-level production facility long enough to produce sufficient material for a bomb. Although U.S. estimates differ, none predict this will occur sooner than five years from now. The danger, therefore, is that Israel will make up its mind to strike Iran before the U.S. has had time to fully consider its options.

Israel will not ask for American permission before attacking Iranian nuclear facilities at Isfahan and Natanz. But the U.S. will be blamed throughout the Middle East as a hidden coconspirator. Retaliation by the Iranian government and by those who sympathize with Osama bin Laden will target not only Israelis, but also Americans and American interests, including oil-tanker traffic in the Persian Gulf.

As Henry A. Kissinger has noted, a defining challenge for statesmen is to recognize "a change in the international environment so likely to undermine national security that it must be resisted no matter what form the threat takes or how ostensibly legitimate it appears." Iran's emergence as a nuclear armed state would constitute just such a catastrophic transformation for the United States. But just as JFK refused to choose between accepting nuclear weapons in Cuba or attacking the Soviet Union during the Cuban missile crisis, the challenge today is to find additional options, short of war, to stop Iran's acquisition of nuclear arms.

PERSPECTIVE 2   Iran: The Logic of Deterrence (2006)

Christopher Layne[2]

At this writing it is not known if the United Nations, when it receives the report of the International Atomic Energy Agency on the status of Iran's compliance with the Nuclear Non-Proliferation Treaty, will impose sanctions on Tehran or whether a last-minute diplomatic compromise will avert—at least for the time being—the need for punitive measures. Neither outcome, however, will bring about a definitive

[2] Source: Christopher Layne, "Iran: The Logic of Deterrence," The *American Conservative*, April 10, 2006. Reprinted by permission of *American Conservative*.

resolution of the deepening crisis between the U.S. and Iran. Washington and Tehran will remain on a collision course that could eventuate in military conflict.

The main source of conflict—or at least the one that has grabbed the lion's share of the headlines—is Tehran's evident determination to develop a nuclear weapons program. Washington's policy, as President George W. Bush has stated on several occasions in language that recalls his pre-war stance on Iraq, is that a nuclear-armed Iran is "intolerable."…

The administration's stance with respect to so-called rogue states was … detailed in its September 2002 National Security Strategy. Here, the offending characteristics of such regimes were defined with specificity. These states "brutalize their own people"; flout international law and violate the treaties they have signed; are engaged in the acquisition of WMD, which are "to be used as threats or offensively to achieve the aggressive designs of these regimes"; support terrorism; and "hate the United States and everything it stands for." Given the nature of the threat, the National Security Strategy concluded that the Cold War doctrine of deterrence through the threat of retaliation is inadequate to deal with rogue states because the rulers of these regimes are "more willing to take risks, gambling with the lives of their people and the wealth of their nations." Moreover, in contrast to the doctrines of the two superpowers during the Cold War, rogue states consider WMD to be the "weapons of choice" rather than weapons of last resort. Consequently, the administration argued, rogue states represent a qualitatively different kind of strategic threat, and the United States "cannot remain idle while threats gather."

… The very notion that undeterrable rogue states exist is [a] … questionable assumption on which the administration's strategy is based. In an important article in the Winter 2004/2005 issue of *International Security*, Francis Gavin points out that the post-9/11 era is not the only time that American policymakers have believed that the U.S. faced a lethal threat from a rogue state. During the 1950s and early 1960s, for example, the People's Republic of China was perceived by Washington in very much the same way as the U.S. perceived Saddam Hussein's Iraq or, currently, Iran. Under the leadership of Chairman Mao Zedong, the Chinese Communist Party imposed harsh repression and killed millions of Chinese citizens, and Beijing—which had entered the Korean War in 1950, menaced Taiwan, gone to war with India in 1962, and seemingly was poised to intervene in Vietnam—was viewed as an aggressor. For Washington, Mao's China was the epitome of a rogue state, and during the Johnson administration, the United States seriously considered launching a preventive war to destroy China's embryonic nuclear program.

In many ways, Mao was seen by U.S. policymakers as the Saddam Hussein of his time. Like Iranian president Mahmoud Ahmadinejad, who has made outrageous comments denying the Holocaust and threatening Israel's destruction, Mao also indulged in irresponsible rhetoric, even cavalierly embracing the possibility of nuclear war. "If the worse came to worst and half of mankind died," Mao said, "the other half would remain while imperialism would be razed to the ground and the whole world would become socialist." Once China became a nuclear power, however, where nuclear weapons were concerned both its rhetoric and its policy quickly became circumspect. In fact, a mere five years after the Johnson administration pondered the possibility of striking China preventively, the U.S. and China were engaged in secret negotiations that, in 1972, culminated in President Richard Nixon's trip to Beijing and Sino-American co-operation to contain the Soviet Union.

The U.S. experience with China illustrates an important point: the reasons states acquire nuclear weapons are primarily to gain security and, secondarily, to enhance their prestige. This certainly was true of China, which believed its security was threatened by the United States and by the Soviet Union. It was also true of Saddam Hussein's Iraq and is true of Iran. As Gavin writes, "In some ways, the Kennedy and Johnson administrations' early analysis of China mirrors the Bush administration's public portrayal of Iraq in the lead-up to the war. Insofar as Iraq was surrounded by potential nuclear adversaries (Iran and Israel) and threatened by regime change by the most powerful country in the world, Saddam Hussein's desire to develop nuclear weapons may be seen as understandable." The same can be said for Iran, which is ringed by U.S. conventional forces in neighboring Afghanistan and Iraq and in the Persian Gulf, and which is a stated target of the Bush administration's policy of regime change and democratization. Tehran may be paranoid, but in the United States and Israel, it has real enemies. It is Iran's fear for its security that drives its quest to obtain nuclear weapons.

The same architects of illusion who fulminated for war with Iraq say that if Iran gets nuclear weapons, three bad things could happen: it could trigger a nuclear arms race in the Middle East; it might supply nuclear weapons to terrorists; and Tehran could use its nuclear weapons to blackmail other states in the region or to engage in aggression. Each of these scenarios, however, is improbable in the extreme. During the early 1960s, American policymakers had similar fears that China's acquisition of nuclear weapons would trigger a proliferation stampede, but these fears did not materialize, and a nuclear Iran is no more likely to start a proliferation snowball in the Middle East. Israel, of course, already is a nuclear power. The other three states that might be tempted to seek nuclear weapons capability are Egypt, Saudi Arabia, and Turkey. But as MIT professor Barry Posen points out, each of these three states would be under strong pressure not do to so. Egypt is particularly vulnerable to outside pressure to refrain from going nuclear because its shaky economy depends on foreign—especially U.S.—economic assistance. Saudi Arabia would find it hard to purchase nuclear weapons or material on the black market, which is closely watched by the United States, and, Posen notes, it would take the Saudis years to develop the industrial and engineering capabilities to develop nuclear weapons indigenously.

Notwithstanding the near-hysterical rhetoric of the Bush administration and the neoconservatives, Iran is not going to give nuclear weapons to terrorists. This is not to say that Tehran has not abetted groups like Hezbollah in Lebanon or Hamas in the Palestinian Authority. However, there are good reasons that states—even those that have ties to terrorists—draw the line at giving them nuclear weapons or other WMD: if the terrorists were to use these weapons against the United States or its allies, the weapons could be traced back to the donor state, which would be at risk of annihilation by an American retaliatory strike. Iran's leaders have too much at stake to run this risk. Even if one believed the administration's hype about the indifference of rogue-state leaders to the fate of their populations, they care very much about the survival of their regimes, which is why deterrence works.

For the same reason, Iran's possession of nuclear weapons will not invest Tehran with options to attack or intimidate its neighbors. Just as it did during the Cold War, the U.S. can extend its own deterrence umbrella to protect its clients in the region like Saudi Arabia, the Gulf states, and Turkey. American security guarantees will not only dissuade Iran from acting recklessly but also restrain proliferation by negating the incentives for states like Saudi Arabia and Turkey to build their own nuclear weapons. Given the overwhelming U.S. advantage in both nuclear and conventional military capabilities, Iran is not going to risk national suicide by challenging America's security commitments in the region. In this sense, dealing with the Iranian "nuclear threat" is actually one of the easier strategic challenges the United States faces. It is a threat that can be handled by an offshore balancing strategy that relies on missile, air, and naval power well away from the volatile Persian Gulf, thus reducing the American poltico-military footprint in the region. In short, while a nuclear-armed Iran is hardly desirable, neither is it "intolerable," because it could be contained and deterred successfully by the United States....

12 International Terrorism

Key Controversy: How Should We Respond to International Terrorism?

Since the September 11, 2001 attacks, terrorism has become one of the critical problems of international relations in the eyes of most Americans. Even though the magnitude of the attacks was unprecedented, terrorism has been around for a long time. So, too, have debates about almost every aspect of terrorism—its meaning, definition, causes, consequences, and morality. This chapter focuses primarily on policy responses to terrorism. It identifies two different strategies of response that emerged in the post–September 11 debate. A *cosmopolitan* approach treats terrorist attacks as criminal acts against humanity as a whole, requiring a legal and international response accompanied by a long-term strategy addressing the root causes of terrorism, such as global poverty and discontent. The cosmopolitan strategy resonates with important strands of liberal, Marxist/radical, and feminist thought. A *statist* approach treats terrorist attacks as acts of war that might require a forceful response not only against terrorist organizations but also against states that actively support or passively tolerate them. Advocates of a statist response are more inclined to see terrorism as rooted in a fundamental conflict of values, not social and economic conditions that can be eliminated by reform. This approach obviously has much in common with a realist worldview. ■

Coming just a few months shy of the tenth anniversary of the September 11, 2001, attacks that made him one of the world's most wanted men, the killing of Osama Bin Laden in April, 2011, served a dramatic bookend for a decade in which Americans worried about international terrorism for the first time. Though no one knows yet what his death will mean for the terror organization he founded and led, we can safely say that it will not mark the end of terrorism: Osama Bin Laden did not invent terrorism and his passing will not bring its demise. The need to understand terrorism and devise appropriate responses is no less pressing now than when he was alive. And the critical questions are the same as they were before anyone ever heard of Osama Bin Laden: What is terrorism? What motivates individuals and groups to engage in terrorism? Can terrorism ever be morally justified? Does terrorism work? What policies and strategies should nations pursue to deal with terrorism? These questions reflect the enduring conceptual, empirical, theoretical, moral, and political issues that come to mind as we try to understand and respond to terrorism. And, as is usually the case, the problems become more complex as we realize how these questions are interrelated—for example, assumptions about terrorist motivations are tied to policy recommendations; and definitions of terrorism influence moral evaluations.

Though the term *terrorism* originated during the French Revolution, the phenomenon is probably as old as political violence itself. It is possible to find acts in the ancient world that would meet contemporary definitions of terrorism. In this sense, the attacks of September 11, 2001, were merely the latest in the very long history of terrorism. Though it is important to place contemporary events in their larger, historical context, it would be a mistake to view the September 11 attacks as "only" the most recent manifestation of an age-old phenomenon. For the United States, of course, September 11 had a special significance because it was the target. The larger significance of the attacks derives from their magnitude. As Martha Crenshaw notes, "the September 11 assaults ... [were] unprecedented in the history of terrorism."[1] The attacks represented more than a minor escalation in the scale of violence; this was violence of another order entirely.

Terrorism: The Definitional Angst

terrorism The indiscriminate use or threat of violence to advance social, political, economic, or religious objectives by creating a climate of fear.

What is **terrorism**? Though this seems like a simple enough question, things are rarely as simple as they first appear. Like so many critical concepts in international relations, terrorism has no universally accepted definition. Paul Pillar sees a "collective definitional angst" among policymakers and scholars dealing with terrorism.[2] It is no surprise that definitional issues are so contentious. It is difficult to think of a more emotionally laden term in the current political environment. Nations and groups are understandably eager to define terrorism so as to exclude their own actions but include those of their opponents. If you can make the *terrorist* label stick to your enemies, this alone is a political victory. One harsh critic charges that in the case of U.S. antiterrorist policy, "the condemnatory label [is] being deployed to the enemies of U.S. interests while being withheld from U.S. friends and clients, no matter how opprobrious their conduct might otherwise be."[3] Even those more detached from contemporary political conflicts have difficulty settling on a definition. One study required more than a hundred pages to survey and compare the various definitions.[4] Walter Laqueur, exasperated by the proliferation of definitions, concludes that "any definition of political terrorism venturing beyond noting the systematic use of murder, injury and destruction or threats of such acts toward achieving political ends is bound to lead to endless controversy." As a result, "it can be predicted with confidence that the disputes about a comprehensive, detailed definition of terrorism will continue for a long time, that they will not result in a consensus and that they will make no notable contribution toward the understanding of terrorism."[5]

In some respects, Laqueur exaggerates the difficulty of defining terrorism. Although some acts may fall within certain definitions of terrorism but not others, most fall unambiguously into virtually all definitions. Minor definitional differences should not obscure the consensus on the basic components of terrorism. What are those components? First, terrorism involves the threat or use of violence. Though people sometimes talk about *cyberterrorism*, in which a society is targeted by having its communications and information systems disrupted, most still see physical violence as a defining feature of terrorism. Second, this violence must be in pursuit of some broader political or social objective. A mugger might use deadly force, but this is usually for personal gain, not a political or social agenda. Third, it usually does not matter *who* is harmed by terrorist violence because "terrorism is specifically designed to have far-reaching psychological effects beyond the immediate victims or objects of the terrorist attack."[6] A suicide bomber who blows up a bus and kills dozens is not trying to kill those people specifically. In this sense the targets are random, and the randomness is what creates fear that leads everyone to worry about whether they might be the next target. Cindy Combs reflects the consensus, defining terrorism as "involve[ing] an act of violence, an audience, the creation of a mood of fear, innocent victims, and political goals or motives."[7]

Moving beyond these essential elements, the controversy heats up. Bruce Hoffman, for example, defines terrorism as something conducted by "a subnational group or nonstate entity."[8] If this definitional amendment is accepted, it inoculates states from charges of terrorism. Given that the term *terrorism* was first used after the French Revolution to describe the revolutionary government's "reign of terror," it would seem odd to argue that states, by definition, cannot commit acts of terrorism. But Louis Rene Beres agrees with Hoffman: "Definitions that do not refer specifically and exclusively to insurgent organizations [nonstate actors] broaden the meaning of terrorism to unmanageable and useless levels."[9] This is the definitional issue on which there is the greatest divergence of opinion.

Terrorism or Terrorisms?

After reaching some measure of agreement on a general definition of terrorism, we need to ask whether it is useful to view terrorism as an undifferentiated phenomenon. The problem is familiar. Sometimes it makes sense to group together similar things, whereas other times it is better to draw some distinctions. For some purposes we might want to lump all felons together, and for other purposes it is useful to differentiate burglars from mass murderers. These distinctions and classifications are neither right nor wrong; they are simply more or less useful. Similarly, sometimes it might be helpful think about terrorism in general, whereas at other times differences among terrorist groups might be critical for shaping policy responses.

In the sense that they have all engaged in terrorism, the Irish Republican Army (IRA), Al-Qaeda, and Aum Shinrikyo can be considered terrorist organizations.

But do these disparate groups really represent the same phenomenon? Not really. They are all different in terms of motives, goals, and objectives as well as the type of terrorist attacks committed. The IRA was/is a fairly traditional terrorist group with relatively modest political objectives, fighting against what it sees as outside domination. Its tactics were also very traditional, involving small-scale bombings that caused several dozen casualties at most. Nationalist or separatist groups like the IRA "have tended to calibrate their use of violence, using enough to rivet world attention but not so much as to alienate supporters abroad or members of their base community."[10]

Al-Qaeda ("the base"), on the other hand, has more expansive political and social goals motivated by a particular form of religious fundamentalism. Not only are its objectives broader and more ambitious than that of IRA, but its tactics and the scale of its attacks are also on a very different level. The IRA had no desire to destroy Great Britain; it merely wanted to get the British out of Northern Ireland. The IRA would never have contemplated crashing airliners into buildings or using chemical, biological, or nuclear weapons. This is what made the attacks of September 11, 2001, so significant, the scale of the attack. Thus, even though the phenomenon of terrorism may be as old as human history, September 11 suggests something very different from what we are used to. This is particularly significant because religiously motivated terrorist activities have been increasing since the 1990s. According to Hoffman, "only two of the sixty-four [terrorist] groups active in 1980 could be classified as predominantly religious in character." The majority were ethnic or nationalist in nature. By 1995, however, religious groups "account[ed] for nearly half (twenty-six, or 46 percent) of the fifty-six known, active international terrorist groups."[11] Thus, the mix of international terrorist groups shifted in favor of those inclined to use greater levels of violence and more unconventional modes of attack.

In addition to organizations that fuse fundamentalist religious doctrine with political objectives, there are also groups such as Aum Shinrikyo (the "Supreme Truth"), the bizarre Japanese doomsday cult responsible for a sarin nerve gas attack on the Tokyo subway in March 1995 that killed twelve and hospitalized almost 5,000. Prior to this attack, Aum Shinrikyo had also released botulinum toxin and anthrax from rooftops and trucks in Japanese cities. Fortunately, these attacks failed. The intent was to spark what the cult's leader predicted would be an apocalypse and nuclear war that would usher in heaven on earth. The cult's members believed they would somehow escape destruction.[12] These organizations may prove particularly dangerous because they possess few, if any, internal constraints on their use of violence. Most terrorist organizations use violence in pursuit of an identifiable objective, and as a result there is usually some level of violence that would be counterproductive. For doomsday cults, there might never be such a thing as too much violence.

This diversity of terrorist groups simultaneously complicates and simplifies the problem. It complicates things because it means that generalizations about terrorism are difficult to come by. As Walter Laqueur tells us, "what can be said without fear of contradiction about a terrorist group in one country is by no means true for other groups at other times in other countries."[13] There is unlikely to be a single explanation that accounts for the IRA, Al-Qaeda, and Aum Shinrikyo. Although this makes

Americans celebrate the killing of Osama Bin Laden just few months shy of the 10th anniversary of the 9/11 attacks.
Source: Spencer Platt/Getty Images

grandiose theories about terrorism problematic, it might be good news in terms of policy responses because it allows us to cut the problem up into more manageable pieces. The so-called war on terrorism can then be transformed into a war on *terrorisms*, particularly those that pose the greatest threat. The goal of eliminating all terrorism might be morally laudable, but also so expansive as to be practically daunting, if not impossible; dealing with just a part of the problem is likely to be difficult enough.

Frameworks for Understanding

What do different perspectives on international politics contribute to our understanding of terrorism? The prevailing wisdom is not very much. John Mearsheimer, when asked what realism says about terrorism, answers, "Not a whole heck of a lot. Realism … is really about relations among states, especially among the great powers. … Al-Qaeda is not a state, it's a non-state actor, which is sometimes called a **transnational actor**.… Realism does not have much to say about the *causes* of terrorism." But merely because terrorist organizations are nonstate actors, there is no reason to assume that theories of international relations have

transnational actor Nonstate actors engaged in activities across national boundaries.

nothing to offer. Terrorist organizations must still operate within states, their targets are often states, their objectives usually involve changing the behavior of states, and their activities take place within the same international system in which states operate. Though international relations focuses on the behavior of states, everyone has always been aware that nonstate actors can affect international politics. It was, for example, the assassination of the Austro-Hungarian archduke in July 1914 by a member of a radical Serbian nationalist (terrorist) group that set in motion the events leading to World War I. Thus, while he concedes the limited relevance of realism for explaining the *causes* of terrorism, Mearsheimer points out that "terrorism is a phenomenon that will play itself out in the context of the international system. So it will be played out in the state arena, and, therefore, all of the realist logic about state behavior will have a significant effect on how the war on terrorism is fought."[14]

We also need to remember that most theories of international relations are built upon a deeper vision of the nature and causes of social conflict. International conflict is simply a specific manifestation of social conflict. Because terrorism is also a form of social conflict, each theory's basic understanding of social conflict will influence its analysis of terrorism. Though they may lack well-developed theories of terrorism, when realists, liberals, Marxists, and feminists approach the issue their underlying beliefs and assumptions provide the intellectual foundation for their analysis. And just as Mearsheimer expected "realist logic [to] have a significant impact on how the war on terrorism is fought," we can expect other perspectives to yield different strategies.

statist Views terrorist attacks as acts of war and assumes that the most effective strategy for combating terrorism requires putting pressure on those states that actively support or passively tolerate terrorist organizations.

cosmopolitan Conceptualizes terrorist attacks as criminal acts requiring an international, multilateral response within the context of international law and organizations. As a long-term strategy, it involves addressing the root causes of terrorism, which are usually identified as poverty, inequality, and discontent.

Focusing on post–September 11 debates, Daniele Archibugi and Iris Young draw a useful distinction between **statist** and **cosmopolitan** responses and "frames of interpretation": "The attacks on the World Trade Center and the Pentagon in September 2001 can appear within two different frames of interpretation. The first [statist] sees them as attacks on the United States as a state and its people. The second [cosmopolitan] views them as crimes against humanity. The difference in interpretation is not merely technical, but political, and each implies different strategies of reaction."[15] The observation that different interpretive frameworks lead to different policy responses is merely another way of noting that peoples' underlying beliefs and assumptions are inevitably reflected in their preferred policy responses. But in terms of international terrorism, what exactly are the different strategies of reaction, and how do they reflect alternative frames of interpretation?

The Cosmopolitan Response

One of the first questions in the wake of September 11 was how the attacks should be viewed. The initial response, quickly embraced by the Bush administration, was to characterize them as acts of war. The language of war was immediately evident. Even those willing to accept the terminology of war, however, concede that it is somewhat problematic. As Nicholas Lehman explains, "Traditional wars are fought by military means and have definite endings ... [but] terror ... will never sit at a desk and sign an unconditional surrender."[16] If this was a war, it was not like

World War II because "war" usually describes armed conflict involving states. But what does it matter whether terrorism is framed in terms of warfare? Steven Metz explains that "casting it as such was a major decision" because "portraying the conflict as a war militarized it. While the American public is accustomed to metaphorical uses of the world 'war'—the 'war on poverty' and the 'war on drugs'—the 'war on terror' was not portrayed this way. It was presented as a *real* war…[and] real wars are resolved by military force."[17] Words matter.

Regardless of the merits, the rhetoric of war stuck. But there are those who remain critical and prefer an alternative framing. The criticism does not arise from the failure of this war to meet the definition found in dictionaries but rather from a concern that the terminology of war brings with it policies that might not be appropriate. As Metz notes, "although September 11 required bold action…it did not have to be a war on terrorism of global reach."[18] But if the attacks of September 11 were not acts of war, how should they be seen? What is the alternative? Archibugi and Young propose that "the events [of September 11] be conceptualized as crimes, not as acts of war."[19] They suggest that we adopt a law enforcement model in response, not a military model. A parallel is drawn to the 1995 bombing of the Murrah Federal Building in Oklahoma City. The U.S. government did not declare itself at war with Timothy McVeigh or the organizations he associated with. Though widely described as an act of terrorism, it was viewed as a criminal act, not an act of war. Conceptualizing the September 11 attacks as crimes against humanity, not merely against the United States, provides a framework for interpretation that leads to a *cosmopolitan* policy response, which has two essential elements.

The first task relates to the culprits and organizations responsible for the attacks. Consistent with a criminal/law enforcement model, the United States and the international community should have sought "the establishment of an international tribunal with the authority to seek out, extradite, or arrest and try those responsible for the September 11 attack and those who commit or are conspiring to commit future attacks."[20] In this vein, Samina Ahmed urged the United States to "refrain from any unilateral and precipitous military action. It must create a unified international coalition, with strong Islamic representation, to bring Bin Laden and other terrorists within the Taliban-controlled territory of Afghanistan to justice."[21] The proposed tribunal would be similar to the one dealing with those accused of human rights violations during the war in the former Yugoslavia. From this perspective, Al-Qaeda and similar groups would be classified as international criminal organizations, and the full range of international law enforcement bodies would be mobilized to pursue them. Though most favoring this strategy admit that international legal and law enforcement institutions are not as strong and well developed as domestic ones, they are seen as strong enough to be effective, and the threat of international terrorism might also help strengthen these institutions further. International legal responses directed at people and organizations involved in specific terrorist acts, however, are something of a bandage approach dealing with terrorism only after harm has already been done. It is bandage, necessary perhaps, but a bandage nonetheless.

Advocates of a cosmopolitan response also urge that we address the deeper causes of terrorism, the *root causes*. According to Andrew Johnston, "You can write off the terrorist attacks of Sept[ember] 11 as the crazed act of a fanatical gang hell-bent on causing mayhem at any cost. Or you can try to understand the attack's root causes by taking a closer look at the world whose fragile ecology of power they upset."[22] The implication, of course, is that the root causes need to be identified in the hope that they can be eliminated or ameliorated. We need a bandage to stop the bleeding, but more is needed to heal the underlying wound.

The general proposition that we should eliminate the root causes of terrorism appears so commonsensical that it is hard to imagine any disagreement. The difficulty is identifying the root causes This brings us back to the diversity of terrorism: There are many terrorist groups around the world with many different agendas. Different manifestations of terrorism may have very different root causes. As a result, it should come as no surprise that the list of potential root causes is quite long, some applying to terrorism in general and others specifically to Islamic fundamentalist terrorism. With regard to the latter, many cite a long history of Western, especially U.S., support for repressive and authoritarian regimes in the Arab world, often placing this pattern in the context of a long history of Western and Christian hostility to Islam reaching back to the Crusades. Israeli treatment of the Palestinians, U.S. support for Israel, and the stationing of U.S. troops in Arab countries (particularly holy lands in Saudi Arabia) are presented as the most recent manifestations of this historical pattern. This combination of historical and contemporary grievances helps explain a widespread sense of frustration throughout much of the Islamic world fueling terrorism focused on the United States and its allies.

At a more general level, terrorism is commonly seen as a response to poverty and economic inequality. This is why Jared Diamond argues that "we must feed the hands that could bite us" to reduce terrorism. "When people cannot solve their own problems," Diamond argues, "they strike out irrationally, seeking foreign scapegoats, or collapsing into civil war over limited resources. By bettering conditions overseas, we can reduce chronic future threats to ourselves." To cope with these underlying causes, he proposes that the United States "single out three strategies—providing basic health care, supporting family planning and addressing such widespread environmental problems as deforestation."[23] Similarly, Robert Hinde is convinced that "overpopulation, poverty and political dislocation are no doubt important background factors in the genesis of terrorism," and warns that "as disparities of wealth and opportunity on our planet widen, the problem is certain to get worse."[24] No less a figure than James Wolfensohn, former president of the World Bank, essentially equates the war on terrorism with a war on global poverty, arguing that "the war [on terrorism] will not be won until we have come to grips with the problem of poverty and sources of discontent." Even though "this war is viewed in terms of the face of Bin Laden ... [and] the terrorism of Al Qaeda ... these are just symptoms" whose underlying cause "is the discontent seething in Islam and, more generally, in the world of the poor. Winning the war means tackling the roots of protest."[25] Archibugi and Young agree. After outlining the steps necessary to strengthen international legal institutions, they settle on just one recommendation as the core of their long-term cosmopolitan strategy: "narrow global inequalities." Despite noting that "there are many poor places that appear not to nurture people who join international terrorist organizations," they believe "there is no doubt that such indifference amid affluence fosters resentment in many corners of the world and endangers peace and prosperity for many outside the shanty towns."[26] In the final analysis, the failure to address the problem of global poverty will come back to haunt the wealthy and powerful: "No justice, no peace."[27]

Others agree with the need to address the root causes of terrorism but identify different root causes. Even Archibugi and Young admit that there is more to it than poverty: "ultimately … the creation of a more peaceful and just world order implies changes in *political, economic and social* institutions [emphasis added]."[28] In a world where political and economic forces are inevitably intertwined, the economic causes of terrorism are not easily divorced from politics. Some emphasize the economic roots, others the political roots. In this view it is not merely poverty that fuels terrorism, but a more profound sense of exclusion and domination at the domestic and international levels. Domestically, the absence of democracy and lack of human rights contribute to a sense of resentment while foreclosing nonviolent means of dissent. Tony Karon argues that "in the long term, eliminating the root cause of terror will involve, if not complete democracy, at least allowing the citizens of Middle Eastern countries some voice [in] their governance."[29] Internationally, the dominance of a handful of nations possessing tremendous economic, political, and military power only exacerbates the problem because "the willingness of the United States to wield [its power] asymmetrically and with only the thinnest veneer of multilateralism elicits hostile reactions from all over the world."[30] Again, the only long-term strategy to deal with the root causes of terrorism is a wholesale reform of those international and domestic institutions, political and economic, perpetuating the inequities and injustices that sustain terrorist organizations by providing fertile breeding grounds of anger and discontent. Attempts to combat terrorism with the sort of forceful response entailed by a war/military model will only exacerbate that problem. As Betty Williams, a Nobel Peace Prize winner, maintains, "From my long experience with terror and violence in Northern Ireland, I know that a war on terrorism and violence cannot bring anything, but breed and increase terror and violence."[31]

The Intellectual Roots of a Cosmopolitan Strategy

What are the intellectual underpinnings of a cosmopolitan strategy? A statist strategy, about which we will have more to say shortly, is obviously informed by realism. Consequently, a cosmopolitan strategy is rooted in the alternatives to realism. The suggestion that a law enforcement model should form the basis of a response to the attacks of September 11 provides one indication of the strategy's underlying assumptions. Those skeptical of the effectiveness of international law, after all, are unlikely to place it at the center of their response to terrorism. Liberals (and constructivists) have historically been more inclined to see international law and organizations as effective embodiments of shared values and interests. Thus, it makes sense to view this component of a cosmopolitan strategy as being derived from an essentially liberal logic of international politics.

The proposal that we deal with terrorism by addressing its root causes is a little ambiguous in terms of its intellectual foundations, potentially reflecting elements of liberalism, Marxism, and feminism. There are several aspects of this approach that resonate with a liberal view. The basic assumption that we can identify and reform the social, economic, and political institutions and conditions that give rise to terrorism is consistent with the liberal approach to social conflict, which contains an element of optimism and faith in the ability of rational people to solve social problems. The guiding vision is that greater material prosperity, respect for human rights, and democratic government (all liberal values) will provide the antidote to terrorism. If the denial of justice leads to violence, the provision of justice will lead to its elimination. The corollary of Archibugi and Young's "No justice, no peace" must be "If justice, then peace."

The cosmopolitan approach resonates with other perspectives as well. Finding the roots of terrorism in poverty and economic inequality is consistent with a Marxist view of social conflict as rooted in economic inequality and exploitation. Even when conflicts do not appear to be economic on the surface, Marxists assume that there is usually a critical economic foundation. Focusing on the Marxist analysis of civil violence more generally, James Rule explains that we should "expect, for every mobilization on behalf of religious or other nonmaterial ends, to find some antecedent frustration to the material interests of groups among whom the mobilization occurs."[32]

Feminists have also expressed sympathy for a cosmopolitan approach and deep reservations about a statist response stressing military force. Not surprisingly, however, feminists are eager to expand the "poverty as the root cause of terrorism" thesis to include all institutions and patterns of domination, including the oppression of woman. It is, they point out, no coincidence that regimes with some of the worst records when it comes to the rights of women (e.g., the Taliban in Afghanistan) are associated with support for terrorism. Amy Caiazza draws the connection: "there are centuries of evidence that physical, political and economic violence against women is a harbinger of other forms of violence." Thus, "we should pay particularly close attention to those who are effective opponents of violence against women. By doing so, we would be more likely to address the root causes of terrorism and violence at home and around the world."[33] J. Ann Tickner (taking the connection between poverty and terrorism for granted) draws our attention to "the poor treatment of women as one of the major reasons for the region's [the Middle East] lack of development."[34] And because poverty and lack of development are the root causes of terrorism, it follows that the poor treatment of women is one of the major reasons for terrorism. Though feminists disagreed about the use of military force against the Taliban regime in Afghanistan, it is fair to say that feminists generally favor a cosmopolitan strategy over the statist approach.[35]

The Statist Response

A cosmopolitan approach frames terrorist attacks as criminal acts, fearing that portraying them as acts of war will lead to counterproductive military action that leaves the root causes of terrorism undisturbed. There is no question that terrorist acts usually violate domestic and international law, making them criminal acts by definition. "The fundamental problem," according to Steven Pomerantz, "is that international terrorism is not *only* a crime. It is also, for all intents and purposes, an act of war, and the United States needs to treat it as such."[36] Although admitting that "my view may [be] in the minority" among his fellow law professors, Anthony D'Amato's assessment is similar to Pomerantz's: "Sept[ember] 11th occasioned an attack on the United States itself by people who seem to be engaged in an outright war against us…. It may be a new concept of 'war,' but it is one that builds upon, and extends, the classic concept."[37] There is agreement that terrorist attacks were not acts of war in the sense that we normally think of war, but they were also not crimes in the way we normally think of crime, either. Neither label is without its problems. Those who prefer to view terrorist attacks as acts of war do not shy away from the implications of doing so. Pomerantz recognizes that this "means, for starters, a significantly more aggressive diplomatic posture."[38] In words that are sure to make Archibugi and Young cringe, Charles Krauthammer argues that "half-measures are for wars of choice, wars like Vietnam. In wars of choice, losing is an option. You lose and you still survive as a nation." The war on terrorism, however, is different: "Losing is not an option. Losing is fatal. This is no time for restraint and other niceties. This is a time for righteous might."[39]

Though it is important to note the critical differences between cosmopolitan and statist strategies, they should not be presented as caricatured alternatives sharing no common ground. Advocates of a statist approach would certainly not object to seeing terrorists before some kind of tribunal, and those favoring a cosmopolitan strategy might admit that in certain instances states may have to use military force. The difference is one of emphasis and general predispositions: Should attacks such as those of September 11 be viewed *primarily* as crimes against humanity or as acts of war? Should international legal and organizational avenues be pursued as *primary* or merely *supplementary* components of an antiterrorism strategy?

A statist strategy would deemphasize, not completely eliminate, the legal and international organizational elements of an antiterrorism policy. It is on this point that the realist basis of a statist strategy starts to reveal itself: Statist criticisms of a law enforcement model echo familiar realist arguments about the limits of international law and organizations. Archibugi and Young correctly note that states often treat terrorist acts as criminal acts, but all of their examples (e.g., the attack in Oklahoma City) are domestic in nature. Pomerantz is in full agreement that "when it comes to terrorism at home, law enforcement and the criminal justice system—our only available options—have been effective." But the suggestion that a similar approach be applied globally ignores the fundamental differences between international and domestic society. At the national level, law enforcement agencies and legal institutions are sufficiently developed and powerful to deal with such problems. At the international level, there are good reasons to doubt the effectiveness of international organizations, where debate often takes precedence over action. In the wake of the 1972 Palestine Liberation Organization (PLO) massacre of Israeli athletes at the summer Olympic Games in Munich, Germany, the United Nations attempted to develop policies dealing with terrorism. The resulting debate and failure to draft or implement antiterror policies demonstrated why the international community accomplished so little before September 11. After protracted discussion, the United Nations could not even get past the point of defining terrorism.

Particularly problematic were the actions of national liberation movements. Activities the United States considered terrorism were viewed by many in the developing world as legitimate responses to oppression and domination. "The resultant definitional paralysis," Hoffman explains, "throttled UN efforts to make substantive progress on international cooperation against terrorism."[40]

Despite these problems, there was modest progress on a few fronts. During the 1960s and early 1970s, several treaties dealt with hijacking and the safety of commercial aviation. The PLO's taking of Israeli hostages at the 1972 Olympics eventually led to the adoption of the International Convention Against the Taking of Hostages (1979), yet even this small achievement was only ratified by ninety-seven nations. And, as with most international agreements, states are free to withdraw (with one year's notice in this case).[41] International police agencies such as Interpol try to keep track of known terrorists, but much intelligence remains in the hands of national law enforcement and intelligence organizations that may or may not share it with others. The general problem here should be familiar by now: it is difficult to craft an effective international response in a world of sovereign states. After a plot to blow up several airliners was thwarted in August 2006, historian Niall Ferguson asked, "Who seriously expects the United Nations to prevent Al Qaeda (or its latest imitator) from trying to blow up passenger planes in the air? Those who dreamed up the 'Lockerbie-meets-9/11' bomb plot clearly did intend 'mass murder on an unimaginable scale.' All the U.N. has to offer in response is yada, yada, yada on an unimaginable scale."[42]

"It's the Clash, Not the Cash"[43]

Statists tend to view the cosmopolitan desire to combat terrorism by eliminating its "root causes" as a deceptively attractive solution. In reality, they often argue, we have no idea what the root causes are. The common hypothesis that poverty and inequality lead to terrorism is usually asserted as matter of faith without compelling evidence. Even Archibugi and Young concede that the link is not straightforward. Most poor societies are not sources of terrorism, and affluent societies are not immune. If we look at terrorists themselves, we find little support for the poverty-causes-terrorism thesis. Economists Alan Krueger and Jitka Maleckova, in one of the few systematic studies of this issue, examined the backgrounds of 126 members of the militant wing of Hezbollah, a terrorist organization headquartered in Lebanon. They found that "compared to the general population from the same age group and region, the Hezbollah militants were actually slightly less likely to come from impoverished households, and were more likely to have attended secondary school."[44] The lack of connection between poverty and terrorism is striking with regard to the attacks of September 11. "Poverty did not breed the terrorists of September 11," Helle Dale tells us, "the politics of radical Islam did." This is evidenced by the fact that "the 19 hijackers were not poor or uneducated, they were motivated by religious fanaticism and apparently some bizarre expectations of their rewards in heaven." And the people who planned the attack did not lack for privilege: "Is Osama Bin Laden a poor man? Certainly not. He's the son of a Saudi family wealthier than most Americans will ever dream of becoming."[45] If those who hijacked the planes and crashed them into their targets are at all representative, Sean Wilentz notes wryly, we would be more justified concluding that "money, education and privilege" are the root causes of terrorism.[46] There may, of course, still be lots of good reasons to work for the reduction of global poverty, but its causal role in creating and sustaining terrorism is, at best, much more complicated than often suggested.

But even if poverty and inequality were the root causes of terrorism, we would face a further problem. Like virtually every other potential root cause, global poverty is not something likely to be eradicated in the next ten or twenty years. The threat of terrorism is in the present, whereas the elimination of global poverty is, being optimistic, sometime in the distant future. As Robert Trager and Dessislava Zagorcheva note, "counterterrorist strategies that attempt to address the root causes ... are strategies for the long run. In the meantime, religious terrorism is on the rise, and the rate of suicide terrorist attacks has increased significantly."[47] What should we do about terrorism between now and the day when justice and equality are finally realized? Too often, statists fear, the demand that we attack the root causes of terrorism is a self-righteous excuse or cover allowing people to avoid meaningful actions and hard choices in the here and now.

From the perspective of most statists, the focus on poverty and inequality as the root cause of terrorism is either wrong, too simplistic, or not terribly useful for shaping meaningful policy responses. This is not to say that statists ignore the issue of root causes. It is hard for anyone to witness nineteen young men sacrificing their own lives to crash airplanes into buildings without wondering about their motivations. But because terrorism is such a varied phenomenon, different manifestations of it will likely have different root causes. In the current context statists prefer to focus on the root causes of fundamentalist Islamic terrorism, because this is the major threat of the moment. What motivates the Basque separatists in Spain might be an interesting intellectual question, but it is not the most pressing. While statists are by no means unanimous in their assessment, they are more inclined to see this terrorism as a manifestation of a fundamental conflict of values and cultures. Indeed, the attacks of September 11 appeared to confirm the warnings made by several prominent scholars in the early 1990s that the post–Cold War era would be one increasingly characterized by a "clash of civilizations." The first to use the phrase and issue a warning about an impending "clash of civilizations" was the widely respected Princeton historian Bernard Lewis, an authority on Middle Eastern and Islamic history. In his influential essay, "The Roots of Muslim Rage," published more than a decade before September 11, 2001, Lewis expressed his growing concern about several trends foreshadowing greater conflict between the West and the Muslim world. Part of the problem was the tendency of many in the West to assume that all other cultures shared Western notions about the appropriate relationship between religion and politics and the separation of church and state. This was simply not the case: "There are other religious traditions in which [relations between] religion and politics are differently perceived."[48] In the wake of the Cold War, some observers predicted a more peaceful world based on the spread of Western values of liberal democracy and capitalism. Lewis was not so optimistic.

But it is not the mere existence of certain religious and cultural differences that worried Lewis. After all, there was nothing new about most of these differences.

What really troubled him was the emergence in parts of the Muslim world of an extreme form of fundamentalist Islam, expressed not merely as a particular interpretation of the faith's tenets but also a deep hostility, indeed "hatred," of the West. On one level, this hostility could be traced to specific policies of the United States and other Western nations—support for Israel, propping up oppressive dictatorships throughout the Middle East that enriched themselves and foreign oil interests at the expense of their people, and the stationing of Western forces on the holy lands of Saudi Arabia during and after the 1991 Gulf War. Lewis, however, saw something deeper at work: "At times this hatred goes beyond hostility to specific interests or actions or policies or even countries and becomes a rejection of Western civilization as such, not only what it does but what it is, and the principles and values it practices and professes. These are indeed seen as innately evil, and those who promote or accept them as the 'enemies of God.'" Pointing to the absence of such sentiments in the history of Islam, Lewis stresses that there is nothing inherent in Islam that leads to such extremism. "But Islam, like other religions," Lewis notes, has "known periods when it inspired in some of its followers a mood of hatred and violence. It is our misfortune that part, though by no means all or even most, of the Muslim world is now going through such a period, and that much, though again not all, of that hatred is directed against us."[49]

clash of civilizations The thesis, popularized by Samuel Huntington, that civilizational conflicts based on competing social and political values are replacing traditional national conflicts as the defining feature of contemporary international politics.

Warnings of a coming **clash of civilizations**, however, did not gain widespread public attention until Samuel Huntington, a Harvard political scientist, advanced a similar argument in *Foreign Affairs* in 1993. Like Lewis, Huntington rejected post–Cold War optimism about a more harmonious world based on Western values of liberal democracy and free markets. Like Lewis, Huntington saw an emerging conflict between the West and the Islamic world rooted in competing religious, political, and cultural values. But Huntington greatly expanded the scope of Lewis's analysis to incorporate more than two world civilizations. Though the world remains divided into sovereign states, the fault lines of conflict will be between civilizations that embrace "different views on the relations between God and man … as well as different views of the relative importance of rights and responsibilities, liberty and authority, equality and hierarchy." Huntington identified seven major civilizations—"Western, Confucian, Japanese, Islamic, Hindu, Slavic-Orthodox, Latin American and possible African."[50]

Huntington's thesis has proved to be very controversial. Some question his characterizations of the different civilizations, while others think he exaggerates the extent to which civilizations can be treated as coherent, monolithic entities. One need look no further than the conflicts that emerged in Iraq after the 2003 U.S. invasion between Shiite and Sunni Muslims to see that conflicts within civilizations can be just as intense as conflicts among them. Nonetheless, many could not help but think that Huntington was on to something, particularly in the aftermath of September 11. "Read in the wake of September 11," Stanley Kurtz muses, "it is more clear than ever that Huntington's book is filled with … useful generalizations…. In large measure the world is already living out the truth of Huntington's thesis."[51] In a similar vein, Michael Howard takes direct issue with the poverty thesis and leans toward cultural conflict explanations for the Islamic fundamentalist terrorism: "This is not a problem of poverty as against wealth,

Representatives of Afghanistan's Taliban regime reject United States' demands to hand over Osama bin Laden and others connected to the September 11 attacks. The Taliban would become the first victim of the statist strategy of "regime change" in the war on terrorism.
Source: Saeed Khan/AFP/Getty Images

and I am afraid that it is symptomatic of our Western materialism to suppose that it is. It is a far more profound and intractable confrontation between a theistic, land-based and tradition culture, in places little different from the Europe of the Middle Ages, and the secular values of the Enlightenment."[52] If a terrorist organization is engaged in an effort to undermine and perhaps destroy secular, liberal civilization, then no concession or change of policy will reduce the threat.

Description of the threat as "intractable" in this context is revealing. Statists are not only skeptical that we can identify the root causes of terrorism, they are also less sanguine about our ability to eliminate those root causes even if we find them. There tends to be a lot more talk of intractable conflict in a statist perspective, and given its realist foundations, this should come as no surprise. When someone describes conflicts as "intractable," there is a good chance we are dealing with a realist. This perspective contrasts with the liberal inclination to view social conflict as a consequence of social, economic, and political conditions that can be altered in a manner that will eliminate the conflict. The notion that we should (or even can) eradicate inequality and injustice in order to end the threat of terrorism strikes statists/realists as a utopian evasion. Thus, on one level this debate can been seen as yet another contemporary manifestation of the enduring clash between liberal optimism and realist (conservative) pessimism on questions of social conflict.

Even though the Bush administration's policies after the September 11 attacks followed the logic of a statist response in many respects, it quickly tried to distance itself from the clash of civilizations logic. Former Secretary of State Colin Powell portrayed the attacks as an assault on "civilization" (that is, civilization in general, not any particular civilization), but he insisted there was "no connection or relationship to any faith."[53] Speaking to the UN Security Council two months after the attacks, Powell was even more explicit in rejecting a Huntingtonesque approach: "This was not about a clash of civilizations or religions; it was an attack on civilization and religion themselves."[54] Publicly, at least, the administration interpreted the attacks as the work of an evil person and organization perverting the values and ideas of Islam. Skeptics were quick to wonder whether these denials were designed primarily to avoid alienating moderate Arab governments whose cooperation might be needed in the short run.[55]

States Still Matter

One may lament the lack of viable alternatives to states acting to defend themselves against threats to their security and citizens, but for statists this is the unavoidable reality of the world in which we live. Responses to terrorism need to be crafted within the limitations of the existing state system. Fortunately, there is much that states can do. Certainly nonstate adversaries pose challenges that more traditional state-to-state conflicts do not, but we should not leap to the conclusion that states are powerless to act against terrorist organizations merely because they are not states. Jack Spencer reminds us that terrorist "groups could never pull off these sophisticated operations if there were no place where they could support their networks." Terrorist groups may not be states, but terrorists, terrorist training facilities, and terrorist financial resources are all located within the borders of states. Consequently, the war on terrorism is "essentially … [a] war with states that support terrorism."[56] Several years before the September 11 attacks, Steve Pomerantz suggested the same course of action: "If a state is the victim of private actors such as terrorists, it [can] try to eliminate these groups by depriving them of sanctuaries and punishing states that harbor them. The national interest of the attacked state will therefore require either armed interventions against governments supporting terrorism or a course of prudence and discreet pressure on other governments."[57]

As the Bush administration tried to give meaning to the "war on terrorism," Vice President Dick Cheney provided the rationale for a statist response: "To the extent that we define our task broadly … including those who support terrorism, then we get at states. And it's easier to find them than it is to find bin Laden."[58] This same sentiment informed President Bush's warning that the United States would "make no distinction between the terrorists who committed these acts and those who harbor them." From the statist perspective, the war on terrorism is, even if indirectly, still a conflict among states. And one deals with this threat according to the same logic that guides responses to traditional threats—by "exacting a price for terrorism so as to make it less likely that terrorist will want to strike again."[59] These costs need to be imposed not only on the terrorists themselves but also on states that provide active support or passively permit them to operate. In President

Bush's words, "we have to force countries to choose."[60] The option of last resort would be "regime change": "If you replace the states that do support terrorism with those that don't, you deny terrorists the kind of support that allows them to mount big operations against us."[61]

This is the crux of the statist response: combating terrorist organizations by using the traditional tools of statecraft against those states within whose borders they operate. Will this allow us to eliminate terrorism? Certainly not. The eradication of terrorism is an unrealistic pipe dream. The focus has to be on weakening or eliminating those particular terrorist organizations that pose the greatest and most immediate threat. Although "we can never be immune from terrorist violence," Pomerantz concedes, "we can … raise the price for those who attack us and the nations that sponsor and support them. In doing so, we can expect to make the cost high enough to significantly reduce the number of international terrorist incidents directed against the United States."[62] This summarizes the statist strategy nicely, and it is easy to see how its underlying logic is quintessentially realist. First, there is the admission that we will never eliminate all terrorism and the hope that we can is a fantasy, reflecting a realist impatience with sweeping declarations of unattainable aspirations. Second, we need to deal with terrorist organizations as threats to the national interest that must be either defeated or deterred. Third, states continue to be the critical players on the global level, even when it comes to controlling the actions of nonstate actors such as terrorist organizations.

Conclusion

Though it helps clarify critical issues of analysis and policy to present statist and cosmopolitan approaches as alternatives, it may also be important to think about how their elements might be combined into a coherent strategy. Perhaps the choice between strategies is a false choice. Might we be better off with a synthesis integrating the best elements of both? One could make a convincing argument that the Bush administration did just that in the aftermath of September 11. We have already emphasized how regime change and a willingness to use force unilaterally reflect an essentially statist response to terrorism. John Lewis Gaddis, however, sees a strong cosmopolitan streak in the strategy because it identifies a root cause of terrorism and seeks to eliminate it. But unlike most cosmopolitan analyses, it does not trace terrorism to poverty and inequality. Instead, the Bush vision sees the absence of democracy and political freedom as the root cause of the disenchantment and frustration that breed terrorism. Gaddis claims that "the Bush strategy deals with the longer-term issue of removing the causes of terrorism and tyranny altogether." Accepting the "emerging consensus within the scholarly community … [that] it wasn't poverty that caused a group of middle-class and reasonably well-educated Middle Easterners to fly three airplanes into buildings," the Bush administration offers a "solution to this problem that is breathtakingly simple: it is to spread democracy everywhere." Though Gaddis does not use the labels *statist* and *cosmopolitan* in his analysis of Bush's strategy, he clearly thinks it combined elements often considered at odds: "it sees no contradiction between the wielding of power and the commitment to principles.... It is optimistic about human nature, and therefore Wilsonian in its worldview."[63] Cronin makes the same point, arguing that "a 'roots' approach is precisely at the heart of current U.S. policy: the promotion of democracy may be seen as an idealistic effort to provide an alternative to populations of Muslim countries, frustrated by corrupt governance, discrimination, unemployment, and stagnation."[64] Will this melding of power and ideas, statism and cosmopolitanism, prove to be an effective response to the challenges of terrorism in a post-September 11 world? More than a decade later, the jury is still out on this most important question.

But whatever the final verdict, neither terrorism nor the debate over appropriate responses is going away anytime soon. In fact, there are important elements of the debate we have not even touched on, such as whether the war on terrorism requires restrictions on domestic civil liberties. If anything, we can probably expect terrorism to worsen before it gets better because "the number of intensely aggrieved groups will almost certainly grow in the coming decades of rapid technological, and hence social, change."[65] And it is this very technological change and the easy dissemination of knowledge that give individuals and groups the ability to cause harm and destruction on a scale previously unimaginable. Technological and social change provides both motives and means.

Policy debates will remain intense for at least two important reasons. First, they reflect competing visions of international society and, at an even more fundamental level, differences about the nature and dynamics of social conflict. Second, and this point cannot be stressed too heavily, "the menu for policy options in the war on terrorism is loaded with short-term/long-term tradeoffs."[66] Examples of these trade-offs abound. Democracy in the Middle East may be an essential part of a long-term strategy to reduce terrorism, but in the short run we might have to deal with some nondemocratic regimes to diffuse the most immediate threats. But if the United States is seen as supporting nondemocratic regimes, this could increase hostility and the risk of future terrorist attacks in the long run. Similarly, the use of military force may be needed to destroy or diminish the capabilities of a terrorist group or its state sponsor; but if this reinforces certain negative images of the United States, long-term threats may increase. Most people are probably attracted to elements of both the cosmopolitan and statist strategies because they each embody desirable short and long-term objectives that may run counter to each other. Policy debates are always the hardest to resolve when they require trade-offs among equally valued and beneficial objectives. But no useful purpose is served by failing to recognize the need to make trade-offs. All good things do not always come together.

CHAPTER SUMMARY

- Although definitions of terrorism are often controversial and politically charged, there is a consensus that terrorism has several essential components: (1) the use or threat of violence to create a climate of fear, (2) indiscriminate targeting of civilians (because the audience is the real "target"), and (3) a larger social or political objective. There is less agreement about whether terrorism should be defined to exclude states and include only nonstate actors as possible perpetrators.

- Even though terrorist acts and groups share some things in common, it is probably more useful to classify terrorist groups according to their motivations, goals, and objectives rather than to treat terrorism as a single, undifferentiated phenomenon. Strategies that might be effective in dealing with some organizations may prove useless for others with different objectives and *modi operandi*.

- In the aftermath of the September 11 attacks, debate naturally focused on possible responses to terrorism. Archibugi and Young argue that two basic alternatives shaped the public debate.

- The cosmopolitan response encompasses both short and long-term elements. In the short term, the specific attacks need to be treated as criminal acts necessitating an international legal response to capture and prosecute those responsible while using the full range of tools available to the international community to destroy the organization's ability to operate.

- The longer-term goal of a cosmopolitan strategy lies in addressing the underlying root causes of terrorism, which are normally identified as the poverty, inequality, and discontent that breed resentment and drive people to desperate acts.

- The suggestion that terrorism be approached from an international legal perspective and the desire to deal with the root causes of terrorism makes a cosmopolitan approach attractive to liberals as well as to many feminists and Marxists.

- The statist response views terrorist attacks as acts of war and threats to national security. Although there may be useful legal and multilateral elements of an effective response, the emphasis must be on destroying the terrorist organization's ability to act by any means available. The focus of these efforts should be not only the terrorist organizations themselves but also the states that support or permit them to operate.

- Although the logic of tackling the root causes of terrorism is attractive, statists are skeptical of the commonly accepted idea that poverty leads to terrorism. At a minimum, the connection between poverty and terrorism is very complicated. Statists are more inclined to see terrorism, especially of the type perpetrated by Al-Qaeda, as motivated by a fundamental conflict of values and visions.

- This view of the underlying conflict and the inclination to view terrorism as a national security issue to be addressed within the framework of state relations resonates more with the realist perspective.

- Even though they are portrayed as alternative approaches, it might be useful to think about whether and how elements of these apparently opposing strategies might be melded into a single coherent strategy. The critical obstacle that must be overcome to achieve this fusion is that many of the short-term responses called for by a statist approach appear to work against many of the long-term goals of the cosmopolitan approach.

CRITICAL QUESTIONS

1. What elements of the definition of terrorism are widely accepted and disputed?

2. Do you think terrorism can ever be justified? Could terrorist acts by opposition groups in Germany designed to undermine the Nazi regime between 1933 and 1945 be justified? Why or why not?

3. To what extent has the Bush administration been successful in creating an antiterrorism strategy combining elements of statism and cosmopolitanism?

4. Why do many see a general "war in terrorism," as problematic?

5. Though a crude "poverty leads to terrorism" hypothesis seems not to fit the evidence, many continue to feel that some connection must exist. How can we think about the relationship between poverty and terrorism in a more complicated and sophisticated fashion?

KEY TERMS

clash of civilizations, 310
cosmopolitan, 302

statist, 302
terrorism, 298

transnational actor, 301

FURTHER READINGS

The literature on terrorism has grown considerably since the events of September 11, 2001, but it is still useful to consult some of the major works that appeared before these events. Alex Schmid's *Political Terrorism: A Reference Guide* (New Brunswick, NJ: Transaction Books, 1984) is still a standard reference. Walter Laqueur's *Terrorism* (Boston: Little, Brown, 1977) remains insightful. Bruce Hoffman's *Inside Terrorism* (New York: Columbia University Press, 1998) is particularly good on the history and evolution of terrorism. For exhaustive coverage of terrorism in the Middle East, see Richard Chasdi's twin volumes, *Serenade of Suffering: A Portrait of Middle East Terrorism, 1968–1993* (New York: Lexington Books, 1999) and *Tapestry of Terror: A Portrait of Middle East Terrorism, 1994–1999* (New York: Lexington Books, 2002). On the rise and dynamics of suicide terrorism, see Robert A. Pape, *Dying to Win: The Strategic Logic of Suicide Terrorism* (New York: Random House, 2006). The classic exploration of the dilemmas terrorism poses for democratic states is Paul Wilkinson, *Terrorism and the Liberal State* (New York: Macmillan, 1977).

It will come as no surprise that many works on terrorism have appeared since September 11, 2001. Bob Woodward's *Bush at War* (New York: Simon & Schuster, 2002) provides a good first look at the United States' response. A controversial reaction from the political left (which has been criticized by many normally considered on the left) is Noam Chomsky, *9/11* (Boston: Seven Stories Press, 2001). Other interesting attempts to come to terms with the broader dilemmas in responding to terrorism include Jean Bethke Elshtain, *Just War Against Terror: The Burden of American Power in a Violent World* (New York: Basic Books, 2003), Paul Berman, *Terrorism and Liberalism* (New York: W. W. Norton, 2003), and Thomas Friedman, *Longitudes and Attitudes: Exploring the World After September 11* (New York: Farrar, Straus and Giroux, 2002). And a recent collection of essays dealing with a range of largely moral and ethical issues is James P. Sterba, ed., *Terrorism and International Justice* (Oxford: Oxford University Press, 2003). A collection of feminist perspectives is Susan Hawthorne and Bronwyn Winter, eds., *September 11, 2001: Feminist Perspectives* (Melbourne, Australia: Spinfex, 2002).

TERRORISM ON THE WEB

www.cfr.org/issue/terrorism/ri135
Section of the Council on Foreign Relations's Web site dealing with international terrorism.

www.fas.org/irp/threat/terror.htm
Section of the American Federation of Scientists' Web site with links to a wealth of resources in terrorism.

www.start.umd.edu/
Web site of the National Consortium for the Study of Terrorism and Responses to Terrorism maintained by the University of Maryland.

www.state.gov/s/ct/
The counterterrorism section of the U.S. State Department Web site.

www.jurist.law.pitt.edu/terrorism.htm
Updates and essays on legal aspects of responses to terrorism after September 11, 2001.

www.ssrc.org/sept11/essays
The Social Science Research Council's Web site containing essays and research analyzing the events of September 11, 2001, and terrorism more broadly.

NOTES

[1]Martha Crenshaw, "Why America? The Globalization of Civil War," *Current History* 100 (December 2001): 425.

[2]Paul Pillar, *Terrorism and U.S. Foreign Policy* (Washington, DC: The Brookings Institution Press, 2001), p. 5.

[3]Conor Gearty, *The Future of Terrorism* (London: Phoenix Books, 1997), p. 34.

[4]Alex Schmid, *Terrorism: A Research Guide* (New Brunswick, NJ: Transaction Books, 1984).

[5]Walter Laqueur, *Terrorism* (Boston: Little, Brown, 1977), p. 79.

[6]Bruce Hoffman, *Inside Terrorism* (New York: Columbia University Press, 1998), pp. 42–43.

[7]Cindy Combs, *Terrorism in the Twenty-first Century* (Upper Saddle River, NJ: Prentice Hall, 2003), p. 10.

[8]Hoffman, *Inside Terrorism*, p. 43.

[9]Louis Rene Beres, "The Meaning of Terrorism—Jurisprudential and Definitional Clarifications," *Vanderbilt Journal of Transnational Law* 28 (March 1995): 90–243.

[10]Council on Foreign Relations, "Terrorism: Q & A," at www.terrorismanswers.com.

[11]Hoffman, *Inside Terrorism*, pp. 90–91.

[12]On Aum Shinrikyo, see Jessica Stern, "Terrorist Motivations and Unconventional Weapons," in *Planning the Unthinkable: How New Powers Will Use Nuclear, Chemical and Biological Weapons*, ed. Peter Lavoy, Scott Sagan, and John Wirtz (Ithaca, NY: Cornell University Press, 2000), pp. 205–209.

[13]Laqueur, *Terrorism*, p. 134.

[14]"A Conversation with John Mearsheimer," University of California at Berkeley, April 8, 2002. Transcript at http://globetrotter.berkeley.edu/people2/Mearsheimer/mearsheimer-con5.html.

[15]Daniele Archibugi and Iris Young, "Toward a Global Rule of Law," *Dissent* 49 (Spring 2002): 27.

[16]Nicholas Lehman, "The War on What?" *New Yorker* (September 9, 2002): 14.

[17]Steven Metz, *Iraq & The Evolution of American Strategy* (Washington DC: Potomac Books, 2008), pp.91 and 92.

[18]Ibid., p. 90.

[19]Archibugi and Young, "Toward a Global Rule of Law," p. 28.

[20]Michael Ratner and Jules Lobel, "An Alternative to the Use of U.S. Military Force," *Jurist: The Legal Resources Network*. Online forum accessed at http://jurist.law.pitt.edu/forum/forumnew32.htm.

[21]Quoted in Foreign Policy in Focus press release, "World Trade Center/Pentagon Attack: Expert Statements," (September 18, 2001). Accessed at http://www.fpif.org/media/releases/2001.

[22]Andrew Johnston, "Disparities of Wealth Are Seen as Fuel for Terrorism," *International Herald Tribune* (December 20, 2001), p. 8.

[23]Jared Diamond, "Why We Must Feed the Hands That Could Bite Us," *Washington Post* (January 13, 2002), p. B01.

[24]Robert A. Hinde, "Root Causes of Terrorism," *Pugwash Online*. Accessed at www.pugwash.org/september11/hinde.htm.

[25]"The War Against Terrorism Will Be Won by Eliminating Poverty," interview with James Wolfensohn (December 7, 2001). Accessed at http://www.worldback.org/html/extdr/extrme/jdwint120701b.htm.

[26]Archibugi and Young, "Toward a Global Rule of Law," p. 31.

[27]Ibid., p. 32.

[28]Ibid., p. 28.

[29]Tony Karon, "Can Democracy Be a Weapon Against Terrorism?" *Time* (September 28, 2001): 18.

[30]Archibugi and Young, "Toward a Global Rule of Law," p. 27.

[31]"Bush and Sharon 'Creating Terrorism,'" *Gulf News* (November 2, 2003). Accessed at http://www.gulf-news.com/Articles/news.asp?ArticleID_77025.

[32]James B. Rule, *Theories of Civil Violence* (Berkeley: University of California Press, 1988), p. 71.

[33]Amy Caiazza, "Why Gender Matters in Understanding September 11: Women, Militarism and Violence," IWPR (Institute for Women's Policy Research) publication no. 1908 (November 2001), p. 1.

[34]J. Ann Tickner, "Feminist Perspectives on 9/11," *International Studies Perspective* 3 (2002): 346.

[35]Another example is Mary Riddell, "Feminised Face of War," *Guardian* (September 23, 2001), p. 24.

[36]Steven L. Pomerantz, "The Best Defense," *The New Republic* (August 31, 1998): 14.

[37]Anthony D'Amato, comment attached to Ratner and Lobel, "Alternative to the Use of U.S. Military Force," p. 2.

[38]Pomerantz, "Best Defense," p. 15.

[39]Charles Krauthammer, "Not Enough Might," *Washington Post* (October 30, 2001), p. A21.

[40]Hoffman, *Inside Terrorism*, p. 32.

[41]Accessed at www.nti.org/e_research/official_docs/inventory/pdfs/hostage.pdf.

[42]Niall Ferguson, "Testing the Limits of the U.N." *Los Angeles Times*, August 14, 2006. Accessed at www.latimes.com/news/opinion/la-oe-ferguson14aug14, 0, 7360876.column? coll_la-opinion-rightrail.

[43]This phrase is found in Daniel Pipes, "God and Mammon: Does Poverty Cause Militant Islam?" *The National Interest* no. 66 (Winter 2001/02): 21.

[44]Alan B. Krueger and Jitka Maleckova, "Economics and the Education of Suicide Bombers: Does Poverty Cause Terrorism?" *New Republic* (June 24, 2002), p. 21.

[45]Helle Dale, "Poverty and Terrorism," *Washington Times* (March 20, 2002), p. 24.

[46]Cited in Pipes, "God and Mammon," p. 17.

[47]Robert F. Trager and Dessislava P. Zagorcheva, "Deterring Terrorism," *International Security* 30, no. 3 (Winter 2005/2006): 88.

[48]Bernard Lewis, "The Roots of Muslim Rage," *Atlantic* 266, no. 3 (September 1990), p. 47.

[49]Ibid., p. 47

[50]Samuel Huntington, "The Clash of Civilizations?" *Foreign Affairs* 72, no. 3 (Summer 1993): 32.

[51]Stanley Kurtz, "The Future of 'History,'" *Policy Review* 113 (June 2002). Accessed at www.policyreview.org/JUN02/kurtz.html.

[52]Cited in Pipes, "God and Mammon," p. 21.

[53]Colin Powell, statement before the Senate Foreign Relations Committee (October 25, 2001). Accessed at www.state.gov/secretary/rm/2001/5751.htm.

[54]Colin Powell, statement before the United Nations Security Council, November 12, 2001. Accessed at www.state.gov/secretary/rm/2001/6049pf.htm.

[55]See Marc Erikson, "It IS a Clash of Civilizations," *Asia Times* (November 28, 2001). Accessed at www.atimes.com/c-asia/CK28Ag01.html.

[56]Cited in David Masci and Kenneth Jost, "War on Terrorism," *Global Issues* (Washington, DC: CQ Press, 2003), p. 80.

[57]Pomerantz, "Best Defense," p. 14.

⁵⁸Bob Woodward, *Bush at War* (New York: Simon & Schuster, 2002), p. 43.

⁵⁹Pomerantz, "Best Defense," p. 14.

⁶⁰Woodward, *Bush at War*, p. 33.

⁶¹The quote is from Dan Goure and is cited in Masci and Jost, "War on Terrorism," pp. 80–81.

⁶²Pomerantz, "Best Defense," p. 14.

⁶³John Lewis Gaddis. *Surprise, Security and the American Experience* (Cambridge, MA: Harvard University Press, 2004), pp. 89–91.

⁶⁴Cronin, p. 42.

⁶⁵Robert Wright, "A Real War on Terrorism," part of nine part series on www.slate.com (September 6, 2002), p. 2.

⁶⁶Ibid., p. 3.

Did September 11 Reflect a Clash of Civilizations?

The thesis of a clash of civilizations advanced by Samuel Huntington and Bernard Lewis in the early 1990s took on renewed significance in the wake of the attacks of September 11. For some, the attacks were a wake-up call, a strikingly violent confirmation of the clash and the magnitude of the threat it poses. Others feared that portraying a conflict with a terrorist group as a manifestation of some larger clash of civilizations was an overly broad and simplistic characterization of a complex problem that ran the risk of becoming a self-fulfilling prophecy. In the essay below, Louis René Beres, writing just days after the attacks, focuses on the attacks themselves and the attackers. For him the magnitude and barbarity of the attacks only makes sense if they are seen in the framework of a much deeper civilizational clash. Amitav Acharya, writing a few months after the attacks, focuses on the reaction in the Muslim world to the attacks and the initial U.S. responses. Though he makes the interesting concession that "civilizational affinities" may have played a "secondary role," he does not see the Muslim reaction as consistent with any fundamental clash of civilizations. To what extent is the disagreement between Beres and Acharya a result of the evidence they focus on? How might one differentiate between civilizational affinities and a clash of civilizations? How might the different positions of Beres and Acharya on the issue of a clash of civilizations lead to different responses to the sort of terrorism witnessed on September 11?

Terrorism and the Global Clash of Civilizations (2001)

PERSPECTIVE 1

Louis René Beres[1]

Terrorism, to be sure, is America's overriding problem for the immediate future. But terrorism is not really our underlying problem. It is rather the palpably barbarous tactic of a methodically planned and determinedly apocalyptic war. Directed initially against Israel and the United States, this fevered attack will soon spread—perhaps uncontrollably—to large cities in Europe and possibly even to various parts of Asia.

This war is a sustained and foreseeable catastrophic Arab/Islamic assault against the West, a civilizational struggle in which a resurgent medievalism now seeks to bring fear, paralysis and death to "unbelievers." It goes without saying that an overwhelming number of Muslims throughout the world are uninvolved in this assault, or even tacitly opposed to it (few Muslims will oppose it openly),

[1] Source: Louis René Beres, "Terrorism and the Global Clash of Civilizations," Israel Insider, October 1, 2001. Online at http://web.israelinsider.com/Views/927.htm. Reprinted by permission of the author.

but many millions of others in many countries are already prepared to enter Paradise by becoming "martyrs." ... [T]he preferred terrorism tactic in this war is likely to involve chemical, biological or nuclear weapons.

Our truest war is not against Osama Bin Laden or even the particular Arab/Islamic states that nurture and encourage his program for mass murder. Even if Bin Laden and every other identifiably major terrorist were apprehended and prosecuted in authoritative courts of justice, millions of others in the Arab/Islamic world would not cease their impassioned destruction of "infidels." These millions, like the monsters who destroyed the World Trade Center and attacked the Pentagon, would not intend to do evil. On the contrary, they would mete out death to innocents for the sake of a presumed divine expectation, prodding the killing of Israelis, Americans and Europeans with utter conviction and complete purity of heart.

Sanctified killers, these millions would generate an incessant search for more "Godless" victims. Though mired in blood, their search would be tranquil and self-assured, born of the knowledge that its perpetrators were neither evil nor infamous, but heroic and "sacrificial." For those millions engaged in an Arab/Islamic war against the West, violence and the sacred are always inseparable. To understand the rationale and operation of current terrorism against the United States, including the September 11th attacks, it is first necessary to understand these conceptions of the sacred. Then, and only then, will it become clear that Arab/Islamic terror against the United States is, at its heart, a manifestation of religious worship known as "sacrifice."

This is the truest meaning of Arab/Islamic terrorism against our country. It is a form of sacred violence oriented toward the sacrifice of both enemies and martyrs. It is through the purposeful killing of Americans, any Americans, that the Holy Warrior embarked upon Jihad can buy himself free from the penalty of dying. It is only through such cowardly killing, and not through diplomacy, that "Allah's" will may be done.

When America has understood that terrorism is only a tactic, and that it is a tactic related to Islamic sacrifice, it will be able to confront a particularly lethal enemy, one that already has within its capabilities the capacity to kill hundreds of thousands or even millions of American men, women and children. Until now, this is an understanding that has lent itself to insubstantial theorizing. Now, immediately, Arab/Islamic terrorism should be recognized, at least in part, as a bloody and sacred act of mediation between sacrificers and their deity.

America is now routinely characterized as a "cancer" in the Arab/Islamic world. A recent article from an Egyptian newspaper speaks of "the cancer, the malignant wound, in the body of Arabism, for which there is no cure but eradication." Such references are far more than a vile metaphor. They are profoundly theological descriptions of a despised enemy that must be excised, that is, "liquidated." Where this "liquidation" would be accomplished by self-sacrifice, possibly even terrorism involving weapons of mass destruction, it would be life affirming for the killers. Naturally, some Arab/Islamic governments and movements would deny such end-of-the-world thinking, but it operates nonetheless.

What is to be done? The truth of the terrorist threat to the United States is vastly more grotesque than what is commonly understood. We face suicidal mass killings with unconventional weapons in the future not because there exists a small number of pathological murderers, but because we are embroiled—however unwittingly—in an authentic clash of civilizations. While we all wish it weren't so, wishing will get us nowhere. Our only hope is to acknowledge the true source of our now existential danger, and proceed to fight the real war from there.

Clash of Civilizations? No, of National Interests and Principles (2002)   PERSPECTIVE 2

Amitav Acharya[2]

The swift collapse of the Taliban regime in Afghanistan under the weight of American military power marks the defeat of one of the more prominent ideas to emerge from the ashes of the Cold War. Samuel Huntington's thesis about a "clash of civilizations."

The Sept. 11 attacks on the United States were the first real test of the Huntington thesis. Amid the initial shock waves of the attacks, many saw its vindication. This view gained strength when George W. Bush used the word "crusade," with its connotations of a Christian holy war against Muslims. The attacks themselves were presented by the perpetrators as Islamic holy war against Christians and Jews.

Yet the response of governments and peoples around the world has proved that this was no clash of civilizations. What emerged was an old-fashioned struggle over the interests and principles that have traditionally governed international relations. Civilizational affinities played only a secondary role.

The world's Muslim nations condemned the terrorist attacks. Many recognized the U.S. right to retaliate against the Taliban for sheltering Qaida. Some offered material and logistical assistance.

From Saudi Arabia to Pakistan, from Iran to Indonesia, Islamic nations denounced bin Laden. In Pakistan, President Pervez Musharraf and his associates denounced the terrorists for giving Islam a bad name. Reversing its long sponsorship of the Taliban and braving the wrath of Islamic extremists at home, Pakistan offered vital logistical support to U.S. forces.

Iran, which for decades had spearheaded Islamic revolutionaries' campaign against the United States, also made no secret of its disdain for the Taliban's Islamic credentials. Iran saw an opportunity to rid itself of an unfriendly regime in its neighborhood.

Each of these nations put national interest and modern principles of international conduct above primordial sentiment and transnational religious or cultural identity.

Pakistan, for example, got badly needed American aid and de facto recognition of its military regime. Indonesia, whose support as the world's most populous Islamic nation was crucial to the legitimacy of the U.S.-led anti-terrorist campaign, received American economic and political backing for its fledgling democracy.

[2] Source: Amitav Acharya, "Clash of Civilizations? No, of National Interests and Principles," International Herald Tribune, January 10, 2002. Reprinted by permission of the author.

In Indonesia and Malaysia, the war against terrorism presented an opportunity for governments to rein in domestic Islamic extremists who had challenged their authority and created public disorder.

Most nations accepted the U.S. counterstrike as an exercise in a nation's right of self-defense. None granted the same right to the Taliban.

Asked to choose between America and the terrorists, nations of the world closed ranks to an unprecedented degree and sided against the terrorists. They did so despite reservations about America's Middle East policy, concerns about civilian casualties in the Afghanistan war and misgivings about U.S. military and economic dominance of the world.

The "clash of civilizations" thesis fares no better in the domestic arena than on the international stage. Appalled by the terrorists' methods and the loss of so many innocent lives, most religious leaders in Islamic societies condemned the attacks as un-Islamic.

Dire predictions were made that countries which acquiesced in or backed the U.S. retaliation would be torn apart by ethnic and religious strife, but such predictions did not come true.

In Pakistan, where the risk was most serious, General Musharraf was able to act more and more boldly against extremists as Islamic protests fizzled out. Hard-core Islamic elements in Indonesia failed in their attempt to rally widespread public support against the American action in Afghanistan. In Malaysia, Prime Minister Mahathir bin Mohamad set aside his rhetoric against American hegemony and made it difficult for Malaysian jihadists to travel to Afghanistan to fight alongside the Taliban.

The international response to the Sept. 11 terrorist attacks shows that religion and civilization do not replace pragmatism, interest and principle as the guiding motives of international relations.

In rejecting the call to jihad issued by the Taliban, Osama bin Laden and their supporters, some Islamic nations acted out of interest and others out of principle. Most were motivated by a combination of both.

13 | The Global Commons

Key Controversy: Is the Global Commons in Danger?

The complex bundle of issues surrounding population growth, environmental degradation, and resource depletion, usually referred to as the *global commons*, are both scientific and political. The scientific debates, which are crucial for understanding problems of the global commons, differ from many of the debates we have examined in that they do not follow the familiar perspectives on international relations. There is no realist or liberal position on whether the earth is warming or why. On the scientific aspects of the global commons debate, the main points of disagreement concern the nature and magnitude of population, resource and environmental pressures, as well as the likelihood that technology and human ingenuity will provide solutions. Some see the problems as dire and express skepticism about technological fixes, while others think the problems are often exaggerated and remain optimistic about technological solutions. On the political side of the global commons debate, the central issue should be very familiar: How do we deal with problems that are global in scope in the absence of the sort of central political authority that helps us solve similar problems at the national level? ∎

In January, 2011, *National Geographic* ran an article with the simple title "7 Billion," referring to the current global population. The subtitle continued, "By 2045 global population is projected to reach nine billion. Can the planet take the strain?"[1] In a similar vein, a *New York Times* headline from the summer of 2008 pointing to rising energy and commodity prices (especially for food) was even more dramatic, asking "Is Doomsday Upon Us, Again?"[2] John Feeney warns that "today's crumbling environment, racked by climate change, mass extinction, deforestation, collapsing fisheries and more is evidence that our total consumption has gone too far. We are destroying our life support system." "To avert catastrophe," he sees no alternative but "to reduce both factors in the equation: our numbers and per person consumption."[3]

Such concerns are nothing new. Periodically throughout human history people have worried about a disjuncture between population and resources. But it was not until the early years of the industrial revolution that some began to portray the problem as global in scale. **Thomas Malthus** (1766–1834) provided an early and influential expression of concern. In his *An Essay on the Principle of Population* (1789), Malthus predicted a dreary future for humankind. The basic problem was that the population was growing geometrically (1,2,4,8,16), whereas food production grew arithmetically (1,2,3,4,5). If these trends were extrapolated into the future, the point would eventually be reached when there would be too many people and too little food. Famine would become commonplace, and this would lead to widespread social and political unrest. Famine and disease would eventually reduce population to sustainable levels, but the process would not be pleasant. It was a gloomy vision.

Fortunately, history has not been kind to Malthus and his predictions. The key flaw was his assumption that existing trends would extend unaltered into the future. Although population growth continued at an even faster rate than Malthus anticipated, revolutions in farming techniques and technology led to an even more dramatic increase in the food supply. Rather than population outstripping the food supply, the reality was exactly the opposite. For more than a century after Malthus, the productivity of the industrial revolution eased concerns about the availability of food and other resources. Economic growth and greater productivity provided the answer to the requirements of population growth.

In the 1950s and 1960s, there was a revival of the concerns expressed by Malthus. Why did people start to worry again? The most important reason was a dramatic increase in global population beginning in the 1950s.[4] During the latter half of the twentieth century, global population grew almost 2 percent a year (see Table 13.2), well above the historical average. The problem seemed even worse when this growth rate was disaggregated. Although 2 percent was the global growth rate, some areas of the world were approaching 5 percent, and this was largely in poor nations considered least able to sustain a rapidly growing population. President Lyndon Johnson even voiced concerns in his 1965 inaugural address, urging his audience to "seek new ways to help deal with the explosion of world population and the growing scarcity of world resources."[5]

In addition to the global population explosion, resource shortages raised concerns about the long-term sustainability of existing levels of consumption. The most dramatic of these were oil and gas shortages in the 1970s that created long lines at gas stations, even though these lines had more to do with politics than with any resource limits. The crisis resulted from OPEC decisions, not some sudden decrease in the global oil supply. But whatever the cause, the oil crisis got people thinking about the fact that some resources were not unlimited and dwindling supplies might one day create real shortages.

The final element in the resurgence of concerns about population growth and resources was the emergence of the modern environmental movement in the 1960s and 1970s. As J. R. McNeill explains, "Between 1960 and 1990 a remarkable and potentially earth-shattering (earth-healing?) shift took place. For millions of people swamps long suited for draining became wetlands worth conserving. Nuclear energy, once expected to fuel a cornucopian future, became politically unacceptable.

Thomas Malthus (1766–1834) Predicted (in 1789) that population growth would soon outstrip increases in the food supply, leading to a host of social, economic, and political crises. Though he proved to be wrong, his arguments foreshadowed many of those made almost two hundred years later by the Club of Rome.

TABLE 13.1
How many people have ever lived on the earth?

Year	Population
8000 BCE	5,000,000
1 CE	300,000,000
1200 CE	450,000,000
1650 CE	500,000,000
1750 CE	795,000,000
1850 CE	1,265,000,000
1900 CE	1,656,000,000
1950 CE	2,516,000,000
1995 CE	5,760,000,000

Source: Population Reference Bureau estimates.

Printed but never used by the United States during gas shortages in the late 1970s, these gas ration coupons reflected growing concern about scarce energy resources.

Source: U.S. Department of Energy

Pollution no longer signified industrial wealth but became a crime against nature and society…. Environmentalism had arrived."[6] One manifestation of environmental activism was an explosion in the number of international environmental nongovernment organizations (NGOs). In many respects this was analogous to the growth of international human rights NGOs during the same period. Organizations such as Greenpeace, the World Wildlife Fund, Friends of the Earth, and the Nature Conservancy have played roles in environmental issues very similar to Amnesty International's role in the area of human rights, especially in terms of increasing public awareness. One of the more remarkable aspects of the rise of environmental NGOs is the extent to which they have actually been incorporated into the processes and institutions that negotiate, draft, and monitor compliance with international environmental agreements. Governments and organizations rely on environmental NGOs because they often possess tremendous scientific expertise on very technical and complex issues. Through their efforts at all levels, environmental NGOs and activists helped focus public and governmental attention on global environmental and resources issues.

Too Many People, Too Few Resources

In 1968, a group of concerned scientists convened in Rome for a project that would shape debate about the problems of population growth and resources. Known as the **Club of Rome**, they wanted to bring together existing knowledge about population growth, technology development, food production, energy supplies and consumption, and the environment in order to examine "the present and future

Club of Rome A group of social and natural scientists created in 1968 to examine the future "predicament" of humankind. Their 1972 study, *Limits of Growth*, helped shape the debate over the interrelated issues of global population growth, resources depletion, and environmental degradation.

predicament of man."[7] The result was a study entitled *Limits to Growth*. On one level, their argument resembled that of Thomas Malthus. The most important similarity was the focus on population growth (see Table 13.1). The basic conclusion was simple: a world of limited resources cannot sustain an unlimited population. Whereas Malthus emphasized the problem of food, the Club of Rome stressed other concerns. The good thing about food is that it is a **renewable resource**—that is, we grow new food all the time and we can figure out ways to increase food production. Much more problematic was the consumption of **nonrenewable resources**. Oil provides an obvious example—there is only a certain amount of oil in the world today and when it is gone there will be no more, at least not for millions of years. Many elements of the environment are also in a sense nonrenewable resources: People need clean air, clean water, and a hospitable environment in order to live. If the environment is destroyed, a resource necessary for life will be gone.

As the title of its study suggests, the Club of Rome believed there was a limit to the number of people the world could support. In the abstract, this is a point with which few could disagree. It would be hard to imagine how the Earth could sustain a few trillion people. But what is the limit, and how close are we to it? The Club of Rome's was unequivocal: "If present growth trends in world population, industrialization, pollution, food production, and resource depletion continue unchanged, the limits to growth on this planet will be reached sometime in the next one hundred years."[8] Once these limits were surpassed, "the most probable result will be a rather sudden and uncontrollable decline in both population and industrial capacity" and a declining standard of living for everyone in the world.[9] The echoes of Malthus were clear.

The Population Explosion

Simply stated, population grows because more people are born than die. If 40 children are born in one year for every 1,000 people and 20 die, the net gain in population is 20 per 1000, or 2 percent. Two percent does not sound like a very high rate of growth: 2 percent interest, inflation, and unemployment would be considered quite low. Until recently, global population has rarely grown by more than 1 percent (see Table 13.2). It is only in the second half of the past century that growth rates approached 2 percent. But we get a better appreciation for the significance of 2 percent growth if we look at **doubling time**, which is the number of years it takes a population to double at given rates of growth. If population grows at 0.5 percent a year, it would take 140 years to double, but when population grows at 2 percent it doubles in only 35 years (see Table 13.3). Thus, if global population continues to grow at 2 percent, the world will go from 6 to 12 billion and maybe even 24 billion people within the lifetime of today's average college student.

The finite nature of many resources and the limited resilience of our environment place a limit on the number of people the world can sustain, which the Club of Rome referred to as it's **carrying capacity**. The only long-term solution is stabilizing population at or below carrying capacity. Eventually the world must achieve

---

renewable resources Resources whose supply can be increased within a meaningful time frame.

nonrenewable resources Limited or finite resources that cannot be replaced once used.

TABLE 13.2

Historical world population growth rates

Period	Annual Percentage Growth
1750–1800	0.4
1800–1850	0.5
1850–1900	0.5
1900–1920	0.6
1920–1930	1.0
1930–1940	1.1
1940–1950	1.0
1950–1960	1.9
1960–1970	2.0
1970–1980	1.8
1980–1981	1.7

Source: Hughes Barry B. World Futures: *A Critical Analysis of Alternatives* pp. 54, table 4.1. © 1985 by The Johns Hopkins University Press. Reprinted with permission of The Johns Hopkins University Press.

doubling time The number of years it takes population to double at a given rate of growth.

carrying capacity Term employed by the Club of Rome to indicate the maximum level of population that the world's resources and environment could sustain.

zero population growth (ZPG). There is no escaping the need for an eventual end to population growth. And because population growth results from more people being born than dying, there are only two logical ways to achieve ZPG: Reduce the number of people being born or increase the number of people dying. Stated in such harsh terms, we begin to see the difficulty of the problem.

Resources and the Environment

Although the Club of Rome worried about the availability of food and arable land, this was not seen as the greatest problem. Some of the resources people consume are renewable in the sense that we can make more of them, and food is one such resource. Other resources are finite in that the available quantity is set. The Club of Rome worried most about nonrenewable resources. While the club's predictions of resource depletion have proven excessively pessimistic, the inevitability of depletion remains.

In no area are concerns about depletion greater than in energy. The problem is that demand for fossil fuels is rising steadily, largely as a result of the growth of the Indian and Chinese economies. With a combined population in excess of 2 billion, it is hard to imagine how the world could produce enough oil if Indians and Chinese start consuming oil at the same rate as Americans. In recent years, the theory of **peak oil** has only exacerbated fears of oil depletion. According to peak oil theory, trends over the past few decades suggest that the world is approaching the point at which it will have consumed about half of the world's oil reserves. Some predicted that global oil production would peak before 2008, though estimates varied (see Figure 13.1). From that point on, demand would surge as production declined, raising the price of oil dramatically, perhaps to hundreds of dollars a barrel, leading to economic recessions and conflicts over resources.[10] The dramatic increases in the price of oil in 2007-2008 and again in 2011 were taken by many as evidence that peak oil was upon us. Existing oil fields were being depleted rapidly and new discoveries were insufficient to meet the future demand. Even many oil industry executives, historically optimistic about meeting demand, have begun to sound the alarm. While some fear an impending crisis, "most experts believe there are still enough oil reserves, both discovered and undiscovered, to last at least through the middle of the century."[11] This leaves about four decades to find an alternative to petroleum.

Availability of resources, however, is only half of the problem, and maybe not the most troublesome half. Even if there were enough land, food, oil, coal, and so on for 15 or 20 billion people, we need to take into account the consequences of this level of consumption. Farming land, burning oil, chopping down forests, and operating factories create by-products, some of which have major impacts on the environment. And our environment is also a "resource" in a broader sense. Clean air, clean water, and a hospitable climate are things people need to survive as much, if not more so, as they need a supply of oil. In this sense, we also consume our environment.

Although the list of environmental concerns is long, the threat of **global warming** (now usually subsumed under the broader rubric of **climate change**) receives the

---

zero population growth (ZPG) A situation in which a population's crude birth rates (number of births per 1,000 people) equals crude death rates (number of deaths per 1,000 people).

peak oil The theory that the world's production of oil is about to reach its peak and decline thereafter, resulting in higher prices that can have damaging effects on the world's economies. This is just one example of concerns that high levels of consumption are depleting critical finite resources.

TABLE 13.3

Doubling time

Growth Rate (% per year)	Doubling Time (years)
0.1	700
0.5	140
1.0	70
2.0	35
4.0	18
5.0	14
7.0	10
10.0	7

Source: Donella H. Meadows, Dennis Meadows, and Jorgen Randers, *Limits to Growth—The 30-Year Update*, p. 23. Copyright © 2004. Reprinted by permission of the authors.

global warming The problem of rising global temperatures brought on by the emission of greenhouse gases (especially carbon dioxide and methane).

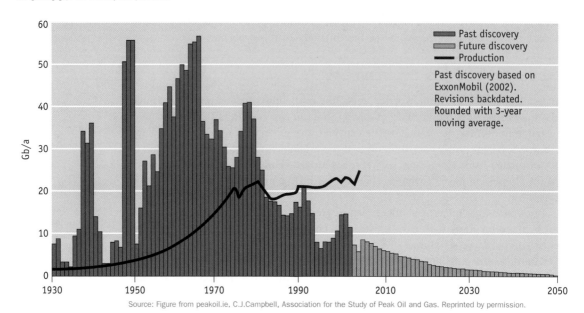

FIGURE 13.1

The growing gap: Oil discovery and production

Source: Figure from peakoil.ie, C.J.Campbell, Association for the Study of Peak Oil and Gas. Reprinted by permission.

most attention. The basic dynamics of climate change are by now familiar, beginning with the burning of fossil fuels releasing carbon dioxide (CO2) and other **greenhouse gases** into the earth's atmosphere. Though some of these gases are absorbed by the world's oceans and forests, the remainder accumulates in the earth's upper atmosphere, preventing the escape of the sun's infrared radiation and causing the earth to warm. This accumulation of greenhouse gases has increased average global temperature over the last hundred years, a period coinciding with the industrial revolution, by about 1° Fahrenheit. Some of the consequences of this warming are clearly discernible, including longer growing seasons, earlier flowering of trees, and shifts in plant and animal habitats. Although the impact of climate change on humans has been limited thus far, if predictions "prove correct, this warming implies vast changes in evaporation and precipitation, a more vigorous hydrological cycle making for both more droughts and more floods. The consequences for agriculture, while difficult to predict, would be sharp. Human health would suffer from the expanded range of tropical diseases. Species extinction would accelerate.... [and] for some low-lying countries, such as the Maldives, it could also be the last chapter."[12]

The scientific consensus is that recent warming exceeds normal historical fluctuations and must be traced largely to human activity. The most comprehensive studies are provided by the Intergovernmental Panel on Climate Change (IPCC), an organization established in 1988 involving more than 2,500 of the world's leading climatologists. The IPCC's 1995 study concluded, "the balance of evidence

greenhouse gases Gases resulting from the burning of fossil fuels, especially carbon dioxide (CO2), that build up in the upper atmosphere. It is the accumulation of these gases that leads to global warming.

suggests that there is a discernable human influence on the global climate." In 2001 the IPCC's judgment was even less equivocal: "There is new and stronger evidence that most of the warming observed over the past 50 years is attributable of human activities."[13] The IPCC's 2007 report was similarly certain, concluding that "most of the observed increase in globally averaged temperatures since the mid-twentieth century is *very likely* due to the observed increase in anthropogenic [i.e., resulting from human activity] greenhouse gas concentrations."[14]

One of the more alarming aspects of climate change is that most of the world's greenhouse gases are produced by a small percentage of its population—those wealthy and technologically advanced enough to support a lifestyle requiring large quantities of fossil fuels. A family of four in Seattle contributes much more to global warming—i.e., has a larger "carbon footprint"—than a family of ten in Bangladesh. As the majority of the world's population pursues economic development and replicates the lifestyles of the industrialized North, the problem will get much worse. A world of 10 or 12 billion people living an American lifestyle would dramatically accelerate climate change if we continue relying on fossil fuels. This is one reason that likely scenarios for the next century indicate more warming than in the past. In 1995, the IPCC predicted that global temperature would increase between 1.8° and 6.3° Fahrenheit, though by 2001 it raised this estimate to an increase of 2.5° to 10.4°.[15] The IPCC's 2007 report narrowed the range of likely temperature increase to between 3.2° and 7.2°.[16]

Though quick to emphasize that it is not the only culprit in climate change (methane gas is another), a number of climatologists have focused on the concentration of carbon dioxide, measured in parts per million (ppm), in the atmosphere as a critical indicator of the magnitude and progression of the problem. They note that between 1959 and 2008 atmospheric carbon dioxide concentrations rose from slightly more than 300 ppm to almost 400 ppm (prior to the industrial revolution the level was about 250 ppm). Those using this measure assume that there is a level at which the concentration passes a critical threshold, a point of environmental no return. Some frame this as a "tipping point" beyond which climate change becomes irreversible and catastrophic. They fear that beyond this point a series of mutually-reinforcing processes will combine to accelerate the already dangerous changes. If rising temperatures melt the arctic permafrost, for example, large quantities of additional carbon dioxide currently trapped in the frozen ground would be released, raising temperatures even more in a rapid, vicious, and uncontrollable feedback loop. With estimates ranging from a high of 550 ppm to a low of 350 ppm, there is little agreement on what the tipping point might be. If the lower limit is correct, the problem is worse than many realize because that threshold has already been passed. But disagreement about the precise threshold should not obscure the more important consensus: A higher figure only lessens the *urgency* of reducing carbon emissions, not the *necessity*.[17]

Global warming may be the most overriding and widely publicized environmental problem, but it is by no means the only one. There is also the erosion of the earth's ozone layer. Though ozone is considered a pollutant at ground levels (major cities issue "ozone alerts" on bad pollution days), a thin layer of ozone in the stratosphere screens out the sun's harmful ultraviolet rays, which contribute to a variety of medical conditions, from skin cancer to cataracts. The depletion of ozone is the result of emissions of chlorofluorocarbons (CFCs). Even though the ozone holes are currently located over unpopulated or sparsely populated areas, this is another potentially dangerous consequence of human industrial activity (though successful attempts have been made in the last two decades to reduce the use and production of CFCs).

We can add to this list concerns about *biodiversity* with the extinction of animal, insect, and plant species; the shrinking of the world's major rain forests; acid rain; the erosion of farmland; the scarcity of fresh drinking water; and the use of toxic chemicals that are finding their way into the human food chain. The technical details and debates involved in many of these issues quickly become a mind-numbing array of data, statistics, charts, and tables that are almost impossible for a nonspecialist to sort out. But the overall picture is that of a fragile ecosystem suffering a series of substantial shocks in a relatively short period as a result of human economic and industrial activity. The combined effect is that we have reached a point where, to paraphrase the title of former vice president Al Gore's environmental manifesto, the "earth is in the balance."[18]

Former U.S. Vice President addresses the 2007 United Nations Climate Change Conference in Bali. Many see climate change as the biggest threat to the global commons.

Source: Mast Irham/Corbis Wire/epa/Corbis

The Tragedy of the (Global) Commons

Before we can solve a problem, we need to appreciate its underlying dynamics. In considering the dilemmas of population growth, resource depletion, and environmental degradation, many have found it useful to think of them as *commons* problems, invoking the metaphor of **the tragedy of the commons** to illustrate these complicated issues in simple terms. Indeed, according to a World Bank discussion paper, the metaphor of the commons has been "the dominant paradigm within which social scientists assess natural resource issues."[19] In discussing the problem of climate change, for example, a recent World Bank study argued that the world's advanced industrial nations "cannot continue to fill up an unfair and unsustainable share of the *atmospheric commons*."[20] The commons metaphor tries to illustrate the incentives that often lead people to act in ways that ultimately destroy something they need to survive.

the tragedy of the commons A metaphor in which actors fail to restrain their use of common resources, eventually depleting those resources for all. Often used to conceptualize the issues of global population growth, resource consumption, and environmental degradation.

The tragedy of the commons metaphor derives from a time in history when many towns had tracts of land open to all referred to as commons. If you have been to Boston, for example, you may have visited its central park still known as the Boston Common. As the name implies, this land was public or communal, not private, property: Everyone was free to graze their animals on the commons. Problems arose because individuals in the community controlled the size of their herds. Because the animals were private property, individual herders enjoyed the full benefit of each additional animal they fed on the commons. In doing so, however, they bore only a portion of the costs because when the animal was fed on the commons the costs were essentially shared by the community as whole. So the benefits of herd expansion were private while the costs were social. As a result, there was always a rational incentive to acquire more animals because the herder enjoyed the full benefits while bearing only a fraction of the cost. But as herds grew larger, eventually too many animals grazed and the commons were destroyed. The carrying capacity, so to speak, of the commons was exceeded, with a predictable result.[21]

Many see our current global problems in similar terms. The commons in this case is not grazing land per se, but all the resources we need to sustain the human herd—energy supplies, food, clean air, clean water, and so on. These are our global commons. If we run out of oil because of excessive consumption, it is gone for everyone, whether you used it or not. If the environment is destroyed, it is destroyed for everyone, regardless of whether you polluted it or not.

Garrett Hardin on Restricting the Commons

If the earth's future hangs in the balance, we are indeed confronting a drastic problem. But do drastic problems require drastic solutions? Some think so, including Garrett Hardin, one of the more controversial figures in debates about population growth and its consequences. Hardin has been influential in framing the issues raised by the Club of Rome as analogous to the tragedy of the commons but on a global scale. He was not as shy as the Club of Rome in proposing solutions.

Hardin begins by pointing out the obvious: If the world has too many people, it is because people are having too many children. The only solution is to have fewer children. Most people continue to believe, however, that procreation is not something that should be subject to government regulation. This is a luxury, Hardin thinks, we can no longer enjoy. Arguing that we need to relinquish the "freedom to breed," he makes his case in the starkest terms: "The most important aspect of necessity that we must now recognize is the necessity of abandoning the commons in breeding. No technical solution can rescue us from the misery of overpopulation. Freedom to breed will bring ruin to all.... The only way we can preserve and nurture other and more precious freedoms is by relinquishing the freedom to breed, and that very soon … only so can we put an end to this aspect of the tragedy of the commons."[22]

What would restricting the "freedom to breed" entail? Visions of infanticide and coerced abortions immediately come to mind, but very few (and certainly not Hardin) suggest such draconian measures. Once there is agreement that procreation is a legitimate target of social or government regulation, several devices to reduce population growth are possible. Interestingly, few people have problems with government policies encouraging people to have more children. In fact, many countries have tax incentives for bigger families, especially in parts of Europe and Asia with low birth rates. People seem more reluctant, however, to use similar policies to discourage large families. But, Hardin would ask, why is it acceptable to offer tax benefits for second and third children but not to impose tax penalties for additional children? The discussion of policy details, however, comes after the acceptance of the legitimacy and necessity of social and political regulation of population growth.

international food bank Proposed as a means of responding to famines around the world. The idea was to create a ready stock of food that could be shipped rapidly to areas in need, thus saving thousands of lives. Opposed by Garrett Hardin because he thought such aid would increase the population of areas that were already overpopulated.

population escalator Garrett Hardin's term to describe the effect of an international food bank. Refers to the steady increases in population that would result every time external assistance was offered to deal with recurring famines.

Even more controversial was Hardin's opposition to proposals for the establishment of an **international food bank** in the 1970s to assist countries in the event of famine. Famine, in Hardin's view, was often a sign of overpopulation. Nations experiencing repeated famines failed to come to grips with the problem of population growth. If the international community rushes in with food aid, this merely allows people to survive and population to grow, resulting in what Hardin refers to as a **population escalator.** Aid only rescues societies from their inability or unwillingness to control their population. Although feeding starving people might seem the moral thing to do, the inevitable result is continued overpopulation and more famines. In typically provocative terms, he advised, "it is essential that those in power resist the temptation to convert extra food into extra babies."[23] Given the limited supply of food and other resources, Hardin viewed the world as akin to a lifeboat stocked with enough food and water to support ten people with fourteen people aboard. In this case there are two options: share the food and water among all fourteen, which means no one will survive, or recognize the need to reduce the population to ten so that some can make it. If we see the world's resources as a commons to be shared by all, the inescapable and logical result, in Hardin's view, is ruin for all.

Needless to say, Hardin's approach is not universally accepted. Even among those who agree with the basic logic and details laid out by the Club of Rome, Hardin's solutions are considered extreme. Most would rather tackle the problem through the less coercive means that Hardin viewed as inadequate. Others reject Hardinesque solutions because they disagree with the underlying assumptions of a looming crisis brought on by global population growth. As a result, they also reject Hardin's metaphor of the earth as a lifeboat without sufficient resources to sustain those on board. If they wanted to be as provocative as Hardin, the critics might suggest that a better metaphor would be that some of the people on the lifeboat want to eat like gluttonous fat pigs on their way to shore and are prepared to deny others food in the process. These critics of Hardin and the Club of Rome see a world of plenty, not a world of limits.

A World of Plenty

Examining competing visions of the future, Barry Hughes distinguishes **neotraditionalist** from **modernist**. The neotraditionalist approach is embodied in the analysis and predictions of the Club of Rome. The label *neotraditionalism* stems from a distinction often drawn between so-called traditional and modern societies. Traditional societies tend to accept a fatalistic view of life as constrained by natural limits, whereas modern societies are characterized by a faith in people's ability to overcome nature's limits. The notion that people need to adjust to inherent limits to growth is, according to Hughes, a traditionalist view rejected by those he calls *modernists*, who believe people have the intellectual and technological capacity to overcome the limits that supposedly restrict human and economic growth. Modernists believe that Hardin and the Club of Rome, like Malthus before them, are wrong, and largely for the same reasons.[24]

Malthus was clearly wrong in his time, and four decades since the Club of Rome's report have not borne out many of its predictions either. Was the Club of Rome merely a little ahead of its time, or were its analyses and predictions fundamentally flawed? Modernists think the latter, arguing that visions of scarcity and ecological disaster have been wrong historically and are likely to continue to be wrong. Modernists do not necessarily reject the principle that there is a limit to the population that the world can sustain; they simply do not think we are anywhere near that limit. The modernist vision of the future rests on a few critical assumptions. First, global population is likely to level off at about 9 billion by the end of the century. Second, many of the supposed limits to growth are likely to be overcome by human ingenuity and technological advances. Third, many of the problems cited by the Club of Rome are the result of bad policies, not any inherent limits to growth. In sum, the predictions of the Club of Rome are likely to be seen a hundred years hence in much the same manner people now see Malthus's predictions: fundamentally flawed because they extrapolate existing trends into the future without accounting for human adaptability, intelligence, and technology.

How Many People Will We Have?

Graphs showing global population growing at rapid rates well into the future are indeed scary. The doubling of population every thirty-five or forty years as far as the eye can see might well be catastrophic. Fortunately, modernists argue, this is unlikely to happen. Adhering to the **theory of demographic transition**, they see population growing in spurts that eventually level off, not in a consistently exponential fashion. The dramatic increase in global population in the middle and latter half of the twentieth century was an anomaly that will not be sustained.

neotraditionalists Those, like the Club of Rome and Garrett Hardin, who believe that the world is rapidly approaching (or is already at) its limits to growth.

modernists Those who reject the analysis presented by the Club of Rome. Argue that even if there is a limit to the population the world can support, it is not even close to that limit. Generally have a great faith in science's ability to solve problems and overcome what are often portrayed as limits to growth.

theory of demographic transition Claims that periods of great population growth tend to be followed by a leveling off of population. The same technological, economic, and social changes that cause population to grow in the first place by reducing death rates usually have long-term effects that result in declining birth rates.

TABLE 13.4

A hypothetical demographic transition (1)

	Crude Birth Rate	Crude Death Rate	Growth Rate (%)
Stage I	40/1,000	38/1,000	.2
Stage II	40/1,000	22/1,000	1.8
Stage III	24/1,000	22/1,000	.2

Source: © Cengage Learning 2013.

According to the theory of demographic transition, high rates of population growth are usually the result of social, medical, economic, and scientific advances that increase life expectancy and reduce infant mortality. As people live longer and more children survive infancy, population grows rapidly. This is what Europe experienced two or three generations ago as a result of the industrial revolution. Increasing life expectancy and decreasing infant mortality, however, are not initially matched by declining birth rates. If death rates decline while birth rates remain the same, population grows rapidly. Eventually, however, birth rates adjust downward, causing population to level off (see Table 13.4 and Figure 13.2). This adjustment might take a generation or two.

Why do birth rates eventually decline? First, the advances that improved life expectancy and infant mortality are usually part of a larger pattern of economic growth that increases wealth and affluence. And if there is an iron law of demography, it is that wealth and fertility (childbearing) are *inversely* related: across societies and within them, wealthy people have fewer children. This might seem odd because wealthy people and societies should be able to afford more children, but the critical factor is the changing motivation for procreation. In poor societies, children are economic assets, often contributing income to the family by their early teens. As societies and people become more affluent, they have children largely for their emotional and psychological benefits. And for many parents, two children provide all the emotional benefits they can tolerate.

FIGURE 13.2

A hypothetical demographic transition (2)

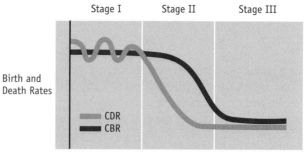

Birth rates also decline for a more straightforward reason. If many children die very young, people need to have more children to assure that some survive to adulthood. In countries like the United States, parents expect every child to outlive them into adulthood: It is a rare tragedy when a parent buries a child. Throughout most of human history and in many parts of the developing world, the death of a child is not unusual. But as infant mortality declines, there is less need to have a lot of children to assure the survival of a few. As children regularly and reliably survive, people start to have fewer.

A final reason for declining birth rates is that economic growth and industrialization also tend to alter the role of women in society. As women become more educated, work outside the home, earn their own income, and gain access to birth control, they tend to have fewer children. This is a point stressed by feminists and nonfeminists alike: improving the status of women is one of the keys to reducing population growth.[25]

On a global level, different regions progress through this demographic transition at different times and rates. The advanced industrialized world has already gone through the cycle. Population grew rapidly during the first half and middle of the twentieth century and then leveled off. In Western Europe many nations are now faced with birth rates so low that they worry about their ability to afford the generous welfare benefits that elderly citizens enjoy.[26] Much of the population growth we see today is occurring in the Third World. Modernists predict that trend will

TABLE 13.5

Forecasted population sizes

Year	Median World and Regional Population Sizes (millions)				
	2000	**2025**	**2050**	**2075**	**2100**
World total	6,055	7,827	8,797	8,951	8,414
North Africa	173	257	311	336	333
Sub-Saharan Africa	611	976	1,319	1,522	1,500
North America	314	379	422	441	454
Latin America	515	709	840	904	934
Central Asia	56	81	100	107	106
Middle East	172	285	368	413	413
South Asia	1,367	1,940	2,249	2,242	1,958
China region	1,408	1,608	1,580	1,422	1,250
Pacific Asia	476	625	702	702	654
Pacific OECD	150	155	148	135	123
Western Europe	456	478	470	433	392
Eastern Europe	121	117	104	87	74
European part of the former USSR	236	218	187	159	141

Source: Reprinted by permission from Macmillan Publishers Ltd.: from Wolfgang Lutz, Warren Sanderson, and Sergei Scherbov, "The End of the World Population Growth," Nature, August 2, 2001, p. 544. Copyright © 2001.

continue and that "demographic transition theory reassuringly suggest[s] that the rest of the world will follow the same path as the industrialized West."[27] Indeed, in many parts of the Third World this already appears to be happening. In Taiwan and South Korea, for example, birth rates in 1960 were about 40 per 1,000. By 2001 they were down to 14 per 1,000.[28] Taking these trends into account, more recent estimates suggest that global population will continue to increase until about 2075, when it reaches approximately 9 billion and will stabilize around that number (see Table 13.5).[29] Thus, though a doubling of population every thirty-five years would be a nightmare, this is almost certainly not going to happen.

But even if one accepts the prediction that world population is likely to level off, 9 billion is still a lot of people. The question remains: Can the world's resources and environment sustain indefinitely a population of 9 or 10 billion people? Modernists think so. An exhaustive survey of modernist responses to resource and environmental concerns is more than we can accomplish here. But let us look at a few issues to get a feel for the modernist perspective: food, energy resources, and global warming.[30]

Feeding the World

Can the world feed 9 billion people when many are starving in a world of 6 billion? Though we might assume people are starving today because food is in short supply, we would be wrong: The world produces more than enough food to feed its entire population. The problem of starvation is one of food distribution, not supply. Over the past few decades, global food production has actually been increasing *faster* than world population. Since 1961 we have seen a roughly 250 percent increase in grain production and a 300 percent increase in meat production. Even more important are the per capita (per person) figures. Because the period since 1961 has been one of unprecedented population growth, it would be amazing if food production kept pace. In fact, the world produced more grain and almost twice as much meat *per person* in 2005 than in 1961.[31] Indeed, "many agronomists think the world could easily support 20 billion or 30 billion people."[32] Because most expect global population to peak at about 9-10 billion, modernists expect the overall supply of food to remain sufficient. We also have no idea of what the genetic revolution will bring. Perhaps we will see a greater reliance on disease-resistant crops or grains engineered to have higher concentrations of essential nutrients (e.g., strains of rice much higher in vitamin A). When these advances are coupled with declining rates of population growth, the problem of feeding the world's people is perhaps the least of our worries.

Until the last few years, this optimistic analysis was the norm. John Parker notes that "By the 1990s most agricultural problems seemed to have been solved. Yields were rising, pests appeared to be under control, and fertilizers were replenishing dried soil." Today, however, this optimism is beginning to wane. Dramatic increases in prices for basic agricultural commodities in 2007-2008 and again in 2011 have revived concerns about the ability to feed the world's people. These increases resulted from a "combination of factors—rising demand in India and China, a dietary shift away from cereals towards meat and vegetables, the increasing use of maize for fuel, and developments outside of agriculture." The immediate result in many poor countries was food riots, bans on the export of foodstuffs, and price controls. A number of analyses saw rising food prices as an important sources of political upheaval throughout the Arab world in 2011. The fear, however, is that rising prices signify a larger and enduring problem—the end of the era of cheap food and new era of scarcity. Parker articulates these concerns that rising agricultural commodity prices "seems to suggest that the world cannot feed its current population, let along the 9 billion expected by 2050."[33]

Fueling the World

We can find ways to grow more food, but other commodities are finite in that once we have used them all, we will have to wait millions of years for the earth to replenish our supply. Fossil fuels are the case in point. There is no doubt we are using fossil fuels more rapidly than the earth is producing them. Consequently, there is no escaping the logical conclusion that we will run out of fossil fuels someday. Even if population stabilizes at 9, 10, or 11 billion people, this does nothing to prevent the depletion of oil, gas, and coal, though it will take a little longer than if we had 15 or 10 billion people. Fewer people simply gives us more time, not more resources.

How do modernists respond to this logic of inevitable resource depletion? There are essentially two major responses. First, the supply of these fossil fuels is likely to be more than sufficient until viable alternatives are developed. Second, we need to differentiate *energy* from *fossil fuels*. Fossil fuels may have provided for most of our energy requirements in the industrial age, but there are other potential sources of energy, many of which are unlimited, and technological advances are likely to allow us to exploit these sources before we need them.

The bad thing about predictions is that they may not come true. Make too many bad predictions and people start to question them all. Few predictions have fared as poorly as those concerning the depletion of fossil fuels. In 1891, the U.S. Geological Survey indicated that it was unlikely there was much oil to be found in Kansas and Texas. As recently as 1981, the U.S. Department of Energy predicted that by the end of the century the price of oil would double or triple.[34] In 1972, the authors of *Limits to Growth* estimated that we would exhaust all known existing reserves of petroleum by 1992.[35] Not only were these predictions wrong, they were shockingly so. Needless to say, we did not run out of oil in 1992. Nor do trends in the price of oil indicate any increasing scarcity. Modernists delight in pointing to past predictions of resource depletion. Until recently there was not even much evidence of price pressure. In constant 2000 dollars (i.e., adjusted for inflation), the price of oil *declined* by more than 50 percent from the early 1980s to 2000.[36] Of course, by the Summer of 2008 and again in 2011 oil exceeded 100 dollars a barrel and gas prices reached new heights, hovering around $4.00 a gallon for some time, leading some to conclude scarcity was finally translating into permanently higher prices, as predicted by the theory of peak oil. Not everyone shared this assessment, emphasizing the role of speculators, political unrest in the Middle East and the declining value of the dollar in pushing oil. In general, modernists think that existing reserves are greater than many assume and that new technologies will allow us to extract a lot of difficult-to-reach oil. Modernists concede, however, that the age of easy and very cheap oil may be approaching an end.

There remains the unavoidable conclusion that one day these fossil fuels will be either exhausted or so expensive as to be not economically viable. We can quibble about how long that will take, but there is no escaping the reality of eventual depletion. What then? Modernists stress that fossil fuels and energy are not the same. Running out of fossil fuels does not mean the end of our energy supply. A host of theoretical alternatives to fossil fuels—hydroelectric, nuclear, solar, wind, biofuels and so on—are available. There are two problems at present. The technologies are not advanced enough and the energy produced is generally more expensive than fossil fuels. But the coming decades are likely to see improvements in the technologies of alternative energy sources, which will help make alternatives more economically viable and environmentally friendly. As the cost of fossil fuels increases, alternative sources will become more attractive and profitable. This is the silver lining of oil over $100 a barrel—prices this high make alternatives economically feasible. We may run out of fossil fuels, but we will never run out of energy. This optimism and belief in technology is expressed by Bjorn Lomborg: "The important point ... on energy is to stress not only that there are ample reserves of fossil fuels but also that the potentially unlimited renewable energy resources definitely are within our economic reach."[37]

The Problem of the Environment

The environmental consequences associated with population and economic growth probably provide the greatest challenge to modernist optimism. There is no single modernist response to this complex range of concerns. In general, however, modernists are skeptical of what they see as exaggerated predictions of imminent environmental catastrophe. To understand the range of responses, let us look at the issue of global warming and break down the issue into several distinct questions. First, is global warming occurring? Second, if so, what is causing it? And third, how much warming are we likely to see and with what effects?

With regard to the fact of warming, almost no one resists the conclusion that global temperatures have risen over the past century. The major points of contention concern the causes, likely extent and consequences of warming. The theory of global warming asserts not merely that temperatures are rising, but that human activity is the cause. Critics are quick to point out, however, that global temperatures have fluctuated throughout history. No one denies this. The issue is whether current warming is occurring on a greater scale or more rapidly than in the past. Unfortunately, no one was keeping records 18,000 years ago, so we need to look at indirect indicators of temperature, such as the accumulation of ice in Greenland, to gauge global climate thousands of years ago. But these indicators are open to different interpretations. A 2003 survey by Harvard scientists concluded that global temperatures appear to have been significantly higher during the Middle Ages than they are today.[38] The problem is that systematic records of temperature begin in the second half of the 1800s. If this period was unusually cool, using it as a baseline for measuring warming might be misleading.[39] There is, however, no genuine disagreement on at least one major point: the concentration of CO_2 in the atmosphere has been increasing due to fossil fuel consumption. Even the Bush administration's Environmental Protection Agency, which was criticized for its equivocal position on global warming, concluded that "there is *no doubt* this atmospheric buildup of carbon dioxide and other greenhouse gases is largely the result of human activities."[40]

Once we get past the fact of rising carbon dioxide concentrations and temperatures, we enter the realm of predictions of future temperature trajectories and consequences. These questions are difficult because answers are derived from complex climatological models incorporating many elements of a very complicated system, including not only greenhouse gases and temperature but also oceans, forests, cloud cover, evaporation rates, precipitation, and so on. Changes in one element of the climate affect others, and no one is sure how they all interact. Remember the IPCC's prediction that global temperature will increase between 2.5° and 10.4° Fahrenheit by 2100. Eight degrees is a substantial range. For some, even the smallest increase is cause for concern. According to Al Gore, "even *small* changes in global average temperatures can have *enormous* effects on climate patterns. And *any* disruption in climate patterns can dramatically affect the distribution of rainfall, the intensity of storms and droughts, the directions of prevailing winds and ocean currents, and the appearance of erratic weather patterns [emphasis added]."[41] In Gore's view, the world's environment is a finely balanced, fragile, and interrelated system in which adverse changes in one area, however small, can have "enormous" repercussions for the larger environment.

Some modernists maintain that small increases in temperature might not be such a bad thing. A few years ago, in a somewhat provocative passage with the title "The Case for Global Warming," Greg Easterbrook even saw some positive consequences of global warming. But Easterbrook also provides an interesting example of how the debate has shifted in the last decade. Admitting that "as an environmental commentator, I have a long record of opposing alarmism," he now concedes that "the science has changed from ambiguous to near-unanimous … [and] based on the data I am now switching sides regarding global warming, from skeptic to convert…. [The] research is now in, and it shows a strong scientific consensus that an artificially warming world is a real phenomenon posing real danger."[42] On the issue of global warming, at least, the ranks of the skeptics appear to be thinning by the day. The debate has shifted to what should and can be done to halt the process of warming.

But even modernists who accept the reality of human-induced warming and the need to halt or reverse existing trends find grounds for optimism in technology. Assuming the need to reduce emissions and stabilize atmospheric carbon dioxide, there are only two options: consume less energy or find sources that generate fewer or, better yet, no harmful emissions. Even in the absence of climate change, we would still need alternative energy sources because fossil fuels are being consumed faster than they are replenished. The question is whether alternatives can be developed and adopted in time, before the consequences of fossil fuel consumption pass the so-called tipping point.

The Good News

Though recognizing some genuine problems, modernists reject the chorus of what they consider Malthusian predictions of gloom and doom. Such predictions have been notoriously wrong in the past and need to be viewed with deep skepticism today. The problems are either nonexistent (food availability), greatly exaggerated (global warming), capable of "solving themselves" (population growth), or amenable to technological solutions (energy). Furthermore, the endless recitation of problems only serves to obscure the evidence of a better life for virtually everyone on the planet. On whatever measure one chooses, human life is better today than it was a hundred years ago. As a result, Lomborg anticipates that "children born today—in both the industrialized world and developing countries—will live longer and be healthier, they will get more food, a better education, a higher standard of living, more leisure time and far more possibilities—without the global environment being destroyed. And that is a beautiful world."[43] The difference in vision between this view and that of the Club of Rome could not be starker.

Global Problems, Global Solutions?

Common resources link people together. In the tragedy of the commons, each herder's prosperity depends on others using their common land responsibly. It is one of the ironies of social relations that interdependence is a source of both conflict and cooperation. If one's behavior had no effect on the fate of others, everyone could afford to ignore one another's irresponsibility. If one herder overgrazes his private land, this would be of little concern to others. But if someone overgrazes the commons, all suffer. Disagreements about the use of common resources are always a potential source of conflict. The need to protect the commons, however, also creates mutual interests requiring cooperation. If the resources and environment needed to sustain life on this planet are really in danger, the prospects for conflict and the need for cooperation are both great.

Environmental and resource problems are not new. In the early 1900s, progressives such as President Theodore Roosevelt spearheaded efforts to protect the environment from the ravages of industrialization. People worried about environmental degradation long before the Club of Rome and global warming. What has changed is the problem's scope. Prior to the 1960s, most environmental and resource concerns were local, regional, or maybe national. Lakes polluted or forests destroyed in one nation had little impact on others. It was really not until the 1960s that people began to recognize the global nature of the problem.

Global problems are always more difficult to solve than similar problems at the national level, where government regulation offers a potential solution. National governments can enforce limits on pollution. The threat of legal sanctions can force factories to limit emissions. Government coercion is sometimes useful for compelling responsible behavior. As we have pointed out repeatedly, however, there is no world government to play a similar role, exacerbating problems of enforcement. As Ruth Bell explains, "Enforcement has always been the Achilles' heel of international environmental agreements, largely because nations submit to international oversight, which they see as a threat to their sovereignty, only with the greatest reluctance."[44] This is not to say that commons problems are impossible to solve in the absence of government, merely that they are more difficult.

Different theoretical perspectives offer varying degrees of optimism regarding the ability to solve international commons dilemmas.

Not surprisingly, realists tend to emphasize the obstacles to cooperation in dealing with problems of the global commons. Anarchy makes it more difficult to reach and enforce international agreements while the finite nature of many resources increases the likelihood of conflict. Scarcity always breeds conflict as actors compete for control of, and access to, the resources they need. Of course, in the popular imagination, the resource most likely to fuel conflict is oil. Because the world's major economies are so dependent on oil, it is not too far-fetched to imagine future conflict among oil-thirsty nations such as China, India, and the United States as they vie for control of Middle East oil. But oil is not the only potential source of conflict. There are other more mundane resources that might create problems. In many parts of the world with large populations and small supplies of fresh water, this most basic of all resources already creates tensions. There has, for example, been a long-standing dispute between Israel and Jordan over their rights to water from the Yarmouk River. There is a similar conflict between the United States and Mexico because the United States uses almost all the Colorado River's water before it reaches the Mexican border. In a world of increasing scarcity, "resource wars" might become commonplace.[45]

On the environmental front, there will also be conflicts over who should bear the burden of protecting the commons. The Kyoto Protocol (1997), which sought to curb global warming by reducing greenhouse emissions, provides an illustration. A central flaw with the agreement in the eyes of critics is its failure to impose restrictions on all nations. Wealthy industrialized nations such as the United States faced substantial reductions while China, India, and other developing nations did not. Opponents saw such disparities as unfair. Supporters, however, thought it was perfectly reasonable that nations responsible for past emissions bear the burden of current reductions. Developing nations fear that restricting their emissions would doom them to permanent underdevelopment. All of this is complicated further by recent studies indicating that some developed countries are "reducing" their emissions simply by shifting carbon intensive production to developing nations and importing the resulting products. As a result, "while Europe may pride itself on emitting less carbon from its own territory than it did in 1990, from a consumption point of view the carbon embodied in imports from China alone all but cancels out the gain."[46] So China can argue that its carbon emissions are increasing largely to meet the demands of foreign consumers. These distributional questions about who is responsible for the problem and should bear the costs of protecting the global commons are likely to remain a continuing source of conflict in attempts to protect the global commons.

Liberals certainly recognize the difficulties in solving global commons problems. International anarchy precludes some of the solutions available at the national level. Conflicting interests make agreements difficult and national sovereignty creates problems for enforcement. No one thinks these are easy problems. Liberals would be quick to note, however, that the history of dealing with international environmental problems is by no means a catalog of failure. The obstacles have not always proven insurmountable. One can point to well over hundred

international regimes A broad term used to characterize the institutions, norms, practices, and decision-making procedures that have been created to shape international behavior in given issues areas.

international treaties and conventions addressing an extremely diverse range of problems including endangered species, the dumping of toxic wastes in the oceans, biodiversity, the exploitation of Antarctica's resources, and acid rain. Nations, international organizations, and NGOs have been able to create rules and institutions to protect the environment and regulate access to resources. In these cases what we have seen is the emergence of successful **international regimes**, a somewhat abstract concept used to describe "sets of implicit or explicit principles, norms, rules, and decision making procedures around which actors' expectations converge in a given area of international relations."[47] Such regimes typically include treaties that specify rules of behavior as well as institutions/organizations that foster negotiation, information sharing, and compliance monitoring.

Many cite the Montreal Protocol of 1987 as an example of success. The origins of the protocol can be traced to the mid-1970s when scientists became aware of a hole in the earth's critical ozone layer. Scientists identified chlorofluorocarbons (CFCs) as the main culprit. Given the widespread use of CFCs in refrigeration, air conditioning, and aerosol sprays, there were reasons for pessimism regarding the prospects for successful regulation. But scientists, environmental activists, and NGOs were able to raise public awareness of the problem and pressure governments and international organizations to act. Negotiations resulted in the 1987 protocol in which twenty-two nations agreed to cut their use of CFCs in half by 1998. When data indicated that the problem was worse than anticipated, the timetable for phasing out CFCs altogether accelerated. Developed nations agreed to end all use of CFCs by 2000 and developing nations agreed to do likewise by 2010. A total of 189 nations have signed the protocol, leaving only six relatively insignificant holdouts (e.g., Andorra, San Marino, and the Vatican). One of the protocol's more innovative provisions was the so-called Multilateral Fund, to which developed nations contributed money to offset the costs incurred by developing nations as they transitioned to CFC substitutes. In many respects, the process appears to have been a great success. Levels of CFCs have either stabilized or decreased and compliance appears to be quite good. As a result, "the global response to ozone depletion is often invoked as a direct policy precedent for dealing with increasing concentrations of carbon dioxide in the atmosphere."[48]

The Kyoto Protocol represented an attempt to replicate the success of Montreal. The results so far, however, have not been encouraging. The agreement's overall purpose is to set targets for the reduction of carbon dioxide and other greenhouse gas emissions. As indicated above, a particularly controversial element of the protocol is the differential obligations. Industrialized nations promised to reduce emissions by 5.2 percent from their 1990 levels by 2010 (which would be about 29 percent below what they would be without Kyoto). Not all countries are required to reduce emissions. Developed nations have targets as high as 10 percent, while developing nations do not have to reduce emissions at all. Though 160 nations signed the Kyoto Protocol, several, including the United States, have refused to ratify the agreement. The reasons for this are many, but usually focus on fears about the economic consequences of reducing carbon emissions. There are even some, especially in the United States and Australia, who question the entire theory of human-induced climate change. And even nations sympathetic to the process have carved out important exceptions—Germany, for example, decided that its coal industry would be exempt from the reduction targets.

While many nations have met the targets of the Kyoto Protocols, there is little evidence that it has had much impact on the overall problem. A recent World Bank study noted that global carbon emissions have actually *increased* by 25 percent since the adoption of the protocols in 1997.[49] It is certainly possible the emission increases would have been greater in the absence of an agreement, but a 25 percent increase in little more than a decade is not very promising if the problem is pressing. And while some European nations have reduced carbon emissions, they have increased by 7 percent in the United States, 17 percent in Russia, and a whopping 102 percent in China.[50] There is also no indication increases in the concentration of atmospheric carbon dioxide are slowing. Despite subsequent climate conferences in Bali (2007), Copenhagen (2009), and Cancun (2010), a political solution to the emissions problem seems far off.

Indian students protest the failure of the United States to ratify the 1997 Kyoto Protocol. The sign also illustrates how just a single person in a developed nation is responsible for more greenhouse gas emissions than dozens or even hundreds of people in developing nations.

Source: © Kamal Kishore/Reuters/Corbis

Skeptics see the fate of Kyoto as a more likely harbinger of efforts to deal with other problems of the global commons. CFC emissions were much easier to eliminate because there were economically viable substitutes. The cost of reducing CFC use was not that great. The same cannot be said for greenhouse gases. The reliance on fossil fuels is far greater and alternatives much more expensive and less developed. Eliminating carbon emissions is a problem of an entirely different magnitude than CFCs. The World Bank explains that with respect to reducing greenhouse emissions, "the tightness of the weave between climate and industrial development suggests adjustment costs are likely to be substantial – and that past comparisons such as acid rain and ozone depletion are of limited relevance."[51]

Conclusion

Few issues are more important than the future of the global commons, and few problems appear more daunting. Attempts to protect the global commons must overcome several obstacles. The first is uncertainty about the nature and magnitude of the problems. Scientists do not agree on such critical issues as the likely course of population growth, the supply of fossil fuels and the viability of alternative energy sources, or the extent of future global warming and its consequences. The second obstacle is the absence of a central political authority to solve problems that are global in scope. Though it is not impossible to deal with global problems in the absence of a central political authority, this undoubtedly complicates matters. This chapter has discussed these scientific and political issues. But there is at least one other feature of many commons problems, especially those that are environmental in nature, that makes them difficult to solve: the lag between actions and their effects.

Focusing on the issue of climate change, Ruth Greenspan Bell notes that "part of the problem is that the threat still feels abstract. Despite accumulating evidence, the full impact of climate change has not yet been felt; for now, it can only be modeled and forecast." As a result, "much of the planning for meeting this challenge has also had a somewhat abstract feeling."[52] The climate change we see today is the result of emissions from years and even decades ago. There is a lag period between the actions that cause some problems and the point at which people finally begin to feel the effects. Solving such problems requires that people change their behavior now, perhaps in very costly ways, to avoid problems that they are told will manifest themselves decades in the future, perhaps beyond their lifetimes. The costly solutions are real and immediate while the consequences of failing to act are distant and speculative. People need to have a very long mental time horizon in order to alter their behavior now to prevent problems in the future. It is often very difficult to mobilize people to solve such problems, even when there is a consensus on their existence and a government to deal with them. Without such a consensus or government, the difficulties are magnified.

The danger, many fear, is that because of the time gap between actions and effects the political will to act will lag behind the need for action. Current emissions will produce future warming and by the time the effects are sufficient to spur nations to action, further warming will be irreversibly set in motion. If people must feel the worst effects of environmental damage before altering their behavior, the will to act may not emerge until the window for meaningful action has closed. "Like the frog in the pan of heating water that does not notice the temperature is rising until it is too late," Bell worries, "human beings have been lulled into believing that they have many years to deal with climate change." But if this assumption is false, "when dramatic changes finally do occur, it will be too late for remedial action."[53] There is no assurance that the political "tipping point" at which action will take place is the same as the environmental tipping point beyond which it is too late. On some levels, threats to the global commons present challenges for scientists who must figure out the nature of, and solutions to, the problems we confront. On another level, the threats pose a challenge to the international community that must find a way to deal with global problems in the absence of a central political authority. But at a deeper level, the most critical challenge might be to people's ability to take an apparently distant and seemingly speculative future into account in shaping their present behavior.

CHAPTER SUMMARY

- In recent decades, people have increasingly begun to worry about the interrelated issues of global population growth, resources depletion, and environmental degradation.

- Though Thomas Malthus feared the consequences of population growth more than two centuries ago, these same concerns emerged in somewhat different form in the 1960s and 1970s.

- The terms of the debate were set in 1972, when the Club of Rome released its study *Limits to Growth*, predicting that in the following century the world would reach the maximum level of population than its resources and environment could support. If population did not level off before that point, the result would be a declining standard of living for all on the planet.

- The issues raised by the Club of Rome are conceptualized using the metaphor of the tragedy of commons, which attempts to illustrate why people often overuse common resources. On a global scale, the "commons" in question are limited natural and environmental resources.

- If this vision of the future is correct, the only long-term solution lies in restraining population growth. Exactly how this is to be accomplished is often a matter of some controversy. Garrett Hardin has argued that the first critical step is recognizing the need for government policies that restrict population and encourage people to have fewer children.

- Not everyone accepts the Club of Rome's analysis of the "predicament" facing humankind. In opposition to this *neo-traditionalists* vision is a *modernists* view.

- Modernists present a more optimistic assessment, claiming the problems highlighted by the Club of Rome are mostly nonexistent, exaggerated, or solvable.

- Drawing on the theory of demographic transition, modernists predict that global population will level off at about 8 to 9 billion by the end of the century.

- On the question of natural resource depletion, modernists are skeptical of predictions of imminent exhaustion. These sorts of predictions have a very poor track record. Most resources (e.g., fossil fuels) remain sufficiently plentiful to sustain our population until scientific progress leads us to feasible and unlimited substitutes.

- On environmental issues, modernists also fear that many problems, such as fears of global warming, are being exaggerated. Those environmental problems that do exist have technological solutions. We have the ability to sustain the world's probable population with a minimal effect on the global environment.

- Even if there is agreement on the scientific questions, there remains the obstacle of crafting a solution to global commons problems in a world without a central political authority. Realists are inclined to think resources and environmental problems will increase conflict, not encourage the cooperation necessary to solve them. Liberals are more optimistic that international regimes can be developed to help deal with commons problems even in the absence of a central political authority.

CRITICAL QUESTIONS

1. What are the essential elements of a commons dilemma and why is this often used as a metaphor for global resource and environmental problems?

2. Why are commons problems so much more difficult to solve at the global level than at the domestic level?

3. Modernists often assume that global population will level off as developing nations replicate the demographic trends of the developed world. What are the assumptions underpinning this optimism? Can you think of reasons why this expectation might not be warranted?

4. Why is the underlying problem of global population growth so difficult to solve?

5. What are the similarities and differences in the problems posed by CFCs and greenhouse emissions?

KEY TERMS

FURTHER READINGS

A good place to begin is with the landmark study that shaped much of the debate for the past few decades: Donella Meadows, Dennis Meadows, Jorgen Randers, and William W. Behrens, *Limits to Growth* (New York: Universe Books, 1972). The Worldwatch Institute publishes a popular collection of essays every year entitled *State of the World* (New York: W.W. Norton, annual) dealing with the issues raised in the larger debate about population growth, environmental problems, and resources depletion. Another fairly comprehensive overview is John Dryzek and David Schlosberg, eds., *Debating the Earth: An Environmental Politics Reader* (Oxford: Oxford University Press, 1998). A popular statement of concern echoing the views of the Club of Rome is Albert Gore's, *Earth in the Balance: Ecology and the Human Spirit* (New York: Houghton Mifflin, 1992). Garrett Hardin's, *Living within Limits: Ecology, Economics and*

Population Taboos (Oxford: Oxford University Press, 2000) is a thought-provoking, if controversial, exploration of many of these issues. The classic response to arguments about growing resource scarcity was presented in Julian Simon and Herman Kahn, *The Resourceful Earth* (Oxford: Basil Blackwell, 1984). Bjorn Lomborg's, *The Skeptical Environmentalist: Measuring the Real State of the World* (Cambridge: Cambridge University Press, 2001) is an extremely controversial attempt to counter what he sees as exaggerated concerns about population growth, resources, and environmental degradation. For a good survey of alternatives to oil, see Michael Parfit, "After Oil: Predicting the Future," *National Geographic* (August 2005): 4–31. A recent analysis of the science and politics of climate change is Roger Pielke, Jr., *The Climate Fix: What Scientists and Politicians Won't Tell You About Global Warming* (New York: Basic Books, 2010).

THE GLOBAL COMMONS ON THE WEB

www.wri.org
Web site of the World Resource Institute dealing with a range of global commons issues.

www.ipcc.ch
Official Web site of the Intergovernmental Panel on Climate Change, the leading organization examining the problems of global warming.

http://e360.yale.edu./content/topic.msp?id=5
Excellent Web site on global environmental issues and debates.

www.climatedebatedaily.com
Useful site that draws together divergent views on the reality, causes, consequences, and solutions to global warming and climate change. Also provides links to literally hundreds of Web sites and blogs on almost every conceivable issue and point of view associated with climate change.

http://dotearth.blogs.nytimes.com/
A wide ranging Web site maintained by reporter Andrew Revkin on issues of the global commons. The site's title gives a hint of its focus: "Nine Billion People. One Planet."

NOTES

[1]Robert Kunzig, "7 Billion," *National Geographic* (January 2011). Accessed at: http://ngm.nationalgeographic.com/2011/01/seven-billion/kunzig-text

[2]Donald McNeil, "Malthus Redux: Is Doomsday Upon Us, Again?" *New York Times* (June 15, 2008), p. WK3.

[3]John Feeney, "Return of the Population Timebomb," *Guardian* (May 5, 2008). Accessed at: http://www.guardian.co.uk/commentisfree/2008/may/05/returnofthepopulationtimebomb.

[4]See Paul R. Ehrlich, *The Population Bomb* (New York: Ballantine, 1968), which is a classic early statement of concern about population growth.

[5]Michael Latahm, *The Right Kind of Revolution: Modernization, Development and U.S. Foreign Policy from the Cold War to the Present* (Ithaca, NY: Cornell University Press, 2011), p. 104.

[6]J.R. McNeill, *Something New Under the Sun: An Environmental History of the Twentieth-Century World* (New York: W.W. Norton, 2000), p. 340.

[7]Donella H. Meadows, Dennis Meadows, Jorgen Randers, and William W. Behrens, *Limits to Growth* (New York: Universe Books, 1972), p. 9.

[8]Ibid., p. 23.

[9]Ibid.

[10]See Kenneth S. Deffeyes, *Hubbert's Peak: The Impending World Oil Shortage* (Princeton, NJ: Princeton University Press, 2003).

[11]Jad Maouwad, "The Big Thirst," *New York Times* (April 20, 2008), p. WK4. For a more alarming assessment see James Hamilton, "Running Dry?" *Atlantic* (October 2007), pp. 42–43.

[12]McNeill, *Something New Under the Sun*, pp. 110–111.

[13]Citations from the Union of Concerned Scientists Web site on global warming: www.ucsusa.org/globalenvironmental/globalwarming/page.cfm?pageID_497.

[14]*Climate Change 2007: The Physical Science Basis, Summary for Policymakers*, p. 10. The report can be accessed at www.ipcc.ch/SPM2feb07.pdf.

[15]Ibid.

[16]*Climate Change 2007*, p. 13.

[17]Roger Pielke, Jr., *The Climate Fix: What Scientists and Politicians Won't Tell You About Global Warming* (New York: Basic Books, 2010), pp. 11–15.

[18]Albert Gore, *Earth in the Balance* (New York: Houghton Mifflin, 1992).

[19]Daniel Bromley and Michael Cernea, *The Management of Common Property Natural Resources*, World Bank Discussion Paper no. 57 (1989), p. 6.

[20]World Bank, *World Development Report 2010: Development and Climate Change* (Washington D. C. The World Bank, 2010), p. 1, emphasis added.

[21]There are numerous statements of the tragedy of the commons. See, for example, Elinor Ostrom, *Governing the Commons: The Evolution of Institutions for Collective Action* (Cambridge: Cambridge University Press, 1990), and Garrett Hardin, "The Tragedy of the Commons," *Science* (1968): 243–248.

[22]Hardin, "Tragedy of the Commons," p. 248

[23]Garrett Hardin, *Managing the Global Commons* (San Francisco: Freeman, 1977), p. 269.

[24]Barry Hughes, *World Futures: A Critical Analysis of Alternatives* (Baltimore: Johns Hopkins University Press, 1985). For more on the distinction between traditional and modern societies, see Daniel Lerner, *The Passing of Traditional Society: Modernizing the Middle East* (New York: The Free Press, 1958). Different labels have also been used to describe these competing perspectives, such as eco-optimists and eco-pessimists, neomalthusians and cornucopians, and so on.

[25]On the theory of demographic transition, see: John I. Clarke, *The Future of Population* (London: Phoenix, 1997), and Hughes, *World Futures*, pp. 73–76.

[26]See Nicholas Eberstadt, "The Population Implosion," *Foreign Policy* (March/April 2001): 42–53, and Carolyn Lynch, "Population Loss Trends Cited," *Washington Post* (March 22, 2000), p. A28.

[27]Latahm, *The Right Kind of Revolution*, p. 96.

[28]Hughes, *World Futures*, p. 75. Year 2001 figures from the Population Reference Bureau (www.prb.org).

[29]Wolfgang Lutz, Warren Sanderson, and Sergei Scherbov, "The End of World Population Growth," *Nature* 412 (August 2, 2001): 543–545. The authors concede a high-end prediction population of about 12 billion. The figures in table 13.5 represent the most likely population figures.

[30]The classic statement of modernism is Julian Simon and Herman Kahn, *The Resourceful Earth* (Oxford: Blackwell, 1984). See also Gregg Easterbrook's, *A Moment on the Earth: The Coming Age of Environmental Optimism* (New York: Viking, 1995), and Ronald Bailey, ed., *The True State of the Planet* (New York: The Free Press, 1995). A more recent study is sure to become the new classic statement of modernism: Bjorn Lomborg, *The Skeptical Environmentalist: Measuring the Real State of the World* (Cambridge: Cambridge University Press, 2001).

[31]See Worldwatch Institute, *Vital Signs 2006–2007: The Trends That Are Shaping Our Future* (New York: W.W. Norton, 2006). Accessed at www.worldwatch.org.

[32]McNeil, "Malthus Redux," p. WK3.

[33]John Parker, "The 9 Billion-people Question: A Special Report on Feeding the World," *The Economist* (February 24, 2011), p. 3.

[34]Hughes, *World Futures*, pp. 104–105.

[35]Meadows et al., *Limits to Growth*, p. 58. There are predictions concerning the depletion of other natural resources as well, not a single one of which has proved correct.

[36]Lomborg, *Skeptical Environmentalist*, p. 123 (figure 65).

[37]Lomborg, *Skeptical Environmentalist*, p. 132.

[38]Brian Matthews, "Middle Ages Were Warmer Than Today, Say Scientists," *Daily Telegraph*, April 6, 2003. Accessed at http://www.dailytelegraph.co.uk.

[39]See Brian M. Fagan, *The Little Ice Age: How Climate Made History, 1300–1850* (New York: Basic Books, 2001).

[40]Accessed at http://yosemite.epa.gov/oar/globalwarming.nsf/content/climateuncertantie.

[41]Gore, *Earth in the Balance*, p 91

[42]Gregg Easterbrook, "Finally Feeling the Heat," *New York Times* (May 24, 2006), p. A27.

[43]Lomborg, *Skeptical Environmentalist*, p. 352.

[44]Ruth Greenspan Bell, "What to Do About Climate Change," *Foreign Affairs* (May/June 2006): 108.

[45]See Michael Klare, *Resource Wars: The New Landscape of Global Conflict* (New York: Owl Books, 2002), and Thomas Homer-Dixon, *Environment, Scarcity and Violence* (Princeton, NJ: Princeton University Press, 2001).

[46]See "Daily Chart: Greenhouse Gases, The Cost of Trade," *Economist Online* (April 26, 2011). Accessed at: www.economist.com/blogs/dailychart/2011/04/greenhouse_gases

[47]Stephen Krasner, ed., *International Regime* (Ithaca, NY: Cornell University Press, 1983), p. 2.

[48]Pielke, *The Climate Fix*, p. 25.

[49]World Bank, *World Development Report 2010*, p. 233.

[50]See "Global Carbon Emissions Since Kyoto." Accessed at: www.guardian.co.uk/environment/interactive/2009/nov/30/copenhagen-summit-world-carbon-emissions

[51]World Bank, *World Development Report 2010*, p. 236.

[52]Bell, "What to Do About Climate Change," p. 109.

[53]Ibid., pp. 105–106.

Where Do We Go After Kyoto?

For perhaps the first time in history, many of the problems facing humanity in the twenty-first century are truly global in scope. As global problems, their solutions require genuinely international and cooperative action. The dilemma is crafting and implementing global solutions in the absence of global government or even international institutions capable of enforcing agreements designed to protect the global commons. On one level, both of the essays below wrestle with the problem of finding global solutions in the context of an anarchic global order. Martin Wolf and Scott Barrett agree on much. They share a belief in the severity of the world's climate crisis. They recognize the need for a realistic solution within the confines of the existing global political order: there are no calls for world government or anything like it. They also agree that previous attempts to deal with climate change, most notably Kyoto, have failed. But do they agree on why Kyoto failed and what to do in its wake? Read the essays focusing on two questions. First, what do Barrett and Wolf see as the underlying obstacles to effective global action that caused Kyoto to fail? Second, how are their analyses of Kyoto's failure reflected in their proposals for future action?

How Not to Repeat the Mistakes of the Kyoto Protocol

PERSPECTIVE 1

Scott Barrett[1]
YaleGlobal, 14 November 2007

WASHINGTON: It's not enough for countries to want to slow climate change. Countries have a much harder task—figuring out exactly how the world can cooperate to counteract climate change. Unfortunately, the Kyoto Protocol is not a model.

The Kyoto Protocol was an early attempt at collective action. However, even if the Kyoto Protocol works exactly as intended, global emissions and atmospheric concentrations of greenhouse gases will continue to rise. Compared with Kyoto's base year, 1990, emissions have already risen 28 percent. Kyoto aims to limit the emissions of only a subset of countries by just 5 percent. Emissions thus continue to rise even as we enter the implementation period next year. To meet a goal such as stabilizing atmospheric concentrations of greenhouse gases, emissions eventually must decline—and dramatically.

Al Gore, who won the Nobel Prize for Peace this year along with the UN Intergovernmental Panel on Climate Change, has said emissions should fall 90 percent by 2050. How can the world move from the current situation, in which emissions are rising steadily, to the desired one, in which emissions are falling—fast?

An effective international agreement for climate change mitigation must do three things.

First, a treaty must attract broad participation. This is not only because all countries emit greenhouse gases. It is also because, should only some countries reduce emissions, comparative advantage in the carbon-intensive industries may move to the other countries, causing these other countries to increase their emissions—a phenomenon known as "trade leakage." Kyoto failed to convince the world's biggest emitter and only superpower, the United States, that it should participate—reason enough to call the agreement a failure.

I blame the agreement rather than George Bush. The Clinton–Gore administration did not attempt to get the U.S. Senate to ratify Kyoto. Nor did it pass legislation to reduce U.S. emissions. And President Bush, the unilateralist, did bend to another international agreement. When the World Trade Organization authorized Europe to impose trade restrictions against the U.S. for illegal steel tariffs, Bush withdrew the tariffs. This is what a good treaty needs to do—change the behavior of states by changing the incentives that cause states not to cooperate. The World Trade Organization does this. The Kyoto Protocol does not.

Second, a treaty must deter countries from not complying. Canada's Parliament ratified the Kyoto Protocol; its participation in the treaty is thus not a problem. Under the agreement, however, Canada must reduce its greenhouse gas emissions 6 percent below the 1990 level through 2008–2012, and in 2005 Canada's emissions were 33 percent above the Kyoto target.

Canada's government has given up on the idea of meeting the Kyoto target. It aims instead to reduce the rate of growth in emissions, hoping that emissions will peak from 2010. However, a government-funded roundtable of experts has concluded that the government's own policies will not meet even this modest goal. Canada's previous government predicted that Canada's emissions would exceed the Kyoto target by 45 percent by 2010. It now looks like that prediction will not be far off.

Why would Canada, a country in good standing in international affairs, fail to fulfill its legal obligations? One reason is that the cost to Canada of complying with Kyoto would be, in the words of the above roundtable, "considerable." Another reason is that, unlike other agreements such as those under the World Trade Organization, Kyoto does not punish countries for non-compliance. A final reason is that Canada's compliance with Kyoto would not prevent the climate from changing and indeed would have almost no discernible effect. Why should Canada undertake "considerable" sacrifice for that?

An effective international agreement must not only tell countries what to do; it must create incentives for countries to do what the treaty says must be done.

Third, an agreement must get countries to participate and comply with an agreement in which substantial action is required. It's easy to get countries to participate and comply with an agreement that requires little. A prime example is the UN Framework Convention on Climate Change. Only four countries failed to ratify this agreement—Andorra, the Holy See, Iraq, and Somalia. However, this agreement does not require that parties reduce their emissions. Similarly, the big emitting developing countries like China and India are parties to the Kyoto Protocol, but that's because the treaty does not require them to limit emissions. Russia is also a party to the Kyoto Protocol, and its emissions are capped, but the cap is so generous that it has no effect.

An agreement that fails to induce the U.S. to participate, that fails to create an incentive for Canada to comply and that fails to limit the emissions of the fastest growing large economies is a failed agreement.

While the world's attention focuses on Kyoto, another international agreement works quietly behind the scenes to make a material difference. This is the Montreal Protocol—the agreement for protecting the ozone layer. Ozone-depleting substances, it turns out, are also greenhouse gases, but the relationship between ozone and climate change is complicated. Ozone is a greenhouse gas, so an agreement that protects ozone will increase warming. As well, in limiting the use of ozone-depleting substances, the Montreal Protocol has caused substitutes—including non-ozone-destroying HFCs, a greenhouse gas—to increase. The Kyoto Protocol controls HFCs. So the Montreal Protocol has positive and negative effects for the climate.

A recent study, however, has shown that the overall effect of the Montreal Protocol on greenhouse gases is helpful. The study by G.J.M. Velders et al., published in the Proceedings of the National Academy of Sciences, calculates that the Montreal Protocol has been, and will continue to be, more helpful than the Kyoto Protocol, even assuming that Kyoto is implemented perfectly. Already, this study estimates, the Montreal Protocol has achieved four times as much as the Kyoto Protocol could ever hope of achieving.

Indeed, only a month ago, the Montreal Protocol was revised again. This time, the agreement to phase out HCFCs, a greenhouse gas, was accelerated. Moreover, manufacture of HCFCs produces HFCs, as a byproduct. Preliminary estimates suggest that the agreement negotiated in Montreal in September will have more than twice the intended impact of the Kyoto Protocol. This is on top of the larger effect Montreal has already had in reducing the concentration of greenhouse gases.

What is the Montreal Protocol's secret of success? One difference between Montreal and Kyoto is that Montreal imposed restrictions on all countries from the start. A second difference is that Montreal created strong incentives for participation and compliance—a combination of carrots and sticks. A final difference is that Montreal created a system for positive feedback, with each step in reducing ozone depletion creating incentives for countries to take yet another step.

Ten years after Montreal was first negotiated, the agreement had been adjusted and amended seven times. Ten years after Kyoto was negotiated, that agreement has not entered the implementation phase. Montreal is doing nearly as much as is possible to protect the ozone layer and much more than Kyoto to protect the climate. Kyoto, meanwhile, has made virtually no difference.

There's a lesson in this for future climate negotiations. Rather than cap aggregate greenhouse emissions directly, attention should turn to the actions that can be taken to limit the emissions of individual gases. Montreal could do it, so why not a different kind of climate treaty? Any new climate treaty must break the problem up, addressing different gases in different ways and focusing on sectors rather than economy-wide targets.

PERSPECTIVE 2 Why the Climate Change Wolf Is so Hard to Kill Off

Martin Wolf[2]

Published: December 4, 2007 Last updated: December 5, 2007

The point of the story of the boy who cried wolf is that, finally, a wolf did appear. I feel the same way about the intellectual heirs of Thomas Malthus. Malthusians have finally found a wolf called climate change. Many now agree. But it is far away and coming slowly. "If the worst comes to the worst," mutter the rich to themselves, "we can always let our children cope."

This is the complacency that the latest Human Development Report from the United Nations Development Programme attacks. It does a good job, too. But does it do a good enough job to turn the Bali climate change conference into a call for effective action? I fear not. This is not because it fails to make a morally sound case. It is rather because humanity will change its behavior only when convinced that the lifestyle the better off enjoy now—and the rest of the world aspires to—remains in reach.

This cynical view of human behavior is fully consistent with what has happened so far. For it is as if the Kyoto treaty had never been. Is this judgment too harsh? Consider just a few of the many facts contained in this report: atmospheric concentrations of carbon dioxide continue to rise at a rate of 1.9 parts per million a year; over the past 10 years the annual growth rate of emissions has been 30 per cent faster than the average for the past 40 years; if the rate of emission were to rise in line with current trends, stocks of CO_2 in the atmosphere might be double pre-industrial levels by 2035; and that, argues the International Panel on Climate Change, would give a likely temperature increase of 3°C, though rises of over 4.5°C cannot be excluded. If the science is right, the world is doomed to significant climate change.

The report takes a temperature increase of 2°C as the threshold of "dangerous climate change". Achieving that means draconian cuts in emissions: "If the world were a single country it would have to cut emissions of greenhouse gases by half by 2050 relative to 1990 levels.... However the world is not a single country. Using plausible assumptions, we estimate that avoiding dangerous climate change will require rich countries to cut emissions by at least 80 percent, with cuts of 30 percent by 2020. Emissions from developing countries would peak around 2020, with cuts of 20 percent by 2050."

The one point in favor of George W. Bush's U.S. or John Howard's Australia is that they were not hypocritical. For the signal feature of most of the commitments made so far has been the failure to meet them. The vaunted European emissions trading system has been more a way of transferring quota rent to a few big emitters than an effective means of emissions control. The U.K. government has, for example, been honest enough to admit that large electricity generators gained £1.2bn in quota rent for 2005 alone.

---

[2] Martin Wolf, "Why the Climate Change Wolf is so Hard to Kill Off," *Financial Times*, December 5, 2007. From the Financial Times. © 2007. Reprinted by permission. All Rights Reserved.

Can the world do better in future? Yes, but it will find it difficult. If we are to understand why, we must confront the fact that the world is far from a single country. This creates three huge problems: collective (in)action; perceived injustice; and indifference.

First, not only does each country want to be a free rider on the efforts of others but none feels wholly responsible for the outcome.

Second, the contributions made by different countries to the problem have been (and remain) enormously different. Collectively, the rich countries account for seven out of every 10 tons of CO_2 emitted since the start of the industrial era. While China is the biggest emitter in the world, its emissions are still only one-fifth of U.S. levels per head. India's are one-fifteenth.

Third, as the report spells out in compelling detail, the heaviest cost will be borne by the world's poor. Among the most frightening consequences are those for rainfall and glaciers: water shortages could become severe across large swaths of the globe. Poor people are far less able to cope with climatic disasters than rich ones. But this, if we were honest, is why the rich are unlikely to make the huge reductions in emissions the report demands. The powerful will continue to act without much consideration for the poor. This, after all, is a world that spends 10 times as much on defense (much of it useless) as on aid to poor countries.

How might this change? The answer is that we must appeal at least as much to people's self-interest as to their morality. Yes, we have a moral obligation to consider both the poor and future generations. Yes, the fact that the changes in the composition of the atmosphere are, to all intents and purposes, irreversible makes early and effective action essential. But acceptance of these points will not be sufficient to obtain meaningful action, instead of pious aspirations and much pretense. A good example of the latter is the proposition that it is enough to lower the carbon intensity of output. Alas, it is not, unless the reduction is very large indeed.

Two things are needed. The first is convincing evidence that the true risks are larger than many now suppose. Conceivable feedback effects might, for example, generate temperature increases of 20°C. That would be the end of the world as we know it. I cannot imagine a rational person who would not seek to eliminate even the possibility of such outcomes. But if we are to do that, we must also act very soon.

The second requirement is to demonstrate that it is possible for us to thrive with low-carbon emissions. People in the northern hemisphere are not going to choose to be cold now, in order to prevent the world from becoming far too hot in future. China and India are not going to forgo development, either. These are realities that cannot be ignored.

The UNDP report argues that the low-carbon future it wants could be achieved at a cost of 1.6 per cent of global output between now and 2030. Such round numbers look attractively modest. But the question people will still ask themselves is what this might mean for their own standards of living. Advocates of change will have to persuade people that living in a low-carbon economy does not mean giving up everything they enjoy. People will not wear hair shirts, whatever they may pretend.

In short, if they are to tolerate radical change in energy use, people must first be frightened and then they must be offered a good way out. The truth, moreover, is that this will happen only if the U.S. also takes the lead. No country will deliver radical cuts if the U.S. does not do so, too. No leaps forward in science and technology will occur if the U.S. is not prepared to commit its resources to those ends. The U.S. can no longer wait for a lead from others. Either it takes the lead now or the cause, in all probability, will be lost. Our children and grandchildren will then find out whether it was a real wolf or not.

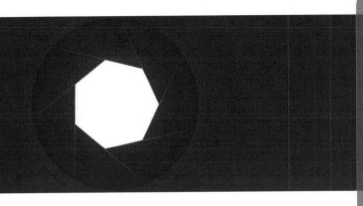

Index